GREENING OF CAPITALISM

GREENING	How Asia Is Driving
OF	the Next Great
CAPITALISM	Transformation

John A. Mathews

Stanford Economics and Finance
An Imprint of Stanford University Press
Stanford, California

Stanford University Press
Stanford, California

Special discounts for bulk quantities of titles in the Stanford Economics and Finance imprint are available to corporations, professional associations, and other organizations. For details and discount information, contact the special sales department of Stanford University Press. Tel: (650) 736-1782, Fax: (650) 736-1784

Printed in the United States of America on acid-free, archival-quality paper

Library of Congress Cataloging-in-Publication Data

Mathews, John A. (John Alwyn), author.
 Greening of capitalism : how Asia is driving the next great transformation / John A. Mathews.
    pages cm
 Includes bibliographical references and index.
 ISBN 978-0-8047-9150-2 (cloth : alk. paper)
  1. Economic development—Environmental aspects—Asia.
2. Sustainable development—Asia.   3. Capitalism—Environmental aspects—Asia.   4. Asia—Economic policy.   I. Title.
 HC415.E5M38 2015
 338.95—dc23
                                                          2014010114

 ISBN 978-0-8047-9316-2 (electronic)

Typeset by Newgen in 10/13.5 Sabon

To the memory of Ed Cohen-Rosenthal, a dear friend and pioneer of industrial ecology—his memory lives on in his work

Contents

Figures, Maps, and Table   ix
Preface   xi
List of Acronyms   xvii

1   Introduction   1

PART I   How We Got to Where We Are

2   The First "Great Transformation"   21
3   Why "Business as Usual" Cannot Continue   49

PART II   Toward a New Eco-Logic for Capitalism

4   From Fossil Fuels to Renewable Energy   79
5   From the Linear to the Circular Economy   114
6   From Generic to Eco-Finance   131

PART III   An Economy of Sustainable Enterprise

7   The Transition to a Green Economy   153
8   From Green Economy to Green Economics   182
9   The Greening of Capitalism   204

Notes   239
Bibliography   293
Index   325

Figures, Maps, and Table

Figures

1.1	China's "black" face: Buildup of thermal power	12
1.2	China's "green" face: Buildup of wind power	13
1.3	China's green and black energy revolution	14
2.1	Growth of per capita income, England, 1200–2000	22
2.2	Real prices of wood and coal in London, 1400–1800	27
2.3	Fossil fuels and industrialization of the United States	28
2.4	Global uptake of fossil fuels	29
2.5	Increasing rates of human activity since the Industrial Revolution	31
2.6	Major world economies' fluctuations over the past two thousand years	36
2.7	China's and India's looming oil gap	39
2.8	Global price of coal, 2001–2012	41
3.1	Plateauing of global (conventional) oil supplies	57
3.2	Carbon dioxide and methane levels over the past thousand years	61
3.3	Measured temperature increase, 1860–2000	62
3.4	China: Projected carbon emissions from power generation, 2000–2040	66
4.1	Wind- and nuclear-generated electricity in China, 1995–2012	82

4.2   Industrial dynamics of electric power capacity in
      China, 2000–2040   84
4.3   Photovoltaic module experience curve, 1976–2011   106
5.1   Emergence of circular economy linkages   124
5.2   Industrial symbioses in Guitang Group, China   126
5.3   Industrial symbioses in Kalundborg, Denmark   127
6.1   Global financial assets, 1990–2012   139
7.1   Emergence of a sixth techno-economic paradigm   156
7.2   Spectral analysis of Kondratiev waves, 1870–2010   161
7.3   Systemic technological transitions following logistic
      industrial dynamics   168
8.1a Neoclassical view of the economy in relation to nature 188
8.1b Biomimetic economy, recognizing natural limits   188
8.2   Sequences of interconnections in the game of Go   194

Maps

3.1   Diminishing Arctic sea-ice cover   63
4.1   China's projected strong and smart electric power
      grid   83
4.2   Asian Super Grid proposal   93
4.3   Desertec proposal   98

Table

7.1   Upswings and downswings in industrial capitalism,
      1760–2011   156

Preface

There comes a point in every writing project when a book passes from being a possibility (one among many) to something that simply demands to be written. That point came for me at the time of the Copenhagen "Conference of the Parties" under the Kyoto Protocol in December 2009. Like much of the world, I had been monitoring the press and the statements from scientists on the looming threat of global warming, and I too was caught up in the enthusiasm that Copenhagen might deliver a global pact to reduce carbon emissions and "save civilization" as we know it. As we found out, Copenhagen delivered no such thing—and apart from the vested interests that blocked any hope for a pact, the Copenhagen conference was marked by the arrival of the Chinese as major participants in the debate and, in the eyes of many, as obstacles to a global agreement. This struck me at the time as grossly imbalanced—for anyone who knew anything about global warming knew that the Chinese were only adding carbon to the massive emissions already released by the Western powers. Had people done their homework, they would have known that China's emissions were rising at the time, precisely because it was expanding its energy system at an unprecedented pace to underpin a massively expanding manufacturing system that in turn underpinned the country's bid to industrialize and raise hundreds of millions of people out of poverty. How could anyone seriously expect China (and India or Brazil, or other countries) to sign up to a pact that would see carbon emissions constrained and then fall while it was still pulling its population out of poverty by industrial growth?

This sense of imbalance prompted me to look more closely at China's energy policies (strategies)—and what I found was even more surprising. While the environmentalists and activists who had been so bitterly disappointed by Copenhagen were blaming China for the fiasco and pointing to its "black" coal-fired industrialization strategy as culprit, in its own quiet way China had in fact been ramping up renewable energy industries at a pace and scale that far exceeded those of any other country. The costs of renewable power were coming down because China was driving the scale of their expansion. If the world was greening, it was mostly because of China. And it was not just energy, but resources generally, with China elevating the notion of a circular economy (in which waste outputs would be channeled as inputs for alternative industrial activities) as a national industrial and development strategy. I learned later that China was also fashioning a novel approach to finance, ensuring that long credit lines were extended to enterprises producing renewables like solar photovoltaics and wind power turbines to enable these industries to grow rapidly and become competitive much faster than if they were powered by market forces alone.

And so what demanded to be written was an account of the issue of the greening of our industrial system viewed not as a moral imperative as seen by the West but as an extraordinary development challenge for China and other newly industrializing nations looking to join the club of industrialized countries—without destroying their own and everyone else's environment. For China it is a matter of fashioning the green growth strategies that are able to balance the black strategies of burning coal and oil and creating unbreathable air in China's cities. My understanding of the issues evolved from an initial concern with climate change and international action to become a concern as to whether China would be allowed by the international community to complete its industrialization without destroying the earth; this led me to think through the fundamental changes to the industrial system that would be called for if such a strategy were to succeed. Seen from this perspective, so much of the outpouring of concern over climate change and carbon emissions is highly Europe- and America-centric, viewing the problem as one of excessive growth and China's concerns as marginal—sometimes quite explicitly condemning China's millions to perpetual poverty by decreeing that their turn at the industrialization wheel would never come. But the argument that formed for me and which is now expressed in this book is that the next phase of industrialization is the one that will be the most critical, because it will determine whether our industrial way of life—with all its capacity to raise incomes and wealth and banish age-old prejudices—can exist in balance with our planetary ecological niche. And central to this phase is China and its emerging green development model—what scholars like Hu Angang call China's "inevitable choice." We are witnesses to the greatest uncontrolled planetary experiment ever undertaken, and we know not whether China's greening will occur in time or at the requisite scale. The future is far from being determined.

As this book took shape, it became more and more about the wellsprings and operating principles of capitalism itself and less about the details of renewable energies or resource efficiencies or eco-finance. And in this way the book became a long argument with economists, many of whom are concerned by the issues but take a narrow view, considering the role of carbon taxes and cap-and-trade schemes as exhausting the possibilities for effective action. In the case of China it is clear that while market-based incentives are playing an important role (e.g., in the Sloping Lands program, where farmers are paid to cease planting crops on steep lands vulnerable to soil erosion), the real factor driving change is the capacity of the state to intervene and change economic incentives. From this perspective I see this book as an imaginary dialogue with a fine economist, Deidre McCloskey. Her current magnum opus on what she calls the virtues of capitalism, elaborated in text after text, adopts a strikingly original position that capitalism has been an unalloyed triumph for humanity and that so much of the opposition comes from a failure not just of imagination but also of appreciation of the evidence. As McCloskey develops the next volumes in this monumental treatise (through the highly innovative approach of posting a draft to the web and inviting comments from serious readers), she drops hints here and there that capitalism would solve all the environmental problems—if allowed to work properly, without government interference. This position echoes that of some economists who call themselves "free-market environmentalists." Since I am calling for the greening of capitalism and not just for a few environmentally friendly policies here and there, it seems only reasonable that I should engage with McCloskey on this point. The big point of disagreement is that I insist that if China and other industrializing powers are to get onto a new, non-fossil-fueled industrial trajectory, it will be only through smart state intervention in the economy, shaping and facilitating the growth of new, green industries. My argument is that prices and markets could indeed shape entrepreneurial decisions once the economy is on a new trajectory—but that state intervention is needed to make the shift, particularly when the vested interests aligned against such a change are as powerful as those of the fossil fuels industry. I come to this position by viewing the issues not through the eyes of the United States or Europe (or Japan) but through the eyes of China and the options it faces. One doesn't have to be an adviser to the Chinese government or an apologist for an authoritarian state to see that China faces formidable problems—and that the way it goes about finding and implementing solutions will have very powerful repercussions for the rest of humanity. This is the starting point for my argument.

As noted, I first started serious work on this book at the end of 2009, at the time of the Copenhagen conference on climate change. As it happened this was also the time when I was taking up the new Eni Chair of Competitive Dynamics and Global Strategy at the LUISS Guido Carli University in Rome. I should like to acknowledge the role of Eni, Italy's largest oil and gas company, in providing me with the freedom (and encouragement) to pursue a renewables teaching agenda at LUISS, including creating a master-level course, "Economics and Management of Energy Business," and inviting me to present an early version of my argument (which had nothing to do with oil or gas) to a seminar at the Eni corporate training center in Milan. My thanks to Giorgio di Giorgio, who made this possible.

My principal debt is to my former doctoral students, Mei-Chih Hu, now a professor at the National Tsinghua University in Taiwan; Hao Tan, now a senior lecturer at Newcastle University in Australia; and Ching-Yan Wu, also teaching and researching in Taiwan. They have been a constant source of encouragement and wisdom on all matters Asian and regular collaborators, as attested by the joint papers cited in this book. Hao Tan in particular has been my principal collaborator and the source of many of the charts utilized in this book; for this I owe him a great debt.

I would also like to acknowledge the input from my esteemed colleagues and collaborators Elizabeth Thurbon and Sung-Young Kim, who read earlier drafts of the book and commented profusely.

Colleagues around the world made important contributions along the way: Keun Lee at Seoul National University, a fellow student of catch-up strategies, who drove me to set the Chinese strategies in a wider developmental context; Sergio Trindade, my co-host at the memorable Conference that we staged on sustainable biofuels at the Rockefeller Foundation's conference facilities at Bellagio on Lake Como; Michael Mann for stimulating exchanges on the feasibility of the next energy transformation; Soogil Young, former head of the Presidential Commission on Green Growth in Korea, who opened the way to comprehending Korea's remarkable policies; my sister Freya Mathews for rewarding discussions on biomimicry; and for their various inputs, Paolo Baroni, Jae-Young Choung, Mark Diesendorf, Rainer Kattel, Mark Kivers, Erik Reinert, Francesco Rullani, Ric Samans, Shahid Yusuf, John Zysman; Myung Kyoon Lee, Darius Nassiry, and Mattia Romani at the Global Green Growth Institute; and finally my colleagues at the Organisation for Economic Co-operation and Development, Andrea Goldstein, Federico Bonaglia, and Annalisa Primi. I would also like to thank Sergio Weguelin, former head of Environmental Affairs at the Brazilian Development Bank, for his clarifying the bank's differential funding strategies. Over the years I have had stimulating exchanges with Sean Kidney, the energetic mover behind the Climate Bonds Initiative, based in London. My thanks also to business colleagues with a greening bent who helped me to formulate the argument: John Harrison (TecEco), Geoff and Phil Bell (Microbiogen), Hans-Joerg Naumer (Allianz Global Investors), and Oliver Yates (Clean Energy Finance Corporation).

Aspects of this book have been tested on numerous audiences at academic institutions around the world, as well as at conferences in Penang on Greening of Urban Growth, and at Hsinchu, Taiwan, on fast-follower development strategies. I have benefited from invitations to participate in landmark conferences on finance, development, and innovation, staged with the support of the Ford Foundation, in Rio de Janeiro (November 2011) and in Beijing (October 2013): my grateful thanks to Bill Lazonick of the University of Massachusetts; Ana Celia Castro of the University of Rio de Janeiro; and Leonardo Burlamaqui, then of the Ford

Foundation for their sound insights and judgment. The argument has also been distilled through numerous contributions to blogs over recent years; for this my thanks to Stephan Richter (*The Globalist*), Andrew Sheng and Pamela Mar (*Fung Global Institute*), Anthony Barnett (*Open Democracy*), Mark Selden (*AsiaPacific Journal: Japan Focus*), Jane Rawson (*The Conversation*), and Giles Parkinson (*Renew Economy*). I was fortunate in the choice of readers by Stanford University Press; my thanks to Dmitri Zhengelis and Rajah Rasiah, both fine scholars who provided penetrating comments and also waived their right to anonymity. Finally, I would like to thank my editors at Stanford University Press for their guidance and patience: Margo Beth Fleming, James Holt, John Feneron, and Katherine Faydash.

As in everything I do, my wife and partner, Linda Weiss, has been a perceptive critic and discussant, sharing all the struggles to bring these ideas to fruition and to scholarly standard even while laboring on her own magnum opus, now published by Cornell University Press.

Acronyms

Conceptual

BAU	business as usual
BCA	border carbon adjustment
BICs	Brazil, India, China (Goldman Sachs's BRICs includes Russia)
C2C	cradle to cradle
CAP	collective action problem
C&CC	circular and cumulative causation
CC&S	carbon capture and storage
CDM	Clean Development Mechanism (under the Kyoto Protocol)
CE	circular economy
CERES	circular economy and renewable energy system
CHP	combined heat and power
CIGS	copper indium gallium selenide (new-generation thin-film photovoltaic semiconductor)
CPR	common pool resource
CPS	circular production system
CSG	coal seam gas
CSP	concentrated solar power
EDCs	emerging and developing countries
EIP	eco-industrial park
EKC	environmental Kuznets curve

EPR	extended producer responsibility
EROI	energy return on (energy) invested
ETR	environmental (ecological) tax reform
EV	electric vehicle
FFI	fast follower innovation
FFV	flex-fuel vehicle
FIH	financial instability hypothesis (Minsky)
FiT	feed-in tariff
FME	free-market environmentalism
FYP	Five-Year Plan (in China)
GGC	green growth capitalism
GHG	greenhouse gases
HEV	hybrid electric vehicle
HSR	high-speed rail
HVDC	high-voltage direct current (for power transmission in modernized grid)
IPP	independent power producer (decentralized electric power generator)
IPRs	intellectual property rights
LCA	life-cycle assessment
LCCR	low-carbon climate resilient economy (OECD)
LTCB	long-term credit bank
MBI	market-based incentive
MFA	material flow analysis
MOE	merit order effect
MST	molten-salt technology (for CSP)
NAMA	National Appropriate Mitigation Action (Kyoto)
NGO	nongovernmental organization
PHEV	plug-in hybrid electric vehicle
PMDD	permanent magnet direct drive (wind power technology)
PTC	production tax credit
PV	photovoltaic
RE	renewable energy
RE^2	renewable energies and resource efficiency
REDD	Reducing Emissions from Deforestation and Forest Degradation
RRR	reduce, reuse, recycle

SETA	Sustainable Energy Trade Agreement (proposed by ICTSD)
SMCS	sound material-cycle society (Japan)
TEP	techno-economic paradigm
TF-PV	thin-film photovoltaic
TGC	tradable green certificate
TPP	tradable pollution permit
UHVDC	ultra high-voltage direct current (power transmission)
WTE	waste to energy
ZEV	zero emissions vehicle

Organizational

ADB	Asian Development Bank (issuer of green bonds)
AfDB	African Development Bank (issuer of green bonds)
APEC	Asia Pacific Economic Cooperation (a grouping of Asia Pacific economies)
ASG	Asian Super Grid
ASPO	Association for the Study of Peak Oil
BRICs	Brazil, Russia, India, China (Goldman Sachs)
BNDES	Banco Nacional do Desenvolvimento (Brazilian Development Bank)
CBI	Climate Bonds Initiative
CBRC	China Banking Regulatory Commission
CDB	China Development Bank
CEDA	Clean Energy Deployment Administration (proposed for United States)
CEFC	Clean Energy Finance Corporation (Australia)
CICERO	Center for International Climate and Environmental Research (Norway)
CTI	Carbon Tracker Initiative
DoD	Department of Defense (United States)
EEG	*Erneuerbare Energien Gesetz* (German Renewable Energy Promotion Law)
EIA	Energy Information Administration (United States)
EIB	European Investment Bank (issuer of green bonds)
ERI	Energy Research Institute (China)
ETS	Emissions Trading System (European Union)
FAO	Food and Agriculture Organization (United Nations)

FP(V)UP	Federal Photovoltaic Utilization Program (United States, 1970s)
GCF	Global Climate Fund (United Nations)
GEA	Green Economy Agency (new UN agency proposed in this book)
GGGI	Global Green Growth Institute (Korea)
GGKP	Green Growth Knowledge Platform (GGGI, OECD, UNEP, World Bank)
IBRD	International Bank for Reconstruction and Development (World Bank)
ICO2	Carbon Efficient Index (traded on Brazilian commodities exchange)
ICTSD	International Centre for Trade and Sustainable Development (Geneva)
IDDRI	Institute for Sustainable Development and International Relations (Paris)
IEA	International Energy Agency (linked to OECD)
IETA	International Emissions Trading Association
IFC	International Finance Corporation (part of the World Bank group)
IIASA	International Institute for Applied Systems Analysis (Austria)
IMF	International Monetary Fund
IPCC	Intergovernmental Panel on Climate Change (United Nations)
IRENA	International Renewable Energy Agency
ITRI	Industrial Technology Research Institute (Taiwan)
Kexim	Korean Export-Import Bank (issuer of green bond, February 2013)
KfW	*Kreditanstalt für Wiederaufbau* (German Development Bank)
METI	Ministry of Economy, Trade, and Industry (Japan)
MIGA	Multilateral Investment Guarantee Agency (part of World Bank group)
ND&RC	National Development and Reform Commission (China)
OPEC	Organization of Oil Exporting Countries
R100PI	Renewables 100 Policy Institute
Ren21	Renewable Energy Policy Network for the 21st Century

SBIR	Small Business Innovation Research program (United States)
SDC	Sustainable Development Commission (United Kingdom, abolished 2010)
SEFI	Sustainable Energy Finance Initiative (UN Environment Programme)
SLCP	Sloping Lands Conversion Program (China)
UNDP	UN Development Program
UNEP	UN Environment Program
UNFCCC	UN Framework Convention on Climate Change
UN-GEA	UN Green Economy Agency (agency suggested by author in this book)
WCRE	World Council for Renewable Energy
WRI	World Resources Institute
WTO	World Trade Organization

1   Introduction

The bourgeoisie, during its rule of scarce one hundred years, has created more massive and more colossal productive forces than have all preceding generations together. Subjection of Nature's forces to man, machinery, application of chemistry to industry and agriculture, steam-navigation, railways, electric telegraphs, clearing of whole continents for cultivation, canalisation of rivers, whole populations conjured out of the ground—what earlier century had even a presentiment that such productive forces slumbered in the lap of social labor?

> —*Karl Marx and Friedrich Engels,* The Communist Manifesto *(1848)*

The Puritan wanted to work in a calling; we are forced to do so. For when asceticism was carried out of monastic cells into everyday life, and began to dominate worldly morality, it did its part in building the tremendous cosmos of the modern economic order. This order is now bound to the technical and economic conditions of machine production which to-day determine the lives of all the individuals who are born into this mechanism . . . with irresistible force. Perhaps it will so determine them *until the last ton of fossilized coal is burnt.*

> —*Max Weber,* Protestant Ethic and the Spirit of Capitalism *(1904)*

Now that mankind is in the process of completing the colonization of the planet, learning to manage it intelligently is an urgent imperative.

> —*Barbara Ward and Rene Dubos,* Only One Earth *(1972)*

The traditional development strategies of industrialised countries all present two distinct features whether in Europe, the United States or Japan, despite their differing national and development conditions. One is that high-speed growth is sustained by high consumption of resources (especially non-renewable resources); the other is that the high-speed growth is stimulated by high consumption of the means of subsistence. We call this a traditional development model. In view of China's

conditions, it is impossible for China to realise modernisation by following the traditional model.

> —*Hu Angang, "Green development: The inevitable choice for
> China" (2006)*

Most books with *greening* in the title would be expected to start
with the observation that we have only one earth and it is subject to increasing stresses from our ever-expanding industrial system. There would
follow an analysis of energy and resource issues, with the aim of showing
that "business as usual" cannot be allowed to continue. Capitalism, with
its unbridled appetite for expansive consumption and the production that
feeds it, would be viewed as the core problem. There might ensue a discussion that critiques the notion of economic growth as something that
cannot continue forever in a finite world, leading to a preferred outcome
of a steady-state economy as the best approximation to a balance between
ecological and economic processes. Whether it is capitalist or not would
be left unsaid.

None of this is wrong; it is all too true. And none of this is new; we
have heard it all before. Something different is needed if we are to make
headway with the greening of capitalism. It requires changes that will *really* matter and will *really* have an effect, and that are based on capitalism
as it *really* operates.

My approach is to start at the opposite end, as it were, with the
current "third phase" of industrialization that is bringing China and India
into the orbit of the industrialized world. As China lifts hundreds of millions of people out of poverty, and India follows a similar course, and Brazil and many other developing countries aspire to do so as well, they open
up a new pathway for development and the prospect of a new kind of
industrial capitalism. There is under way a process of "shifting wealth,"
whereby the center of gravity of the world economy is shifting east (and to
some extent south), thereby raising the prospects for hundreds of millions
more to be lifted out of poverty.[1] But no sooner do these extra millions
and eventually billions seek to achieve their share of industrial wealth (as
did the West through the first and second industrial revolutions) than they

encounter a most inconvenient truth. Can the development model that served the already-industrialized countries—with access to the cornucopia of fossil fuels and unlimited resource flows—scale to accommodate the new demands?

The process of industrialization has lifted close to one billion people in Western Europe, North America, and Japan out of the "Malthusian trap" that pinned income to population and set them on a trajectory of rising per capita wealth. This created a "great divergence" between the West and the "rest," accounting for the extreme disparities in wealth, income, and power that have characterized the modern world. In the twentieth century, while serious efforts were made to industrialize in many parts of the world, it was only in East Asia that catch-up, or convergence, was achieved. Now in the twenty-first century these efforts have spread to China and India, and a "great convergence" is under way, reversing the trajectories of the past two hundred years.[2] So the key question is, Can the industrial model that served the West so well now be adapted to meet the new demands? Can it meet the needs of up to six billion people who are looking to achieve middle-income status by 2050 (as envisaged by economists such as Michael Spence)?[3] Can it do so—without subjecting the planet to irreparable harm?

The scale of the changes involved in this next "Great Transformation" is immense. The original Industrial Revolution lifted the population of Great Britain to double the per capita income over a period of around 150 years; the subsequent industrialization of the United States took around 50 years. Now China has doubled its per capita income in 12 years, and India in 16 years. Moreover, China and India are starting from a population of more than one billion, compared to around ten million for the United States and the United Kingdom early in the nineteenth century. So the pace of industrialization in this third round has picked up tenfold, and the number of people involved has expanded a hundredfold—meaning that the current transition involving the new industrial giants China and India is a thousand times more intense than the original Industrial Revolution. Can the same model of dependence on apparently unlimited fossil fuels and resource abundance underpin this latest industrial transition at such a level of intensity?

To pose the question in this way is really to answer it. As soon as the material, resource, and energy requirements needed to expand the present industrial system along conventional lines are spelled out, the impossibility of pursuing such an approach becomes clear. Industrial capitalism is rapidly "filling" the planet. Something therefore needs to be done in a way that is consistent with the engine of wealth generation that drives the capitalist economy. To borrow the phrase made famous by Karl Polanyi, who described the process of industrialization as the "Great Transformation," we may characterize the changes that would allow industrialization to spread worldwide, in a manner that respects ecological realities, as the "Next Great Transformation."[4] Its current drivers, as well as the obstacles that stand in its way, are the subject of this book.

In this work I examine efforts under way in East Asia and Europe that seek to carve out a new development pathway. Insofar as its material foundations are based on a less resource-intensive approach to growth, we might call that pathway "green." Eminent Chinese scholars like Hu Angang see such a development as the "inevitable choice" for China and, by extension, for the rest of the developing world.[5] Thus, rather than beginning with the problems of carbon emissions; devastation of forests, fisheries, and agriculture resources; and degradation of soils and other problems, my approach is to look to "greening" of development strategies and to ask what may be the consequences for the myriad problems of environmental mismanagement that are widely discussed. The difficulty encountered in framing the issue in the conventional way, which starts with the problems, is that it appears to place the burden of solving problems created by the developed world on the shoulders of developing countries; this makes "green growth" strategies thereby suspect in the eyes of some. After all, why should developing countries have to bear the burden of higher costs for renewable energies while the developed world goes on burning cheaper coal? *Why* indeed? That there is considerable debate and some opposition to green strategies in the developing world is hardly surprising.[6]

A different starting point is possible, and indeed necessary. Instead of listing the well-known problems created by capitalism, one can begin by celebrating its achievements. Capitalism is an extraordinary social, political, and economic innovation that has been world transforming. The modern global system, powered by industrialization, is quite unlike anything that came before. New gigantic productive forces have been conjured into existence, in the phrase immortalized by Marx and Engels.

Mortality rates have been drastically reduced, leading to a population explosion that has in turn enhanced productivity and innovation potential. Income levels have exceeded population growth, breaking humanity free of the Malthusian trap that constrained everything before.

On the whole, the arrival of industrial capitalism has been associated with profoundly positive results. Food has become cheaper and more abundant; extraction of resources has grown, and their prices relative to wages have plummeted. Early experiences of pollution and environmental degradation have been reversed. Scientific and medical breakthroughs of the first order—anesthesia, antibiotics, vaccines—have relieved humanity from age-old burdens (although those breakthroughs are not yet universally shared).

Recognition of the many achievements of industrial capitalism has sparked its emulation and rapid diffusion worldwide—in Latin America, India, East Asia, and now in China. All these countries have been industrializing on a conventional resource-intensive and fossil-fueled model first—as did the West. As industrial capitalism powered by fossil fuels and extensive resource throughput spreads worldwide, so its impact on ecological processes becomes more obvious, more intrusive, less avoidable.

The costs of continuing with "business as usual" (to use the terminology of the International Energy Agency and the Intergovernmental Panel on Climate Change) are becoming apparent—and it is in the developing countries that these costs are encountered with greatest force, as ecological limits are breached with abandon. The polluted air of Beijing and the clogged waterways of Mumbai are ever-present reminders of the toll being taken by such a pathway of industrialization, where massive resort to coal and fossil fuels leads to the fouling of the air and waterways, and equally massive throughput of resources leads to chemical pollution on a scale unprecedented.

It is therefore perhaps not surprising that the strongest response is also to be found in these developing countries. China in particular is emerging as a leader in building renewable energy industries and advancing the frontier of resource efficiency technology. After all, the conventional view has been that it would be the most advanced countries that would be supplying the technologies needed to clean up the planet. The fact that in many ways it is the latecomers like China that are taking the lead, while the advanced countries remain locked in by their carbon investments, is at odds with this conventional view. It throws up one of the most challenging issues to be resolved by the social sciences.

How can we account then for this unanticipated development? I advance a response in this book that integrates three major lines of argument, each associated with a pioneering thinker of the twentieth century. First, the argument I advance is neo-Schumpeterian, in that it evolves through repeated episodes of creative destruction, which turns on the capacity of firms to drive change, subject to the institutional incentives and barriers created by the prevailing techno-economic paradigm. The latest such shift may be identified with the surge of investment in renewable energies and low-carbon technologies. It amounts to a complete change in techno-economic paradigm and creates unprecedented opportunities for the firms (and countries) that grasp the challenge. Second, the argument is neo-Gerschenkronian, in that it focuses on the latecomers to industrialization and how they draw advantages from adopting a green development model. China is the clear latecomer that is arguably adapting fastest to the demands of a greening of capitalism. Finally, the argument is neo-Olsonian, in that it takes account of the tangle of institutional blockages and vested interests that block and delay the transition in the most advanced countries—what is memorably described as "carbon lock-in."[7] This implies that the initiative in shifting to a new kind of industrial system will most likely pass to the countries that have contributed least to the present problems.

From these three perspectives an argument is distilled whereby it is the latecomers like China that have the most pressing need for green growth strategies, given the terrible environmental catastrophes they are experiencing, and that have the greatest incentive to implement an alternative development model. What is equally important is the fact that the state centered on Beijing has the capacity to do something about those problems. The country's current Twelfth Five-Year Plan provides as close a template as one is likely to find for greening an industrial economy. In a similar move, South Korea, another East Asian practitioner of state-guided industrial transformation, has initiated its own green growth industrial strategy. By contrast, the lead countries, and particularly the United States, which came of age in the oil era, have the densest thicket of rules and institutions favoring fossil fuel interests. These rules and interests are proving to be exceedingly difficult to undo. In Europe, however, the German *Energiewende* (energy transformation) may have wider ripple effects as it demonstrates a middle way.

The Focus of Change: Renewable Energies, Resource Efficiency, and Finance

The variety of problems we are confronted with—the peaking of oil and gas supplies; environmental spoliation; depletion of soil and water; long-term systemic disturbances exhibited in such miscellaneous phenomena as loss of biodiversity, collapse of coral reefs, mass extinctions—all call for specific kinds of solutions. But underpinning these solutions there is a common cause—and that is the "business as usual" (BAU) kind of capitalism that has brought us (effectively so far) to this point. The argument of this book, then, is that it is changes to the rules of *this particular kind of capitalism* that are called for—not changes to the rules of capitalism as such, insofar as it works well on foundations of property rights, markets, and innovation. Indeed, the "free-market environmentalism" school of thought would have it that if these foundations could be extended and built on more completely, then all the problems would disappear. As Jeffreys puts it, "Free market environmentalism can save the planet." Faith in market fundamentalism, however, has not been well rewarded, as the blowback from deregulated financial markets amply testifies.[8]

The problem is to get from a BAU trajectory to something quite different involving renewables, resource efficiency, and eco-finance—a zone in which markets may be expected to work well. The transition is, however, most unlikely to be brought about by market forces alone (such as through consumer demand, perhaps buttressed by carbon taxes) because the carbon lock-in is simply too strong. In this case there is a necessity for the state to take action to drive the system onto a new trajectory with new rules and standards that make the system more "sentient," more attuned to the scale and scope of interaction between economic and ecological processes. Specifically, there will need to be new rules for the transition to a new kind of green growth capitalism—and these new rules will have to engage directly with the details of energy, resource throughput, and finance, replacing the existing trajectories with new state-mandated renewable pathways.

In short, the capitalist tools of property rights, markets, and creative destruction can be expected to work effectively—as claimed by the proponents of free-market environmentalism—but only after the system has been given a reboot and is embarked on a new course that results from smart state intervention. Such intervention can be expected to take the form of publicly stated and enforced "default options" in the form of renewable energies and resource efficiency and recirculation principles, effected through differential tax rates, penalties and subsidies, differential interest rates, and other instruments. (Since I will be referring to "renewable energy and resource efficiency" principles repeatedly, let us agree to refer to them as RE^2 principles.) The refounding has to be genuine, and has to be seen to be genuine. It has to be public in order to generate systemwide change and adherence by capitalist entrepreneurs. It has to be enforceable if it is to have the desired effect—and that means backed by strong state capacity. Weak governments giving weak commitments or backsliding too easily will not produce the desired effect.

Now the free-market environmentalist critics respond that all this is unnecessary; if there is a profit to be made in the new RE^2 sectors, then capitalist interests will dictate that entrepreneurial initiatives flow in these directions. The flaw in this assumption is that it ignores time and scale. There is an urgency to dealing with the problems created by the conventional model that demands a timely response. A leisurely reliance on, say, common law procedures for sorting out conflicting property rights claims as between fossil fuel burners and those affected by the emissions cannot hope to achieve resolution before the problems become unmanageable. Such court procedures advocated by free-market environmentalist authors can tackle incremental problems but not comprehensive system transformations.[9] The intensity of the carbon lock-in presented by the BAU system is such that only a government-mandated shift to a new regime could succeed in creating the conditions for genuine competition in energy and resource industries. To rely solely on private-sector entrepreneurial initiative in a context where Olsonian vested interests are so powerful is to condemn the system to inertia for decades.[10]

Other critics might respond that in advancing the case for RE^2 to be the default option, we are "picking winners" on a grand scale. Why not leave it to the market to sort out what kind of post–fossil fuel energy system and resource operations might prevail? The response is that it will indeed be the market that determines which specific options—including particular renewable energies and resource recirculation pathways—will be chosen and adopted. But a flood of new investments in these various options will come into being only after the alternative option of investing in destructive fossil fuels and resource exploitation has been phased out by governments' introducing of new rules that favor green trajectories. It is the character of these rules—and not the individual technologies of energy generation and resource circulation—that will make the difference in countries' effectively dealing with these issues.

Once a new direction is signaled and followed through, with policy resetting that mandates a new renewable trajectory, then entrepreneurial initiative can be expected to take over and investments in the new options to start flowing on a large scale. In this sense there is little difference between myself and advocates of "pure capitalist" solutions like Deidre McCloskey or the free-market environmentalists.[11] If there is a difference, it is that I recognize the need for smart state action *to set the system on a new trajectory*—an inescapable precondition—and that such a new trajectory will not be brought into being without state involvement. Insofar as the advocates of free-market principles deny the need for state action, they deny the power and potential of capitalist tools to really do the job in driving the system onto renewable pathways. Indeed, they condemn the tools of a greener capitalism to be working forever against the inertia and vested interests of business as usual, becoming blunted and thereby never succeeding in bringing about a more sustainable economy.

This is where the case of China makes a powerful entrance. In the terms of a detective novel, China has both motive and means. It has the motive in wishing to clean up its own environment and to avoid the endless geopolitical conflicts that a continuation of the fossil-fueled pathway promises. And it has the means in the form of a strong (in this case, authoritarian) state that is prepared to make tough decisions and implement them. I make this statement as an observation, and not as an endorsement of authoritarian rule.

China's Green and Black Model

Some will no doubt find it an "inconvenient truth" that it may well be China—widely condemned for its industrial pollution—that is

leading the way toward a renewable alternative. The key point to highlight is that while China has been expanding its fossil-fueled energy system at an unprecedented rate, at the same time it has been expanding
its alternative renewable energy systems and resource-efficient circular
economy, also at an unprecedented rate. From 2005 it was doubling its
wind power capacity each year and is now continuing to double it every
two to three years, creating by far the world's largest wind power sector
(turbines and components) and largest land area of wind farms. It has
been scaling up its solar photovoltaic (PV) systems in a similar way, so
that its solar PV production industry is by far the largest in the world. In
the period of the Eleventh Five-Year Plan (2006–2010), its investments
in a strong and smart electric power grid that can collect and distribute
power from a variety of fluctuating renewable sources were doubled, so
that they outranked investments in power generation; this process is accelerating under the Twelfth Five-Year Plan. By 2013 China had by far the
largest renewable energy industry in the world, outranking the entire German and French power systems. There is still a reluctance to acknowledge
this point, and some leading climate scientists discount Chinese efforts,
promoting nuclear as the only alternative to fossil fuels.[12]

As China succeeds in building this new RE^2 trajectory, it can be
expected that India will follow, with perhaps a ten-year lag.[13] If India
pursues a trajectory with a clear focus on renewables and resource efficiency, and it shows many signs of doing so, then it, too, will be focused
firmly on a development pathway that can scale. Likewise in the case of
Brazil, there is already a high reliance on renewable energies, including
bioenergy, and emergent green investment strategies being developed by
the Brazilian Development Bank. In the West, too, Germany is now firmly
committed to such a course, whether through competitive emulation of
China or through its own ambitions, and Japan is now reviewing its commitments to nuclear power after the Fukushima shock. But it is China
that is the main story.

If its stated ambitions offer a reasonable guide to the future, then
the Chinese leadership is determined to set the country on a greener
course. At an Association of Southeast Asian Nations conference staged
in Beijing in 2006, the vice minister of environmental protection, Li Ganjie went on the record to state that "green development is an inevitable
choice" for China and for developing countries generally. The vice minister

noted that in the short term, promoting green development acted as a stimulus for the economy; in the medium term, it improved resource efficiency (reducing the scale of resource usage and imports), reduced emissions, and reversed environmental degradation; and in the long term, it promoted a different kind of sustainable industrial system. Since these words were spoken, China has surprised many with its commitment to green development, establishing renewable energy industries at a pace unheard of in the West, putting in place the building blocks of a circular economy by turning wastes into raw materials and by directing finance to support such investments via differential interest charges levied by state-owned banks.

The obvious contrast to be made is with the China model that everyone recognizes—the "black" development model, based on coal. Since 2001, when it joined the World Trade Organization, China has built the world's largest manufacturing system powered by the world's largest energy system—and fueled, for the most part, by coal and other fossil fuels. In this respect, China has merely been replicating the steps of earlier industrializers, from Great Britain to Europe and the United States, and in the twentieth century, to Japan, Korea, and Taiwan. All these countries utilized fossil fuels to build their formidable industrial systems. China is doing the same, but on a much grander scale than anyone else—adding 50 billion watts of coal-fired electric power each year (or a 1 gigawatt [GW] thermal power station a week), as well as scouring the world for coal, oil, and gas supplies. Indeed, China is now burning nearly as much coal as the rest of the world combined—nudging 3.5 billion tonnes per year.[14] Its rapid ramping up of coal consumption and fossil fuel electric power generation follows a well-known course (Figure 1.1).

The Chinese leadership appears to recognize that this strategy will not scale, because it will call for coal production and oil imports that will force China to go out into the world in search of resources and impinge too openly and aggressively on other countries' claims. China has a clear interest in avoiding resource-based confrontations (at least away from its immediate neighborhood) because it has a strong commitment to achieving standards of living comparable with those of the West through peaceful development, without the waste of war. If resource confrontations are to be avoided, Beijing realizes that renewable energy industries will need to be built as fast as is physically and technologically possible.

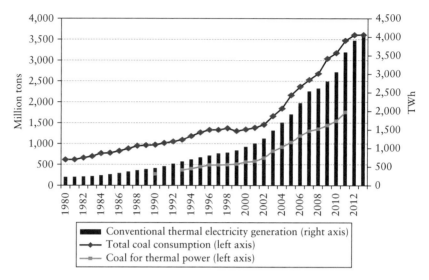

FIGURE **1.1**   China's "black" face: Buildup of thermal power
SOURCE: Adapted from Mathews and Tan (2013).

Current efforts seem directed precisely toward this goal, as we shall see in more detail in Part 2 of this book. In anticipation, consider just one example. In wind power, China rose from a marginal position in 2005 to double its wind power capacity each year, becoming world leader by the end of 2010 (Figure 1.2). This is what might be recognized as its "green" development model.

By 2013, China was adding more power-generating capacity in hydro and "new" renewables than in conventional nuclear and thermal power stations—an extremely important milestone, both for China and the world. Its Twelfth Five-Year Plan has notable goals of raising those levels. In terms of electric power, China's leadership (in the form of the planning body, the National Development and Reform Commission) anticipates that by 2015 no less than 30 percent of electric power capacity will be generated from nonfossil sources (including a small amount of nuclear)—up from less than 5 percent in 2001.[15] By 2012 wind power capacity already exceeded that of nuclear power. This can be described best as an energy industrial revolution.[16]

Beyond 2020, confidence in this continued uptake of renewables can only increase because of cumulative industrial dynamics.

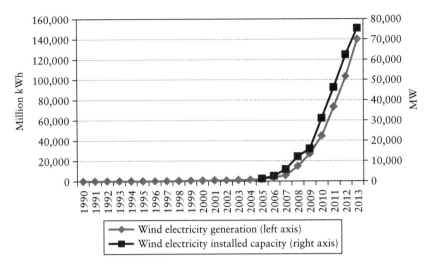

FIGURE **1.2**   China's "green" face: Buildup of wind power
SOURCE: Adapted from Mathews and Tan (2013).

A logistic (or S-shaped) curve captures the industrial dynamics involved in China's adoption of a succession of renewable energy and nuclear technologies that can be expected to progressively substitute for its use of various fossil fuels, in particular coal. One can make this statement with a degree of confidence because China is already embarked on such substitution; it also has policies and commitments in place to carry the momentum forward to 2020 and beyond. We know from the history of technological substitutions—such as open-hearth steelmaking furnaces in the nineteenth century, and compact discs' displacement of vinyl records in the twentieth century—that once such substitution reaches a certain threshold, it then continues, following the well-known logistic, or S-shaped, curve trajectory (discussed in Chapter 4, on renewables).

If China meets its goals, which is highly likely, then the country would be well on course to becoming the world's first to complete its industrialization with a greater reliance on renewables than on fossil fuels.[17] Following industrial logistic arguments, the process through which the green will supersede the black may be envisaged as in Figure 1.3— an image that represents the future of China as much as of the planet as a

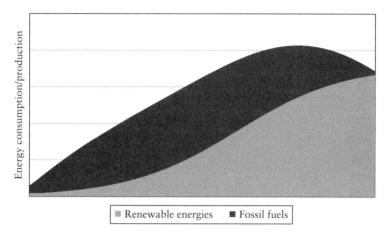

FIGURE **1.3**   China's green and black energy revolution
SOURCE: Tan and Mathews.

whole. The wider implications, in terms of reducing geopolitical tensions and social and environmental costs, need little elaboration.

Debates and Contested Positions

In the chapters to come, I engage with many of the debates raised by the energy-environment issue and the emergence of a new, green techno-economic paradigm. The intensity of such debates—over the costs and feasibility of renewables, the costs of building new infrastructure versus the costs of doing nothing, the character of a green economy and whether growth can continue, and the role of state versus the market in driving the transition—is clear to all who have participated. Rather than restate the terms of those debates, this book offers a distinctive perspective based on the argument I have outlined here. For example, the trading of emissions permits and the creation of so-called carbon markets is a topic that has generated heated discussion—with advocates insisting that such market-driven creations are the cheapest and most effective means of changing behavior, while critics point to the Olsonian barriers and weakness of incentives created by realistic carbon taxes. When we examine the experience of China, the issue becomes clearer. There it is recognized that determined state intervention is needed to drive investment into new energy sources. Between state and market there are of course numerous institutions that play a role in shaping the directions of investment. Once a new line of development is under way, then finessing carbon taxes and emissions trading schemes becomes feasible—as witnessed by the launch of pilot schemes at the provincial level in China. When introduced without prior state direction (as occurs in much of the West), carbon markets function simply as a means to create carbon bubbles. China seems determined to avoid such outcomes.

The feasibility of renewables themselves has been hotly contested on various grounds, such as their costs, lack of technical maturity, resource impact, and even technical complexity. Again, the experience of China is instructive. The fact that China has been able to take certain technologies that are already dominant and scale them up to levels unprecedented elsewhere has demolished many of these arguments. What were previously seen as costs are now seen as business opportunities as new markets are created by Chinese interventions—as in the case of smart-grid technology and its components, or new city-lighting systems based on light-emitting diodes (LEDs). Indeed, the very success of China's exports of renewable energy systems around the world has grown the market for these products and thereby driven down costs much faster than anticipated. This has sparked emulation and a new realism in entrepreneurial business models and competitive dynamics. Green growth is truly shifting from religion to reality.[18]

What, then, are the implications for growth—or for "degrowth"? Is it possible to be green and to grow? There are increasing numbers of people in the West who advocate "zero growth" or "degrowth" as the option of choice to take the world in a genuinely green direction. Again, the experience of China allows us to review the issue in a fresh light. It has to be conceded that the degrowth choice would stop industrialization in China and India in its tracks. So on immediate political grounds, it is extremely unlikely that these new industrial giants would come out in support of zero growth. That means the concept would apply only to the already advanced countries—clearly a politically unpopular option if ignored everywhere else.[19] On those grounds, it just won't fly.

Even if a way could be found around these political difficulties, zero growth is not really an option for capitalism. On one hand, we have a planet with resources that are neither infinite nor always readily or harmlessly available. On the other hand, we have a perpetual growth machine in the form of a capitalism that thrives on innovation and expansion. How can these two observations be reconciled? In what respect does it make sense to talk of green growth? A strict adherence to the idea of steady state would rule out such a possibility, at least in the medium term. But is a capitalist green growth economy a feasible proposition?[20] Can we envisage a form of growth that enables incomes to rise while restricting the growth of resource throughput—leading eventually to a steady state in material terms while enabling innovation and income growth to proceed? This would be a form of growth that not only does less damage to the planet but also accommodates the needs of large industrializing countries like China and India while still taking the industrial world as a whole closer to the ideal of a steady-state economy. An argument to be developed in Chapter 8 is that growth in capitalism actually derives from interconnected capitalist firms generating increasing returns from their combined manufacturing activities, and not necessarily from expanding resource flows.[21] The fact that growth in the industrial experience of the West has indeed been associated with increasing resource throughput (as measured by gross domestic product) does not mean that growth must always follow such a course.

These considerations lead me to specify what I mean by "green growth capitalism." It is an economic system that is greening itself through preferred investment in RE^2 activities, and in which the growth registered in output, productivity, and incomes is achieved without extending the resource base. Green growth capitalism captures increasing returns generated by manufacturing, where manufactured devices like wind turbines and solar cells are utilized to harvest power from renewable energy sources. The creation of an energy system grounded in manufacturing and its increasing returns (manifested in rapidly falling costs) stands in marked contrast with the securing of energy by extractive activities (mining, drilling), which are always associated with diminishing returns (rising costs).[22] And just like its nongreen relative, the emergent green growth capitalism is also highly dependent for its emergence on active state intervention. It will operate through creative destruction: as one sector expands, another will be destroyed, but incomes will continue to rise, on the basis of improving productivity generated by increasing returns.

While this pattern has recurred over the past three hundred years, growth has been "extensive," necessitating rising levels of resource throughput. Such a nongreen growth model of capitalism seemed to make sense in an era when resources were assumed to be inexhaustible and fossil fuels promised endless supplies of cheap energy. In our own era, however, this model's environmental and ecological costs are more widely understood, and not least the political costs as nations line up to fight one another for the dwindling supplies exacerbated by the arrival of so many latecomers to the industrialization game. The threat of resource wars triggered by further pursuit of a BAU trajectory must be a factor as China looks to balance geopolitical pressures, created by its intrusion into new regions in pursuit of resource security, through building renewable industries at home that will lessen the potential threats from abroad.

The green growth model, by contrast, is one that looks to secure energy and resource efficiency through building sophisticated energy and resource industries, utilizing technology specific to the purpose, and grounding strategies for export growth in future on such new indus-tries. Energy (and economic) security in such a model is underpinned by the fact that devices for capturing renewable energy sources are manufactured—and manufacturing is, in principle, open to anyone. I refer to this as a "green growth" model, borrowing the terminology used in Korea.[23] In contrast to both the advocates of free-market environmen-talism and of zero growth, I emphasize that determined state action is required to shift the system from its present trajectory to a renewable pathway—and that without such intervention, the transition will not be accomplished. Indeed, we see emerging a renewed debate on industrial policy and structural change and the possibilities for greening of indus-trial policy not just in the emerging countries, but increasingly in the advanced industrial countries themselves.[24]

The chapters to come elaborate on and substantiate these arguments. In the first part of the book, I ask how we got to where we are as an indus-trial civilization, with its "business as usual" features and fossil fuel de-pendence. An alternative to BAU capitalism has to be found and deployed if the aspirations of billions are to be met.[25] Part 2 is the substantive core of the book, devoted to the three fundamental sectors of capitalism—

energy, resources, finance—in which new approaches are most needed, and in which the seeds of change are already being sown. Part 3 draws the threads together to discuss the driving and opposing forces shaping the emergence of a green growth capitalism, with a focus on how these are playing out in the important case of China.

I   *How We Got to Where We Are*

2   The First "Great Transformation"

Day by day it becomes more evident that the Coal we happily possess in excellent quality and abundance is the Mainspring of Modern Material Civilization. . . . Coal alone . . . commands this age—the Age of Coal.

  —*W. Stanley Jevons,* The Coal Question *(1865)*

How could this unprecedented swarming of people on a small, offshore island be made consistent with a rising standard of living? It was impossible on the fixed area of English cultivable land, whatever miracles English technological progress in agriculture might accomplish. The way out was for England (through a transportation revolution and international trade) to endow itself with the equivalent of a vast extension of its own land base. Because it was the first to switch from wood fuel to fossilized fuel, it was able to become the workshop of the world and exchange the industrial fruits of its new technology for abundant cheap food from newly settled overseas countries.

  —*Joseph Schumpeter,* Business Cycles *(1939)*

[A] market economy implies a self-regulating system of markets; in slightly more technical terms, it is an economy directed by market prices and nothing but market prices. Such a system capable of organizing the whole of economic life without outside help or interference would certainly deserve to be called self-regulating. These rough indications should suffice to show the entirely unprecedented nature of such a venture in the history of the race.

  —*Karl Polanyi,* The Great Transformation *(1944/2001)*

The modern world is indeed the product of industrialization—and it is industrialization that all countries now seek to achieve as their highest priority. The reason they do so is apparent from a glance at Figure 2.1, which provides a summary economic history of the world. There clearly occurred "something" between 1760 and 1860 in Britain that changed that country forever, and then changed the world.

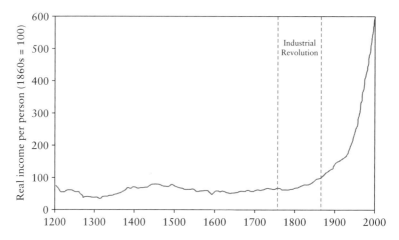

FIGURE **2.1**   Growth of per capita income, England, 1200–2000

SOURCE: Gregory Clark, *A Farewell to Alms: A Brief Economic History of the World.* © 2007 by Princeton University Press. Reprinted by permission of Princeton University Press.

Yes, something very important for the world economy clearly occurred during the approximately hundred years from 1760 to 1860. In England in these years, population doubled but income rose fourfold—so that *per capita income actually doubled.*[1] This was the first time that there had been a sustained breakout from what has come to be known as the Malthusian trap—after the English political economist, Rev. Thomas Malthus and his *Essay on the Principle of Population* (1798). Malthus had argued that as income increases, so population would increase at a greater rate until the population would outgrow its resource base and trigger a famine—thus keeping per capita income more or less constant. This is just what has happened throughout history—going back hundreds of years. A dramatic illustration of this thesis occurred in China at the very time that Malthus was writing. Under the Qing dynasty, food production systems were rationalized and intensified, leading to improvements in agricultural productivity—but those improvements were then followed by explosive increases in population. Indeed China's population increased from 100 million in 1750 to 283 million in 1890.[2] Poor harvests and bad weather led to famines in 1810 and 1811 then again in 1846 and 1849 (with up to 40 million dying), triggering the Taiping Rebellion that started in 1850; and then in 1875 and 1876 harvest failures led to a great famine in 1876–79, one of the worst ever experienced in China. Clearly China had not broken out of the Malthusian trap, whereas Britain, with its access to fossil fuels, had done so. In the Malthusian trap, the limiting condition was the price of food, which depended on agricultural return. But in Britain the price of fuel—particularly coal—became more important as regulator of an industrial economy.

In the years 1760 to 1860, incomes rose in excess of population increase in Britain, and then kept on rising. This was the totally unexpected feature of industrialization. Earlier debates had focused on the question of whether the rise in incomes actually improved people's lives. One group of pessimists argued that standards of living actually fell—but more recent work would seem to have settled the matter in favor of a rise.[3] In any case, it is clear that as each successive wave of countries seeks to industrialize, they do so in the expectation (and reality) of incomes and national wealth improving. Industrialization is clearly an enormously powerful social and economic tool—as recognized by numerous scholars, including Joseph Schumpeter in the epigraph to this chapter.

Karl Polanyi put it best, describing the transition from agrarian to industrial capitalist society as the Great Transformation.[4] Because that is what it was. The agrarian economy, with its settled ways of doing things (interrupted assuredly by innovations that had long-term effects) was sundered by the tumultuous changes unleashed by industrialization—essentially the harnessing of capitalist rules and institutions and the introduction of "unlimited" power from fossil fuels. Polanyi insisted on the radical disjuncture—the rupture—that capitalist industrialization represented. In his 1944 book *The Great Transformation*, he described the resulting social form as market society, and developed the argument that this "market society" was essentially an ideological construction based on three "fictitious commodities"—land, labor, and money. They are fictitious, according to Polanyi, because they are treated as real and independent, and yet they have no existence apart from their role in the market system created by strong state intervention.[5] This is the enduring legacy of Polanyi's work—that industrial capitalism was not "natural" but an amazing outcome of deliberate policies and state actions.

The appeal of Polanyi's *Great Transformation* lies in its insistence that the creation of a market economy was essentially an ideological and political construction and not, as depicted in mainstream economics, an outgrowth of markets and liberalism.[6] Mainstream economics identifies categories such as "labor" and "land" in order to discuss their interaction in market settings, but for Polanyi these are abstractions that have had to be divorced from their flesh-and-blood counterparts; the economic discourse disguises the transformation involved in their appearance as semiautonomous economic categories. He insisted that they had appeared not spontaneously, but only through decisive state intervention, in the form of the enclosures (that created an economic category of "land" free of traditional encumbrances) and likewise state intervention to overthrow traditional parish-based labor regulation, to create a free market in something called "labor." His argument is given greater salience by his demonstration that each of these aspects of the Great Transformation evoked countermoves (what he called the double movement, or what we now call feedback loops) such as the Speenhamland system of labor support—the last vestige, as he saw it, of the English squirearchy's efforts to deal with the emerging industrial system, prior to the rise of workers' own trade unions.[7]

In contrast, Polanyi's scholarship has not stood up to sustained analysis. In focusing on the "fictitious" commodities of labor and land, he missed the equally important role played by energy and resource throughput. In his later years he engaged in a long-running debate over the extent to which markets were to be found in precapitalist societies—and his position that markets are a very recent phenomenon is now found to be untenable by most serious scholars of economic history.[8] Does that mean that the concept of the Great Transformation is vitiated? Not at all. This term best captures the flavor of the enormity of the transition, and it announces in advance (in 1944) why the rest of the world would be so keen to share in the process and enjoy its fruits.

Leaving to one side any critique of Polanyi and his work, what exactly was this "Industrial Revolution" or "Great Transformation" that generated such a sustained increase in incomes, allowing one country after another to escape the Malthusian trap? This is indeed an important question—because the way we answer it shapes the way we seek to understand the next "Great Transformation" that is clearly under way and already transforming emerging giants like China and India.[9]

Going beyond Polanyi (but in a way of which he would surely have approved), I propose to discuss the first Great Transformation under three headings: energy (the switch to fossil fuels); resources (the tapping of industrial commodities well beyond the organic local materials traditionally used); and finance, which made the whole transformation possible. We will then investigate how these all came together in Britain in the last decades of the eighteenth century, launching the industrial era. This approach provides the prelude to our utilization of these three categories as driving the "next" industrial revolution in the twenty-first century.

The Drivers of the First Great Transformation

Energy—Resort to the "Cornucopia" of Fossil Fuels

Largely unremarked on by economic historians, England underwent an energy revolution from 1650 to 1750 that preceded by a hundred years the innovations in mining, textiles, iron, and so on, and the factories that are generally reckoned as constituting the Industrial Revolution.[10] The economist W. Stanley Jevons had already captured the over-riding significance of coal to Britain's industrial success in his 1865 monograph— and this too should properly be considered as fruit of an energy revolution that preceded what is commonly described as the Industrial Revolution (which was really a revolution in the application of steam power to new sectors of production like textiles) from 1750 on. The significance of the "energy revolution" that saw a complete transformation in the fuels and power systems used in Britain from an economy largely powered by organic sources (particularly wood and charcoal) to one involving inorganic (particularly coal—with a minor role played by peat in the Netherlands) is now clear.[11] It is essential to grasp this prior energy industrial revolution because it is changes in energy production and consumption that preceded the shift to industrialization in every subsequent country. Energy, and in particular the rise of fossil fuels, starting with coal, is inseparable from our understanding of industrialization.

How did this energy transition come about? By around 1750, after decades of upheaval, Britain was largely a coal-based economy. Its annual coal production was ten million tonnes, far in excess of any other country. This put Britain on an inorganic fuel footing that had never been achieved before in human history. Coal production had grown threefold over the previous half century, having been around three million tonnes in 1700—

itself well in advance of any other country, including China. As shown so clearly by the German historian Sieferle, this was achieved only by the most arduous process of substitution of coal for wood and charcoal in one industrial sector after another—such as in salt making and soap production, and culminating in iron production, with the development of the coke iron furnace by Abraham Darby in Coalbrookdale around 1709.[12] The crowning achievement of this series of innovations involving coal was unquestionably the development of the atmospheric steam engine, unveiled to the public by its developer, Thomas Newcomen, in 1712. Most historians of the period agree that Newcomen's demonstration of his beam engine, to be used for pumping water from coal mines, was the single biggest breakthrough—a work of extraordinary genius.[13] It quite literally changed the world.[14]

The economic historian Robert Allen, professor of economic history at Oxford, has uncovered the price shifts that helped to drive this transformation. As pressure on wood supplies sharpened in the seventeenth century, so prices of wood (and hence charcoal) rose—all while the price of coal remained more or less the same, meaning that supply could increase as fast as demand rose. One of Allen's major contributions to the debate is contained in Figure 2.2, which reveals how the price of wood (in London) rose rapidly in the decade 1650 to 1660 to reach three times the price of coal. This was a "price shock" in seventeenth-century England that was every bit as severe as the Organization of the Petroleum Exporting Countries (OPEC) oil "price shock" of the 1970s was for the global economy in the twentieth century. The shift to coal began in earnest in the middle of the seventeenth century with the rise in wood prices, opening up a considerable gap between coal and wood prices. By the year 1700 the transition from wood to coal was well under way.[15]

Fossil fuels, then, created a cornucopia for the early industrializers. Rolf Peter Sieferle captures the effect neatly in calling the fossil fuel reserves a "subterranean forest" that vastly expanded the energy resources available to the early movers. These resources gave them a lead over the rest of the world, and that lead has become institutionalized and maintained for decades, even centuries. The great drama of industrialization, now captured in the modernization of China, India, and Brazil, concerns the continuing efforts of these latter countries to tap into the cornucopia for themselves. But here they encounter problems that were evaded by

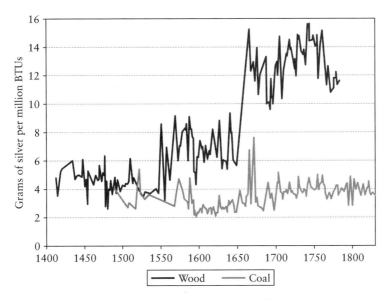

FIGURE **2.2**   Real prices of wood and coal in London, 1400–1800
SOURCE: Allen (2009). Reprinted with the permission of Cambridge University Press.

the early movers in industrialization. They encounter problems in terms of energy security, economic security, and environmental security. These problems will prove to be central to the argument developed in this text; they call for a more sophisticated approach to issues of energy-material transformation underpinning industrial expansion.[16]

The subsequent story tells itself through the data on fossil fuel application and industrialization. Consider first the case for the United States and then for the rest of the world (Smil 1994). Figure 2.3 shows how coal rapidly displaced wood and charcoal in the United States in the early decades of the nineteenth century. Chandler (1972) makes a powerful case that the US industrial revolution got under way only after anthracite coal fields in Pennsylvania were opened up, allowing coal to be supplied at cheap rates to the northeastern states, which then became the epicenter of US industry.

Before 1900, the United States had overtaken Britain as the world's most significant user of fossil fuels. In the 1920s the Soviet Union, after the Russian Revolution, started its climb to industrialization, again

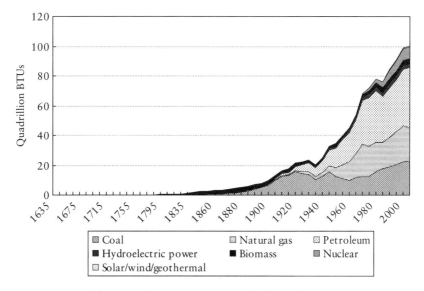

FIGURE **2.3**   Fossil fuels and industrialization of the United States
SOURCE: US Energy Information Administration.
NOTE: Time and scale are not uniform for reasons of space.

powered by fossil fuels. Then China followed the same pathway in the 1950s. Figure 2.4 shows how fossil energy utilization has expanded *three-hundredfold* in the past century and a half of industrialization. If any doubt remains as to the source of the industrial expansions in Europe and the United States in the nineteenth century as lying in the application of fossil fuels, those doubts must be cleared when we look at the cases of the industrial revolutions of the twentieth century, in Japan and East Asia, and even more so when we look at the industrial revolutions now under way in the twenty-first century in China and India—all dependent on fossil fuels.

In the face of this evidence, one must really wonder why it has taken economic historians so long to acknowledge the critical role played by fossil fuels in the industrialization process—particularly in the diffusion of industrialization from one country to another, and from one industry to another. It is worth posing the counterfactual, what would have happened if Britain had not moved inexorably to a coal-based economy in the seventeenth century? The evidence from China, or from the

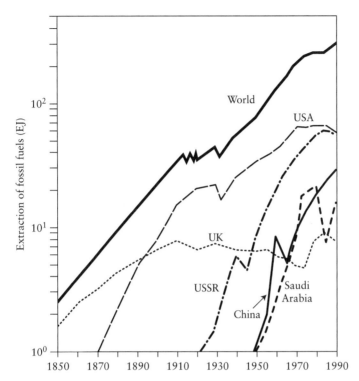

FIGURE **2.4**   Global uptake of fossil fuels
   SOURCE: Smil (1994). Used with permission.

Netherlands, where peat provided an intermediate fossil fuel that was rapidly exhausted, is that any moves toward industrialization would have been short lived. The shift to coal use in Britain really was a one-off event in world history, from which there is now no turning back. The issue is, can countries (particularly China and India) continue to industrialize— but on the basis of renewables rather than fossil fuel energy sources?

Resources—Tapping into Colonial Possessions and New Lands

Industrialization—this wild, three-hundred-year ride—was not just about coal and fossil fuels. There was also the vastly increased access to raw materials consequent on European dominance of world markets that was in turn secured by its military superiority. Coal was available in

England itself (while increasingly wood and charcoal had to be imported from Scandinavia). The case of cotton was central—and its logistics shaped the history of the nineteenth century. Indeed, cotton was the first among these new "industrial-scale" commodities; it drove the economic development of the American South, and it was closely intertwined with the political maneuverings that led to the US Civil War.

The scale of the resource utilization, which dwarfs anything seen in the preindustrial era, indicates the qualitative shift involved. Technological improvements such as the spinning jenny and Eli Whitney's cotton gin (both names being derived from *engine*) combined with Britain's increasing control over a new kind of global supply chain—with cotton being purchased from colonial plantations, then processed into cotton cloth in the textile mills of Lancashire, and then exported in British ships to the outposts of empire.

Paul Kennedy, in *The Rise and Fall of the Great Powers*, puts it well:

> What industrialization, and in particular the steam engine, did was to substitute inanimate for animate sources of power. . . . The consequences of introducing this novel machinery were simply stupendous: by the 1820s someone operating several power-driven looms could produce twenty times the output of a hand worker, while a power-driven "mule" (or spinning machine) had two hundred times the capacity of a spinning wheel . . . the vital point for our purposes was the massive increase in productivity, especially in the textile industries, which in turn stimulated a demand for more machines, more raw materials (above all, cotton), more iron, more shipping, better communications, and so on. (Kennedy 1987, 145)

Of course the European countries had the advantage that they could expand their resource base beyond their own borders through the conquest of overseas possessions—whether held as colonies or as trading posts. The successive waves of European colonization, from the Spanish and Portuguese to the Dutch, English, and French, and finally the Germans and the Japanese, have no explanation other than as the quest for more and more extensive supplies of raw materials—as well as captive markets for finished goods. The scale of resource use since industrialization began in earnest reveals a relentless and uniform pattern, right up until the point of peak use followed (in many cases) by collapse (Figure 2.5).

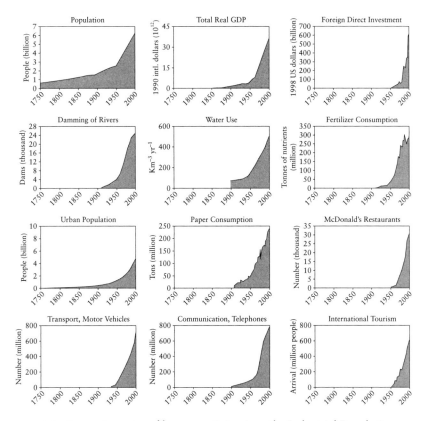

FIGURE **2.5**   Increasing rates of human activity since the Industrial Revolution

SOURCE: Springer and *AMBIO*, volume 40, issue 7, November 2011, page 742, "The Anthropocene: From Global Change to Planetary Stewardship," by Will Steffen et al., figure 1a. © Royal Swedish Academy of Sciences 2011. With kind permission from Springer Science and Business Media.

Resource extraction, and throughput, continues to grow exponentially. Indeed the emphasis on gross domestic product (GDP) "growth" as a goal of economic policy, by governments and institutions like the World Bank and International Monetary Fund, means that resource throughput is expected to continue indefinitely—as if resources were infinite. This is "business as usual."

The economic geographer J. C. Smith captures the scale of the problem in his book on the trends over the coming four decades unleashed by population, global warming, natural resource usage, and globalization. He poses the dilemma of expanded resource use clearly, asking how the entire world might be brought to the same level of material consumption as that enjoyed by North Americans, Western Europeans, Japanese, and Australians today. His conclusion is that global consumption would need to rise *tenfold*—as if the world's population were to suddenly expand from 7 billion today to 72 billion. If the time frame is extended to 2050, then the equivalent population would rise to 105 billion people.[17]

Can the planet afford another ten North Americas? Clearly, if things continue as they are, the answer must be no. The impact on the planet's capacity and recovery systems would be exceeded—many times over. It would be the end of our industrial civilization. The industrial model that has served the advanced world so well, raising living standards in Europe, North America, and Japan to unprecedented levels, cannot and will not scale to encompass further billions in China, India, Brazil, and elsewhere without straining and ruining the planet's resources. This is indeed an "inconvenient truth"—and one that can be dealt with only through a radical change in resource circulation patterns, from a linear to a circular model.[18]

Finance—The Rise of Debt and Credit Instruments

Finance now bestrides the world like a colossus; it created the system we call capitalism, and so it must be involved in creating a successor system. The elements of capitalism that financed all the energy and resource innovations of industrialization, in a new "mode of production," had deep historical roots, going back to the Chinese and Islamic world business empires of the eleventh to fourteenth centuries as they were imported into Italy. Many of the techniques developed (such as double-entry bookkeeping) were then diffused to small city-states in Italy, northern German provinces, and the Netherlands (Venice, Florence Genoa, Bremen, Hamburg, Antwerp, Amsterdam) through the thirteenth to sixteenth centuries.[19] These institutional innovations included a monetary economy, free labor (wages), manufacturing industry, banks, stock exchanges, bills of exchange, insurance, and ultimately the joint stock corporation. The nation-states of Europe were slower to latch on to these social and economic innovations, but they started to do so in Britain and France in the sixteenth century and increasingly in the seventeenth century, ahead of Spain and Portugal, where the Catholic Inquisition and periodic expulsions created terror and social upheaval that disrupted economic development. The center of gravity started to shift to the new nation-states, in particular to Britain, with its constitutional monarchy as opposed to the absolutism of France.[20]

The evolution of financial instruments has already moved through several major innovations and adaptations, from the invention of giro banks and then credit-creating banks to the securitization of government debt via bonds and the subsequent innovations involving shares (equity) and markets in which such instruments can be exchanged and liquidated. Bonds issued by Renaissance Italian city-states, such as the *prestanze* of Florence or the Venetian *prestiti*, proved to be financial innovations of the first order, in that they created debt securities that had the same status as traditional fixed property.[21] In time they came to be called "mobile property" (as in the later French innovation of *credit mobilier*)—which corresponds to what we now call negotiable securities. Eventually the bond market expanded to accommodate issues from private firms (known as debentures) backed by the reputation and market strength of the leading merchant banks (like Barings in London and Goldman Sachs in New York), which acted as their underwriters. Bonds are now the capitalist instrument of credit par excellence, facilitating the large-scale flow of investment funds into the industries created by the first Great Transformation. Bonds, debentures, and other forms of securitization have underpinned the expansion of the entire industrial system.

As discussed in Chapter 6, the scale of the global financial system is truly awesome, totaling $225 trillion in 2012. The bond markets account for $100 trillion, whereas equity markets are half this size, at $50 trillion. Yet neither of these markets has been utilized at scale so far in the funding of a green revolution. The most likely route for finance to become involved is via institutional investors—pension and superannuation funds, insurance funds, and hedge funds—viewing green investments as safer than their business-as-usual counterparts. The sums under the control of such institutional investors are colossal, and certainly capable of meeting the scale of investment required for the green transition; the Organisation for Economic Co-operation and Development (OECD) estimates that they exceed $71 trillion.[22] Clearly, once financial instruments are devised to tap into such funds (and give institutional investors sound investment projects), the prospects for renewable energies and clean technology generally will be transformed. But that is to get ahead of our story.

So—this first Great Transformation was effected through changes in the markets for energy, for commodities and for finance. My task in this book is to trace the comparable process that is already under way in the markets for energy, commodities, and finance in the twenty-first century, in what I am calling the *next* Great Transformation. The prelude to this is the process through which industrialization is diffusing worldwide to become the dominant business and economic process of our time.

Global Expansion of Industrial Capitalism

Once Britain had found the formula, bringing together capitalist institutions and rules, together with fossil fuels and access to overseas resources, it entered a period of unprecedented expansion in industrial output, which fed a growing domestic population and overseas markets, increases in productivity, and the improvements in per capita income that we associate with the Industrial Revolution. The same combination was rapidly replicated in places where coal deposits were readily available—particularly in the Ruhr Valley in Europe (Belgium, German states) and, after the 1830s, with the opening of the Pennsylvania coalfields, in the United States, enabling these countries to rapidly catch up with the early leader, Britain.

The kind of capitalism that quickly took over the world was an expansionist, acquisitive, and ruthlessly rational kind of economic system, one that had been in its totality quite unknown in previous epochs. It employed rational calculation in place of moral or community values and practices.[23] It regarded nature as an objectified entity to be plundered at will (and it likewise regarded nature as a limitless sink into which waste could be disposed). It sought to turn existing products and practices, with their community links and associations, into commodities that could be bought and sold—starting with manufactured products, then encompassing services such as insurance, freight handling, stockjobbing, and extending eventually to health care and education. And it regarded labor as likewise a commodity to be bought and sold, in extreme cases in the form of slavery and child labor. Above all, it recognized no limits to its expansion, given its access to fossil fuels and the cornucopia they generated. For all its faults, this was an incredibly successful system that liberated those who enjoyed its benefits from manual labor, from famine, and from what Marx called the "idiocy of rural life." It effected what Polanyi called, with good reason, the Great Transformation.

Contemporaries at the time of the Industrial Revolution saw it as a liberation from drudgery and from localism—although the shift to coal as fuel in Britain was everywhere resisted; it succeeded only through its economic (cost) superiority. There were of course romantic opponents, who castigated the "dark satanic mills" for reasons that are entirely understandable (they were, after all, dark and satanic), but they missed the bigger picture by focusing on the details. It now becomes clearer as industrialization spreads its influence worldwide, and more and more parts of the world take up its dynamic (the latest being China), that the romantic critique carries little weight when set against the advantages of becoming integrated into a world industrial system; the benefits of industrialization and modernization are felt as liberation from obscurantism, from poverty, and from age-old injustices and superstitions (a caste system in one country, the subjection of women to their menfolk in another). The issue is, can these benefits be separated from the destructiveness of the ruthlessly rational, acquisitive, and expansionist war launched against a country's and the world's resource base (its biosphere) as that country takes its place in the capitalist world order?[24]

After the successful bridging of the income gap by countries in East Asia in the second half of the twentieth century, it is now the turn of China, India, and Brazil to move up the ladder of development, each with its own distinctive pattern—China as manufacturing "workshop of the world"; India in information technology and software services, as the "back office of the world"; and Brazil as agro-industrial giant, the "farm of the world." Yet the significance of energy to this world-historic transformation is little understood. The 2003 Goldman Sachs report *Dreaming with BRICs: The Path to 2050*, made the celebrated prediction that by 2050, China would be the world's largest economy, India the third largest, and Brazil the fifth largest. This report was a wake-up call for many, showing where growth would likely take today's developing countries to world leadership by halfway through the century (and successive updates bring the deadline closer). Yet curiously, the Goldman Sachs report made no mention of energy—not of fossil fuels or of any renewable energy resource. With the double influence of peaking of global oil supplies, combined with the rising apprehensions related to emissions of greenhouse gas emissions, such neglect of fundamental energy questions is no longer tenable.

Diffusion of Industrialization: From Great Divergence to Great Convergence

The Industrial Revolution transformed the economic prospects for Britain—but this needs to be seen in its historical context. When we examine world per capita income over several hundred years, we observe that the rise of the West is relatively recent—coinciding in fact with the Industrial Revolution. Europe's share of world GDP did not overtake that of China until after the Napoleonic Wars, in 1820—as shown in Figure 2.6.

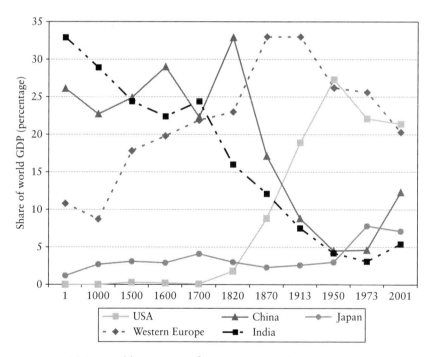

FIGURE **2.6**   Major world economies' fluctuations over the past two thousand years

SOURCE: Maddison (2001).

Figure 2.6 captures two thousand years of economic history. It shows that India and China dominated the world economy right up until around 1700, when Europe started to pull away from India but did not catch China until after 1820. In 1500, for example, China and India accounted for slightly less than half of the global economy (Maddison 2001). By the nineteenth century China was falling in terms of per capita income, as it started its decay under the Qing dynasty that continued right up until the Revolution that created the republic under Sun Yat-sen in 1911. European (Western) world dominance in per capita income terms is thus relatively recent.[25] Of course, Europe had achieved military superiority well before that and was already benefiting from colonial conquests, through which Britain and other European countries received resources far beyond their domestic capacities.

Economic historians like Pomeranz (2000) term this period the "Great Divergence," when Britain and then other Western countries pulled away decisively from both China and India. This Great Divergence has been the single most important feature of the world system for the past three hundred years, accounting for the current distribution of wealth and power that so favors the West.[26] But the second half of this third century of industrialization, in the years 2000–2050, is already starting to see the first signs of the Great Convergence, as China (and to some extent India) employ catch-up strategies to bridge the gap between themselves and the Western leaders. This is the dominant process of our time—dating from China's historic "opening" to the world, which put it on a new economic and industrial trajectory, in 1979.[27] Four of these fast-growing economies (Brazil, Russia, India, and China) were famously labeled as the "BRICs" by Goldman Sachs in 2001—and they have lived up to their name as the fastest-growing nations on the planet over the past decade. China became the world's largest exporter of manufactured goods in 2009, beating out Germany, and the world's largest manufacturing country in the year 2010.[28] On the negative side, China has also become the world's largest emitter of carbon dioxide, principal of the greenhouse gases identified by the Intergovernmental Panel on Climate Change (IPCC) as sources of "anthropogenic" climate change. China is now converging back on the West in the twenty-first century—a process of convergence that is reversing the previous Great Divergence.[29]

Shifting Wealth

The phenomenon of shifting wealth (otherwise known as a "great convergence" by contributors to the *Financial Times*) is reshaping not just debates on production possibilities in emerging and developing countries (EDCs) but also the possibilities for creating a new kind of production and consumption model. The emergence of such a "green growth" model as an alternative mode of development, and as framing an industrial strategy in EDCs, is one of the most striking features of our time. The OECD captures the process in its notion of shifting wealth, by which the OECD countries' share in manufacturing value-added has declined from 84 percent in 1990 to 60 percent in 2010, whereas that of non-OECD countries (for which read China) has increased from 16 percent to 40 percent over the same period.[30]

In the twenty-first century, China has outperformed all the world's economies in terms of GDP growth; China is following in the footsteps of Japan and then Korea in closing the gap with the United States and advanced countries in terms of per capita income. The trajectory followed by Japan and Korea is clearly the trajectory that the Chinese leadership intends to pursue. As Martin Wolf of the *Financial Times* puts it, this "great convergence" that is reversing the previous "great divergence" is "far and away the biggest single fact about our world."[31]

Energy and Resource Challenges for Development

As China and India ramp up their share in the world's manufacturing activities, so they necessarily increase their exploitation of the world's resources in order to feed their ever-expanding industrial machines and to pursue double-digit growth. As the impact on the planet's resources grows, so the vulnerability of China and India grows with it. The constraints under which China and India are developing industrially cannot be illustrated better than by revealing their growing dependence on imports of oil—a disastrous dependence, in terms of both the sums that have to be paid for the imports, and the energy insecurity it engenders (Figure 2.7). India's gap is relatively larger, while China's is much larger in absolute terms.

(A) China

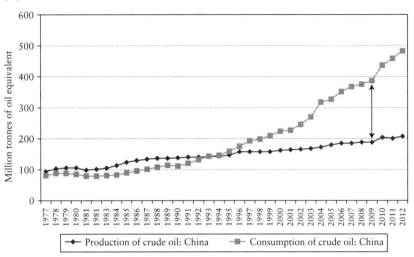

(B) India

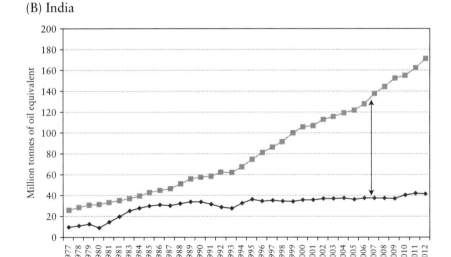

FIGURE **2.7** China's and India's looming oil gap

SOURCE: US Energy Information Administration.

NOTE: Arrow between production and consumption indicates gap that must be made up for by imports.

In 2013 China emerged as the world's largest oil importer—a dubious distinction.[32] The more that countries like China and India become dependent on oil imports, while the Western countries (United States and Europe) and Japan themselves remain highly dependent on oil imports, the closer the world gets to a century of resource wars and oil wars in the twenty-first century. It is now understood that the Iraq War, launched by the Bush (junior) administration in 2003, was largely fought to secure oil supply lines for the United States, as was the previous Gulf War, launched by the Bush (senior) administration in 1991. In both cases, China and India were prepared to play a passive role—but that cannot be assumed to be the case in future. India's situation is even worse than China's, in that the gap between production and consumption is relatively even larger (shown in Figure 2.7).

So, how we got to where we are is a story of the discovery and then reckless exploitation of the fossil fuels and endless resources cornucopia. Bringing the story up to the present, as in the charts on China's and India's growing dependence on oil imports, we are led to consider the motives behind China's juggling of green and black industrialization pathways.

The Impact of China's Fossil Fuel Reliance

As China moves to expand its energy system that powers its vast manufacturing system, so its impact on global fossil fuel prices must be expected to become clear. Its impact on coal prices is already apparent, as shown in Figure 2.8.

Figure 2.8 reveals that the long-term trend in the price of coal is upward, with the price doubling over the past decade from less than US$40 to more than $80 recently (and leaving out of account the extreme price peak associated with the onset of the global financial crisis). This long-term price trend must be associated with China's vast appetite for coal, so that the long-term downward trend in coal's usage and price is being reversed.[33]

Anti-Malthusian resource optimists like Julian Simon used to make bold predictions about the direction of resource price and supply trends. The cover of Simon's (1998) revised version of his 1981 best seller *The Ultimate Resource* says it all: "Natural resources . . . pollution . . .

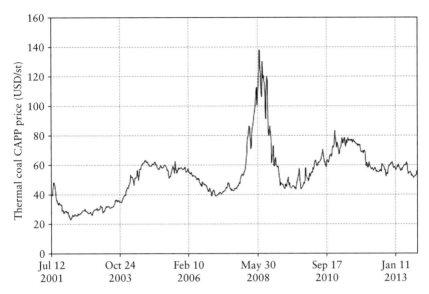

FIGURE **2.8**   Global price of coal, 2001–2012
SOURCE: www.infomine.com. Used with permission.

world's food supply . . . pressures of population growth. . . . Every trend in material human welfare has been improving—and promises to do so, indefinitely." Until his untimely death in 1998, Simon had been a tireless opponent of pessimistic forecasts of resource shortages, and he won many famous bets, such as his wager against the "population bomb" scholar Paul Ehrlich that prices of a selection of metals chosen in 1980 would decline over the subsequent decade; Simon won the bet. But Simon was writing and publishing prior to the literature on peak oil (and peak coal, peak everything else) and, above all, prior to the rise of China as a serious manufacturing center and consumer of energy and resources.

There can be no expectation that the long-term trend in the price of coal (and other minerals) will be anything but upward—and I would be prepared to bet on this with Simon if he were still alive. The reason is that China's extra demand is coming on top of an already-stretched system. Simon's thesis was that industrial capitalism would keep prices of commodities falling because of its capacity to find alternatives and substitutes for basic commodities.[34] It might have worked while the system was still expanding into a frontier—but the frontier has been reached, and China's demand is proving to be the tipping point.[35] Further demand from later industrializers like India, and then the countries of Africa, South America, and elsewhere in South Asia, can be expected only to further compound the problem.[36] This is not "neo-Malthusianism" (an argument based on population outgrowing material resources) but a realistic appraisal of the real resource and energy trends needed to maintain a capitalist industrial system as it globalizes along conventional, fossil-fueled lines.[37] Behind the dry statistics and charts of a growing gap between fossil fuel production and consumption for both India and China (resulting in growing share of imports as shown in Figure 2.7), there lurk the geopolitical realities of increasing fossil fuel dependence: war, revolution, and terror. These are prospects that are incompatible with China's goal of fifty years of peaceful development.

That is why a different model of growth is needed—why it is essential, why it has to be developed—and why it has to be developed in the first instance by China, India, and the countries coming after them. Fundamental changes to the rules and institutions of what Peter Nolan (2009) aptly calls "wild capitalism," which has now filled the earth, are called for.

The Alternative "Beijing Model" of Green Development

China's "green development model" is attracting the intellectual notice of scholars, such as Hu Angang, a member of the Chinese Academy of Social Sciences and influential with the Chinese leadership. He has been arguing now for several years that "green development is the inevitable choice for China."[38] Hu contends that China is being forced to adopt an alternative to the model of industrialization that the West was able to pursue, for several reasons: because China is a latecomer and faces an international economic situation that is already crowded; because it is lagging in conventional fossil-fueled technology but as a latecomer can leapfrog to the lead with green technology; because it has such a huge population for which the traditional model would not scale; because it cannot pursue resources abroad through colonialism and armed conquest—unlike its Western predecessors; and because basing its development model on increasing resource intensity will come up against inevitable resource constraints (such as the peaking of oil and coal supplies). Any one of these constitutes an adequate reason for searching for a development alternative based on security grounds. Taken as a group, and when combined with the prospect of facing increasing international pressure on carbon emissions, these considerations become overwhelming, and indeed make green development "an inevitable choice for China"—and by extension, for Brazil and India as well. Green development has to be seen, then, as the *necessary* and *unavoidable* industrialization path forward for the BICs.[39] The alternative would be relentless resource wars; terrorism; increasing insecurity; and dependence on fuel imports, whose price will inevitably rise.

By contrast, a green development strategy offers notable advantages. It taps into energy resources that are abundant and that call for the use of sophisticated technologies that can then serve as the core of export-oriented new industries. So it is economically rational. The renewable energy resources themselves are abundant and widely dispersed, so that the BICs cannot be held to ransom by fossil fuel powers and can generate all the power needed to drive their industrial strategy without fuel costs. The possibilities for leapfrogging in renewable energies and low-carbon technologies are there to be captured, particularly if implemented with latecomer strategies that exploit indigenous standards and the domestic market. Green growth industries are based on manufacturing, which generates increasing returns (as costs fall), in contrast to extractive industries, which produce fossil fuels where diminishing returns prevail (and hence rising costs and prices).[40] The development of green industries can generate employment and livelihood in rural as much as in urban settings, so contributing to balanced development. A green development strategy involving circular economy initiatives (e.g., recycling, turning wastes into inputs) offers the prospect of reducing resource flows and hence dependence on virgin resource imports and resultant strains on the balance of payments, as well as leapfrog advantages in capturing resource efficiencies. And finally a green development strategy sees green industrial initiatives not as a cost but as an investment, calling for green financial instruments and a central role for banks and financial institutions—in place of reliance on tax-based resources (i.e., public finance), which have been a barrier to effective initiatives in dealing with climate change. Whatever cost disadvantages are incurred by renewables and circular economy initiatives are being rapidly eroded, with cost advantages swinging toward the RE^2 strategies, as discussed in subsequent chapters.

This list has not even mentioned as yet the advantages that green development offers in terms of reducing carbon emissions, and so combating global warming. In this sense, green development is a "no regrets" strategy; it offers a range of tangible benefits apart from its savings in terms of carbon emissions. Even if the dangers of global warming turn out to be overstated (itself highly unlikely), the BICs would in any case accrue enormous advantages by adopting green development strategies, simply in terms of their offering greater security, resilience, and development potential.

Therefore, China and the world have everything to gain by going with a renewable energy and circular economy goals, and little, if anything, to lose. Indeed, what China and the rest of the world "lose" is the prospect of endless war over fossil fuel resources, endless pollution and waste generation, and the dwindling of energy resources as supplies peak and prices spiral out of control. This is indeed a favorable "Pascal wager."[41]

While the international community has been busy debating global warming, and scholars and activists have been putting forward proposals for strengthened international treaties as a way of dealing with the problem of resource-intensive capitalism (e.g., Kyoto Protocol), China appears to be motivated by quite different considerations. After China's membership in the World Trade Organization had been finalized in 2001, the country's leadership could already see a surge in investment in manufacturing activities for export. Such an export-oriented manufacturing machine called for a huge expansion in energy, and initially the only energy source available was coal. So the Chinese Communist Party made some tough decisions about expanding coal-fired power generation and the expansion and rationalization of the coal supply industry. But the industrial expansion also called for oil and gas. Since China had already peaked in these supplies, it was dependent on overseas expansion for oil security.

Then came 9/11, unleashing a terrorist attack in the heart of New York by Saudi nationals, triggering the "war on terror" as response. How might such an event have been viewed from Beijing? It is entirely plausible that the Communist Party leadership would have associated further expansion of their oil and fossil fuel interests with endless risk of war and terror, involving conflict not just with host nations in the Middle East but also with the United States and its seemingly unlimited appetite for Middle Eastern "energy" (meaning "oil").[42] Under such circumstances, an alternative energy pathway involving rapid buildup of renewable energy devices tapping into renewable sources would have seemed rational and justifiable.

That is indeed what can be observed. After a lag of a couple of years, China's investments in renewables, initially wind power and solar thermal, increased dramatically after 2005 at rates unprecedented in economic history. Under the Eleventh Five Year Plan, covering the years from 2006 to 2010, investments in renewable energies were ramped up to become the largest in the world. Now under the current Twelfth Five Year Plan (2011–15), capacity in renewables is set to expand further, and by the conclusion of the plan period renewable energies are anticipated to account for 30 percent of China's electric power generation—an enormous shift in an enormous industrial machine, thus turning China into a renewables superpower.[43] While state-owned corporations remain the bedrock of the energy system, in coal and oil and gas and in electric power generation, it is new, privately funded corporations that are being allowed their entrepreneurial head in the renewables sector generally, as we witness hundreds of companies eagerly piling into the new wind power, solar photovoltaic (PV) and solar thermal sectors, as well as various forms of bioenergy and alternative fuels.

Of course, China's backing of fossil fuel expansion continues apace, at a rate of roughly one thermal (coal-fired) power station of 1 billion watts (1 GW) per week. But increasingly this investment is being matched by expenditure on renewables, so that already the character of the energy sector is changing. Importantly, a strong domestic constituency is being created that promises to drive further development and expansion of the renewables sector. China's backing of renewables is entirely pragmatic and driven by national security as well as economic concerns. But it does have implications for environmental effects, and in particular for global warming concerns. China's emissions of carbon particulates (making the air in industrial cities practically unbreathable) is continuing to rise but can be expected to plateau in the 2020s and then start to decline, as cleaner energy sources take over (both "clean" coal and renewables).[44] China's greenhouse carbon emissions can also be expected to keep rising, plateauing in the 2020s or 2030s, and then starting to decline—significantly decline. (This aspect of China's energy industrial revolution is taken up in the next chapter.)

So, as a matter of necessity, China is embarking on a different growth path, one that emphasizes a new awareness of the earth's ecological limits and the building of an economy that is explicitly designed to operate within these limits.[45] I submit that a full appreciation of the impact of the Twelfth Five-Year Plan goes beyond its immediate goals for 2015, impressive as these are. If we take the perspective of industrial dynamics, then what we see being established in China is new energy and green (low-carbon) industries that will follow a familiar S-shaped uptake curve. This pattern of S-shaped growth (or logistic growth) has been seen repeatedly in previous technological substitutions and can with confidence be anticipated as the pattern of uptake of renewable energies and low-carbon technologies in China, between now and midcentury—by which time the momentum in favor of such substitution will be unstoppable and create an economy fully converted to RE^2 principles by the end of the century. This Beijing approach to building an alternative industrialization pathway is bound to be attractive for other industrializing countries. India and Brazil are likely to be serious candidates for adopting a "Beijing Consensus" on alternative development pathways. Indeed, the evidence is overwhelming that they are already embarked on such a pathway. Brazil is now a world leader in building an alternative energy pathway as a tropical country on the basis of its agro-resources, creating bioenergy industries that would conquer world fuels markets if only the United States and European Union would lower their tariff barriers targeted at Brazilian exports of sugarcane-based ethanol.[46] And India is rapidly building eco-industrial parks on the model of those achieved already in China, as part of its push to create industrial clusters gathered together in special economic zones, and is promoting green industries at the state level as fast as it allows for a huge expansion of its fossil fuel sector. Other countries, in Central and South America, in Southeast Asia and Africa—and in the wake of the Arab Spring, in North Africa and the Middle East—are more than likely to follow suit, since this new pathway promises real industrialization, a process that can lift billions out of poverty, without costing the earth.

China's achievements have not gone unnoted. Germany is the first of the advanced countries already paying China the compliment of emulating its approach to serious buildup of green industries. Germany announced in June 2011 a radical about-turn in dropping its previous reliance on nuclear (which had been retarding the renewables option for decades, as deplored by scholar-activists like Scheer)—triggered by the Japanese Fukushima disaster of 2011. This was then followed up with successive announcements on its planned buildup in renewables industries—in what the Germans call the *Energiewende* ("energy transition" or "transformation"). Germany has moved on from its heavy promotion of renewables markets, via its feed-in tariff system embodied in the Renewable Energy Sources Law of 2000 and earlier incarnations, to the far more significant promotion of renewable energy industries themselves—exactly as is being done by China.[47] Although for various reasons more problematic, Japan also has the makings to pursue a similar course. Japan has a track record of building a circular economy and providing strong backing for renewables earlier in the 1970s and 1980s, until lower oil prices discouraged such initiatives. So before too long we could see Germany and China and perhaps Japan and Korea as serious proponents of green industries, both for domestic consumption and for export. Between them, these industrial powers would represent an unstoppable force turning the global industrial machine from its present addiction to fossil fuels into something quite different.

Such a story cannot be told for the United States, where the country is counting the costs of a lost decade after the events of 9/11. It may be argued that US foreign policy has been shaped by oil ever since its domestic supplies peaked in 1970, while more and more ambitious plans for securing and protecting oil supply lines were being formulated in the 1990s, then put into effect under the Bush administrations of 2000 to 2008. The terrorist attacks hardened US resolve to secure the oil supply lines, triggering the invasion of Iraq under the pretext of hunting for "weapons of mass destruction." But this strategy went horribly wrong, with Osama bin Laden escaping to Afghanistan and enticing US Armed Forces into a long and fruitless war on that terrain (where there is no oil!). Meanwhile a Sunni uprising in Iraq tied US forces down, preventing any other potential incursions in the Middle East or the Central Asian region around the Caspian Sea oil basin. Potential invasion of Iran was negated by Beijing's forging of a strong alliance with Teheran to secure its own oil supplies—while expanding its supplies from African countries like Namibia, Sudan, and Nigeria, beyond the US sphere of influence.

Meanwhile the US Congress has passed fitful and episodic support for renewables while refusing to dismantle fossil fuel subsidies, thus frustrating efforts to develop meaningful cap-and-trade schemes for reining in carbon emissions that would also have provided incentives for renewables. During this "lost decade," US dependence on oil has actually increased.[48] Its major industrial competitors in the East (China) and in the West (Germany) are moving in a quite different direction. While the US Congress was debating climate change and blocking energy reforms, its chief competitors were building the renewable energy systems and circular economy processes that would establish their technological leadership and, for those who follow suit, make resource wars redundant in the twenty-first century. Kant's predictions of "perpetual peace" might finally become credible once grounded in this new industrial pathway.[49]

It is the argument of this book that such geopolitical considerations lie at the root of the greening of capitalism. The emergent industrial model that is being driven by China and increasingly emulated by Brazil and India, as well as Germany, is one that can offer realistic prospects of holding back and actually diminishing carbon emissions while reducing the throughput of resources (e.g., iron ore, cement, aluminum) via circular economy initiatives and policies. This emergent model is being driven not by Kyoto-style rhetorical statements as to anticipated carbon emission reductions, nor by professed concern for the future of industrial civilization. Rather, it is being driven by national self-interest and a long-term view of the role of state initiative and competitive dynamics in a sustainable industrial system. It may come as a surprise to Greenpeace and Friends of the Earth that the most serious student and practitioner of their policies turns out to be the Communist Party of China. It may also come as a surprise that it is the US military that is also taking a serious interest in renewables, for the very good reason that they are increasingly aware of the vulnerabilities of long supply lines for oil and other fuels.[50] It is strong states and powerful organizations that are driving the technological transitions that will define the twenty-first century.

3   Why "Business as Usual" Cannot Continue

The issue we face . . . is not how to facilitate environmental quality by limiting economic development . . . , but how to create a system of production that can grow and develop in harmony with the environment.

—*Barry Commoner,* Making Peace with the Planet *(1990)*

The strategic green-technology investments of the kinds that the Chinese government is now undertaking—and that the American Energy Innovation Council and the President's Council of Advisers are recommending for the United States—will not be sufficient, by themselves, to end the global struggle for control of the world's shrinking supplies of vital materials. . . . Like the current scramble for the world's last remaining resources, the race to adapt will spell doom for slow-moving companies, and will cause a grand reshuffling of the global power hierarchy. But it is not likely to end in war, widespread starvation, or a massive environmental catastrophe—the probable results of persisting with the race for what's left.

—*Michael Klare,* The Race for What's Left *(2012)*

For that which is common to the greatest number has the least care bestowed upon it.

—*Aristotle,* Politics

God blessed them [Adam and Eve] and said to them, "Be fruitful and increase in number; fill the earth and subdue it. Rule over the fish in the sea and the birds in the sky and over every living creature that moves on the ground."

—*Genesis 1:28*

While acknowledging the extraordinary changes wrought on the world by the advent and now global diffusion of industrialization, we must take stock of the costs involved. While industrial capitalism was still small in comparison to the enormity of the planet (think of Mimi in *La Bohème* singing of "la mare infinita," or the endless and bottomless sea), and while it was expanding into a frontier beyond which wilderness and undisturbed nature still prevailed, the encroachment of cities on their natural surrounds could be tolerated. But as the system globalizes and oil prospectors tap ever deeper into the earth's crust and extend their operations to untapped areas (offshore wells and Arctic refuges), as cities consume ever more of their hinterlands, as industrialized agriculture carries away millions of tonnes of topsoil from the river valleys of China and elsewhere, so we see industrial capitalism changing to a system that is now filling the world and despoiling it.

So great is the destructive power of this "wild" version of industrial capitalism, unrestrained and encompassing the globe, affecting biological and geological processes globally, that it has inspired a name: the Anthropocene epoch. But it is not just "man-made"; it is a product of industrial capitalism equipped with fossil fuels. The term was coined by the Nobel Prize–winning atmospheric chemist Paul Crutzen in 2000.[1] In a follow-up paper published in *Nature* in 2002, Crutzen gives as good a summary as one is likely to find of the awesome scale of the impact of our industrial civilization on the planet's recovery processes:

> During the past three centuries, the human population has increased tenfold to more than 6 billion and is expected to reach 10 billion in this century. The methane-producing cattle population has risen to 1.4 billion. About 30–50% of the planet's land surface is exploited by humans. Tropical rainforests disappear at a fast pace, releasing carbon dioxide and strongly increasing species extinction. . . . More than half of all accessible fresh water is used by mankind. Fisheries remove more than 25% of the primary production in upwelling ocean regions and 35% in the temperate continental shelf. Energy use has grown 16-fold during the twentieth century. . . . More nitrogen fertilizer is applied in agriculture than is fixed naturally in all terrestrial ecosystems. . . . Fossil-fuel burning and agriculture have caused substantial increases in the concentrations of "greenhouse" gases—carbon dioxide by 30% and methane by more than 100%—reaching their highest levels over the past 400 millennia, with more to follow.[2]

More recently, a group of climate scientists, led by Will Steffen and including Paul Crutzen as well as the environmental historian John McNeill, updated the story, framing their narrative as our growing stewardship responsibilities in this new epoch of the Anthropocene.[3] While the term itself is somewhat controversial, the features it describes are beyond dispute: we are indeed living in a man-made era, during which human action transmitted via capitalist operations transforms everything it touches.[4]

Industrial Capitalism: A Frontier System That Expanded to Fill the Planet

There are all too many indications as to how the present industrial economy cannot reproduce itself and how in fact it is creating the conditions for its own destruction. The substitution of fossil energy sources— coal, then oil and gas—for earlier "organic" sources of energy, a process that began in England in the second half of the eighteenth century and has become global in scale and scope, brought untold benefits through liberating humankind from earlier Malthusian constraints. But it has created in turn a series of problems that instead of being local are global and civilizational in character. The industrial superstructure that we created has now—literally—filled the planet.[5]

The destructive potential of this system can be seen in terms of the rising levels of resource spoliation; by increasing levels of pollution; by waste generation and the fouling of air and water; and ultimately by global warming, a truly planetary phenomenon that is caused by fossil fuel combustion and that threatens total destruction of our industrial civilization.

Take the case of China, which encapsulates all that is bad about our industrial assault on the environment and that has compressed a process that took a couple of centuries in the West into the space of just a few decades. China has been pursuing its "black" revolution, to the point that it threatens massive destruction—giving China's leadership the most potent motive for developing a "green" counterpart to its black, fossil-fueled economy. Study after study indicates the catastrophic extent of the problems, from depletion of resources, including the tonnes of soil lost each year, the spoliation of the urban and rural environment, the depletion of water tables, and the acrid pollution of the air in cities. It is clear that China's "business as usual" (BAU) path forward is utterly unsustainable—as admitted even by its senior ministers.[6]

A devastating account of the problems in their entirety is provided by US scholar Elizabeth Economy in her 2005 book *The River Runs Black*.[7] As the *Financial Times* put it in a review of Economy's book:

> The statistics and the anecdotes recounted . . . are worse than ominous: China has six of the ten most polluted cities in the world; just by breathing, some children are smoking the equivalent of two packets of cigarettes a day; acid rain affects a third of the territory; more than three-quarters of the river water flowing through urban areas is unsuitable for drinking or fishing; each year, 300,000 people die prematurely as a result of air pollution; in one part of Guangdong Province, where circuit boards had been processed and burned, levels of lead in the water were 2,400 times the guideline level set by the World Health Organisation.[8]

The horrifying picture reflects the reality of double-digit growth promoted for decade after decade. It is the Chinese themselves who feel the toll most immediately, and who understand why a different form of growth model is necessary. China is certainly developing a "green development" model to offset the horrors of the "black development" strategy—but the toll taken will doubtless continue for several decades.

More generally, the Western model of industrial development is resource intensive and environmentally destructive, on the cheery assumption that there is something called "nature" that acts as an endless resource for raw materials and repository for wastes. The scale of the human impact, and its exacerbation as the process of industrialization diffuses, is revealed in the data on accelerating materials uptake in one sector after another, as shown in Figure 2.5.

"Overshoot and Collapse" Character of Resource Usage

Another perspective on the way our industrial civilization interacts with its natural setting is to review the process through which resource extraction proceeds at a moderate rate—then, once "industrialized," it accelerates, and then "peaks" and collapses. This "overshoot and collapse" mode of interaction has been documented over and over again. As just one example, consider the Newfoundland cod fishery, which was relatively stable in its yields up until the advent of factory-scale industrial trawlers, which were brought into production in the postwar period. This drove up the level of catches to an unsustainable level—and then collapse. The fishery has never recovered.[9]

This issue of growth versus sustainability has dominated public debate on the future of industrial civilization, ever since the report to the Club of Rome, *Limits to Growth*, was published in 1972—sparking furious debate and turning it into the founding document for the modern environmental and ecological movement. The two sides to the debate have largely talked past each other. There are, on the one hand, what Friedrichs (2011) calls the Cornucopians, with a vision of endless growth fueled by the power of economic substitution and price-driven choices; and on the other hand are the neo-Malthusians, with a strong sense of the reality of finite stocks of resources, which at some point must induce collapse if endless extensive growth is allowed to proceed. What such collapse looks like in reality, as opposed to computer simulation models, is well illustrated by the Newfoundland cod fisheries, which were wiped out in 1992. The point is that there was ample warning of this eventuality, but no institutional means through which collective action to maintain the fish stocks could be taken. Without such institutional restraints—or in the memorable words of Garrett Hardin, coiner of the parable of the tragedy of the commons, without "voluntary restraint mutually agreed" there can be no sustainability.[10]

The thing that all these episodes have in common is the industrial scale of the exploitation. When resource exploitation took place in a limited manner, confined to some region and constrained by human labor, it was rare that a single resource could be completely wiped out. Now, at an industrial scale, it is rare that a resource can survive.[11] And the process goes on. A recent casualty of this endless dance of industrial expansion leading to collapse was recorded in the marine salmon farms in Chile. Here it was reported (in July 2011) that a virus known as "infectious salmon anemia" had been killing millions of farmed salmon in Chile, devastating one of its showcase industrial success stories. What made it so lethal was overcrowding in the fish pens at industrial scale and the raising of salmon in their own excrement.[12]

Our assaults on the global environment are distinguished from past experiences only in their scale. The historical record is starting to be tapped for evidence on past civilizational collapses and the modes in which societies succumbed to the devastation that they (usually) brought upon themselves. Jared Diamond, for example, in his 2005 book *Collapse: How Societies Choose to Fail or Survive*, assembles a vast range of materials on societies and civilizations that collapsed, including the Maya, the Anasazi (Pueblo cultures), and Easter Island—making the point that the collapse sometimes came swiftly (within a fifty-year period) and occurred as a result of practices that had seemed to be rational and warranted but turned out to have the most serious environmental consequences. The parallel with our own industrial civilization, with its far greater complexity but no less pointed vulnerability, is powerful and immediate.

The reconstruction of a "green history of the world" that brings out these features is now in its early stages.[13] There is lively debate between synthesizers like Diamond and specialists in particular societies, and with those who favor alternative accounts.[14] The real issue, as brought out in the work of Steffen, Persson, and colleagues (2011), is whether short-term responses to environmental pressure in these preindustrial settings brought about changes to institutions that further undermined vulnerability to severe changes.

Anthropological and archeological evidence is being amassed to shed light on past anthropogenic disasters and social collapses—indeed, on civilizational collapses such as those that befell the Maya in the thirteenth century, or the Pueblo culture of Chaco Canyon in the twelfth century, and earlier collapses in Mesopotamia and that of the Harappan civilization of the Indus Valley. A strong case can be made that self-induced ecological collapse was very much a factor in these instances of civilizational unraveling—as in sequences of deforestation, overintensive exploitation of the soil, falling water tables and salination, crop failures, social aggression, warfare, and ultimate collapse. It has to be admitted at the outset that this is a deeply contested field of scholarship, with strong proponents of self-induced collapse, like Diamond (2005), meeting equally strong critiques from scholars such as Tainter (2006), who insists on the priority of the social processes themselves, even if the end result is agreed to be the same. But through all the argument there are undeniable facts concerning sudden collapses—of populations, of cities, of civilizational complexity (to use Tainter's preferred definition).

The case of Easter Island may be taken as exemplary. It is by now well studied as a case of preindustrial social collapse. Although European "discovery" of the island in 1722 hastened the decline of its then-small population, the main damage had already been self-inflicted. Easter Island is now a UNESCO World Heritage site, on account of its unique stone heads facing out to sea—the *moa*. The island is a speck in the South Pacific Ocean, around two thousand miles west of Chile.

Easter Island was settled by Polynesian seafaring colonists who are thought, from archeological and carbon-dating evidence, to have arrived around AD 1000.[15] There is little argument over their almost-immediate wholesale deforestation, using timber for housing, for boats, and as rollers to transport their carved *moa*. As the timber supply started to decline, the climate of the island changed, with more wind and less rain, resulting in poorer conditions for agriculture and loss of fishing as boat-building declined; social pressures intensified, with new cults emerging, together with rising levels of aggression and competition between warring clans. Diamond is surely not alone in asserting that this constituted a downward spiral from which there seemed no escape for the inhabitants themselves—constrained as they were by a culture that knew no writing, that had no sense of history and was consumed by a devastating sense of isolation from their Polynesian roots. The arrival of Europeans, and over subsequent years the devastation wrought by disease and slave raiders, only accentuated a decline that was already in progress.

An evolutionary perspective on these experiences—the rise and fall of the Mesopotamian civilizations, the Maya, the Anasazi (Pueblo) cultures, and isolated examples like Easter Island—is salutary. The ways in which the complexity of social structures is assembled are varied, as are the processes through which they adapt to changes in their environment (external changes or self-induced changes); likewise the ways that these complex societies and civilizations collapse are varied.[16] But they all have in common an inability to control their resource exploitation. There are precious indicators here for our own industrial civilization, which also appears to be prone to overshoot and collapse as the dominant means of relating to our ecological environment.

Fossil Fuels Exhibiting Overshoot—The Peaking of Oil and Other Resources

It is fossil fuels themselves that present our industrial civilization with the greatest and most serious case of overshoot and collapse—the peaking of oil, and of coal and gas as well. We must briefly review this situation, because it is so central to the transition now being forced on the "wild" ride of industrial capitalism and its assumed ready access to a cornucopia of fossil fuels.

Peak Oil, Peak Everything

"Peak oil" is a phrase that was introduced by the American oil geologist M. King Hubbert in a remarkably prescient prediction, made in 1956, that US oil production would peak fourteen years later in 1970.[17] Hubbert was ridiculed at the time (in the heyday of the US oil boom) but was actually correct, even to the year.[18]

Natural resources in a finite planet cannot go on being exploited forever. That much is clear. But how far ahead is "forever"? The debate over whether global oil supplies are now peaking or not is a case in point. Ever since the retired oil geologist Colin Campbell put the world on notice that oil supplies had probably already peaked in the first decade of the twenty-first century, the issue has been the "slow burner" that the oil industry itself is reluctant to discuss.[19] Some go so far as to say that there are still plenty of oil fields to discover (just think of Iraq, they exclaim) and that the twenty-first century will be one that will "overflow with petroleum."[20] Others like the late, lamented Matt Simmons point to the absence of giant oil fields like Gawar in Saudi Arabia as underlining the imminent decline in oil supplies—or at least the increasing expense and difficulties in extracting oil from more and more difficult locations.[21] For this is the point: it is not that the resource is about to give out, but that its extraction will call for more effort after the peak has been passed, so that the operations become more dangerous, riskier, and more costly.

The Association for the Study of Peak Oil (ASPO) has been formed to promote peak oil scholarship, and it is a very active body, staging regular conferences and issuing considered statements on the future of oil supplies that are given wide coverage.[22] The key to the idea of peak oil is simplicity itself: as discovery of new oil fields declines (as it has been since the mid-1960s), so the decline in oil production must follow, with a lag of around thirty to forty years. This is the basis for the prediction that world oil supplies have already peaked and are in a "holding pattern"—neither growing nor falling.

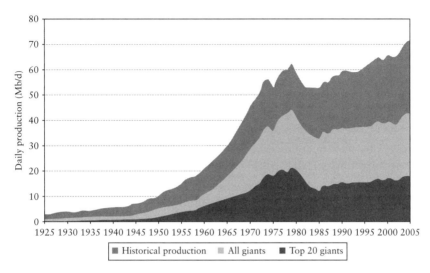

FIGURE **3.1**   Plateauing of global (conventional) oil supplies
SOURCE: Höök, Hirsch, and Aleklett (2009). Used with permission.

Has oil production in fact reached a plateau? It would seem so. Figure 3.1 may be taken as evidence for the end of the cheap oil era. Alternative sources of oil—think of tar sands or shale oil—will inevitably be more expensive, and environmentally much more damaging.

The peaking of oil supplies is felt not solely in terms of shortages but also in terms of oil being harder and more dangerous to get. The upside of the peak oil depiction (as in Figure 3.1) shows the oil that is easy to find and easy to exploit. But on the downside what dominates is the more inaccessible oil—found in hard-to-access deposits such as tar sands in Canada or in deeper and deeper offshore wells—even extending well beyond the continental shelf. These are the "unconventional" oil supplies—the dirtier, nastier, more costly, and more dangerous supplies.

Extreme Resources: Shale Oil, Coal Seam Gas, and Their Promised Bonanza

As the world moves onto the "descent" of the peak oil curve, resort to "tight oil" or "alternative fossil sources" becomes much more widely discussed. These alternatives include shale oil, tar sands oil, coal seam gas—all extracted utilizing dangerous and dirty methods. Oil from tar sands or gas from coal seams is what Klare (2012) calls "extreme resources"—in the sense that they are extremely difficult to extract, extremely dangerous, and extremely dirty.[23] Extracting oil from tar sands requires far more resource destruction than even oil and gas drilling, which itself is staggeringly wasteful; and extracting oil from tar sands releases three times the carbon that producing "normal" oil would release.[24] Tar sands oil pollutes not just the land where it is extracted but everything downstream as well—including, it seems, the media.[25]

This is the cue for entry by Canadian companies that are involved in producing tar sands oil, and their lobbyists, to relabel their activities as "ethical oil"—because it is produced in a democracy![26] A campaign along these lines ignores the environmental costs of extracting oil from tar sands; it simply contrasts oil produced in Canada with oil produced by Saudi Arabia or Iran. Yes, it is true that oil produced by authoritarian "petro-states" feeds a Western addiction at the expense of suppressing human rights in these states (until overthrown by the revolutions of the 2011 Arab Spring)—but the smart conclusion is to swing behind renewable energies, not those from even dirtier sources of oil such as those from the tar sands (or coal seam gas).

There can be little doubt that it is the "dirtier" oil from tar sands and other such sources that is viewed by the oil industry as allowing for continued high levels of supplies. A report released in Washington, DC, by the US Environmental Integrity Project in 2008 indicated that (from official filings) two-thirds of projected expansion in refining capacity in the United States was designed to handle dirtier, heavier oil products— precisely the kind being produced from Canadian tar sands.[27]

Oil from tar sands and coal seam gas secured through hydraulic fracture ("fracking") represent simply the most outrageous of the problems to be posed by the peaking of fossil fuels and the search for dirtier alternatives. The world is likely to be inundated not with fossil fuels themselves but with stories of how to get rich by exploiting various kinds of alternatives to standard-issue oil, gas, and coal. The *International Herald Tribune* carried a supplement with Reuters on the energy business in late October 2011, with the headline "Energy discoveries [read, "alternative fossil fuels"] reshape politics and economics worldwide," which gushed with praise for investment possibilities arising from drilling in deepwater reserves, exploiting oil sands, and resorting to shale gas production and other such delights.[28] The latter is worth mentioning: coal seam gas (CSG) production utilizing hydraulic fracturing (i.e., fracking) threatens to bring gas production right into the center of towns and disrupt farming wherever CSG prospectors find signs of the gas that is now considered so desirable. Never mind that fracking destroys local water tables and is suspected of triggering earthquakes in such unlikely spots as the US East Coast.[29] These "alternative" fossil fuels—more costly, more dangerous, more environmentally hazardous than even conventional fossil fuels—come to the fore precisely because the conventional fuels are peaking and moving into the downside of the peaking curve. If the fossil fuels industry could be described as reckless on the upside of the peak curve, it will become worse than reckless on the downside.[30]

The twin issues of China's search worldwide for new sources of fossil fuels and Canada's development of its tar sands came to a head at the beginning of 2013, when the final hurdle in the acquisition of Canadian tar sands company Nexen by China National Offshore Oil Corporation (CNOOC) was given final regulatory approval. At $15 billion, it is China's largest-ever foreign takeover. And the acquisition gives CNOOC access to oil resources not just in the North Sea, the Gulf of Mexico, West Africa, and the Middle East—but now in Canada as well.[31] It is richly ironic that it should be China that provides the final endorsement of and access to Canada's dirty oil resources rather than the Western oil and gas companies. China is thereby expanding its "black" energy industrial revolution, from coal to dirty oil, making it that much harder (and that much more urgent) to ramp up its complementary green energy revolution.

Bad as these problems are, they pale when set against the monster problem of global warming, which has emerged as the existential threat posed by the entire fossil-fuel-burning culture of industrial capitalism—a problem made much worse by the widespread resort to dirty oil and gas by North American and now Chinese fossil fuel interests.

Global Climate Change

There are many deadly pollution outcomes resulting from the burning of fossil fuels—from acid rain to particulate carbon pollution in cities. But by far the greatest of the pollution crises is that caused by the "greenhouse" effect. The sequence is clear: rising levels of carbon dioxide (from the burning of fossil fuels) drive up global temperatures and thereby induce global climate change. This is the planetary disaster that will bring down our industrial civilization unless confronted and acted on swiftly.

Global warming is the incontrovertible end point of unconstrained use of fossil fuels over the past three hundred years, and of the ever-growing reliance on fossil fuels anticipated over the next fifty years. This is, as Al Gore famously notes, an extremely *inconvenient truth*. How "convenient" it would have been if the world could have gone on following the Western way, with its reliance on endless supplies of fossil fuels to drive ever-more-extravagant lifestyles. But it is now known, through the dedicated work of climate scientists and their UN-coordinated publications via the Intergovernmental Panel on Climate Change (IPCC), that the sharp surge in anthropogenic carbon emissions is having a relentless and destructive impact. This is where externalities become more than mere local and regional aberrations; they are global charges on economic activity that threaten to bring down the whole system.

Notwithstanding the famous remark from Lord Stern, namely that climate change represents the greatest market failure of all, it is not just as a case of "market failure" that global warming should be viewed.[32] Yes, it takes the notion of externality to a wholly new level—but market "failure" has the (perhaps intended) connotation that market "success" is the rule and failure the exception. To get to grips with climate change, however, involves setting markets in their correct place, as good servants but bad masters. The perspective that informs my critique is that mainstream economic analysis is as much to blame for the current incipient disasters as are business practices themselves—and both need to be changed. What a green economics might look like is a topic taken up in Part 3 of this book.

There are certain "facts" concerning global warming that are now accepted by the overwhelming majority of scientific opinion and that are contested only by those guided by vested interests or doggedly contrarian tendencies.[33] The central fact concerns the sudden increase in atmospheric carbon dioxide levels (along with those of other greenhouse gases such as methane)—widely agreed, and depicted in Figure 3.2, from Australia's CSIRO.

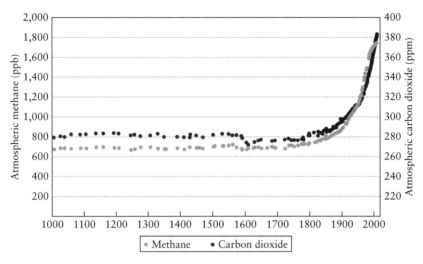

FIGURE **3.2**   Carbon dioxide and methane levels over the past thousand years
SOURCE: © CSIRO. Used with permission.

The real issue concerns associated rise in temperature—as summarized in a famous chart from Mann, Bradley, and Hughes (1999).[34] The argument concerning the rise in atmospheric ground-level temperature over the past century and a half is also a widely accepted fact; namely, temperatures have been rising up until the year 2001 with an accelerating rate, rising from 0.1°C per decade in the first half of the twentieth century then moderating and rising again at 0.1°C per decade from 1980. From around 1900 to 2000 the global air temperature increased by 0.9°C—or close to a rise of 1°C per century (Figure 3.3).

The point of the historical and prehistorical records is to demonstrate that our geological epoch (the Holocene) is "only" 5°C warmer than during the last ice age. So a temperature rise of 1°C per century is no small deal. Over just a couple of centuries such a rise would completely change the world's pattern of climate, agriculture, sea levels, incidence of floods, fires, tornadoes, and many other potentially cataclysmic events.

The first decade of the twenty-first century shows a dip in the trend toward warmer and warmer decades. This "fact" has given rise to much public debate over the reality of global warming. But there is in fact a ready explanation for such a dip in the accelerating temperature

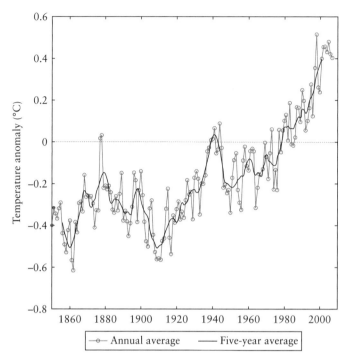

FIGURE **3.3**   Measured temperature increase, 1860–2000
SOURCE: Hadley Centre.

increase—and it concerns the huge increase in coal burning engaged in by China. This spurt of coal burning, involving billions of tonnes of carbon being consumed, has emitted not just billions of tonnes of carbon into the atmosphere (with greenhouse effects) but also billions of tonnes of particulate emissions of sulfur dioxide from the dirty coal. The sulfur dioxide particles act as reflective barrier, and exert a counter-greenhouse effect, dubbed the "global dimming" or "aerosol cooling" effect.[35] The sulfur particles remain in the atmosphere for only a few months or years— whereas the carbon dioxide remains for decades, even centuries. So as China cleans up its coal-burning act (as it almost certainly will), then it can be expected that the increase in temperature will resume—at an even faster rate—unless something drastic is done to change fundamental energy patterns.

Charts like those in Figures 3.2 and 3.3, now famous all around the world, represent the culmination of extraordinary scientific efforts in retrieving ice cores from Arctic and Antarctic sources as well as from Greenland. The *fact* that carbon emissions have been rising relentlessly, leading to ever-increasing levels of carbon dioxide in the atmosphere (now reaching 400 parts per million, or ppm, by volume in early 2013), is hardly in dispute. It is the greenhouse effect of these rising levels and the resultant climate change (global warming) that bring on the most vituperative debate. The theory of the greenhouse effect is barely more than a century old, first formulated by the Swedish scientist Arrhenius.[36]

This warming has multiple effects, but one of the clearest is the impact on the extent of sea ice and glaciers. Map 3.1, from the National Aeronautics and Space Administration (NASA), shows the extent of the polar ice cap in 1979 and its extent in a recent satellite photograph, which shows how much the polar ice has been reduced. The ice is also getting

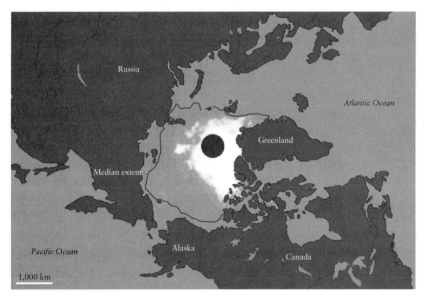

MAP **3.1**   Diminishing Arctic sea-ice cover

SOURCE: NASA.

NOTE: This image taken by NASA shows the extent of Arctic sea ice in August 2012. The line beyond the ice shows the median extent of ice cover between the years 1979 and 2000.

much thinner. While this might be viewed as a positive by Russian oil and mineral interests, keen to engage in exploitation of deposits in the Arctic Sea, and by shipping lines keen to open up summertime transit via the Arctic, it is an unwelcome indicator for the rest of the world of the global impact of the warming induced by burning fossil fuels.

It is worth recalling that it was the West with its fossil-fuel-driven mode of industrialization that is responsible for the carbon emissions that are now taking their toll. While China and India are now coming to share the spotlight in terms of current emissions, the historical responsibility for the carbon that is still in the atmosphere at elevated levels, and that will remain there for decades and centuries to come, is clear. In reality, more than 80 percent of the cumulative emissions come from the developed world.

If carbon emissions constitutes the problem (as any sane person would believe to be the case), then the most recent trends are alarming. According to estimates published by the US Carbon Dioxide Information Analysis Center (part of the Department of Energy), the situation by the beginning of 2013 was that the world was emitting 10 billion tonnes of carbon each year and had driven the CO_2 concentration to more than 400 ppm. Emissions from burning liquids (oil) and gas have been rising steeply, as have emissions from production of cement. But the real kicker is emissions from coal, which have risen steeply since 2001 and now account for around 3.5 billion tonnes—with much of the increase coming from China. This raises an important question: will China's industrialization be the "last straw," or will China manage to tip the world into a new "green growth" trajectory?

A Global Limit to Carbon Emissions, and China's Impact

The simplest way of envisaging the problem of carbon emissions is to see them as having to be limited to 1 trillion tonnes. This is a level of atmospheric contribution that, with 25 percent certainty, would result in global warming of 2°C—the limit suggested by the studies coordinated by the IPCC. As the letter to *Nature* reporting this result states:

> Policy targets based on limiting cumulative emissions of carbon dioxide are likely to be more robust to scientific uncertainty than emission-rate

or concentration targets. Total anthropogenic emissions of one trillion tonnes of carbon (3.67 trillion tonnes of CO_2), *about half of which has already been emitted since industrialization began*, results in a most likely peak carbon-dioxide-induced warming of 2°C above pre-industrial temperatures. (Allen et al. 2009, 1166)

Thus, according to these scientists, around half a trillion tonnes of carbon had already been emitted into the atmosphere by the first two hundred years of industrialization. What, then, can we expect will be added by China's massive burning of fossil fuels—before the substitution by renewables is completed?

My collaborator Dr. Hao Tan and I have spent much effort on this issue. Our picture of China's likely energy trajectories, revealing a slow (convex) outer curve of total energy buildup, and two curves within it depicting fossil fuels' usage (rising steeply then falling away) and renewables (rising steadily along logistic industrial dynamics), is displayed in Chapter 4. This enables us to make a quantitative estimate of China's future carbon emissions. Hao Tan and I expect that the carbon emissions from China's electric power sector will continue to grow until around 2025, and then will start to decline thanks to the takeoff of the renewable energy used in the sector. This means that, for all its efforts to reduce energy intensity and carbon intensity, China is likely to be increasing its total carbon emissions from generating power for another decade or more (Figure 3.4)—as elaborated on in Chapter 4.

China's contribution of around 140 billion tonnes carbon needs to be compared with the cumulative contribution from the countries of the West as they industrialized; these countries emitted around 500 billion tonnes carbon over the 250 years from the Industrial Revolution to the present, and they drove up carbon dioxide concentrations from the pre-industrial level of 280 ppm to around 380 ppm by the year 2000 and to 400 ppm by 2013.[37] China's own cumulative emissions from electric power generation can be expected to push these concentrations even higher.

It is a reasonable assumption that the rest of the world, led by India, could industrialize up to an acceptable standard of living (and energy utilization) for the same amount, and that the West, inspired by China, might be able to scale back to this level over the course of the twenty-first century. The global implications could be a further 500 Gt of carbon being released this century. This would bring the world dangerously close to

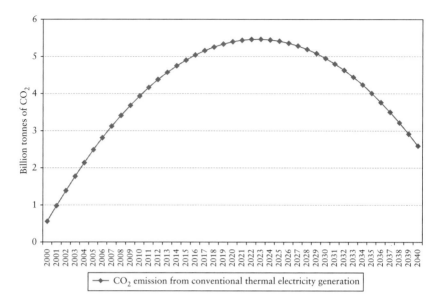

FIGURE **3.4**   China: Projected carbon emissions from power generation, 2000–2040
SOURCE: Mathews and Tan.

the "ceiling" of 1 trillion tonnes described by Allen and colleagues (2009) as likely to drive up carbon dioxide concentrations from their preindustrial level of 280 ppm to a level around 510 or 520 ppm, and, according to the recent papers published in *Nature*, to drive global temperatures up by 2°C. *This would appear to be the minimum possible disturbance to the earth's carbon dioxide atmospheric concentrations* consistent with China's and the world's industrialization and most practicably rapid rate of take-up of renewable and low-carbon energy sources.

It is not even the case that global warming is the most serious consequence of the rises in carbon dioxide levels since industrialization— extremely serious as these may be. The real long-term problem promises to be ocean acidification, which will have dramatic impact on marine species biodiversity—that is, it will kill the vast majority of current marine species. Then there are other horrors in store for us—the unfreezing of methane clathrates from the Arctic tundra (releasing vast amounts of the potent greenhouse gas methane); the rising sea levels as ice sheets melt;

the altering of river courses as glaciers disappear; and the devastation caused by desertification, hurricanes, intense bush fires, and floods—to name just a few. While these potential "civilization destroyers" have been utilized by the mass media as "scare stories" and have led to a degree of fatalistic capitulation, my argument in this book is that this is precisely the kind of response that one might envisage was raised during debates on Easter Island as to what to do about reducing forest cover. Who was it on Easter Island who chopped down the last tree—and no doubt had a rationale for doing so? The correct response to our dilemma is to examine the rules and institutions that bring about this kind of behavior, and then institute stringent changes to those rules—before it is too late. It is the rules of capitalism itself that have to be examined—and amended.

New Challenges, New Promises

There are any number of arguments and convenient "parables" that would seem to offer solutions to the conundrums raised by the globalization and further deepening of industrialization, particularly its massive take-up by China and by other countries coming after China. It is necessary to consider these—if only to see why they fail to provide the fundamental responses that will guide the real changes needed. It is the complexity of our industrial system, and the inadequacy of our responses framed for an earlier, simpler context, that constitutes the principal challenge.[38]

Among the dangerous promises held out to avert the damage done by unrestrained "wild" capitalism as it fills the earth are the following: rising prosperity as the cure for social "bads" (the environmental Kuznets curve); the resort to carbon markets; and a series of technological fixes, among which carbon capture and storage (CC&S) is the most egregious.

Rising Prosperity Won't Solve the Problem

A convenient parable to deflect concern over these mounting problems has been devised, in the form of the environmental Kuznets curve (EKC)—an environmental extension of the notion of the Kuznets curve. The idea, first elaborated by Simon Kuznets (who gave the world gross domestic product as a measure of economic activity) is that as income rises, a particular "bad" rises and then falls—in an inverted U shape. His original work concerned income inequality, but it has now been extended to environmental bads such as pollution.[39]

It is an incontrovertible fact that some "bads" rise and then peak and fall as incomes increase. Close to our current concern, this fact can be demonstrated for energy intensity, which in historical experience rises and then peaks and falls as countries grow wealthier and as their energy efficiency increases. All countries as they industrialize have followed a characteristic trajectory in which their energy intensity (energy consumed per unit GDP) rises, peaks, and then falls. Great Britain was the first to follow this pathway, peaking in 1880; then the United States peaked around 1920, and Germany around 1930; then in the postwar period, Japan peaked around 1960. Countries are less energy efficient as they industrialize, and then they become more energy efficient as they grow wealthy. Moreover, the successive peaks are lower for each country. There are good theoretical reasons for observing such a pattern, based on secular improvements in the efficiency of energy technologies being deployed. Through the history of industrialization, the peaks in energy intensity of "follower" countries have been always lower than those of their forerunners, which suggests that less energy-intensive industrialization paths become available to the latecomer. China is now living through this transformation.[40]

It is a beguiling idea that countries need make no further effort than to enrich themselves to "solve" all their environmental problems. Of course the framers of the original conception (Grossman and Krueger 1995) were careful not to be seen to be saying as much; nevertheless, they left open such an inference. The World Bank devoted its *World Development Report 1992* to the topic "development and the environment," focusing much of its analysis (without using the terminology) on the EKC. The report notes, "As incomes rise, the demand for improvements in environmental quality will increase, as will the resources available for investment" (World Bank 1992, 39). Many commentators took this to mean that economic growth alone could provide the solution to environmental problems—missing the qualifications that the leading authors insisted on, including economists.[41] Of course, if the EKC narrative were to be relied on by China and India, without specific and stringent goals targeted at energy intensity and carbon emission reductions, then all the problems associated with "business as usual" pathways would become manifest, long before the rising prosperity was supposed to have worked its magic. The EKC really becomes meaningless once the discussion focuses on global problems like rising carbon dioxide levels and climate change.

While individual countries can claim to be reducing their energy intensity (energy utilized per unit of GDP), this is frequently achieved simply by relocating the most energy-intensive industries to another country. When a global perspective is taken, it appears that with the rapid uptake of fossil-fueled energy systems in India and China since the year 2000, the correlation between rising GDP and rising energy use is close. In other words, there is no overall decline in energy usage as revenue rises (with efficiency improvements countermanded by greater consumption levels). This is the real situation faced by the world as industrialization spreads.

Carbon Markets Won't Solve the Problem

Another beguiling idea is that carbon markets will, through the securitization of pollution permits and certificates of "saved" carbon emissions, lead to the substitution of low-carbon industrial processes for the dirtier incumbents. Now of course it has been a signal feature of the evolution of capitalism that previously tangible entities like land and commodities could be turned into securities such as certificates of ownership that could themselves be traded. But the idea of trading certificates representing pollution, and building a market for such certificates, takes this process a long way farther—and into some very dangerous territory, particularly when envisaged as operating in a global setting.[42]

There has been strong support for such market-friendly mechanisms, from leaders of the UN Framework Convention on Climate Change (UNFCCC), from national governments, and (of course) from the banks and trading houses that look forward to profiting from such trading. But the problem with artificially created credit instruments is that they can be artificially manipulated—or "gamed" by unscrupulous operators. The UN Kyoto Protocol's Clean Development Mechanism (CDM) is an unfortunate case in point. Very few of the thousands of carbon emissions mitigation projects launched around the world have actually received UN endorsement. And many turn out to have been created solely to game the CDM process rather than to address global warming. The gas trifluoromethane, HFC-23, for example, is a greenhouse gas that arises not from transport or industry but from refrigeration. Many manufacturers (particularly in China) found out how profitable it could be to produce quantities of HFC-23 only to "avoid" its emission through use of CDM carbon credits. One study reported that payments to refrigerant producers and carbon market investors by governments and by purchasers of compliance certificates for HFC-23 exceeded €4.7 billion—whereas the costs of abating the gas directly would not have exceeded €100 million—a forty-seven-fold inflation.[43]

OK, this might be an extreme case of market pathology—but it makes clear the priorities of the participants who flock to any market once it is created, particularly one that operates beyond the bounds of national jurisdictions and subject only to weak UN oversight. Of course some carbon markets could play a positive role in encouraging reductions in carbon emissions—as in initiatives such as carbon-related stock market indices designed to attract investments from funds traded on exchanges.[44] In contrast, many of the carbon markets can be expected to constitute a severe distraction from the business of getting behind renewables and circular economy initiatives, providing opportunities for speculation (more carbon market bubbles?) and for companies to "greenwash" their carbon-emitting practices, if not block effective policies for decarbonizing economies altogether.[45] The objections to carbon markets continue to be that they lack transparency, being based on additionality; that they fail to promote innovation; and that they lack a moral foundation.[46] But the fundamental objection is that they offer little in the way of amelioration potential and ample opportunity for creating speculating bubbles. There is no getting around the fact that policies have to aim directly at the goal of promoting a rupture with fossil fuels and linear economic thinking in favor of renewable energies and circular economy material initiatives—and not at creating artificial carbon markets.

Technical Fixes Won't Solve the Problem

In this context it is also useful to consider some of the technical fixes that have been advanced to deal with global warming—geo-engineering "solutions" such as constructing artificial trees to absorb carbon dioxide or erecting space barriers to "shield" the earth from incoming solar radiation (and thereby unwittingly curtailing photo-synthetic uptake of carbon dioxide). The technical fix par excellence—carbon capture and storage (CC&S)—is based on the tenuous evidence of one case in which it has been shown to work, namely in the Sleipner area of the North Sea. Norway's Statoil has been capturing and pumping back carbon dioxide into this deepwater field to help maintain the pressure of the issuing oil. Almost all other CC&S projects that are announced are quietly discontinued (including the much-heralded FutureGen project in the United States under the Bush administration) or their development is passed from the oil companies to public-sector R&D support.

It is a mystery why CC&S has been passed off as a solution to the problem of carbon emissions when one considers that if it were to work, every atom of carbon that is burnt would have to be collected and disposed of—which would imply building an infrastructure for CC&S at least as large as the existing fossil fuel infrastructure. Building an entire infrastructure in this way would presumably be beyond even the oil industry—which is no doubt why the buck is passed each time the industry has an opportunity to step forward and bear the costs.[47]

Corporate and Social Responsibility Won't Solve the Problem

Many companies are today pursuing business strategies of corporate and social responsibility, arguing that this is good for their bottom line as well as for the planet. No doubt many of these initiatives are well intentioned, effective, and have a positive effect. No doubt it is equally true that many of these initiatives are simply cases of "greenwashing," by which companies instigate minor changes to reap public relations benefits. The case of offsetting carbon credits is one such story. Nevertheless, companies and their "corporate sustainability" strategies and "sustainability alliances" are building momentum, and they are backed by a solid body of empirical research that indicates the beneficial impact on corporate profits of maintaining stringent environmental standards.[48] Yet the point is that for every firm that is doing the right thing, there is another that is profiting by opportunities to do the wrong thing—and there will be no change until there is strong state action to guide the way to collective behavior that produces genuinely sustainable outcomes.[49] One positive step forward would be for commodities exchanges and stock markets to develop indices composed of shares of firms that agree to participate, and by doing so agree to certain minimum disclosure rules for their carbon emissions: the Brazilian Carbon Efficient Index (ICO2) is one such important initiative.[50]

Is There "Unburnable Carbon"?

The Carbon Tracker Initiative in London has formulated the useful notion of unburnable carbon, which views the fossil fuel reserves amassed by oil companies as too large to burn—and yet these reserves underwrite the stock market valuations of these companies and are being actively expanded through exploration.[51] The power of the concept lies in its focus on the most vulnerable and sensitive feature of the oil companies, namely their stock price. The argument goes that as public concern grows over continued use of fossil fuels, with their propensity to drive global warming, so the companies that carry most responsibility for this situation will feel the pressure through diminished stock prices, responding to the "stranded assets" of unburnable carbon on their balance sheets. This is an argument that is addressed to the capitalist character of the economy rather than the neoclassical fiction of an economy without institutions, financial system, or modern firms. A similar line of argument has been advanced by the German scholar Hans-Werner Sinn in his 2012 book (translated from the German) *The Green Paradox*, in which he argues that existing policies to curb greenhouse gas emissions have been ineffective largely because they are focused on the demand side (such as carbon taxes). He argues that this generates the "green paradox," in which the owners of fossil fuel resources are thereby encouraged to accelerate their exploitation, thus resulting in even higher levels of emissions. The solution as Sinn sees it is for the world to opt for supply-side policies on a collective basis, involving a gathering of all consumer countries into a cartel (a "counter-OPEC"), and their adoption of a global cap-and-trade system supported by the levying of taxes on capital, designed to hurt the financial assets of fossil fuel corporations.[52] Even if Sinn's proposals are breathtakingly unrealistic, they nevertheless bring attention right back to the issue of global problems and global solutions—which is where they should be focused.

Will the "Tragedy of the Commons" Destroy
Our Industrial Civilization?

Capitalism has long comforted itself with the parable of the hidden hand, first adumbrated by Adam Smith (1776), as a convenient alibi for the social justification of selfish behavior—an extension of Mandeville's 1714 *Fable of the Bees; or, Private Vices, Public Virtues*. But such parables ignore resource and environmental constraints. A more relevant story is Garrett Hardin's tragedy of the commons—updating the usual story of the hidden hand that coordinates self-interested behavior to achieve a socially optimal outcome. When the self-interested behavior reduces a commons, it cannot hope to achieve an optimal social outcome absent associated interventions, such as institutional (contractual) interventions, privatization, or state regulation.

The tragedy of the commons is a parable in which private ownership without regard to social purpose or public responsibility unleashes destructiveness. Hardin's 1968 article published in *Science* has been one of the most read and cited papers ever to appear in that journal; it has generated—for very good reasons—an enormous secondary literature. Yet its argument is hardly an advance on the quip from Aristotle, namely, "For that which is common to the greatest number has the least care bestowed upon it."[53] Hardin characterizes the "tragedy" simply as the dilemma that arises when many individuals sharing a common resource, acting individually and rationally in their own self-interest, ultimately deplete the resource, even when it is clear that it is in no one's interest to do so. (The reasoning goes as follows: why should I hold back while others do not, and thereby secure a short-term advantage?)

The earth's atmosphere is the ultimate commons in that all are dependent on it; all add noxious elements to it, most of which are recycled and absorbed; and all draw from it in subtractive fashion, in the sense that one person's use reduces the scope for another person's (or organism's) use. This is why destruction of the atmosphere's powers of regeneration is of such concern.

We have to ask what the forces are that drive the level of destructiveness creating such tragedies. Clearly there is something about the "spirit of capitalism" that is involved, in its perspective on the environment as simply a resource to be plundered—and dumped on. It is an objectivized, rationalized, and dehumanized resource that is assumed to be infinite in its capacity to provide raw materials and infinite in its capacity to absorb wastes. Very clearly, none of these assumptions holds true.

Unlike commons usually dealt with in the literature, where privatization and rule by contract can be useful and effective ways of mitigating the tragic reduction of the common-pool resource, a global commons like the atmosphere presents intractable problems. Rules involving bilateral and multiparty contractual agreements are difficult to reach; where the number of users rises (as in the billions of organisms making use of the atmosphere), coordination presents insuperable problems.[54] In the terms posed, there is no solution to this problem. The two "solutions" advanced by Hardin, namely privatization on the one hand and state ownership on the other, seem to be inapplicable—even if we allow for hybrid institutional forms that have emerged since Hardin was writing.[55] Ownership is not an option in the case of the atmosphere.[56]

So yes, the unrestrained emissions of carbon into the atmosphere, unrestrained by any sense of prudence that comes with property rights (to paraphrase McCloskey), will lead to destruction on a planetary scale. There is no easy solution at hand in the form of global government, or even formal international agreement to curb carbon emissions. The world has been discussing the issue for at least three decades, in the setting of the UN Framework Convention—and progress is zero. This is no doubt due less to negotiators' failure of vision than to deliberate obstruction by the vested interests involved.

A different way forward has to be found. And this is where "green growth" makes its reappearance. For China, India, and others are well aware that they cannot hope to complete their industrialization utilizing the wasteful and fossil-fueled BAU model, which will lead them inexorably into resource wars (with each other and with the already-industrialized countries), into endless economic problems created by peaking of resources, and into the environmental tragedy of the commons created by burning fossil fuels and exploiting resources in non-renewable fashion.

A kind of market-relevant response that is called for is exemplified by China's Sloping Lands Conversion Program (SLCP), a huge program to reverse the soil destruction caused by smallholders bringing steeper and steeper lands under cultivation in China's largest river valleys. This program, which has run for the past decade (from 2002) and targets nearly fifteen million hectares of sloping lands, is backed by a budget of $40 million—making it by far the largest "payment for eco-services" program ever launched.[57]

The program was instigated to deal with catastrophic levels of soil loss, with rains sweeping vast tonnages of soil from the valley sides and taking it downriver, causing floods and other damage. The problem was vast and so was the response, involving strong state direction to set agriculture in the Yellow River and Yangtze River valleys on a new trajectory. But it was not just the heavy "visible" hand of the state issuing orders, but a sophisticated program offering inducements to farmers to change their practices and to improve the value of their own land. Thus, it revealed state power in setting a new trajectory, combined with use of capitalist instruments (which I am calling market-based incentives) to ensure adherence with the new trajectory. Something similar is needed worldwide in dealing with the range of issues created by the expansion of industrial capitalism.

The convenient parable of the "hidden hand" ensuring that all is for the best in a capitalist world is no longer an option once the world is "full" and every action from one party inevitably has repercussions on every other party. The convenient parable of the environmental Kuznets curve won't come to our rescue: we can't just assume that to grow wealthy is to get cleaner and more resource efficient. The various technical fixes that have been proposed—such as CC&S—simply don't hold water (or carbon!). The carbon markets that are supposed to generate worldwide incentives for mitigation will no doubt enrich their creators but will do little in the way of real mitigation. Endless calls for R&D without complementary efforts to expand markets for renewables, to drive down prices, may be viewed as a distraction.[58]

Global warming as a real tragedy of the commons stares us in the face unless we can rouse ourselves to change the rules of the game through which people pursuing their self-interest inflict so much damage on themselves and on everyone else. We can trace all the problems to the basic DNA of industrial capitalism—fossil energies allowing for unlimited enjoyment, non-satiety and resource spoliation, finance divorced from ecological realities. Thus, a reworking of capitalism has to address these issues *and resolve them.*

Like the late lamented Barry Commoner, I see the solution to our problems not in terms of fantasies involving global population reduction (which no matter how couched, must always result in some form of famine, pestilence, or war as the reducing force) but instead in terms of changes to the way we generate energy, in the way we produce and circulate resources, and in the way that we allocate finance. Changes in the rules and institutions governing these processes are feasible and necessary—and they are already under way. In one sense, we are more fortunate than when Commoner penned *The Closing Circle* in 1971, in that he was clear as to what needed to be done—a closing of the circle—but dubious as to our prospects for achieving such alignment between capitalist economic cycles and geo-ecological cycles.[59] Now perhaps the situation is clearer, and we can see both sides of the issue: how capitalist industrial dynamics are driving us toward renewable energies, circular economy linkages, and eco-finance; and how capitalist interests are throwing up barriers to the process, such as the buildup of fossil fuel reserves ("unburnable carbon") on the balance sheets of companies and which underpin their stock market valuations—a "wicked" problem if ever there was one. Population, by contrast, appears to be a relatively soluble problem; it will (more or less) look after itself—particularly as the world industrializes and urbanizes and as women become better educated and exercise greater control over their own reproductive activities.

We need a new parable—something like a "closing of the circle," as Commoner suggested, or a "greening of capitalism" or a "green development model"—something that evokes the necessity to live in harmony with the great cycles of the biosphere and within the limits they impose, rather than in ignorance of them and flouting them (as if God had really decreed that man is to be master of the earth). It is to these issues that we now turn.[60]

II *Toward a New Eco-Logic for Capitalism*

There is no substitute for energy. The whole edifice of modern society is built upon it. . . . It is not "just another commodity" but the precondition of all commodities, a basic factor equal with air, water and earth.

—*E. F. Schumacher,* Small Is Beautiful *(1973)*

Fossil resources brought the industrialized countries their prosperity. Yet now that their cost outweighs their benefits, fossil resources may bring those self-same countries to their knees. It is [my] principal thesis . . . that renewable energy, by contrast, brings greater social benefits the more widely it is used, to the point where it fully replaces all fossil energy.

—*Hermann Scheer,* The Solar Economy *(2002)*

The sun is the spring that drives all. The sun maintains all human life and supplies all human energy.

—*Nikola Tesla, "The problem of increasing human energy— with special reference to the harnessing of the sun's energy" (1900)*

We are like tenant farmers chopping down the fence around our house for fuel when we should be using Nature's inexhaustible sources of energy—sun, wind and tide. . . . I'd put my money on the sun and . . . I hope we don't have to wait until oil and coal run out before we tackle that.

—*Thomas Edison, in conversation with Henry Ford and Harvey Firestone, (1931)*

In the market for energy, old and new technologies based on harvesting renewable sources (solar, wind, hydro) are emerging, as a new age of renewables dawns. The sun is finally being viewed as the source for all practicable and sustainable sources of energy (sourced directly as in photovoltaic systems and solar thermal, and indirectly through wind and hydro systems)—as anticipated by the great rivals in inventing the modern world, Nikola Tesla and Thomas Edison.[1] These new systems are being facilitated by investments in smart grids that enable fluctuating sources to be matched across the grid, as well as by new energy storage technologies (e.g., molten-salt systems in concentrating solar power stations, to be discussed in a moment) that overcome problems of intermittency. The capitalist spirit here is harnessed to invest in these new energy sources in the pursuit of profit, driving down the costs through the experience curve, as well as through finance that is becoming cheaper as the energy security of such investments becomes more attractive than fossil fuel investments.[2] China is rapidly taking a leading position in all aspects of these new energy sources, driven by its extreme need, extreme pollution problems, and exuberant capitalist spirit, and it is building export markets for its renewable energy systems around the world.[3] Through the magic of logistic industrial dynamics, the more that Chinese renewable energy industries build momentum, the more certain their eventual supersession of the current energy system becomes.[4] When we add in China's planning system, which directs finance toward favored investment, it could well have an energy system based on hydro, renewable, and nuclear that generates more electric power than fossil fuels by around 2020 and eclipses fossil fuels as primary energy source by 2030. Because China is making such a dramatic impact with its energy industrial revolution, it is best to start our overview of the global energy transition with this signal case.

China's Energy Industrial Revolution

China's rapid buildup of renewable energy industries and projected phase-out of reliance on fossil fuels—within the next couple of decades—has captured the world's attention. China's motives for effecting this energy industrial revolution have more to do with national energy security than with any concerns over the global environment (although those concerns are certainly prominent). Just what is driving China's energy strategy?

China's gross domestic product (GDP) has been on a steep rise since its opening to the world in 1979, averaging 9.9 percent growth over three decades.[5] But it really went into accelerated mode after joining the

World Trade Organization (WTO) in 2001. In the five years following, China doubled its GDP, then doubled it again by 2011–12. What underpinned this extraordinary rise, unparalleled in economic history, was the rise of manufacturing industry—and what powered this rise was the increase in energy, and specifically in coal-burning electric power.

Figures 1.1 and 1.2 (in Chapter 1) tell the story in terms of electric power generation (which accounts for 50 percent of China's carbon emissions).[6] China's electric power generation doubled between 2001 and 2006, and then doubled again. By 2011 China had built the largest electric power "machine" in the world, surpassing that of the United States and rated at more than 1 trillion watts (1 TW) by 2011. This machine generated close to 5 trillion kWh by 2012—of which 3.9 trillion kWh (nearly 80 percent) came from burning coal. The serious buildup in energy capacity began after China joined the WTO in 2001.

At the same time, China has been building up its renewable energy industries—initially hydro as the main source and to some extent nuclear (slowed after Japan's Fukushima disaster of 2011), and increasingly wind and solar. Figure 1.2 (in Chapter 1) shows that China's buildup in wind power started around 2005 and doubled every year, making the country the largest wind power generator in the world, in terms of both production of turbines and their installation in wind farms. China's wind power companies—including Goldwind; Sinovel; and the latest, privately owned addition, Ming Yang—are now globalizing at a rapid rate and moving to the top of the world's leading wind energy companies. China's wind power companies are indeed moving rapidly from imitation to innovation. Goldwind's direct traction wind turbines, eliminating the use of gears, are cheaper and more reliable than their more complex competitors.

A similar story can be told for solar photovoltaics, where early leaders (some of whom have been in financial difficulties) are being joined by later arrivals such as Hanergy and Giga Solar, which are growing and globalizing rapidly. China has yet to make its mark in concentrating solar power (CSP), but initial interest could rapidly translate into world leadership, taking over from Spain. Indeed, China has announced that as part of the Twelfth Five-Year Plan it will drastically expand CSP capacity, reaching 1 GW by 2015—comparable to what the rest of the world has created so far.

And while the choice between nuclear and "new" renewables has not yet been made definitively in China (as it has in Germany, to be

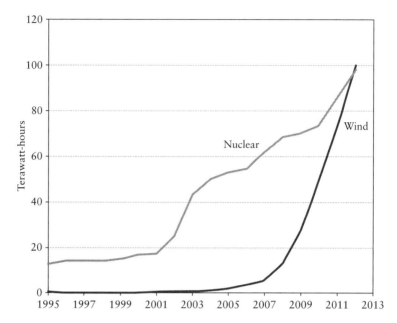

FIGURE **4.1**   Wind- and nuclear-generated electricity in China, 1995–2012
SOURCE: Earth Policy Institute, using data supplied by BP, WPM, and IAEA.

discussed in a moment), it is clear where the trends are taking China. Figure 4.1 compares electricity generated from nuclear with that from wind
power. China's targets are for an ever-increasing proportion of electricity to come from wind, far surpassing whatever might be derived from
nuclear sources.

China is not just building new energy-generating products (and
energy efficiency improving systems); it is also investing vast sums in updating the electric power grid to accommodate a variety of such sources.
China calls this the "smart and strong" grid, in that it will be IT-enabled
and able to carry prodigious quantities of electric power from the deserts
of the west, where wind and solar power abound, to the country's eastern
seaboard, through new high-voltage direct current (HVDC) cables, which
conserve much more power in transmission than conventional AC lines.
The targets for investment in grid upgrading by the State Grid Corporation of China (SGCC) are emblematic of the huge push to accommodate
renewables. SGCC is the world's largest utility, and one of the ten largest
companies worldwide—and yet it is still barely known outside China. Its

grid covers over a billion people in China, complementing that supplied by the Guangzhou-based Southern Power Grid Co.[7]

This upgraded and strengthened grid is becoming China's great twenty-first-century national infrastructure project—the equivalent of the railways in Europe in the nineteenth century or the interstate highway system in the United States in the twentieth century. In Map 4.1 I reproduce a chart from China that shows how the grid will change as the SGCC investments are implemented. The upgraded grid will have several east-west and north-south "trunk routes" for carrying ultra-high-voltage cables. Clearly, provinces that are not depicted as being connected to these HVDC long-distance links will nevertheless be connected to the upgraded grid. And the grid can be expected to be modular and cellular,

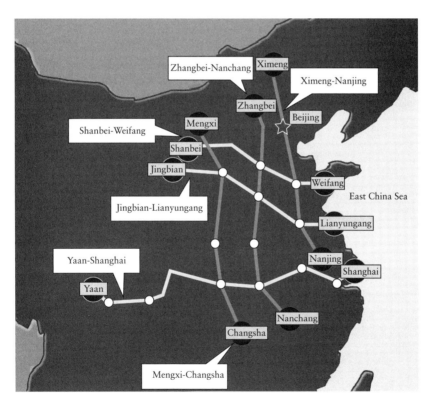

MAP **4.1**   China's projected strong and smart electric power grid
SOURCE: State Grid Corporation of China.

making it eminently robust and resilient. China sees vast new business opportunities opening up with its smart grid, and it is already gearing up the technical standards that will fashion international competition in this sector.

There are several reasons to expect that these changes unleashed in China will be permanent and will lead to still further changes favoring renewables over both fossil fuel and nuclear power systems.

The first concerns industrial dynamics. China's buildup of renewables will not follow a simple linear progression but can be expected to follow logistic, or S-shaped, industrial uptake curves. This means that as investments in renewable systems accumulate, they will become self-reinforcing and lead to further such investments. With my collaborator Dr. Hao Tan, I have plotted China's recent electric power investments in Figure 4.2 and carried them forward to 2020 and to 2030, in accordance with official projections, but fitting logistic curves to them. We follow a distinctive procedure in mapping out the total electric power curve as an outer envelope, following a parabolic trajectory, and renewables trajectories within it, following logistic dynamics. This represents, in other words, a nonlinear approach to capturing energy industrial dynamics.

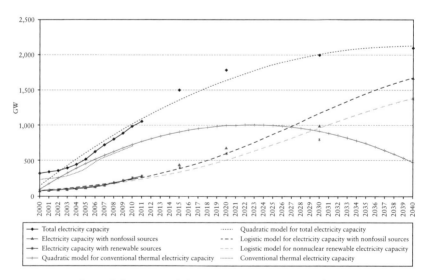

FIGURE **4.2**   Industrial dynamics of electric power capacity in China, 2000–2040
SOURCE: Mathews and Tan (2013).

Hao Tan and I depict China's energy trends in terms of three curves—an outer convex curve representing total electric power, with an inner parabolic curve representing buildup and then decline of coal, and a logistic curve representing the buildup of renewables. For the outer parabolic curve, we have a total electric power trajectory that follows historical points up to the year 2012 (reaching 1145 GW, shown as diamonds in Figure 4.2), and then further points spaced out to 2015 and 2020 according to the most recent official projections, and then to 2030 and 2040 based on publications from the Energy Research Institute. Capacity reaches just over 2000 GW (2 TW) by 2040. We then draw through this our own smooth parabolic curve (quadratic model for total electricity) to indicate the shape of China's likely total electric energy trajectory up to the year 2040.

Hao Tan and I depict coal-burning thermal electric power generation in Figure 4.2, showing it increasing from 758 GW in 2012 to 1030 GW in 2020, then peaking and declining to 1000 GW in 2030—that is, peaking at sometime between 2020 and 2030. In accordance with nonlinear industrial dynamics, the significance of fossil sources can be anticipated to decline rapidly thereafter.[8]

For the inner logistic curve, we depict first the historical points for nonfossil energy sources (including nuclear) up to the year 2012, and then points beyond this date (as triangles) based on official projections. We draw our own logistic curve through all these points (logistic model for nonfossil sources). We have a pair of curves for nonfossil energy sources excluding nuclear, that is, genuinely renewable sources—again shown as historical points up to 2012 and then projected outward (shown as crosses in Figure 4.2) according to official sources, together with our own smooth logistic curve capturing the essence of the trajectory.[9]

I submit that Figure 4.2 provides a plausible and realistic model of China's likely greening of its electric power sector—the source of 50 percent of its carbon emissions. Renewables would account for half of the total power generated by 2022 or 2023—just over a decade hence.

A second point worth underlining is that from these electric power trends we are able to make reliable predictions of China's carbon emissions. In 2012, China burned around 3.4 Gt coal, of which 1.5 Gt were burnt in thermal power stations to generate 4 trillion kWh of electricity. On the basis of Chinese estimates for carbon emissions from thermal

power generation, we would expect this level of power generation to result in 3.1 Gt carbon dioxide—or 0.84 Gt carbon.[10] If we add up *all
anticipated carbon emissions* from China's future generation of electric
power (accounting currently for no less than 50 percent of China's total
carbon emissions), then we can expect the carbon emissions from China's
electric power sector to continue to grow till around 2025, and then start
to decline thanks to the takeoff of the renewable energy used in the sector.
This means that, for all its efforts to reduce energy intensity and carbon
intensity, China is likely to be increasing its total carbon emissions from
generating power for another decade or more—as shown in Figure 3.5 in
Chapter 3—but then carbon emissions would swiftly decline.

The third point is that the eventual decline in thermal power generation and consequent eventual decline in carbon emissions is firmly
grounded in China's industrial strategy, which is to build renewable energy industries as the foundation of future export success and prosperity.
Other countries have built renewable energy markets—such as Germany's efforts to enhance consumer demand for renewables via feed-in
tariffs. But China has, from the start, focused on building the manufacturing industries that produce renewable energy systems, together with the
value chains of components and materials suppliers. The Twelfth Five-
Year Plan states explicitly that China's seven targeted industries for its
clean technology revolution will account for 8 percent of GDP by 2015,
rising to 15 percent by 2020 and expanding rapidly thereafter. The plan
calls for China to move increasingly from imports of technology to indigenous innovation.[11] Only Korea has formulated a comparable green
growth industrial strategy, focused on the building of green industries as
a platform for the future.

I could give many more examples of such renewable energy initiatives under way in the BICs (Brazil, India, and China)—such as India's Jawaharlal Nehru National Solar Mission, launched in 2011 with
an ambitious target of installing 20 GW of solar power within a decade.
The program is entrusted to India's Ministry of New and Renewable
Energy—itself a significant latecomer institutional innovation. And there
are Brazil's recent initiatives in wind power (taking advantage of the
strong and regular wind energy received in parts of the country), which
complement the country's already-high dependence for electric power
on hydro—making Brazil unique among industrializing countries for its

high levels of renewable energy production and consumption. The federal government staged the first auction for wind power licenses only in 2009, and in the intervening period no fewer than 140 wind farms have flourished, powered by companies like Renova Energia.[12] The motives for these initiatives—which could be multiplied—are clear: these countries need to expand their energy systems by 100 percent or more over the course of the coming decade to keep up with their anticipated growth, and they cannot do so utilizing fossil fuels—for economic as much as for energy security reasons. Renewable power systems created by manufacturing provide an obvious alternative.

The implications of this are profound—they imply a sound approach to building new industries through market expansion and cost reduction, via mass production. This is to be contrasted to the conventional approach in the West, which is to focus on innovation rather than market expansion utilizing standardized products that are suitable for rapid scale-up. This is what I have described as a "clash of civilizations" in the fostering of clean technologies.[13]

China (together with India or Brazil) is not alone in effecting an energy revolution. These countries are being paid the compliment of emulation by none other than Germany, preeminent industrial power of the European Union, with its *Energiewende*, or "energy transformation," through which nuclear power is being phased out and renewables are being installed at a rapid rate.

Germany's *Energiewende*

The Japanese Fukushima nuclear disaster struck on March 11, 2011. While Japan was still clearing away the rubble, Germany was already rebuilding its energy system. Within a month, Chancellor Angela Merkel had reversed an earlier decision to slowly phase out nuclear power, and in June the German parliament voted to abolish nuclear power altogether. This marked the beginning of the most fundamental transformation in energy infrastructure unleashed by any advanced industrial economy—what is called in German the *Energiewende* ("energy transition," or "transformation"). Is it a real revolution?[14]

Nuclear power is now a dead issue in Germany. Its phase-out will of course take time. Generation of nuclear power still accounted for

16.5 percent of total German electricity in 2013—but it is falling and will doubtless continue to fall. Seven reactors were shut down immediately as a result of the chancellor's announcement. No new reactors are to be brought on stream, and all existing reactors will have been completely phased out within ten years. Following the turnaround on this issue by the Christian Democrats and Chancellor Merkel, there no longer appears to be any political support for reviving the nuclear industry in Germany.

To plug the gap, renewables are being ramped up at a tremendous pace. Generation of solar PV electricity increased to 29.7 TWh in 2013, whereas wind power held steady at 47.2 TWh—with both accounting for 13.7 percent of all electricity generated in 2013. The proportion of renewables in capacity additions for 2013 is higher and increasing, indicating that renewables will be taking more and more of the load. It is notable that Germany's promotion of renewables has moved on from market expansion policies (like feed-in tariffs) to industry promotion policies—taking a leaf out of China's book.

True, in the interim there are "bridging" power arrangements that have involved marginally more coal being burnt—so that coal accounted for 45.6 percent of electricity generated (up from 44.7 percent in 2012), but coal as a fuel is destined to fall quickly as the renewables are ramped up, and fewer new coal-fired power stations are envisaged. Gas has been forced out of the German (and most European) electricity market because of high prices, and because there has been no "fracking" revolution (as yet) in Europe. To claim that the *Energiewende* means simply that more coal is being burnt—and more carbon emitted—is to miss the point that fossil fuels are marked for elimination.[15]

As in China, the national power grid in Germany is being drastically upgraded to enable it to accommodate higher and higher levels of fluctuating (renewable) power sources. Official estimates are that €20 billion will need to be invested in grid upgrading over the course of the coming decade, with the Bundestag opting for three major north-south connections to be built first—consisting of high-voltage (380 kV) lines.[16] Installing and equipping the smart grid is the huge new growth opportunity in Germany.

The *Energiewende* and the years leading up to it have witnessed the reduction in influence of the former German power generation oligopoly, which had been dominated by four large firms over many years. In 2010 these four once-mighty firms accounted for only 6.5 percent of *renewable electricity* generated in Germany—with their role being supplanted by hundreds of local co-ops, municipally owned generators, and small-scale producers that have sprung into existence.[17] This is a democratization of economic power unprecedented in the industrial world. Indeed, German cities are already taking back the grid into public ownership, through referenda (as in the case of Hamburg in September 2013) or where cities had not privatized electric power supply in the first place (like Frankfurt and Munich)—and they are doing so expressly to accelerate the uptake of renewable sources.[18]

So there is no doubting the scale of the changes unleashed by the *Energiewende* and their long-term impact. Within the next decade Germany will have shifted from a coal- and nuclear-powered industrial economy with four large, centralized power producers to a thriving, decentralized system generating power from renewable sources all over the country, and managing it all through a modernized and IT-enhanced smart grid. All this has been and is being accomplished without a central energy czar.

Of course there are critics—and not just from interests aligned with the four oligopolistic power producers and coal and nuclear interests. There is fierce debate over whether the costs of the transition can be justified, whether the feed-in tariff system has run its course, and whether a predominantly renewables-driven energy system will be up to powering a modern industrial economy. This is a healthy debate, of course—it could hardly be a revolution without such a debate.

Some neoclassical economists are reaching for unprecedented hyperbole as they denounce the whole enterprise—calling it the beginnings of an authoritarian dictatorship in Germany (because the feed-in tariffs are imposed by the federal government) or saying that there will be a "costs tsunami"—thus seeking to reverse the symbolism of the Fukushima disaster away from nuclear power and toward renewables.[19] But opinion polling in Germany shows a public unmoved by such rhetorical flights.

From the perspective of this book, the most arresting issue is the contrast between Germany and China—the two industrial nations that are most advanced in bringing forward a new energy system based largely on renewables. Both have made forceful and determined commitments to the new energy systems while maintaining and then moving toward phasing out their existing commitments to a "black" energy economy. Both see the upgrading of the grid as the key to accommodating higher and higher levels of renewables in the electric power mix. Both are encouraging a swarm of entrepreneurial new ventures into the power generation space, thus making it more competitive and vibrant than any power system before it.

China is doing all this through the leadership of the State Council and the Twelfth Five-Year Plan, enrolling state-owned banks to make the needed investments and credit allocations, with provincial and local administrations competing fiercely to attract new green energy industries. Germany is accomplishing the same result without any central planning or energy "supremo"—but with comparable local and *Länder*-level competitive promotion of the new industries with their job-creation potential. The closest that Germany has had to an energy leader would be the late Hermann Scheer—champion of solar and father of the feed-in tariff—but he was such purely in an ideological sense.

All of this is being done in the name of the low-carbon economy. Yet it is striking how quickly "low-carbon" acquires an economic dimension once the industry-promotion stakes are entered. The new green growth strategies emerging in China and Germany will prove to be far more effective at lowering carbon emissions than the Kyoto Protocol, with its nominal carbon reductions. And this is as it should be: the cleaning of the industrial economy was always going to be a state-mandated, industry-policy-driven strategy involving capitalist calculation.

A Military Perspective on Renewable Energies

If China and Germany are two of the surprises in the rapid adoption and promotion of renewables, another unexpected candidate must be the US military, which is emerging as a principal driver of the transition—for its own logistic and security concerns. Picture, if you will, long supply lines snaking across remote desert roads, carrying fuel to frontline troops, who could just as easily (and more safely) generate their own power using solar devices. Or naval and air craft utilizing biofuel additives to protect themselves against vagaries in fossil fuel supplies. This is why the military is emerging as a far more active and effective proponent of renewables than either the US Congress or the US administration and its Department of Energy.

In October 2010, the 150 marines of the Third Battalion, Fifth Marines, were the first to take a full battle "energy kit" consisting of portable solar panels, energy-conserving lights, solar tent shields that provide shade and electricity, and solar chargers for communications and computer equipment into the rugged outback of Helmand Province in Afghanistan.[20] This is the first of many such initiatives designed to relieve the military of the burden of defending its fuel supply lines and dependence on increasingly unreliable oil supplies. And it is not just the army and marines that are interested. In 2009 the navy introduced its first hybrid vessel, the USS *Makin Island*, an amphibious assault vessel that can run on electric power as well as fuel. The navy is ordering up supplies of alternative fuels as well; in 2010 the navy took delivery of the first alternative fuel (ethanol) made from algae—on the understanding that algae-generated fuels can be produced anywhere they are needed, without long supply lines. The air force too is certifying its fleet of aircraft to fly on aviation biofuels.

Now the US Armed Forces are driving initiatives across the whole spectrum of renewables, energy, and resource efficiency. Consider the aptly named SPIDERS program—standing for "Smart Power Infrastructure Demonstration for Energy Reliability and Security"—a project designed to maintain critical military facilities in operation in case of grid outages while accommodating renewable power input into the microgrids at a level up to 90 percent of all sources. A joint facilities project led by Sandia National Laboratories, the project is quite explicitly aimed at proving the feasibility of a similar organizational architecture for the civilian grid—making it resilient as well as flexible and adaptable.[21]

The military has both motive and means to transition away from fossil fuels. The motive is clear: the US Armed Forces, which once sought a military advantage in building global oil supply lines, now find them a burden. The forces are by far the largest consumers of oil in the United States and are for this reason the most vulnerable of organizations. The means is also clear: the military does not have to wait for Congress to act but can move of its own volition to adopt alternative fuel and energy solutions. Indeed, the military can adopt innovative approaches that are likely to have widespread repercussions in the civilian markets. One such initiative is termed waste-to-energy (WTE), in which in place of loading and transporting and dumping waste, the forces instead turn it into synthetic gas and biofuels for low-grade use (e.g., fuel for generators and military trucks). An experimental device called the Tactical Garbage to Energy Refinery, which converts up to 1 tonne of garbage per day to synthetic fuel (synfuel) that can power a generator set, has already been tested in Iraq.[22] The military is now a hotbed of research, testing, and experimentation in alternative fuels and renewable energies.[23]

A New World of Tradable Renewable Electric Power

Meanwhile there are ambitious plans afoot to transform the world of electric power to make it tradable across borders, in a way that far transcends today's limited experiments. Desertec is one such proposal (to be discussed in a moment, under the rubric of concentrating solar power). An even more ambitious proposal comes from Japan—the Asian Super Grid. Japanese businessman Masayoshi Son (founder of Softbank, Japan's equivalent of Apple) announced the Asian Super Grid as one of the first projects of his newly established Japan Renewable Energy Foundation (JREF), set up in May 2011 immediately after the Fukushima disaster. Son recruited the former head of Sweden's National Energy Agency, Tomas Kåberger, to head up the JREF. At an important conference staged in Tokyo on the first anniversary of the Fukushima disaster, the JREF launched the proposal for an Asian Super Grid, in conjunction with the Desertec Foundation, which is backing a similar proposal linking sites generating renewable energy in North Africa with European power grids. The breathtaking scope of the Asian Super Grid proposal is of a piece with the other far-reaching initiatives taken by Son's SoftBank Renewables and the JREF, including a series of solar farms in Japan designed to take advantage of the new feed-in tariffs launched in Japan on 1 July 2012. Indeed, the JREF and Son's companies have been driving the debate over the phase-out of nuclear and accelerated uptake of renewables in Japan.[24]

The core idea, as shown in Map 4.2, is that wind farms (and possibly solar farms as well) in the Gobi Desert can be linked via high-tension transmission lines to Korea, Japan, and possibly Russia; to China; and

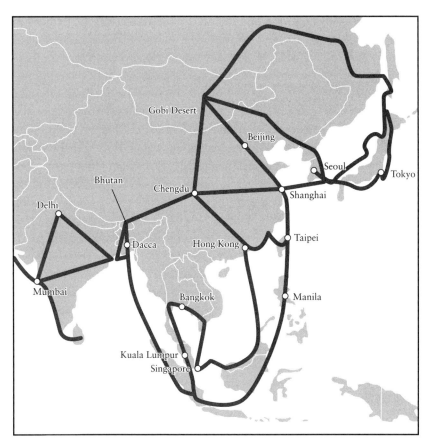

MAP **4.2**   Asian Super Grid proposal
SOURCE: Japan Renewable Energy Foundation.

thence (more speculatively) to Taiwan, Thailand, the Philippines, and even India. The costs of generating power in the desert locations would be low, and provided that the transmission costs can be kept low enough through utilization of high-capacity HVDC lines (which China is installing under its plans for grid upgrading under the Twelfth Five-Year Plan), the power delivered in the various countries would be competitive with thermal or nuclear power.[25]

When I discussed the proposal for the Asian Super Grid with Son at the Global Green Growth Summit in Seoul in May 2012 (where we were both speakers), he was confident that the proposal was sound and could be implemented. He outlined to me the basic concept that drives it—free trade in electric power.

Free Trade in Renewable Electric Power: The Proposed Asian Super Grid

The core driver of the Asian Super Grid (ASG) is the proposal to link the electricity grids of China, Mongolia, Japan, Korea, and possibly Russia into a vast interconnected power system. Such an IT-enhanced interconnected grid will be able to accommodate the fluctuating inputs from various renewable sources and match them to fluctuating demand, thereby enabling renewable sources to be scaled up to a level exceeding incumbent fossil-fueled systems. As in Son's earlier ventures into IT, computing, and telecommunications, his strategy is to tackle established monopolies and take advantage of liberalization to create effective competitors that sow the seeds of Schumpeterian creative destruction. In the case of the ASG the established firms are the large electric power firms (like Tepco in Japan and the Chinese giants like China Datang and China Southern Power Grid Co.), and the concept depends on being able to break their quasi-monopolistic control over electricity markets by trading electricity as a commodity between the established (and enhanced) national grids.

Trading electricity! Son put this revolutionary idea on the table in Japan in hearings before the Diet in April. "Let's connect Japan to other countries and make them compete," he said. "We import oil and gas. What's wrong with importing electricity?"[26]

Indeed, what's wrong with the idea? In our discussion in Seoul in May 2012, Son told me that he had asked officials from the Ministry of Economy, Trade, and Industry (METI) whether it was "illegal" to import electric power, in competition with the established monopolistic power generators like Tepco. He said they were nonplussed. They told him that it wasn't legal, in the sense that there were no regulations covering it—but neither was it illegal. His intervention evidently sparked a scramble at METI to deal with the prospect of a supercompetitive electric power market able to import renewable power from sites such as Mongolian wind farms. This is meat and drink to Son, who sparked such scrambles in his earlier interventions via SoftBank into the information technology, personal computer, and telecom markets in Japan.

There is one immediate obstacle. Japan's Electricity Business Act has an article restricting foreign companies from supplying electricity in Japan—so that represents a legislative hurdle that would need to be cleared for the ASG to become a reality.

Assuming that Son gets the go-ahead to import electric power, he foresees a relatively simple initial step as involving a link between Japan's southern island of Kyushu and Korea—calling for a 400-kilometer high-tension cable embodying the latest 700 kV HVDC technology. This cable length is comparable to the existing link in Europe between Norway and the Netherlands (two of the rare countries that have actually interconnected their power grids), which is 580 kilometers long and was completed in 2008. This was fourteen years after the two countries agreed in principle to link their grids. Obviously Son intends to move at a faster pace than that.

The way would then be open to build the infrastructure that would carry current at very high amperage levels from renewables hot spots like the Gobi Desert to the industrial centers in China, Korea, and Japan. But just as important as the infrastructure would be the political agreement to allow free trade in electric power between the grids. This might be a (relatively) small step for the countries concerned, *but it would be a giant leap for mankind.* For it would bring a resolution to the logjam that has been holding back renewable energy, keeping it as a marginal player in individual countries with their powerful vested interests in fossil fuels. Free trade in electric power would break that logjam very effectively—just as Son's business models have broken incumbent oligarchies in IT, PCs, and telecom in Japan. The Asian Super Grid would then open the way to similar grand proposals, linking North Africa and Europe, and the US Southwest to the US East Coast.

The reason this is such an important initiative is that the empowered grid, rendered "smart" with IT to moderate intermittent power supplies with fluctuating demand and "strong" through the deployment of new HVDC cables to carry renewable power long distances, is the backbone of any substantial push toward a renewable energy future. Over and above what can be done with individual renewable energy technologies and sources, the grid itself has to be enhanced and rendered competitive, so that a multitude of small power generators can be enabled to supply power to the grid, which would be able to accommodate them. Feed-in tariffs complement such a strategy perfectly—which is why they have been so effective in Germany and are going to prove their worth in Japan (since the new feed-in tariffs, or FiTs, were introduced in 2012) and in China (where provincial-level FiT experiments were also introduced in 2012).

Indeed, the free-market approach being championed by Masayoshi Son in Japan complements the approach to market expansion favored by feed-in tariffs, in that both envisage renewables expansion as stemming from the cumulative and aggregate effect of thousands and eventually millions of decentralized decisions over what to connect to the grid and how to do so. China's huge investments in the smart grid are needed to accommodate such decentralized power generation, and its promotion of vast quasi monopolies in power generation (e.g., the State Grid Corporation of China) will eventually work against such a process. For now, the SGCC plays a positive role in upgrading China's grid and equipping it to accommodate varying renewable inputs—including those from new sources such as wind farms in Mongolia.

What is surely worth noting is that many of the sources of tension within East Asia—such as the disputes over territorial claims to the sea around remote islands involving China, Japan, and Korea—turn on access to fossil fuels. These are international disputes that stem from the conventional model of industrialization and its assumption that access to fossil fuels is the critical factor in successful transition to modernity. But the clean-tech or green growth paradigm represents a sharp break with this thinking and, with it, reduces the potential for such disputes. There is therefore much at stake in the success of the free-trade approach to clean technology being championed by business leaders such as Masayoshi Son from Japan and Zhengrong Shi of China.[27]

Beyond Intermittency: The New Surge in Concentrating Solar Power

It will be clear that I do not wish to clutter this chapter with endless technical details of energy sources and the complex technologies that are evolving for generation of power from renewable sources. I am re-fraining from discussing details of wind power, solar photovoltaics, geo-thermal, bioenergy—even though these will all be important as the fossil fuel era gives way to the renewables era. But one topic does deserve men-tion, and that is the new surge associated with large-scale generation of solar power—or concentrating solar power (CSP). All it involves is fields of mirrors and lenses.

In retrospect the month of October 2011 will prove to be of enormous significance. This was the month when the world's first CSP installation with molten-salt heat-storage technology providing uninter-rupted industrial-level power for twenty-four hours per day came on line. Thus was opened a new era in renewable power generation. The Tor-resol Gemasolar plant in Seville, Spain, is a 19.9 MW plant that covers 185 hectares; it counts as a baseload plant with heat storage of fifteen hours (giving uninterrupted power supply). The plant is operating with 75 percent capacity factor, meaning it comes close to coal, nuclear, and natural gas facilities.[28] A further step forward was the larger Solana gen-erating station in Gila Bend, Arizona, which came on stream at the end of 2013. Built by the Spanish engineering firm Abengoa, with Abengoa's technology, this plant generates power at 280 MW and utilizes molten-salt storage, allowing power to be generated for six hours after sundown. I agree with my Australian colleague Mark Diesendorf (2011) that CSP is on the cusp of an enormous global expansion.

CSP with Molten Salts: 24/7 Reliable Renewable Option

Concentrating solar power (CSP) plants are operated not with photovoltaic cells, but with arrays of lenses and mirrors that focus the sun's rays and generate heat that can then be turned to steam to drive a conventional turbine to produce electric power. They use optical technol-ogy, which is well understood and relatively free of risks; they are mod-est in their demands for resources, and even for land they have modest requirements. To take the case of a recent CSP plant constructed, the Shams 1 plant based in Abu Dhabi came on stream in March 2013; it is a 100 MW plant utilizing a field of parabolic trough mirrors covering 250 hectares, or 2.5 square kilometers. If this were scaled up to 1 TW, to become a major source of electric power, it would call for a land area of

25,000 square kilometers—about the size of Burundi or Rwanda in Africa, or Macedonia in Europe.[29] Such a land area would be but a pinhole in the vast deserts of North Africa if connected by high-tension power cables as proposed by the Desertec project.[30]

It is precisely such a political initiative that could turn the possibility of generating abundant electric power and industrial heat from CSP in North Africa into an export commodity for Europe. The Desertec consortium, formed at German initiative and involving major German firms, aims to link concentrating solar power facilities to be built in North Africa with an extended European "super grid"—as shown in Map 4.3.[31] Prospects for the Desertec project have only been enhanced by the Arab Spring, which fosters newly reformed countries like Libya and Tunisia as likely beneficiaries, as well as other Maghreb countries like Morocco and Algeria. A smart national policy on the part of such developing North African countries would view Desertec as a means to create infrastruc-

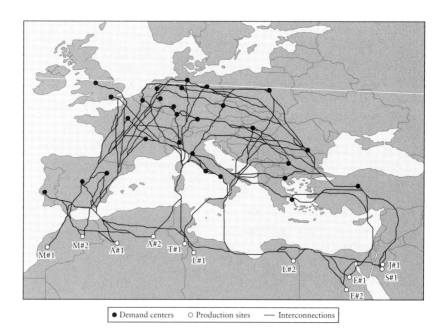

MAP **4.3**   Desertec proposal

SOURCE: Trieb et al. (2012). Used with permission.

NOTE: M: Morocco; A: Algeria; T: Tunisia; L: Libya; E: Egypt; S: Saudi Arabia; J: Jordan.

ture for solar power development, which could be used to drive domestic development as well as earn export revenue.

The comparable proposal for Asian countries is the Asian Super Grid, launched by the Japanese Renewable Energy Foundation. As discussed earlier, the Asian Super Grid would link large renewable power projects in Mongolia (wind and solar) with the grids of China, Korea, Japan, and Russia, through high-voltage direct current lines. Already the Japanese businessman Masayoshi Son has formed a joint venture in Mongolia with a wind power company (Clean Energy company, part of the Newcom Group) as a first step to creating such a visionary infrastructure.

So CSP technology is diffusing around the world—with China entering the field and promising to transform it.[32] China leads the way, with its announcement that it intends to build 1 GW of CSP installations by 2015, ramping up to a projected 3 GW of commercial-scale activity by 2020. This is likely to have a dramatic impact on the learning curve, driving down costs of components and systems—just as China's large-scale entry into solar PV had a dramatic impact on costs in that sector. But China is not alone. Both India and South Africa are scaling up their interest and have opened up reverse auctions for new CSP licenses that are also helping to drive down costs. The Middle Eastern and Gulf states are moving in a big way into CSP, to complement and offset their dependence on oil, with Saudi Arabia announcing a massive 25 GW goal to be met by 2030, and Qatar (currently the world's largest gas exporter) to reach 1.8 GW of CSP capacity by 2020; the United Arab Emirates is also committed and has already brought on stream the world's most efficient CSP plant, the 100 MW Shams 1 plant in Abu Dhabi. India promises to be a major player in CSP, with land banks becoming available, and with solid backing from the Ministry of New and Renewable Energy.[33] The demonstration potential of CSP projects in southern Africa is likewise considered enormous; Eskom estimates that the potential of CSP in South Africa alone as being close to 40 GW, and replication of this in Namibia and Botswana could double the potential, providing copious power for the industrialization of the whole of southern Africa.[34] Altogether, informed commercial expectations are for a hundredfold expansion over the coming decade and a half, reaching 100 GW by 2025.[35]

Concentrating solar thermal energy and storing it with molten-salt technology answers many of the negative charges leveled at solar power and renewables generally—that they are fluctuating, cannot meet baseload, are too diffuse, and are resource consuming. It is revealing to see how CSP with molten-salt technology (CSP-MST) meets these charges head on—and triumphs. CSP with molten-salt technology delivers baseload, dispatchable, regular power.[36] The key fluctuation with solar power has always been that it is available only during the day, and so requires some kind of storage system to carry through to other times. But CSP with molten-salt technology produces heat that lasts for fifteen hours or beyond. It can be used to generate electric power or industrial heat continuously—and at industrial scale levels of 100 MW to 1 GW that, when aggregated, is more than enough for baseload power. Thus, all the talk of needing gas-fired turbines as backup can be dismissed as so much "hot air." The idea that solar energy is too diffuse comes from early critiques of solar PV power by physicists (many of whom were tied to the nuclear and fossil fuel industries); but concentrating solar power meets that charge head on by explicitly *concentrating* the power, thus combating diffuseness.[37]

There is the distinct possibility that CSP will generate sufficient heat that it can be used directly for industrial processes such as producing the aluminum and glass needed for the CSP arrays. This might be a small step for the industry concerned—but again it would be a giant step for humankind. Because it would mean that the industrial process for producing CSP equipment would be *totally self-sustaining and independent of fossil fuels*—with renewable energy equipment being used to generate heat and power needed for production of further renewable energy equipment, and so on, around and around. Moreover, it is almost certain that the materials themselves would be little short of 100 percent recirculated (such as steel, now 99 percent recycled), and so the resource impact of a large-scale (i.e., giga-scale) CSP program would be minimal.

So, what is driving the energy industrial revolution that is already well under way in China and Germany and within the US military, and that shows every likelihood of diffusing rapidly around the world through tradable green electric power and other developments? The best way to consider this issue is to rebut the extraordinary range of charges brought against renewables—turning the charges against the chargers and demonstrating how renewables emerge as superior energy option on every count.

"Real Men Don't Do Renewables"

There has been a strong current of machismo running through the energy debates that have dominated policy discussions over the past decade. I recall a debate in Rome just three years ago, on the future of energy supplies for Europe, in which any suggestion that renewables might take over from oil and gas was greeted with polite disbelief—the underlying assumption being that real men *really* don't do renewables. While countries could dabble in renewables—a small wind farm here, a few solar PV arrays there—when it came to serious, industrial scale, and baseload power, the only sources worth discussing were fossil fuels and nuclear.

How times change. Now we find the US Armed Forces emerging as the single largest adopter and promoter of renewables in the United States—for reasons that have nothing to do with machismo, but everything to do with securing energy supplies in hostile terrain, where more casualties are inflicted from transporting oil along lengthy supply lines than from enemy fire.

Now we also find China (and from 2011, Germany) investing in "industrial-scale" renewable energy baseload power, where the real innovation is correctly viewed not as the sources of power harvested from renewable sources themselves but as the strong and smart grid needed for collecting and distributing power from highly decentralized sources. We find investments in renewable options like concentrating solar power, which with molten-salt technology can generate power 24/7, and for which the CSP power stations are envisaged as spanning continents, as in the Desertec proposal linking North Africa to Europe via HVDC power lines, or the comparable Asian Super Grid proposal. These constitute the electric power generating systems of the future—clean, cheap, and reliable, and based on free trade in dispatchable, renewable electric power.[38]

These practical initiatives are the real answer to the endless debating points made by a vast chorus of naysayers who argue that renewables could not be "trusted" because of their fluctuating nature, their lack of reliability, their dependence on gas-fired backup generators, their excessive usage of land, their impact on traditional business models, and on and on. None of these charges (except the last, as renewables are indeed creatively destroying traditional electric power business models) are true.

The costs are coming down to approach grid parity, through the learning-curve effect; the storage capacities are growing, both through decentralized means in molten-salt CSP power stations and through interlinked smart grid investments, such as those that will link German electric power systems to Norwegian hydropower systems, with offshore wind power moving from Germany to Norway during the night and power returning to Germany during the day.

What are these debating points leveled against renewables? Do any of them stack up? Take the case against renewable energies made by Jesse Ausubel, a professor at the Rockefeller University in New York who has long been a proponent of radical fossil fuel and nuclear options, and a vociferous opponent of renewables. In his "Renewable and nuclear heresies" Ausubel (2007) considers (and attempts to dismiss) the "renewable idols: hydro, biomass, wind and solar." He claims to make his critique as a green, as one who cares about "leaving land for Nature" (Ausubel 2007, 232). So let us take Ausubel as a sparring partner, and subject his arguments to the critical perusal that he would no doubt welcome.[39]

Renewable and Nuclear Heresies

Taking Ausubel's (2007) renewable "heresies" in reverse order, on solar power Ausubel considers just photovoltaics (PVs) and then only the first generation, ignoring concentrating PV as well as non-PV solar such as CSP with molten salt. On this false basis, he claims that solar PV remains "stuck" at 10 percent efficiency (despite the clear evidence available then, and certainly now, that standard efficiency in real settings is around 25 percent) and claims further that power generated is around 5–6 watts per square meter, with no economies of scale. Ausubel gives no examples, so let us take a real case, such as the recently completed Montalto di Castro PV power station in Italy. It is a flat-panel PV installation, consisting of 78,720 modules, operating at a capacity of 72 MW and covering 80 hectares. That's a power rating of 90 MW per square kilometer, or 9 watts per square meter, indefinitely extendable. Montalto di Castro is efficiency rated at 25 percent. On the basis of his defective data, Ausubel argues that present US electric consumption would call for a land area of 150,000 square kilometers, which he presumably thinks sounds impossibly large. Actually, using real data from Montalto di

Castro, setting US electric power consumption at 1 TW would call for land of just over 10,000 square kilometers (1 billion over 90 million kilometers squared)—or just 0.1 percent of the US land area of 9.6 million square kilometers. And the land required would be found in the deserts of the US West and Southwest.

Likewise for Europe, a 1 TW renewable grid would call for land area of just over 10,000 square kilometers, or less than half the size of Belgium. Again, such an area could be easily accommodated within Southern Europe (as in Sicily and elsewhere) and certainly within the North African coastal strip, if it is linked by HV direct current cables to the European grid, as in the Desertec proposal.

But of course nobody is saying that the entire electric power of the United States—or China, or India—would be generated by PVs on their own. It is their very diffuseness that makes them ideal as decentralized sources of electric power, particularly in places where it is difficult for the grid to reach. The actual land required for serious solar production would be a lot less than 10,000 square kilometers in the United States because the real options to be utilized will doubtless be concentrated PV or CSP (with their drastically reduced land requirements).

Ausubel then advances the point that electrical batteries (presumably considered necessary for his version of solar PV) "weigh almost zero in the global energy market" (2007, 234). One has only to look at the figures for lithium-ion battery production in China and the East Asian countries, where the new industry is roaring ahead, to see how wide of the mark is such an assertion—or at the creation by the US government of the US Battery Consortium, to help American firms enter this prized industrial sector of the future.[40]

Moving on from the falsely presented land intensity of solar power, Ausubel then considers other resource issues—that solar cells are "black" and would cover deserts with black absorbers, and that they contain nasty elements such as cadmium. Again, the idea that the deserts would be "covered" by black PV cells is a fantasy, particularly as CSP with mirrors and lenses is introduced, neither of which is black. Yes, the nasty materials used in some kinds of solar PV cells (such as thin-film cadmium-telluride cells) are indeed a cause for concern and will doubtless promote further rounds of recycling to contain their environmental impact. There is already considerable progress in getting off these cadmium-telluride cells toward plastic-film flexible cells, which have nothing like the toxicity.

Ausubel's final point is that renewables in every form "require large and complex machinery to produce many megawatts" (2007, 234). Yes, fabrication facilities that produce solar cells (and mirrors and lenses, and molten-salt piping) are technically sophisticated. This is what makes them interesting; they create an industrialization challenge for both advanced and the newly industrializing countries like China and India to master. It is hardly something to be held against the renewables. Ausubel finishes with some data on the steel and cement requirements needed to produce a year's supply of wind turbines—neglecting to add that these requirements are only a small proportion of those utilized by the current global automotive industry, for example. And again, no one would claim that complex technical products would be produced with zero resource usage. But one might hazard the prognostication that such renewable energy products would be accompanied by an advanced level of recycling, which would drastically reduce their impact on raw materials supplies.

Ausubel makes similar points against hydro, wind, and biomass—but again the data presented are easily shown to be false, and the conclusions drawn erroneous. This is not to say that anyone wishes to see whole countries given over to growing corn for first-generation ethanol plants operated by Shell or BP, or vast new dams being constructed for hydro on the scale of the Chinese Three Gorges Dam. There are clear limits to what can be produced using such options. But to utilize these negative examples as a means of damning the entire transition to renewables is surely misplaced zeal—even for a self-confessed "heretic."

Such debates leave out of the picture the real benefits of swinging behind renewables. These are worth spelling out. Their fundamental advantage is that they are clean; they tap into inexhaustible supplies of renewable energy; and their running costs (once they are built) are exceedingly low, since they need no fuel. Moreover they are diffuse. Rather than being pilloried as a defect, this is their great strength, in that they can power a decentralized industrial system, allowing farms and farmers to become involved in power generation in a way that was simply not possible with big, centralized fossil fuel stations in the past. In developing countries their diffuseness is a boon, for it can underwrite the extension of electric power generation and usage beyond the reach of the grid—an enormous advantage for small communities that have never had access to electric power before. Fundamentally, renewables offer real energy security, to both developed and developing countries, precisely because they are based on manufacturing of devices such as turbines that can be used (in principle) to generate power almost everywhere. Manufactured devices promise an end to the era when energy security was tied closely to geopolitics and the projection of armed muscle (Klare 2012).

The resistance to the renewables revolution is relentless, profound, and utterly ruthless. It really is as if "real men don't do renewables." There seems to be something at gut level that drives the extraordinary efforts to undermine renewables, not just by the immediately affected fossil fuel and nuclear interests, but by a host of associated social, economic, and ideological interests that are well captured in the phrase "carbon lock-in."

The most common charge brought against renewables is their higher cost. But this is the weakest case that can be brought against them, because it is costs that are decreasing fastest, at astonishing annual reduction rates. By contrast, for fossil fuels the expectation can be only for rising costs, as one source after another peaks in a world where industrial activity fills all available niches. Of course, one has to distinguish between capital and running costs. The renewables still suffer from relatively high capital costs (hence financing charges), but they rapidly make up for these in their much lower running costs. The tide is turning.

Declining Costs—Learning Curves

Many governments (and international organizations) still harbor an outdated view that renewable energy, and in particular solar PV energy, is more expensive than traditional thermal (coal-fired) energy. But in reality the costs have been falling at a rapid rate. In many parts of the world the cost of generating electric power from wind or solar PV is now less than or comparable to the cost of producing power from gas, and it will very soon (by 2015) be comparable with the cost of power from the cheapest, dirtiest coal.[41] The view that the choices are difficult because of the costs is now an outdated view.

The data that now need to be considered in framing any development strategy are those relating to the falling costs of power produced

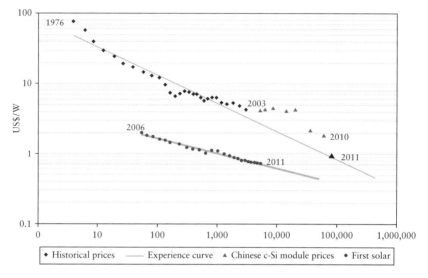

FIGURE **4.3**   Photovoltaic module experience curve, 1976–2011
SOURCE: Bazilian and colleagues (2013). Used with permission.

from renewable sources. The driving influence is that of the learning (or experience) curve, which depicts how costs fall as experience accumulates. Consider Figure 4.3 (Bazilian et al. 2013), which shows falling costs for solar PV over the past thirty-five years.

In Figure 4.3, based on and updating the chart on experience curves contained in the 2012 IPCC report on renewable energies, the overall experience curve is shown in the upper line, indicating that costs had reduced to the *long anticipated point of $1 per watt* by the end of 2011 and bringing solar PV power within the range of almost all emerging and developing countries. Costs reduced from around $76 per watt in 1976 to around 76 cents per watt in 2011—a 10,000 percent reduction in less than four decades! The years immediately preceding 2011 show that costs hovered for several years (from 2004 to 2008) at around four times this level ($4 per watt)—a phenomenon now understood to be due to suppliers being able to command feed-in tariff rates locked at these levels, while restricted silicon supplies meant that there was little price competition. It was this that led many to believe that costs of renewable energies would always exceed those of conventionally fueled power.

But as silicon supplies became more flexible, so manufacturers reduced their prices, which in turn reduced input costs for solar cell producers, and their prices fell as well. The second lower line represents the cost curve for thin-film solar cell producers, dominated by the US firm First Solar. Because thin-film PV cells utilize much lower quantities of silicon, their costs have always been lower—but they are not yet enjoying the economies of scale of amorphous silicon cells. The message is clear: the costs of solar PV cells are falling dramatically.

In many countries with above-average insolation (which means countries right across the tropical belt) this means that producing electric power from solar PVs is now cheaper than producing power from, for example, stand-alone diesel generators. Global investment banks such as UBS are now openly talking of the "unsubsidized solar revolution."[42] The reason that such countries would go on utilizing the unreliable and polluting diesel generators, which offer no developmental momentum of their own (in terms of building new industries), must be inertia. Here is where capitalist industrial dynamics can really play their role, destroying the old inefficient energy systems and ushering in the new through the power of relentless cost reductions and creation of new, competitive enterprises. For developing countries in particular, these cost reductions mean that building power systems that utilize solar input received within the country (rather than fossil fuel imports, with all their energy insecurity implications) become more attractive as underpinning development strategy. The cost reductions also mean that building new solar power production industries becomes more attractive, based as they are on manufacturing with its increasing returns.

Wind energy also exhibits powerful learning-curve advantages, with costs declining for onshore wind at an annual rate of 7 percent. Wind power is well on the way to having a generating capacity of 1 TW—the size of the current entire US or Chinese generating capacity. As it does so, the 7 percent cost reduction curve will make wind power more attractive for countries endowed with the resource. Again, such cost reductions make it inevitable that this power source will eventually be adopted as a default option, ousting its fossil fuel competitors.[43]

Other green technologies such as batteries display comparable experience curves and dramatic cost reductions—as demonstrated in numerous studies and most recently by the IPCC (2011) itself in its study of renewable energies, in which it is stated that with adequate government support, renewable energies should be accounting for slightly less than 80 percent of primary energy inputs by 2050. In the case of batteries, the earlier-generation nickel-metal-hydride batteries have largely exhausted their learning-curve advantages, and the newer lithium-ion batteries have substantial learning-curve cost reductions already achieved and anticipated for the future. These cost reductions for batteries will in turn mean cost reductions for electric vehicles, and thus the cost-driven capitalist processes of substitution will diffuse, from manufacturing and power generation to transport and beyond.[44]

Ultimately renewables will triumph over fossil fuels because of lower costs. The impact of near-zero marginal costs for generation of renewable sources such as wind and solar power is already having a dramatic impact on electric power grids and the business models of conventional operators. In accordance with the merit-order effect (favoring the least-cost renewables over conventional sources), the pattern of grid supplies is already changing, and the emphasis in discussions at power generation meetings is shifting from the dangers of intermittency associated with renewables to the dangers implied to current business models by the merit-order effect.

Is the Transition Impossibly Demanding?

There is by now widespread agreement among energy policy experts that there is a need for a wholesale replacement of the current fossil-fueled power system by one operating on renewable energy sources—and that the process of transition is already under way. The IPCC in 2011 saw the possibility of alternatives to business as usual resulting in 80 percent replacement of fossil fuels by 2050. Some recent contributions see such a transition as occurring as early as 2030 (e.g., Jacobson and Delucchi 2009, 2011). These latter authors spelt out the scale of the technical challenge in meeting their energy system based on water, wind, and sun—in terms of numbers of wind turbines, numbers of solar cells, or numbers of heliostats in solar thermal systems. The issue is, how to scale them so that they become comparable with existing kinds of manufacturing activity?

Among the wider intellectual community, however, there remains strong skepticism as to the feasibility of such a transition. The implicit (and sometimes explicit) objection to a wholesale changeover to renewable energy resources in the coming two decades is the question of availability of land resources, and the construction of what appear to be impossibly large numbers of industrial products such as turbines, solar cells, mirrors, and lenses.

Let me take the recent volume from world-renowned sociologist and historian Michael Mann as a case in point. I choose Mann not because he is an energy specialist but precisely because he is *not* such a specialist, and he draws his data from the published energy policy and sociology literature. In his latest volume 4 of *Sources of Social Power*, in the chapter "Global Crisis: Climate Change," he states:

> The global economy currently uses about 16 TW of electric power generation. To get that total without the aid of fossil fuel from a mixture of current alternative technologies would involve massive industrial complexes spread over very large land masses. Solar cells in the required quantity might spread over about 30,000 [square] miles of land. Solar thermal sources might require about 150,000 [square] miles, biofuels might occupy over 1 million square miles. Then there are wind turbines, geothermal sources, and nuclear power plants. One can play with the relative weights of each of these but, overall, the currently available alternative energy sources would require a space about equal to that of the United States. This would be a theoretical possibility but not a practicable one. (Mann 2013, 386)

I cite this passage not to enter into a dispute with Michael Mann (who as a nonspecialist relies on his sources) but to indicate the extent of the mismatch between the potential of currently available renewable energy technology and the public perception of the obstacles. To state that a land area equal to that of the United States would be required to scale up renewables is to concede that the project is impossible, that the barriers are too high. This would be a depressing conclusion—if it were true. Mann himself is pessimistic.

When we investigate further, we find that Mann has based his statements on a passage from a chapter by Barnes and Gilman (2011), authors who are extremely negative in their view as to the scale of the technical challenges involved in meeting climate change. They cite data presented by the Australian technologist and entrepreneur Saul Griffith on the kinds of technical feats needed to meet the renewable energy challenge.[45] Griffith is actually concerned with presenting the scale of the challenge as an exercise in realism, but he has been interpreted in decidedly pessimistic tone by Barnes and Gilman as presenting the impossibility of making a real transition, and thereby leading Mann to make the pessimistic judgment alluded to earlier.

So just what are the engineering and technical features of moving to a renewable world? If we take CSP as a good candidate, and project that at least 2 TW of CSP will be built around the world over the coming two decades (along with, say, 2 TW of wind power and 2 TW of solar PV), then we have a clearly specifiable technical and materials challenge—very large, but feasible. Let us specify the challenge of building 1 TW of CSP installations in ten years. We can scale up the Shams 1 CSP plant, which to generate power at 100 MW calls for 258,048 mirrors covering a reflective area of 0.63 square kilometers (it's a big field, approximating a square with sides 800 meters). So 1 TW would call for 6,300 square kilometers of reflective mirrors to be constructed and installed over ten years—or 630 square kilometers per year.

We could frighten ourselves and express this as a challenge of building approximately 2 square kilometers of reflective surfaces per day over a ten-year period—a task that seems daunting, near impossible. Or we could compare the challenge with what the industrial world already achieves. Nokia and others build around 1.75 billion mobile phones a year—or around 5 million every day. That's a lot of phones, incorporating many of the features that would be needed in CSP and PV plants constructed at comparable scale. At a similar level, Coca-Cola, Pepsi, and others make around 200 billion aluminum cans for soft drinks every year; if cut in half and extended, that would approximate the challenge of producing parabolic mirrors at the required scale.[46] It's a matter of building incentives so that companies would set about the task in the same business-like way that Coke and Pepsi build soft drink cans. And the world automotive industry builds around 84 million cars and commercial vehicles every year (or 2,300 vehicles globally every day, day after day)— again an enormous technical and materials challenge that is accomplished without fanfare and that dwarfs the challenge of producing CSP, wind turbines, and solar PV at the scale needed to replace our present fossil-fueled systems.

To drive the point home, consider the material requirements of building 1 TW of CSP plants in ten years. We know that such parabolic trough plants call for large quantities of glass and steel and cement. The steel is needed at a scale of 240 tonnes per MW—or 240 Mt per TW in ten years, or 24 Mt per year. Again 24 million tonnes of steel sounds a lot—until we realize that the world currently produces and uses around 1.5 billion tonnes of steel in a year (i.e., sixty-two times the quantity of steel used in one year as would be needed by CSP plants over ten years). From that perspective, the task of producing the steel (and the glass and cement) for the terawatts of CSP, wind power, and solar PV start to look reasonable—large, yes, but feasible.[47] We really have entered a new era, where there can be no valid objections to pursuing the renewable option with all available speed.

A New Default Option

Through these developments—in China, in Germany, in the US military, in the relentlessly rising capacity and investment data, in the breathtaking proposals for international renewable electric power inter-connection, in the dramatically falling costs—it is clear that renewables are emerging as the new default option for the energy markets. After taking into account the "revenues" (the power generated from renewables) and the "costs" (the power still generated from fossil fuel sources) the balance is shifting. The trend toward renewables is clear and palpable.[48] The shift is already dramatic and is building momentum, particularly as countries like China and Germany invest their trade surpluses in renewables in a serious way, at "industrial strength."[49] The objections to renewables continue to surface at every available opportunity—but as this brief review has shown, all of them turn out to be flimsy and without foundation.

Yes, the fossil fuels sector is still strong and is extending its life across a range of business sectors, from coal seam gas to tar sands to deepwater drilling. But these are all getting harder, more costly, and more dangerous (as seen in BP's Deepwater Horizon drilling disaster in the Gulf of Mexico). Ditto with conventional nuclear power, where the Japanese Fukushima disaster indicates the limits to first-generation boiling water reactors built decades ago by General Electric. A world competing for ever-less-accessible fossil fuels is one destined to be waging endless resource wars—like the "peak oil" wars fought by the United States in the Gulf and Iraq. It would be a world of terrorism and further restraint of civil liberties in the name of dealing with terrorism; a world of military exercises on a vast scale in defense of oil supply lines; a world of endless intrigues, aggressions, and international tension over the securing of new supply lines.

By contrast, a world of renewables promises something approximating to Kant's perpetual peace—because they are based on technological sophistication in generating power from abundant energy supplies available to all, rather than on defending unfair and unreasonable resource endowments and their capture by developed countries. The renewables stand as they have always done, as the energy option with the *longest life*, the *cheapest running costs*, the *lowest risks*, the *most widely dispersed availability*, the *most resilient modular design*. And they *generate power with zero carbon emissions*. Why the world took so long to adopt them as the default option is not so much a mystery as a triumph of vested interest over long-term rational choice. But the choice has been made and is becoming irreversible.[50] Adoption of renewables as the default option will release the energy imagination, making feasible previously unthinkable projects like that for artificial photosynthesis or a new solid-state ammonia synthesis pathway (linking energy to agriculture via fertilizers).[51] The ultimate breakthrough would involve linking renewable energy systems such as CSP with water desalination to produce fresh water, which could then be applied to irrigate crops to produce a triple dividend of power, water, and food. Pilot versions of this concept are already available.[52]

More generally, a world running on renewables can be expected to be a world in which peace is more likely than war. War arises usually because nations find themselves cut off from the resources they deem to be essential, or because they or others are making preemptive moves inspired by such considerations. But renewables are available almost everywhere; to tap them one needs simply the technology required. There is, moreover, a huge incentive for a country to seek to take itself to the cutting edge in such technology acquisition and development, to generate power from abundant energy sources most efficiently. Renewables have a built-in bias toward innovation, toward technological learning and peaceful coexistence. Fossil fuels, by contrast, invoke the opposite kinds of behavior—militant guarding and hoarding of resources, and the adoption of warlike postures in securing such supply lines, cat-and-mouse relations with other nations in seeking advantage in terms of material resources, and the playing off of geopolitical advantage with a view to securing resource hegemony.[53]

From the perspective of 2050, when the shift to renewables will be well under way and acquiring unstoppable momentum, it will appear preposterous that we could mortgage the future of our industrial civilization to a finite resource whose exploitation made countries the pawns of those endowed by chance with supplies, encouraged brutal dictatorships to protect them, and whose burning was effectively poisoning the planet.

The turn to renewables is one of the *ruptures* currently marking a transformation of industrial capitalism and framing the transition to a new era. What will play a further role in the building of the renewable energies economy is the parallel shift toward resource recirculation and the circular economy. This is the topic to which we now turn.

5 From the Linear to the Circular Economy

The economic process, like any other life process, is irreversible (and irrevocably so); hence, it cannot be explained in mechanical terms alone. It is thermodynamics, through the Entropy Law, that recognizes the qualitative distinction which economists should have made from the outset between the inputs of valuable resources (low entropy) and the final outputs of valueless waste (high entropy).

> —*Nicolae Georgescu-Roegen, "Energy and economic myths" (1975)*

If people are to prosper within the natural world, all the products and materials manufactured by industry must after each useful life provide nourishment for something new. Since many of the things people make are not natural, they are not safe "food" for biological systems. Products composed of materials that do not biodegrade should be designed as technical nutrients that continually circulate within closed-loop industrial cycles—the technical metabolism.

> —*William McDonough and Michael Braungart, "The NEXT industrial revolution" (1998)*

Knowledge of kinds of waste streams can provide a means to determine potential linkages. But this does not link them; decisions by people do. Turning wasted materials into potential new enterprises is an elegant idea. But enterprises are started by entrepreneurs, not printouts. Computerized linkages can provide information and computer models can illustrate possibilities, but the best they can do is stimulate imagination, not bring about the connections.

> —*Edward Cohen-Rosenthal, "A walk on the human side of industrial ecology" (2000)*

Industrialization has everywhere meant an enormous increase in the scale of usage of raw materials and the components fashioned from them. Finding a way to curb the relentlessly increasing throughput of resources, with their damaging extraction at one end and the problems created by their disposal at the other, is now the subject of the second major revolution that is transforming our system of industrial capitalism. In a word, it is changing the economy from a linear to a circular construct. The new patterns of interlinkage, whereby wastes from one process can be transformed into inputs to another, are studied in a new discipline of industrial ecology.

The traditional linear model of the economy, in which raw materials come in at one end and waste goes out at the other, reflects a long-standing and deep-seated assumption as to the way that the economy, and more recently the industrial economy, is embedded in a limitless entity called "nature" with limitless supplies of resources and limitless capacity to absorb wastes. This is indeed the founding assumption of the traditional ("Western") model of industrialization, as well as of mainstream economics. Indeed, it is the assumption underpinning the universally recognized measure of economic prosperity, namely gross national product (GNP), which measures linear throughput in an economy—where the emphasis is always and everywhere on the extent to which this measure of throughput has "grown." The influential authors Braungart and Mc-Donough christen this linear style of thinking "Take, make and dispose."

Such is the viewpoint that has led to so much grief as the world comes up against the reality of natural limits, both to the extraction of resources (at one end) and to the disposal of resources (wastes) at the other. The problems currently being encountered with fossil fuels and oil in particular—with peaking of oil presenting a limit at the input end, and greenhouse gas emissions and global warming presenting a limit at the output end—are simply the most pointed and concentrated of the problems. But the problems are general and endemic, and they are getting worse. Just to take the case of water, an even more fundamental element to life than energy: the usual classification was fresh water or salt water, but now it has to include "sweet water," as more and more industrial sweeteners used in food penetrate the environment and permanently modify its composition, thus threatening another planetary disaster.[1]

In keeping with the picture of a closed-cycle planet ("only one earth") and the endless biological and ecological processes that circulate nutrients round and round ("waste equals food"), there have in recent years been determined efforts to reframe thinking, by pioneers such as Cohen-Rosenthal (2000), and to bring these cycles that operate so successfully as carriers of life to the center of the industrial system—before it is too late.[2] The most academically sound initiative comes in the field now known as industrial ecology, or industrial symbiosis, where the emphasis is on measuring flows of real materials and energy, as opposed to the fictional flows of income measured by economic aggregates such as GNP.[3] This has also spawned a series of studies in what is called material and energy flow accounting, which defines such aggregates as total material requirement (popularized by the Organisation for Economic Co-operation and Development (OECD), in a series of publications, conferences and workshops).[4]

The world of business has seized on another concept, that of eco-efficiency, which has now been taken up by the World Business Council for Sustainable Development and adopted by a number of leading firms, such as DuPont and others.[5] But eco-efficiency, while emphasizing reduced resource usage (as embodied in its classic RRR formulation—reduce, reuse, recycle), does not capture the full force of the cyclical metaphor. It is simply a means of modifying the present industrial model without providing an alternative. In an influential article published in the *Atlantic* in 1998, the German chemist Michael Braungart (former head of Greenpeace's chemical safety initiatives) and American architect William McDonough described eco-efficiency initiatives in withering terms as simply replicating the same industrial model but in more "efficient" terms—terms that would in any case be swamped by growth in resource usage (just as energy efficiency measures are swamped by growing energy utilization overall—the Jevons paradox).[6] They argued that the world had to do better than merely achieve eco-efficiency with its life-cycle, or cradle-to-grave, thinking.

"Cradle-to-Cradle" Thinking

Braungart and McDonough coined an expression that captures the spirit of their critique. In place of "cradle to grave," which characterizes eco-efficiency (i.e., by focusing on the life cycles of materials and the responsibility of producers covering the entire life cycle), they offer "cradle to cradle" as the appropriate metaphor (which I call here C2C thinking).[7] The essence of C2C thinking is captured in the three tenets that McDonough and Braungart have been promoting now for a decade or more:

> Waste equals food: all industrial wastes can in principle be recirculated as inputs into other industrial processes, just as natural biological cycles operate; Use current solar income: maximize the use of renewable energy sources; Celebrate diversity: in place of industrial monoculture and mass production, C2C thinking follows healthy ecosystems in promoting diversity.[8]

Indeed, so effective has their mission become that they registered "cradle to cradle" as a trademark and formed a joint venture company, McDonough Braungart Design Chemistry, as a vehicle for certifying other companies' initiatives in applying C2C principles to their product redesign.[9]

Apart from this overhasty commercialization of their terminology and private certification initiatives, there is much to commend itself in the C2C approach promoted by McDonough and Braungart. They picture the industrial economy as being driven by three kinds of material processes—the circulation of biologically active materials (as in composting); the circulation of nonbiological but technologically nontoxic materials; and the accumulation of toxic waste, to be disposed of. Their argument is that good industrial design can promote the first two cycles and reduce or eliminate the accumulation of toxic waste. They have illustrated this approach to industrial design through a number of cases drawn from their consulting work. The wider literature refers to such initiatives as clean production or "cleaner" production. China, too, is actively promoting such ideas.

In looking for a name for the alternative concept or framework, which will characterize the rupture with the linear economy, we can do no better than adopt the simple and straightforward idea of the *circular economy*.[10] This is the terminology now favored in China, where it is being promoted most assiduously—precisely because China has most need of such an idea (given its poor resource efficiency and its buildup of toxic wastes) and the means to implement it, through its national planning system overseen by the National Development and Reform Commission.

When one views the economy as a circular material flow, in which the outputs of one process become the inputs for another process, either within the same organization or through interorganizational linkages, then supportive policies present themselves more easily. Such an economy can be called a *regenerative economy*, in that resources are regenerated within each iteration of a cycle, or a *closed-cycle economy*, because it operates with closed-loop cycles of materials.

Circulation of Resources

The idea of circularity encompasses all such possibilities. When the Belgian Minister for the Environment Joke Schauvliege assumed the presidency of the European Union Environment Council in July 2010, she lost no time in putting sustainable "closed-loop" resource management systems at the top of her political agenda.[11] If any proof were needed that this kind of circular economy thinking has now entered the mainstream, it was provided by the newly created Ellen Macarthur Foundation, which staged its first public event in Bradford, United Kingdom, in 2010 on the theme of the circular economy. Since then, the foundation has emerged as a champion of the concept in Europe.[12]

In Germany, the circular economy concept (*Kreislaufwirtschaft*) has been taken up at the national level and by the state of Rhineland-Palatinate, making it the first province in the West to adopt the circular economy as its development goal.[13] Germany has been one of the pioneers of the closed-loop (or circular) economy, enacting legislation as early as 1996, in the Closed Substance Cycle and Waste Management Act. The act introduced the concept of product responsibility to German manufacturing industry—a regulatory requirement that has resulted in German companies achieving the world's highest recovery quotas.[14] In Germany there have been determined efforts to link waste policy with renewable energies—as in the linkage between waste wood, previously treated as a nuisance waste, carrying a negative price (i.e., companies would have to pay to have it removed) to carrying a positive price, where it is perceived as a useful bioenergy source. Other examples are initiatives such as the Zero Emission Campus at Birkenfeld, where biogas is generated from waste food and greenery residues and cogeneration is encouraged from wood chips.[15] Tough regulatory standards for recycling are seen, correctly, as giving German companies a competitive edge—and so the regulatory scope of the 1996 legislation continues to be widened, as in the 2006 Electrical and Electronic Equipment Act, which requires producers to take delivery of their products once discarded.

In Japan circular economy initiatives have been taken even further than in Europe, guided by the Basic Law for Promoting the Creation of a Recycling-Oriented Society, passed in the year 2000. In Japan, where the preferred term is *sound material-cycle society*, the government, through the Ministry for Economy, Trade, and Industry (METI), has coordinated the activities of leading corporations so that regulatory requirements to reduce resource throughput, reuse materials, and recycle components have been extended from one industry to another. For the past two decades, METI has been coordinating the response of Japanese industry to the circular challenge and guided initiatives such as extended producer responsibility and life-cycle assessment of products. A subtle feature of the Japanese approach has been that recycling is held to occur only when the extracted materials are reused; otherwise, the material flow is counted as waste. In other jurisdictions recycling is interpreted more broadly, and hence with less effect.[16]

China, as the latecomer, has learnt from these practices and gone beyond them. China has similarly adopted a law for the promotion of the circular economy, in 2008, modeled on the Japanese legislation, but it has taken the concept further, adopting it as a national development goal. China is setting itself ambitious targets in terms of energy and materials (or resource) efficiency. To achieve those goals, China is specifying a range of means, including the implementation of circular economy— through interconnecting the chains of resource and energy utilization so that wastes from one process can be captured and used as raw materials for another, with energy generation being shared along the value chain.[17] This makes the idea of the circular economy far more ambitious and effective than mere recycling, which simply calls for the redirection of expended articles from waste to industrial input; the circular economy, by contrast, envisages the interconnection of all industrial processes, particularly those that lead up to the final product.

In mid-2008 the Chinese People's Congress passed a national circular economy law, the Law for the Promotion of the Circular Economy, which came into effect on 1 January 2009. While inspired by legislation in other countries, such as in Japan and Germany, the law in China seems to be the first in the world putting circular economy as a national strategy of economic and social development. The Chinese law provides a framework within which incentives and disincentives (penalties) may be developed, at multiple levels, to encourage firms and municipalities to take eco-industrial initiatives, and for the creation of networks of by-product exchange. The framework of the circular economy is now incorporated into the country's Twelfth Five-Year Plan; new resource consumption efficiency measures as basic measures of eco-efficiency are included, to reinforce the impact of the 2008 circular economy law.[18]

China Creates a New Model of How the Economy Works

The twentieth-century witnessed the first fundamental changes in industrial production systems, from craft production to mass production systems—pioneered by the Ford Motor Company. Then in the postwar period a second fundamental transformation was driven through—the lean production system, with Toyota as the lead firm. Now in the twenty-first century there is occurring the third such industrial transformation, which we might dub the circular production system.[19] If the United States was the pioneer of the first (MPS), and Japan the pioneer of the second (LPS), then China is the uncontested leader of the third—the CPS. And each transformation involves a wider and wider circle of interacting firms, with the CPS involving whole regions and eco-industrial parks, and correspondingly more complex interrelationships needed to achieve collective efficiency.

China may be characterized as the most pragmatic exponent of circular and eco-responsible thinking—even as it grapples with the worst forms of industrial pollution. This is the "green and black" paradox of China, again. China's Twelfth Five-Year Plan consolidates previous efforts to promote resource recirculation, after the pattern of the 3Rs—reduce, reuse, recycle. China has adopted these goals not just as an "environmental" policy but also as a mainstream development goal. China's national leadership appears to have understood that continued development in the traditional linear manner, starting with resources taken from nature at one end and proceeding via production processes to the creation of wastes disposed in nature at the other end, is simply no longer feasible. It is destructive to the point of ruin, at both ends; it is costly to both secure fresh resources all the time and lose resources in the form of waste. It is also geopolitically dangerous to scour the world for resources. It is, in other words, economically, politically, and ecologically inefficient. It is not sustainable.

Eco-Industrial Parks

While eco-industrial development is a relatively new phenomenon in China, it is accelerating and promises to become one of the main industrial development models in its application. A number of eco-industrial initiatives have been designed and implemented for the purpose of the circular economy since the concept was first introduced by Chinese scholars into China in the late 1990s (Zhu 1998). For example, in 2005 the National Development and Reform Commission in conjunction with five other ministries launched the first batch of national pilot demonstration projects; a second batch was launched in 2007.[20]

Nevertheless, the point has to be reiterated that China is making progress in circulation of resources precisely because it has the most distressing problems associated with linear resource throughput and wastage, particularly of water.[21] Grand schemes such as the North-South Water Transfer project treat the symptoms; stronger enforcement of water recycling in industry in accordance with circular economy thinking would doubtless pay better dividends.

Eco-Industrial Linkages and the Formation of Circular Economy Patterns

The literature on industrial ecology (IE) is concerned at the macro level with bringing the industrial economy and the environment—or the economy and its natural limits—into some form of harmony, and at the micro level with the identification and analysis of a wide variety of "eco-industrial initiatives" that reduce the energy and resource intensity of industrial activities, largely through converting wastes from one process into inputs to another industrial process. At the macro level, the IE literature is concerned with identifying the processes through which this grand harmonization between industrialization and its natural limits may be effected, and with the kinds of measurement indices that might be used to plot progress (or lack of progress) in approaching such a goal. At the micro level, one of the key concerns of the IE literature is to identify cases of synergistic interactions between firms, or industrial symbioses, through which wastes are converted into inputs, on the biomimetic model of the great natural cycles that have evolved on planet Earth. The literature has identified certain canonical cases of such industrial symbiosis, including Kalundborg in Denmark and emerging cases such as Kwinana and Gladstone in Australia; increasingly there are cases from China.[22]

The eco-initiatives (or cases of industrial symbiosis) carried out in China have been seen as a key part of the solution for China's battle in addressing its environmental problems while maintaining its economic growth.[23] The goal of the eco-initiatives is to eventually establish a circular economy, or what is otherwise known as a closed-loop economy. Such an endeavor is supported by a range of institutional and legal arrangements. In general, closed-loop initiatives are taken at three levels. There are those that are confined to a single enterprise or group of enterprises, enhancing energy and resource efficiency; this is what is generally recognized as "cleaner production." At the second level are initiatives taken at a cluster level, or supply-chain level, where a group of colocated firms (e.g., in an eco-industrial park) share certain streams of resources and energy and so enhance their collective energy and resource efficiency. This is one of the key concerns of industrial ecology, described as industrial symbiosis, along with others such as identifying energy and material flows that could be described as industrial metabolism (as in combined heat and power, or CHP, schemes). In either case the model is the cycles of nature that keep replenishing the basic requirements for life, such as water, carbon, nitrogen and so on. When colocated in an industrial area, and planned as such, they are sometimes known as eco-industrial parks (Lowe 1997).

The third level, so far found mainly in China, involves a whole city, or whole municipal area, in which recycling and interconnected processes are promoted through economic and administrative incentives; conversely, failures to recycle and to make industrial connections are penalized in some way. Demonstration sites are now found throughout China.

An account of the emergence of the circular economy starts with an evolutionary perspective—as is proper to the biomimetic economy. The kind of theory that needs to be developed in the realm of circular economics has to do with the creation of closed loops and the moves toward them, as illustrated in the three panels of Figure 5.1.

The first panel depicts the economy in its traditional linear configuration, with raw materials and energy coming in at one end of a linear process and generating goods and waste (which are a transformed version of the raw materials and energy) along the way. Note that this configuration is couched not in terms of commodities at the input end but in terms of the constituent energy and materials, whose progress can be tracked using tools of material flow analysis (MFA) and energy accounting. Industries A, B, . . . F are depicted as parallel processing systems, without interaction, as in the traditional formulation of the production function in mainstream economic analysis.

Now we introduce some linkages, as shown in the second panel of Figure 5.1. The goods produced by industry A are divided into final goods (for consumption) and intermediates or by-products, which find a use as raw material for another industry B. This industry too utilizes raw materials and energy, as well as these intermediates from industry A to produce goods (for consumption) and inputs that find a use in industry C. Another such chain of activities is found through linkages between industry D and industry E, while industry F is depicted as remaining completely disconnected from the rest of the economy.

A more advanced degree of linkage and evolution toward a circular economy is depicted in the third panel of Figure 5.1, where the linkages between industries are more extensive, with industry A being connected to industry B, and B to C, C to D, D to E, and E to F. But the interesting feature of this panel is that it demonstrates the possibility of a closed loop emerging—linking industries B, C, D, E, F and back to B (bypassing industry A). This hypothetical closed loop, which I propose be named an *industrial hypercycle* (after the hypercycles discovered in biology by Eigen and Schuster [1979]), provides the material foundation for a strong notion of a circular economy.[24]

A well-evolved circular economy would be expected to contain many such closed loops, or industrial hypercycles. By analogy with the idea of hypercycles as introduced into biochemistry as a means of explaining the origins of life without any "god-like" external intervention, we may envisage sequences of industrial activities—where the outputs of one serve as inputs to another and where eventually the loop is closed—forming an industrial hypercycle. The search for such industrial hypercycles should be seen as one of the prime topics of industrial ecological research.

(A)

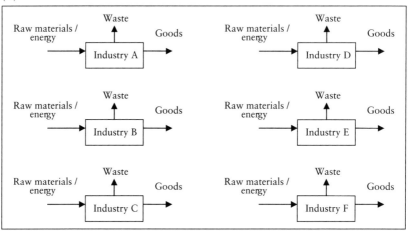

(B)

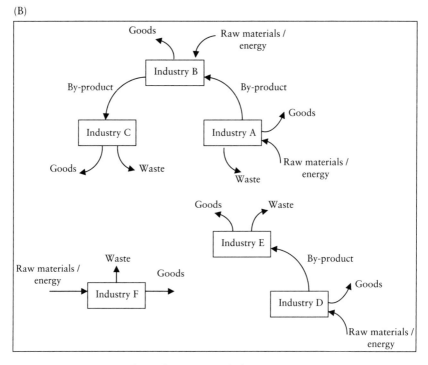

FIGURE **5.1** Emergence of circular economy linkages
SOURCE: Mathews and Tan (2011).

(C)

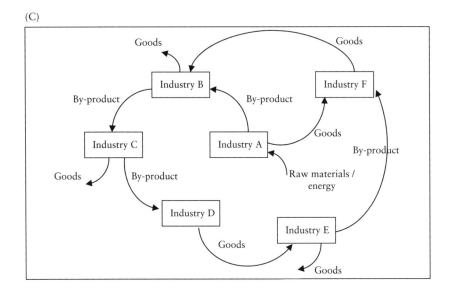

A real version of the process depicted in Figure 5.1 would be, for example, the interrelated material and energy flows associated with the Guitang sugar complex in China, as shown in Figure 5.2.

In the case of Guitang, a group founded as a state-owned sugar producer in 1954, the evolutionary steps toward closed loops have been documented. It began as a conventional sugar mill, but in time it developed new loops to make use of wastes or by-products, creating new value chains that are now propagating through the local economy. There is the sugar process itself, linked to an ethanol production facility, which has closed the loop through wastes from the ethanol plant (vinasse) being converted into fertilizer and recycled back to the cane farms. The other main chain is concerned with paper, which starts with the crushed cane (bagasse) as raw material, converting this to a pulp that is then turned into paper and sold to the wider economy. Since 1998, the group has started the operation in using the filter mud (after being dried) generated from the sugar refinery process as a raw material for cement production, thus creating a new value chain. Furthermore, there is recycling of bagasse as fuel for the production of the heat and power that is used in all the other industrial processes of the Guigang group. This eco-complex

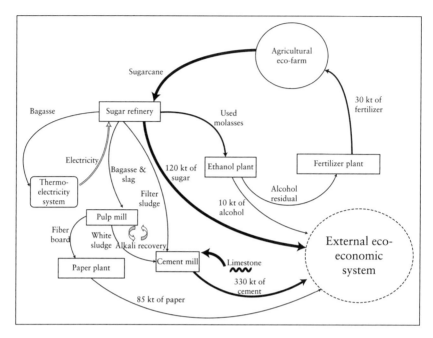

FIGURE **5.2**   Industrial symbioses in Guitang Group, China

SOURCE: Adapted from Mathews and Tan (2011). Redrawn by my collaborator, Hao Tan, and myself, based on sources in the literature.

received recognition in China in 2001 by being designated as the country's first eco-industrial park.

The concept of an eco-industrial park originated in Europe as a spontaneous grouping of geographically colocated enterprises, sharing energy and resource flows to reduce costs and resource intensities. One of the first was the set of interfirm relationships established in the Danish town of Kalundborg, involving linkages between generation of power and heat (combined heat and power system), oil refining, plasterboard production, and soil remediation (Figure 5.3).

Several other such geographically linked clusters involving shared energy and resource flows have been identified, such as at Gladstone and Kwinana in Australia, at Kawasaki in Japan, and at Ulsan in Korea.[25] The idea is gaining real industrial traction; it is beyond the phase in which it might be described as "demonstration projects." China in particular clearly has every intention of drawing competitive advantages from its

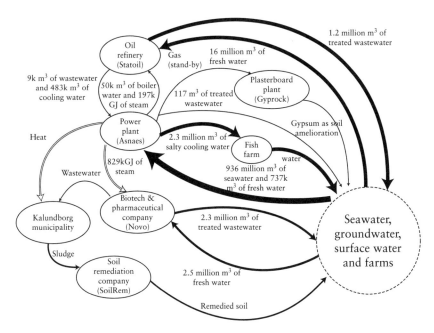

FIGURE **5.3**   Industrial symbioses in Kalundborg, Denmark
SOURCE: Adapted from Mathews and Tan (2011).

mastery of circular economy thinking in its creation of new, clean eco-parks as complements to its building of new, clean eco-cities. A new industrial techno-economic order is being constructed, from the ground up.

Bringing About Circularity: Eco-Tagging

The traditional fossil fuel economy treats raw materials and wastes as generic commodities—without identity, without history, without any moral obligation. A first corrective to this is to provide a means for the tracing of commodity flows within the industrial economy.

It is commodities markets that make industrial capitalism go round, and it is by changing the operations of the commodities markets that the circular economy will become entrenched—so that any alternative will become unthinkable. The story of development of the commodities markets is fascinating, culminating as they do in the great markets of Chicago and New York, which are global in their reach. Commodities are traded with much information provided as part of futures contracts—but much that is not provided. It is in remedying this defect that a giant stride would be made toward embedding the economy in its ecological setting.

How, then, are the eco-linkage ideas of the circular economy to be assimilated with the operation of commodity markets more generally? What is required, I submit, is that commodities need to certify their origin, and in particular whether they are virgin commodities or contain some element of recirculation. For example, a futures contract for oil would be 100 percent "virgin," whereas a futures contract for steel could be almost 100 percent recirculated, derived from scrap iron and biomass ingredients (in place of coal for coking). No commodities market at this point (to the best of my knowledge) offers a commodities futures contract that is differentiated in terms of its origins, identifying the degree to which it is a product of recirculation.[26] The day that such a contract is offered, it will acquire an extra ecological dimension, thereby making all existing futures contracts appear to be generic. The "eco-futures contract" will have that added dimension, just the way that a copyright- or patent-protected product has an extra dimension provided by intellectual property rights—and both will be expected to trade at a premium as a result. Although recycling is still frequently associated with low value-adding activities such as glass and container recycling, or scrap-metal operations, it is destined to become more significant as resources are sought not in virgin mining operations but in "mining" the waste flows generated by industrial activities.

The goal would be to shift from commodity trading in which eco-labeling would provide a source of differentiation to eco-labeling of all *manufactured and processed products*. This would be a situation in which every traded product would have its own eco-history, revealing its origins and the extent to which it is recirculated. One would expect that governments would tax the "virgin" products most heavily and leave the 100 percent recirculated products with zero tax (or a social subsidy).[27]

Technologically, the foundation for such a (near) future situation would be the "Internet of things," with the idea that every product would have its own IT history, just as websites do in the current version of the Internet.[28] A start has been made toward such a situation, with familiar technologies like radio-frequency identification (RFID) being utilized; the Internet of things can be expected to move ahead rapidly, now that it has been conceptualized, to become the norm. Under these circumstances, adding the product's eco-history is just one extra step, requiring no real technical barrier. The capitalist feature of eco-history labeling, or tagging, resides in its providing a source of differentiation that will translate into competiveness differentiation, with green products displaying their eco-history and thereby securing a tangible competitive benefit over companies that stick with generic "non-eco" product designation.

It bears repeating that the traditional framing of economic activity places it in a linear setting, with raw materials being mined at one end and wastes generated and discarded at the other end. The unspoken assumption is that nature provides a limitless source at one end and a limitless sink at the other. All mainstream economic analysis is predicated on such a model. It is assumed that this is a least-cost way of conducting industrial activities. Yes, the scale of linear industrial processes has increased, and costs have reduced—so if a circular alternative is to be developed, its costs will have to come down to comparable levels, through various kinds of incentives. This is why grid parity is so important in the energy sphere, and why a comparable "circular flow parity" is needed for the resources sphere. Initially, state mandated targets are needed to break the lock of existing practices and their artificial low costs. Another way is to utilize consumer pressure in favor of eco-tagged products and commodities. Eco-tagging of resources would give them a "history" and promote a sense of responsibility among users of resources, commodities, and the products into which they are fashioned. This eco-tagging is likely to become one of the strongest factors in the transition to an economy of recirculated resources, one that can be designed as an "intelligent economy" or smart economy.[29]

A New Default Option

It cannot be emphasized enough that the concept of the circular economy represents a radical break—a *rupture*—with the conventional linear economy, in which raw materials are mined or extracted at one end and wastes are dumped at the other—both ends exploiting a sink called "nature" without thought or restraint. Indeed, the very concept of national accounts, measured by gross domestic product (GDP), is an expression of the linear economy. Growth in GDP—in the absence of increasing returns—means growth in throughput. This has become the unofficial religion of industrial capitalism, and any proposal that might interfere with extensive growth, through interfering with GDP growth, is ruled out of order.

In Chapter 8 I am concerned to demonstrate that capitalist growth depends not on throughput expansion but instead on the capture of increasing returns that are generated through multiple linkages between firms; and I will demonstrate that a focus on the linkages in the economy, and in particular the circular economy, can indeed generate growth from a steady-state resource base, via increasing returns. But in this chapter I have been concerned with elaborating on what is meant by circularity in economic relations, and on the eco-linkages that are created as firms connect together, one taking the waste of another as a raw material.

The smart circular economy provides a radical alternative to the linear, nonintelligent economy conception—one that will only gain in relevance as moves toward the green economy gather strength. Indeed, the circular economy—or smart economy—may be viewed as the second of the fundamental *ruptures* currently transforming industrial capitalism and driving the transition to a new system. But I have emphasized that the new trajectory embodying resource efficiency and circularity cannot be expected to establish itself; it will only foster something akin to green growth if it is mandated as a new trajectory by determined state action. Once such a new trajectory is created (as arguably is happening in both China and Korea), then the capitalist tools of property rights, markets and creative destruction via innovation can be set to work. Again, these tools of free-market environmentalism can be expected to achieve their results only if applied in a new, state-mandated renewable and circular economy trajectory. And they will achieve these results only if sufficient finance flows to the new firms making the investments needed to establish the new trajectory. So we finally turn to the third of the ruptures that are needed, namely the shift from generic financing of investments to eco-targeted credit and finance.

6　From Generic to Eco-Finance

The money markets—the engine room of capitalism

> —*Joseph Schumpeter,* The Theory of Economic Development
> *(1912/1934)*

Capitalism is an evolving and dynamic system that has come in many forms and even now different forms coexist. For the United States, the financial stages of American capitalism can be characterised as: commercial capitalism; industrial capitalism and wild cat financing; financial capitalism and state financing; paternalistic, managerial and welfare state capitalism; money manager capitalism.

> —*Hyman Minsky, "Uncertainty and the institutional structure of capitalist economies" (1996)*

Though governments understand that decarbonising the economy will require large sums [of money], many are also realising that further recourse to private capital is required. With their USD 71 trillion in assets, institutional investors—including pension funds and insurance companies—potentially have an important role to play in financing clean energy projects.

> —*Christopher Kaminker and Fiona Stewart (2012)*

We think [green bonds] is going to be a cornerstone market in three or four years—that's the signal we get from investors.

> —*Christopher Flensborg, Skandinavska Enskilda Banken (April 2013)*

Climate Bonds provide for large scale issuance of long-term debt to overcome medium term investment barriers to achieving economies of scale in low-carbon industry sectors. The bonds can thus finance that global transition at speed and at scale.

> —*Climate Bonds Initiative (2009)*[1]

Let's say you are managing a multibillion-euro pension fund (or insurance or sovereign wealth fund), and you have two energy investment projects on your desk. One involves a company with projects that promise soaring costs, investor turbulence, and potential litigation; the other a company with projects that promise regular returns and steadily diminishing costs with rising consumer and government support.

Put this way, the choice to go with the renewables projects, with their declining cost curves and greater investment certainty, is a no-brainer. The problem is that investment-grade securities have not been available—apart from a few multilateral offerings, such as the green bonds, crafted to "test the waters," issued by the World Bank's International Finance Corporation (IFC).

That situation has begun to change, with the issuing in February 2013 of a US$500 million green bond by the Korean Export-Import Bank (Kexim), where the funds are going toward financing low-carbon initiatives, including renewable energy, energy efficiency, and clean water projects. The bond was targeted at and taken up by institutional investors like yourself.

Let us count the ways that this constituted a significant step. It was the first time that a national bank issued such a green bond. Previous initiatives had all come from multilateral banks such as the World Bank, the Asian Development Bank, and the European Investment Bank. Important as these issues have been in testing the waters, they had not involved any national government in offering a public commitment to funding green projects. The Kexim offering did just that.

Second, the bond was offered globally, to the standards of the US Securities and Exchange Commission (SEC), with underwriters Bank of America Merrill Lynch and the Scandinavian Skandinavska Enskilda Banken (SEB) (which has also been linked with the World Bank green bond issues).[2] As a global security it commands a strong resale value, thus enhancing its credibility in the eyes of institutional investors. Above all, it is "investment grade." Third, the bond was offered as a $500 million, five-year security, and it attracted $1.8 billion in demand, with 60 percent being taken up by institutional investors. This revealed the latent, untapped demand on the part of professionals for medium-term green investments that may now be viewed as safer than fossil fuel investments.[3]

Fourth, the Kexim bond was backed by an assurance that all funds would be channeled to green investment projects. The projects are certified by a reputable third party, the Center for International Climate and Environmental Research in Oslo (CICERO). This is designed to protect the professional investor from future legal liability. All the projects are found outside Korea and involve major Korean firms involved in infrastructure projects such as the building of hydroelectric dams or the construction of wind farms.

This bond issue therefore demonstrates that institutional investors will purchase green financial securities if they are presented in the right way, with suitable global reach and certification, and at investment grade. Green bonds are moving from the realm of being curiosities to mainstream financial products. Now, why is this so important?

Bonds are indeed the core of the capitalist system—its engine, to use Schumpeter's graphic phrase. It takes countries decades, if not centuries, to build effective bond markets. Bonds enable governments and leading corporates to raise funds on the strength of their credibility and reputation. They are investment-grade securities, meaning that they are offered only for large amounts (the $500 million of the Kexim green bond is typical)—and so their value for green finance is that they can aggregate across a large number of small projects, none of which on its own would be likely to attract funding. Diseconomies of scale associated with small projects are decisively overcome by the reach of a green bond.

Financing of clean-tech projects via green bonds makes for low-cost capital, since the interest charges will always be just a little above sovereign loans and thus lower than for conventional bank finance. This means that renewables and energy efficiency projects that might have been put out of the running because of high cost of capital or the unwillingness of banks to expose themselves to risks suddenly become viable. The Kexim bond issue was also "sweetened" by the bank in its decision to pay the bond coupons out of its consolidated revenues rather than out of the income generated exclusively by the green projects, thereby effectively switching the risk from investors to the bank.[4] The diffusion of green energy and resource projects has therefore been accelerated. Of course, such a process depends on government support, which in turn reduces investor uncertainty.

Bonds are serious financial instruments that are not to be toyed with. If a country's bonds lose their value, then the country faces ruin. (Technically, the country would be unable to meet its payments and would have to default—a desperate step.) Hence a green bond issued with a national government's imprimatur (as is the case with this new bond issued by Kexim) means that the bond will hold its value only if the projects really are an investment in a green future and really do have the backing of the government. The bond markets will see through any shenanigans and punish the issuer severely.

So here is a novel situation in which the bond markets could emerge as vital players in the transition to a green economy. Their enormous investment potential is there to be tapped in order to finance green investments. Likewise, the equity markets (trading in stocks and shares) will also play a significant role—through initial public offerings (IPOs) and venture capital. The vast resources of the finance sector will inevitably be drawn on—and in this way the ideological insistence of the United Nations and the parties to the Kyoto Protocol that all green investments emanate from tax-based public sources (which could manifestly not finance the transition in any realistic manner) will finally be overcome.

The big investors—institutional, pension and insurance funds, hedge funds, and sovereign wealth funds, which have between them more than $70 trillion in investable funds, according to the Organisation for Economic Co-operation and Development (OECD)—are now actively involved.[5] So the big guns of capitalism, then, are about to be employed.

The contrast with carbon trading has to be underlined. The idea that pollution allowances could be traded and that the "carbon markets" so created might drive investment in the desired direction has been shown to have little potential—given the dismal performance of the emissions trading system (ETS) in Europe and collapsing carbon prices elsewhere. But to tap into the bond markets is a real form of green finance, and one in which Seoul and the Kexim Bank may just have seized the initiative away from Wall Street, Frankfurt, and London.

No great transformation is feasible without the participation of the finance sector. Any notion that a transformation can be engineered by public finance (tax dollars) alone is a fantasy. The heart of finance is the system of bonds—the capitalist instrument of credit par excellence.

It is astonishing that this central player in the financial system has been largely sidelined (until now) by debates over how to mitigate climate change.

The financial system has evolved since the early *prestanze* and *prestiti* created by the Italian city-states of Venice and Florence in the thirteenth century, and which underpinned their commercial success. These early signposts to the capitalist money markets were "forced loans" imposed on the populace by the commercial republics (in lieu of taxes)— and in the entrepreneurial spirit of the times, the notes carrying these assessments could then be traded in secondary markets. In the case of Florence, the public debt was founded in the early fourteenth century, whereby sums owing to the Commune could be transferred to third parties (i.e., sold). These secondary markets are the direct antecedents of the bonds markets of today; they are the origin of the modern notion of securitization. The initial issuer had to have the power to compel uptake of the bond issue (as in the first cases, in which the bonds were a form of tax) or the sovereign status that would inspire confidence that an assurance of paying a coupon (fixed interest) of, say, 5 percent per annum for twenty years, would indeed be complied with. A true public debt in the sense of voluntary as opposed to forced loans to government arose in Venice in the sixteenth century, whereby citizens could invest in interest-bearing securities issued by the republic—known as *prestiti* to create a sense of continuity with earlier means of finance.[6]

Once the genie was out of the bottle, further financial innovations followed swiftly. There were letters of credit and giro banking, which enabled the trade fairs of early Europe to flourish; there were innovations such as joint-stock corporations, which could divide the ownership into parcels (shares) that in turn became negotiable (i.e., could be traded on markets that arose for this purpose).

In the industrial era, the most notable innovations have been new kinds of industrial banks, such as the Crédit Mobilier bank in France (1854) and the Deutsche Bank in Germany (1872). *Crédit mobilier* was a clever innovation that enabled banks to lend against "mobile property" (transferable property, as opposed to landed property, the traditional security demanded)—or what would today be called negotiable securities. Various privileges were conferred on the Crédit Mobilier bank by its charter, including the ability to acquire shares in public companies and to pay calls on its own resources by creditors through issuing its own notes (i.e., bonds). This was a financial innovation of the first order, paving the way to the bonds markets and making Paris a center of capitalist financial activity.

Deutsche Bank was likewise founded as an industrial bank (as opposed to the prevailing commercial or merchant bank) able to make large credit appropriations to industrial enterprises against the security offered by their future earnings rather than the land and buildings that were required as collateral by commercial banking. Germany also pioneered the concept of covered bond, meaning a debt instrument that is backed by a designated set of assets whose value underpins (or "covers") the value of the bond. Likewise in Japan in its catch-up phase, a large bank-based system of finance developed, initially by allowing banks to work as credit providers to groups of linked firms (i.e., the zaibatsu) in the late nineteenth and early twentieth centuries—and then, after defeat in the Pacific War, by designating certain banks as long-term credit banks and issuing a select few banks with a long-term credit license. The three banks so designated were the Industrial Bank of Japan, the Nippon Kangyo Bank, and the Long-Term Credit Bank of Japan.[7]

All these institutional innovations (what Gerschenkron [1962] characterized as latecomer, or "catch-up," institutions) enabled the latecomer countries to catch up with the early leaders by aggregating financial capital and channeling it toward investments in large-scale industrial undertakings—in a way that was quite beyond the commercial banks of the early modern era. Aggregation was the key to applying new financial instruments to the challenges of mobilizing investment in the industrial era of the nineteenth and twentieth centuries—just as it is proving to be in creating the new, green era in the twenty-first century.

From Creditworthiness to Eco-Worthiness

The financial "engine room" of capitalism has been operating with scant regard to the dangers of global warming or any of the other hazards faced by our present industrial order; the ship sails toward the reefs with little sign of awareness from the "financial engineers." Indeed, if we can go by the Wall Street excesses of recent years, and the global financial meltdown of 2008 and 2009, then it would seem that the engine room was in serious disarray, as the "engineers" all put their own exaggerated financial interests before those of the ship or the crew. The scale of the misappropriation is staggering—amounting to trillions of dollars of "lost" finance.

There are many calls to curb the financial system of its obvious appetite for taking excessive risks with "other peoples' money" (a situation that calls for more stringent return to trade-off between concession of limited liability in return for submission to regulation): "If you want the freedom to run big bets, then accept unlimited liability."[8] An even deeper problem concerns the role of finance in underpinning and perpetuating the reign of fossil fuels. Every time a new energy project is brought to the markets for funding (e.g., a bank loan, an overdraft, a corporate bond issue, an IPO), it is evaluated and approved purely on the basis of the creditworthiness of the borrower—without regard to the eco-worthiness of the project. This is the situation that has to change—and is indeed starting to change (as when investments in fossil-fueled projects come to be viewed as "stranded assets" or "unburnable carbon").[9]

It is open to any particular country to allow several institutions to play a new role, licensing them as green banks in an analogous way to the Japanese approach to framing long-term credit bank legislation in the 1950s—and then letting banks themselves take the initiative of seeking such a license. This would no doubt prove to be preferable in the eyes of conservative treasuries to the creation of new green banks using public funds as their seed capital.

Along with markets for energy, resources, and products, the market for finance (investment capital) is thus being transformed, in small steps for the moment but in ways that promise to expand in the near future. Increasingly, large investors (e.g., pension funds) in financial instruments such as bonds are looking to guarantee the security of their investments by placing them in projects that do not suffer from projected resource or fossil fuel shortages and carbon risks. In this way they are becoming much more interested in green investments that promise greater long-term security, and therefore in the financial instruments targeted at such investment projects (e.g., green bonds, climate bonds). As the demand for these green investment vehicles grows, so their price in terms of interest rates can be expected to fall relative to those of financial instruments targeted more generically at any project, without discrimination. In this way a new market for "eco-securities" is being created, to finance investment in specifically green and low-carbon projects for which the energy and resource security involved is greater.[10]

Banks and other financial institutions will in the future be looking for ways to ensure that the finance they generate be targeted and labeled as "green," as opposed to the generic bonds and securities issued now that can be used for any purpose. Thus, the criterion of creditworthiness will be joined by a second (and more important) criterion of eco-worthiness, which will attach to the projects to be financed rather than to the issuer of the bonds or other financial instruments. This is an important shift. Green bonds will come to play an important role in aggregating various small-scale renewable energy and recycling projects, thus giving them the advantage of economies of scale and further reducing the costs of investing in such projects. In these ways, investing in the green economy will come to be far more attractive than investing in the old fossil fuel economy.

What we see emerging are the *new shoots of a green financial system* in which the emphasis will shift from creditworthiness to eco-worthiness. The emphasis will shift from the qualities of the projector (the creditworthiness of the issuer of the bond) to the qualities of the project itself, and to whether the project is climate-friendly or not. Such a shift can be manifested in a positive sense, where green financial instruments (e.g., green bonds, green loans) are presented as a preferred option, carrying a lower interest charge; as well as in a negative sense, where projects that prop up the fossil fuel economy are presented as nonpreferred options and as such carry a financial penalty.[11]

Greening the Bond Markets

Let us be clear as to the size of the global financial system and its capacity to fund investments at scale in renewables and resource efficiency. According to McKinsey Global Institute, financial assets in 2012 totaled $225 trillion—as good an estimate of the size of the global capitalist system one is likely to get. Of these vast sums, $50 trillion was accounted for by equity capital (stocks and shares traded on the world's stock exchanges), whereas bonds in total accounted for twice that sum,

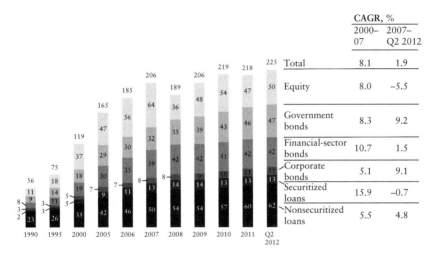

		CAGR, %	
		2000–07	2007–Q2 2012
Total		8.1	1.9
Equity		8.0	−5.5
Government bonds		8.3	9.2
Financial-sector bonds		10.7	1.5
Corporate bonds		5.1	9.1
Securitized loans		15.9	−0.7
Nonsecuritized loans		5.5	4.8

FIGURE **6.1**   Global financial assets, 1990–2012 (in US$ trillions)

SOURCE: McKinsey Global Institute. Used with permission.

NOTE: End-of-year figures for a sample of 183 countries, based on constant 2011 exchange rates. Figures may not sum to totals because of rounding. CAGR = compound annual growth rate.

or $100 trillion.[12] The balance was made up by loans, both securitized (capital markets) and nonsecuritized (bank lending) (Figure 6.1).

Just where are these $225 trillion in funds being invested? Obviously, most are going to prop up business as usual in the fossil fuel economy—through the world's stock markets ($50 trillion), through the bond markets ($100 trillion), and through bank lending. These are the capital markets—the true drivers of capitalism—and the markets that have to be tapped if the world is to make any progress in shifting to a low-carbon industrial trajectory. The OECD has made the case in favor of targeting the bond markets and institutional investors to drive investments in green infrastructure, in both developed and developing countries, where the size of the potential investment pool available from institutional investors is definitively estimated at $71.1 trillion in 2010, and growing rapidly, drawing from investment funds, insurance companies, and pension funds. An OECD working paper gives sustained attention to the barriers standing in the way of the deployment of such funds at scale in accelerating the uptake of renewable energies around the world.[13]

Most of the projects that professional fund managers find themselves being presented with involve fossil fuel energy systems and unacceptable levels of carbon emissions, and for this reason such projects present unacceptable risks of default. For the most part, the kinds of low-carbon projects that they would like to invest in are unsuitable, in that they are small, or underinsured and guaranteed, or are found in emerging markets where risk spreads are high.[14] So there is scope here for some innovative financial institutions to step forward with investment vehicles (bonds) that overcome these obstacles.

Advantages of Green Bonds

Green bonds are able to lump together several projects, each one of which might be quite small and have difficulty in securing funding on its own. First, if aggregated or bundled into a single portfolio of similar (but carefully scrutinized) projects, they are much more attractive to investors. In this way, green bonds promise to overcome the liability of smallness (diseconomies of scale) through aggregation. Second, they overcome the problem of guarantees by arranging for government or multilateral guarantees of the bonds, as part of their design and implementation. The bond-issuing institution plays the role of agent, securing the necessary guarantees on the basis of the creditworthy character of the projects it is investing in. And third, most projects will in fact be found in emerging market countries, where the renewable resources of sun, wind, water, and land can be found in abundance, and where risk premiums would act as a block on investment without safeguards. Again, it is the job of the bond-issuing financial institution to arrange for such safeguards, taking responsibility to test the market with bond issues that pay less attention to traditional risk premiums and more to the low-carbon character of their underlying investment projects. A credible standard certifying to the "green" character of the bond is needed—such as the standard issued by the Climate Bonds Initiative.[15] If the market does not accept such bonds at just a few basis points above normal, then the exercise will have failed and the world will still have a problem on its hands.

Let us take a hypothetical example (based on the real case of the Kexim green bond) to see how access to the international bond markets, attracting the interest of institutional investors (e.g., insurance companies, pension and superannuation funds), could play an important role in green development in countries such as Mozambique (which has vast renewable resources but is currently tied to a black economy). Let us say that the Development Bank of Southern Africa (DBSA) or the African Development Bank (AfDB) floats a US$1 billion climate bond on the New York and Tokyo bond markets, with backing from the Mozambique government and the World Bank's Multilateral Investment Guarantee Agency (MIGA)—giving the bond the prospects of investment grade rating. When discussing ordinary government securities, such as treasury certificates, the government backing the issue commits to repaying investors out of its revenue streams, usually taxation. In the case of a climate bond, a different kind of commitment is called for, both in relation to sources of revenue (e.g., from revenues accruing to providers of renewable energies) and in relation to specified actions to mitigate climate change or assist in adaptation to anticipated climate change (e.g., "ring-fencing" the funds raised by the bond for climate-related activities). These commitments would have to be clearly visible to investors and backed by guarantees and audit reviews, to ensure that funds will actually be expended as advertised. After all, investors are interested in a return commensurate with the risk that they are prepared to take.

In the context of developing countries and their desperate need for funding for new green projects to counteract the black projects that are already under way, the role of green financing (and facilitating it through policy interventions) is critical. Individual projects related to raising the level of renewables in the national energy mix that might otherwise be rendered unachievable through high interest charges would become feasible when financed out of the proceeds of the bond. This mechanism would provide a means to overcome diseconomies of scale, allowing small projects to go ahead (through aggregation), whereas they might be frustrated if pursued individually through, say, ordinary bank loans or equity investments. This is where leapfrogging can really mean something—let us call it "green leapfrogging." There is the vast, largely untapped pool of capital under management by institutional investors (running to $71 trillion in 2010) and the need for such investors to find carbon-neutral or carbon-positive investment projects that will generate long-term returns. And there is the vast, as yet largely unrealized pool of renewable energy projects, spanning wind, solar, and bioenergy, to be found in the tropical emerging developing countries, with their vast natural resources. Until now there have been few institutional mechanisms for bringing together these two classes of economic actors—investors looking for scalable projects and firms looking to finance their green projects. The institutional vehicle that meets this need is the green bond, issued by development banks on international bond markets and couched in such a way that it meets the investment-grade needs of institutional investors and provides aggregated funding to green projects.

The critical issue with regard to low-carbon projects is their viability and real sustainability (i.e., their contribution to real reductions in carbon emissions). This is where standards come to play an important role. It is open to any organization—such as the Climate Bonds Initiative, for example, acting as a de facto industry agency, or CICERO as in the Kexim case—to issue a set of standards that viable and sustainable investment projects would be expected to meet. Close auditing of projects financed by green securities would be needed to ensure that they deliver what they promise. This in itself is a means of ensuring that green finance calls for close supervision and regulation, both to deliver what is promised to investors and to make it more attractive, and less uncertain, than its "brown" alternative. This too is a way of keeping green finance in close touch with the real economy and with its ecological cycles—to prevent the runaway financial innovation that fed on itself and ultimately led to the 2008–9 global financial crisis.

It is the power of the *relative interest charges* (or differential interest rates) that will determine whether green shoots in the real economy are allowed to emerge. If a way can be found to reduce interest charges on green projects, bringing the eco-worthiness of the project alongside the creditworthiness of the projector as criterion for granting the finance, then there are indeed grounds for optimism. And this is exactly what we see emerging in the practices of the Brazilian and Chinese Development Banks, to which we now turn.

Green Banks at Work

We can see a system of green finance emerging from the examples already at hand, in China and Germany and Brazil, and how they interact directly with entrepreneurial interests in renewable energy and circular economy initiatives, in a process of mutual reinforcement best described as a chain reaction.[16] Let me illustrate with the case of green financing in China and Brazil, utilizing the countries' development banks.

China Development Bank

The China Development Bank (CDB) has emerged as the world's largest development bank, dwarfing the World Bank and other multilateral banks such as the Asian Development Bank and the African Development Bank. As a policy bank, it does not take deposits from savers, and instead it raises finance on the Chinese bond market (in the process stimulating the creation and expansion of such a bond market). Apart from its definitive interventions within China's own development (driving the process of urbanization through turning land into collateral), it operates as the principal arm funding both China's outreach to develop oil and gas supplies from around the world, and it provides strong credit lines to renewable energy companies (wind and solar PV initially), thus underpinning their rapid rise in international competition.[17] The CDB makes loans at preferential interest rates to projects that fall within the designated "strategic industries" of the current Twelfth Five-Year Plan, thereby effectively operating a loan system that is biased toward eco-finance.

Brazilian Development Bank

The Brazilian Development Bank (BNDES), founded in 1952, is one of the world's largest national development banks (and it, too, is larger than the World Bank). It is a highly important institution that has been at the forefront of Brazil's development efforts; it raises finance for Brazil's development through multiple channels, including the issuance of bonds on European capital markets.[18] Now it leads as well in the fostering of green finance, or the financing of green development.

The BNDES is moving from a process by which the evaluation of funding proposals was largely focused on the "financials" (e.g., risk, guarantees, creditworthiness of borrower) to one that also captures sustainability of the projects themselves and contributes to the formation of a green economy (i.e., what could be called eco-finance). Both aspects are important: the bank is developing a series of socio-technical guides as to what constitute the criteria by which sustainability may be evaluated, as well as financing initiatives that contribute to green development, such as reforestation, building value chains for renewable energies, and promotion of green technologies.

The key idea is that loans from the bank would carry a sliding scale of charges, with the lowest charges for projects that meet all sustainability criteria and the highest for those that fall short. To implement this strategy, BNDES has been preparing a series of guides that document the socio-technical best-practice benchmarks for low-carbon and ecologically sustainable production, sector by sector. These are to be utilized to provide parameters against which funding proposals may be judged. The idea is that applicants for funding who can demonstrate their compliance with these socio-technical sustainability criteria would be charged the bank's going rate; those that can do better (contributing to raising the bar, or improving the benchmark) would be offered loans at discounted rate (say, 1 percent lower). The bank would reserve the option to raise the socio-technical standards from time to time, even above those required by minimal legal or environmental standards. Agreement would be sought with the industry in most cases.

This promises to be highly effective as a means of encouraging business to raise its green standards—a way that is much more effective than, say, a carbon tax or cap-and-trade scheme. The reason is that it is imposed at the point where funding decisions are being taken. It carries no bureaucratic overload; it is transparent and fair, in that a company can see what the designated sustainability criteria are and whether it meets them or not; and it is applied at the point of investment rather than after the fact (such as a carbon tax), when extra expenditure might be required after the production system has been set in place. Moreover these guides are adapted to the conditions in which industry is conducted in Brazil; they are not imposed by some external authority.

These guides are anticipated to become the defining documents of the green economy as it develops in Brazil. They are highly practicable, in that they have input from trade and industry associations and are based on prior discussions with experts in the industry. They require board approval by the bank prior to being implemented in lending decisions. In this way they would carry authority and be rendered immune from legal challenges that construe the practice as discriminatory. In effect, these documents potentially provide a baseline or standard that firms need to reach if they are to qualify for loans.

The practice of graduating loan charges depending on adherence of applicants and projects to socio-technical guidance is in its infancy in Brazil.[19] But its application is imminent and demonstrates enormous potential. The closest parallel to it is graduated charges imposed by state-owned Chinese banks such as CDB to projects that are targeted by the current Five-Year Plan as opposed to those that are not. It is worth pointing to these practices as genuine "market-based incentives" that operate at the point of investment, or the point of change in a production system, rather than at the point at which the system is already in operation and hence carries inertia or "carbon lock-in."[20]

Regulatory Initiatives

While Brazil's regulatory encouragement of eco-finance is as yet partial, China's is becoming mandatory, with systematic procedures being established to ensure that funds are routinely supplied preferentially to green investment projects. This is accomplished under the "Green Credit Guidelines" of the China Banking Regulatory Commission (CBRC). It might sound a mouthful—but the guidelines, which were being implemented in 2013 as mandatory standards, promise to be the key drivers of China's greening of its development model.[21] Provincial-level environmental protection authorities are being empowered to monitor the lending practices of banks in their region, and they provide the data directly to the CBRC, which will be able to change the credit available to banks depending on their adherence or otherwise to the guidelines.

Think for a moment about what this means—a policy tool that operates at the point of investment, when financing decisions are being taken, driving them toward eco-investment. As such, it is so much more effective than a carbon tax or similar instrument, which operates after critical investments have already been taken, at the point of production. Which strategy promises to be more effective—influencing investment decisions prior to building new plants or influencing production decisions after the plants have been built? To pose the question is to answer it.

A Cautionary Perspective on Green Finance

The last thing one would wish to create with the emergent green finance sector is opportunities for further speculation and financial bubbles—of which the past few centuries have given ample demonstration.[22] So strong regulation is called for. This is indeed a "Minsky moment"—in the best sense of the term—in that it was Minsky who drove home the argument that the capitalist financial system is inherently unstable and prone to bubbles and crashes, but can be made to operate more smoothly if adequately and stringently regulated.[23]

This is what may be anticipated for green finance. Far from seeking to ward off regulation (as done so fiercely by the "brown finance" competitors, in the interests of protecting the possibilities for making private fortunes), the green finance sector is likely instead to welcome it. This would be expected to have a twofold effect. It would protect the green finance sector itself from unscrupulous practices and speculative activity that would induce such bubbles and crashes—through early detection and elimination of what Minsky called "Ponzi scheme" finance.[24] And second, it would make the green finance sector less risky, and therefore more attractive, for investors. Thus, through stringent regulation the green finance sector can expect to develop returns that are superior to those earned in the brown finance incumbent sector (returns across the sector rather than individual earnings and bonuses) because of the greater certainty associated with green investments. And that can be expected to exert a profound knock-on effect on the brown finance sector itself, inducing more responsible behavior through competitive emulation.

It goes without saying that this "green finance stability" hypothesis would meet with stringent opposition from existing Wall Street institutions, with their immense financial muscle and powerful political lobbying interests. It is another instance of the general principle espoused in this text—namely, that the best way to initiate change in a capitalist economy is to split the ranks of capitalists, and thereby ensure that one group of capitalists see their prospects for profits enhanced by the mooted change. The challenge can be expected to arise from elsewhere than Wall Street or the city of London, such as in São Paulo or Seoul, and to exert its competitive emulation pressures indirectly.[25] We return to this topic in the final chapter, with the idea that in a green economy, finance is to be treated and regulated as a utility.

Obstacles and Vested Interests

Of the many obstacles standing in the way of the emergence of a genuine green finance sector, let me highlight just two—the continuing diversion of carbon markets, which are attempting to "merge" themselves with green finance, and the system of rules governing cross-national investment that have grown and proliferated under the WTO.

First is carbon offsets. The problematic effects of resorting to carbon markets as a means of mitigating carbon emissions were alluded to earlier. In the present context it is worth examining how proposals of carbon offsets would strangle climate bonds markets at birth. To take a specific case, in June 2010 the International Emissions Trading Association (IETA) issued a draft discussion paper on linking climate bonds to carbon offsets.[26] While welcome as a means of furthering discussion on green bonds and how they might be used to accelerate investment in renewable energies and energy efficiency, the paper betrayed the top-down thinking that poisoned the Kyoto process and made the Clean Development Mechanism almost useless as a means of reducing real carbon emissions on any scale (a point on which the IETA itself surely agrees)—even if some individuals and organizations have managed to make money out of it. Along the way, the IETA proposes financing mechanisms—supposedly to be used by emerging industrial giants like China, India, and Brazil—that would involve these countries agreeing to subordinate their efforts to (1) having their bonds approved by an international body; (2) demonstrating compliance by the bond with standards issued by the international body covering monitoring, reporting, and verification (MRV) processes; (3) issuing of green bonds to be circumscribed by an overarching allocation of Guaranteed Carbon Collateral Units that would set a ceiling on the range and volume of climate bonds to be issued; and (4) investors such as pension funds being expected to accept carbon credits as means of payment in addition to equity or interest payments. Frankly, these are four impossible conditions that would undermine any real climate bond initiative.[27] Nothing more has been heard of regarding these proposed green bonds.

A second and more serious roadblock is constituted by the terms of bilateral investment treaties. Of even greater salience is the system of tight rules governing transnational investment (bilateral and multilateral investment treaties, and specifically the General Agreement on Trade in

Services) that have proliferated under the WTO. Under these complex rules and procedures, which are enforceable under contract law, countries are tightly constrained in what they can and cannot do. It is therefore conceivable that a country seeking to introduce green finance provisions that depend on differential interest charges might find itself—if these extend to foreign investors—in breach of some such agreement or treaty, and thus liable for compensation. This is not what a green finance program would be looking to achieve. As countries move toward green finance, then, they will have to submit their international agreements (bilateral and multilateral) and treaties to close review, to ensure that the agreements and treaties do not end up strangling the green initiatives.[28]

A New Default Option

Financing initiatives designed to raise funds internationally for infrastructure projects in developing countries (e.g., dams, railways, waterworks) have to overcome investment concern about heightened risks in underdeveloped countries—uncertain rule of law, wild currency fluctuations, illiquid securities markets, absence of insurance coverage, and corruption at various levels of government. The cost of finance can become prohibitive, without government guarantees and particularly multilateral (effectively developed country) guarantees. I am not claiming that the need for a risk premium will disappear just because climate bonds will target low-carbon investments. Such a premium is a fact of life in a country on the margins; the sovereign risk to which the investor is exposed will call for the payment of such a premium as part of the price of the bond being issued.[29]

Ultimately, what will drive the shift to eco-finance will not be the good intentions of investors, or the framing of smart policies for capturing large flows of capital by banks and developing countries, but the fact that green finance will become cheaper than generic, or fossil-fueled, finance. This will partly reflect the fact that development banks will become centrally involved, benefiting from quasi-sovereign status as they do so. But this on its own would not undo the "risk premium" that attaches to loans to banks in Brazil or southern African nations.

In the wake of the 2008–9 global financial crisis, investors in the developed world are looking to find ways to invest in what are viewed as safe and sustainable energy projects. Long-term investors would rather see their funds going to energy projects based on the wind and the sun, which in aggregate are always available, rather than on increasingly problematic sources such as coal, oil, and gas—if offered comparable investment opportunities promising equal returns. There is an increasing awareness among investors that fossil fuels are subject to too many economic and political risks (e.g., unpredictable supplier regimes, wildly fluctuating prices and projected price increases as fossil fuels reach the peak of their supply curves, and unburnable carbon). The volatilities involved make these fossil fuel assets less attractive as objects of long-term investment. The low-carbon and renewable energy projects in the developing countries are correspondingly becoming more attractive.

One may view climate bonds (or green bonds), then, as the financial instrument of choice in channeling funds from the vast investment pool represented by institutional investors in the developed world to the equally impressive array of attractive, low-carbon investment projects in the developing world; in this sense, the bonds play the role that financial instruments have always played, in channeling funds to be pooled and directed to the projects where they are needed. The climate bond adapts and updates this old idea to the new situation of the world's search for climate-friendly and low-carbon investment projects in the developing world, with development banks in emerging markets looking to play a positive role in terms of the financial intermediation required.

There is a striking parallel here between the emergence of a constituency of fund managers looking for "safer" investments that offer long-term eco-security, on the one hand, and the emergence of constituencies of entrepreneurs prepared to make investments in renewable energy sources and in circular economy initiatives on the other hand. In each case we see the emergence of a small group of trailblazers who form islands of eco-activities; they then make connections to each other, thus expanding the islands into archipelagoes, then continents, and ultimately displacing the entire fossil fuel apparatus. This is what I describe in Part 3 as a process of circular and cumulative causation; its effect is to "split" the conventional opposition to such initiatives, as fresh capitalist interests are created through the success of such eco-initiatives and act to counter the inertia (or carbon lock-in) of vested capitalist interests. Thus emerges the new default option of eco-finance.

We have now examined the prospects and dynamics of transformation in each of the three fundamental markets in industrial capitalism—for energy, for resources and commodities, and for finance. It is time to see how the system fits together and how the transition is likely to be accomplished.

III   *An Economy of Sustainable Enterprise*

History provides many examples of technological revolutions that have reshaped the world. None have run their course without encountering massive resistance; no change has been brought about in consensus with those on the losing end, and none has been the subject of an international treaty, even when its effects were felt on a global scale. Nevertheless, many of these revolutionary changes have needed a political framework or targeted help at their inception in order to develop and showcase the economic and cultural benefits. The list includes railways, electricity grids, the car society, shipping and aviation, nuclear power and telecommunications.

—*Hermann Scheer,* The Solar Economy *(2002)*

[In Britain] the landowning elite, which controlled political power before 1850, contributed little to the Industrial revolution in terms of technology or entrepreneurship. It did not, however, resist it.

—*Joel Mokyr,* The Lever of Riches *(1990)*

There is one force [innovation] inherent in the economic process which will cause it to progress or advance in a wavelike fashion. . . . Take, for instance, the railroadization of the Middle West as it was initiated by the Illinois Central. While a new thing is being built and financed, expenditure is on a supernormal level, and through a normal state of incomes we get all those symptoms which we associate with prosperity. When such a period of advance has gone on for a time . . . [we see] the way in which progress is accomplished in capitalism and the old eliminated.

—*Joseph Schumpeter,* Business Cycles *(1939)*[1]

If it is true that there is under way a vast transformation of the global economy, toward a new set of rules and institutions favoring renewables over fossil fuels, and resource recirculation over the linear economy, as well as eco-finance over generic finance, then it will have to involve an equally vast disruption to political and economic institutions that are already in place. The green economy will bring new economic and entrepreneurial forces into play, creatively destroying the established industrial order. Such a transformation cannot be expected to be achieved quickly or easily. And it might well be reversed.

Daron Acemoglu and James Robinson provide one of the conceptual keys needed, in their distinction between economic and political losers in economic transitions. Using the example of the Industrial Revolution, they point out that the aristocracy (or landed interest) was everywhere an economic loser from the rise of manufacturing and the new manufacturing towns. In some parts of Europe—Russia and Austria-Hungary—they perceived this rise as a threat to their political power and blocked it; but in other parts (Britain and Germany) the landed interests accommodated to the new order, in such a way that they maintained their political power. As Mokyr put it, to not oppose industrialization was their great contribution.[2]

In the specific case that we are discussing in this book, involving the transition to a new, green techno-economic order (renewable energy and resource efficiency, or RE^2), there is a name already given to the socioeconomic-cum-political resistance to change; it is "carbon lock-in." This phrase is shorthand for the whole battery of interests that are linked to the fossil fuel economy and its extraction and waste of resources.[3] These interests are formidable, and indeed can appear to be overwhelming. Yet they are on the wrong side of history, and eventually they stand to lose. We can say this with some confidence because this is not the first time that a group of interested parties has opposed change. Indeed, it has happened in a broad way at least five times already since the advent of capitalist industrialization as the dominant economic system.

The process of industrialization brought in its wake an entirely new phenomenon—a cyclical pattern to industrial growth that came to be known as business cycles. The characterization of periods of upsurge (upswings) and downswings, across the entire global capitalist economy, is subject to a great deal of strenuous scholarly effort and disagreement— and so in the absence of any definitive study of the economic history of the industrial era, we have to pose our assertions with some degree of caution.[4] But most scholars agree that there was an upsurge in investments starting around the 1770s and 1780s associated with the application of power and mechanization (water power and some steam) to previously craft production, and with drastic improvements in transport (involving canals and turnpikes)—followed by a downswing from the 1820s to 1840s as the new industrial systems spread across Europe and through the United States. Then there was a new upswing dating from the 1840s associated with the investment surge in steam power, railroads, and iron and steel, followed by a downswing from the 1870s to the 1890s, as again these new technologies became widespread throughout the industrial world. A third such upswing began in the 1890s, driven by a surge in investments in electric power and electric motors, and a downswing following the First World War associated with the diffusion of mass production and the automotive industry, leading into the depressed 1930s. Most scholars would also recognize a fourth upswing following the Second World War driven by huge investments in oil-based expansion of industry, transport, suburbanization, and the spread of mass consumption. Some scholars have identified a fifth such upswing since the late 1980s, associated with information technology, computerization, and telecommunications.[5]

In such a framework, it is possible to see a new round of investment in renewable energy and low-carbon technologies as picking up from around 2010, or building on (or cutting short) the previous cycle. Whatever the periodization and the identification of such upswings and downswings, there have clearly been periods of upsurge associated with a new general technology that enables costs and prices to be drastically reduced. The dating of the main waves (as generally accepted) is given in Table 7.1.[6]

The pattern is seen most clearly if we confine ourselves to stock market indices. Allianz Global Investors has demonstrated five clear industrial cycles in the S&P 500 Index, through rolling ten-year yields, and the beginnings of a sixth such cycle, as shown in Figure 7.1.[7]

The world has been enjoying a boom associated with the recovery phase of the long fourth K-wave since the late 1970s, leading into the upswing of the fifth K-wave since the second half of the 1980s, generally linked with the massive adoption of microelectronics, communications, and information technologies. This long boom is viewed as leveling off in the years leading up to 2010, exacerbated by the global financial crisis that occurred in 2008–9. What is to follow this peaking (or the possibility of a second, minor upswing in the 2010s driven by renewable energies) is a matter of current "great debate."

TABLE **7.1**   Upswings and downswings in industrial capitalism, 1760–2011

Long-wave number	Phase	Onset	End
1	A: Upswing	1780s	1810–17
	B: Downswing	1810–17	1844–51
2	A: Upswing	1844–51	1870–75
	B: Downswing	1870–75	1890–96
3	A: Upswing	1890–96	1914–20
	B: Downswing	1914–20	1939–50
4	A: Upswing	1939–50	1968–74
	B: Downswing	1968–74	1984–91
5	A: Upswing	1984–91	2008–10?
	B: Downswing	2008–10?	?

SOURCE: Based on Korotayev and Tsirel (2010), tables 1–2, p. 2.

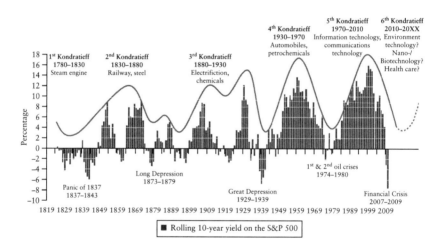

FIGURE **7.1**   Emergence of a sixth techno-economic paradigm
SOURCE: Allianz Global Investors. Used with permission.

Is There a New Long Wave in the Making, Driven by Renewable Energies?

It is difficult now to recall the excitement that greeted the announcement by Perez and Freeman, writing in a neo-Schumpeterian tradition, that the surge in IT investments witnessed in the early 1980s were not just technology-specific developments but actually embodied a shift in techno-economic paradigm. Their argument was that the countries that best adapted to and exploited the potential of IT were those that made the structural adjustments to an economy in which IT provided the pervasive driving technology. They identified this shift as the fifth that had occurred since the Industrial Revolution, and they characterized it as a techno-economic paradigm (TEP) shift, insofar as its dominant technology enjoyed falling costs, was underpricing its incumbent technological competitors, and was pervasive in its effects. Perez and Freeman went further and characterized the organizational features of the emerging fifth TEP shift, such as flexible departures from the rigid hierarchies associated with successful fourth TEP ("mass production") firms, arguing that the firms, regions, and countries that adopted these organizational principles would be the ones that did best in the new IT era. It was no accident that others such as Piore and Sabel (1984), with their similar notion of flexible specialization were writing at the same time and employing a similar kind of analysis.

Fast-forward three decades and we face a comparable situation. There is a new surge of investment in a new technological wave, associated with renewable energy and clean technology. There is a strong case to be made that this new technological wave enjoys (dramatically) falling costs, that it will shortly be priced at well below its fossil-fueled incumbent competitors, and that it will prove to be pervasive in its effects. Going further, it is feasible to argue that this emerging technology wave has very different organizational foundations from its fossil-fueled predecessor, in that it favors decentralized renewable energy generation and open competition between a variety of energy generating systems, as well as an emerging international market for renewable electric power. Put these ingredients together, and you have an emergent, sixth techno-economic paradigm shift.

The mystery is why so little scholarship is devoted to teasing out the implications of such a view. In this book, I take the position that there is indeed such a transition under way—based on a reading of the evidence accumulated to date. We may take the features identified by Freeman and Perez and associated with the fifth TEP shift as benchmark, and then test to see whether the current shift to renewables and clean technology satisfies the same conditions. The argument is cemented by demonstrating that it is consistent with other accounts of the emergent clean-tech era, such as a third energy industrial revolution (Rifkin 2011) and the demonstration by Korotayev and Tsirel (2010) that the global economy is currently on the cusp of a second subwave of investment as the world moves from the fifth to a successor TEP. The emergence of a new sixth TEP shift opens up new possibilities for quick-witted entrepreneurs to take advantage of the new trends, with their IT applications and possibilities for putting manufactured devices to work in harnessing renewable energy sources and circular economy opportunities. There is also ample scope for relevant research on the part of the neo-Schumpeterian community—research that will engage with big issues including climate change, the emergence of China as a new industrial power, and the processes of technological transition.

Technology Cycles and Techno-Economic Paradigm Shifts

The most widely accepted theoretical framework for discussing technological change, and the periodic "technology surges" and the creative destruction they generate, doing away with the old and creating space for the new, is that of techno-economic paradigm shifts, as expounded in numerous works by Freeman and Perez, and which is in turn based on a close reading of Schumpeter's business cycles and Kondratiev long wave theory.[8] Perez (2002) provides the key to making the connection in her notion that while the dominant TEP moves through its mature phases (late deployment and decline), the new paradigm is gestating and moving into early-phase installation (Drechsler, Kattel, and Reinert 2009). My argument is that this is precisely what is occurring with the case of the upsurge in investments in renewable energies.

Emergence of a Sixth Techno-Economic Paradigm

In the Freeman-Perez argument, a novel techno-economic paradigm is characterized by three defining criteria: (1) changes in cost structure, with the emerging technological regime enjoying strong and increasing cost advantages; (2) expanded perception of opportunity spaces, creating multiple entrepreneurial opportunities for the application of the emergent bundle of technologies; and (3) new organizational models, where the new is better fitted to the emergent technologies and generates massive gains in terms of efficiency over those linked (or constrained) by the dominant paradigm. I propose to take three characterizations as definitive: falling costs, costs lower than incumbent technology, and pervasive effects.

In the case of renewable energies or clean tech, one can make the case that two out of three of these fundamental conditions are already satisfied—falling costs and pervasiveness—whereas costs lower than incumbent fossil fuel sources are close but have not yet been achieved ("grid parity").[9] On the issue of falling costs, the uptake of REs is driven by a learning curve (or experience curve) of costs that are falling drastically. The case of solar PV power generation was discussed in Chapter 4, and the drastic declines in costs revealed in Figure 4.3. Wind power has shown similar cost reduction trends, if somewhat less intense. Because these systems are manufactured, the expectation is that learning curve effects will continue to drive down costs—to *below those of the incumbent fossil fuel technologies*. By contrast, costs for the fossil fuel and incumbent nuclear energy producers can be expected to rise, and to continue rising as the challenges and risks of securing supplies continue to mount while demand intensifies.[10]

On the pervasiveness of the carrier technology (and the generation of entrepreneurial opportunities), the RE^2 paradigm shift is already well advanced. The entrepreneurial and business openings are being created in the immediate sector of RE generation systems themselves (wind power generators, solar PV generators, concentrating solar power towers and linear arrays of lenses and mirrors), together with the supply chains that are created to feed these new end products; and then in associated business activities that utilize renewable energies as priority, such as electric vehicle charging systems and green buildings in cities; and finally in the range of totally new activities associated with renewables, such as new and smart grids, new metering systems, new energy storage systems, new transport systems such as electric vehicles (EVs) and their associated infrastructure (charging systems), new industrial heating systems utilizing concentrating solar power, new designs for "green cities"—and so on.[11]

For each new paradigm, there is coevolution between productive and finance capital. Specifically in the case of renewables and low-carbon technologies in the 2010s, one may see the role of finance in inventing new eco-targeted bonds (green bonds, or climate bonds), which can be expected to attract major institutional investors and to aggregate projects to the scale of index-oriented investment (Mathews and Kidney 2010, 2012). At the same time, it is necessary to acknowledge that the resistance posed by corporations and institutions associated with the fourth TEP (fossil fuels and centralization) is fierce, aptly characterized as carbon lock-in, and is actively slowing the diffusion of renewables and clean tech as a result.[12]

Despite these difficulties, the current surge in renewable energy and clean-tech investments and capacity additions is real and is having real socio-techno-economic effects—particularly in China and Germany, where its adoption is most intense.[13] It is the harbinger of a sixth TEP, with renewables as driving factor, in which we see the new paradigm emerging from its gestation phase and entering the installation phase, where finance capital is more daring than productive capital. If Perez is correct in her formulations, we can expect this RE^2 paradigm to blow out into a speculative financial bubble, which might be dated (according to previous sequencing) sometime in the period 2015–20. That gives the probability of several more years of booming RE investments, with the adoption of new systems moving along a logistic industrial trajectory to become, by the time of the bursting of the bubble, the new "conventional wisdom" in energy generation. This would pave the way to a true deployment phase of renewable energies and energy-service innovations, driven by investments in productive capital. It can be anticipated that China will be a leader in this transition.

Insights from Spectral Analysis of Long Waves

An intriguing empirical starting point is provided by the spectral analysis of long waves conducted by Andrey Korotayev with his collaborator Sergey Tsirel.[14] These Russian scholars analyze the current situation as moving in one of two different directions. The background to this analysis is provided by spectral analysis of the third, fourth, and fifth waves, as shown in Figure 7.2.

The Russian scholars interpret their reconstruction of the long waves, utilizing their spectral analysis, as revealing a strikingly consistent long-wave pattern, with a shortening of the wave period closer to the present time. The current period, which looks like the peaking of the fifth

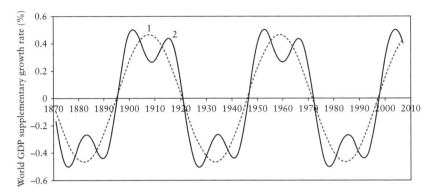

FIGURE **7.2**   Spectral analysis of Kondratiev waves, 1870–2010
SOURCE: Korotayev and Tsirel (2010). Used with permission.

K-wave, could indeed be such—and the global financial crisis of 2008–9 would be taken from this reading as the signal for the downturn. But the authors also offer an alternative and most intriguing reading—namely that the current period may be interpreted as a temporary depression between two peaks of the upswing. By extrapolation, they predicted (in 2010) that such a temporary upswing might begin around 2012–13 (i.e., already) and reach its maximum by 2018–20. The source of such a temporary upswing is left unsaid in their paper. What might it be?

Korotayev and Tsirel (2010) discount the role of communications and IT, which are thought to have exhausted their reserves of fast growth. One factor that they do point to is the acceleration of convergence (of East on West) through "acceleration of the diffusion of the extant high technologies to the populous countries of the World System periphery" (Korotayev and Tsirel 2010, 19)—of which China would have to be taken as prime exemplar, and in which green technologies would have to be identified as prime candidates. While expressing the appropriate caution, this does in fact seem to be the authors' implied candidate. However, there is also strong evidence that the more obvious interpretation, that world GDP had just gone through its K-wave peak, is also plausible. The authors conclude: "At the moment it does not seem to be possible to decide finally which of those two interpretations is true" (Korotayev and Tsirel 2010, 19–21). So their perspective is consistent with the idea that there will be a surge of finance-led investment in renewables and clean technology, accelerating through this decade and culminating in a bubble bursting between now and 2020.

In more general terms, the notion of clean tech as developed by Pernick and Wilder (2007) applies to the characteristics of the sixth TEP. Some forward-thinking consulting firms are also engaging with these issues. Merrill Lynch sees the shift to clean tech as involving both renewables and biotech, or more generally, the industrialization of natural resources. Likewise the Allianz report of 2012 views the sixth paradigm as being driven by clean tech, biotech, nanotech, and "holistic health care"—but the case is not made that these may be viewed as fundamental carrier technologies (not yet). Thus, these contributions focus on contingent features of the renewable energies technology surge and do not (as yet) add theoretical depth to the notion of TEP already formulated by neo-Schumpeterian scholars.[15]

The polymath author Jeremy Rifkin adopts a stance that is complementary to a sixth TEP in his concept of the third industrial revolution, based on renewable energies. In his 2011 book Rifkin identifies what he calls five pillars of this next industrial revolution, specifically (1) a shift to renewable energies; (2) the conversion of buildings into power plants (e.g., by solar panels); (3) the introduction of hydrogen and other energy storage technologies; (4) smart grid technology (Internet-based); and (5) plug-in, electric, hybrid, and fuel-cell transportation. Until recently, such views were considered utopian. Such a perspective is now supported by the emerging literature regarding renewables as providing an anticipated 100 percent replacement for fossil fuels within a reasonably short time frame, such as by around 2030.[16] Rifkin's five pillars are undoubtedly fundamental features of the current shift—as is a shift to energy-efficient and energy-saving innovations as an equally important feature of this fundamental transformation.[17]

So there is a notable coincidence of neo-Schumpeterian and other scholarly views, albeit starting from different premises and using different methodologies. All seem to be converging on the view that what is needed now is an accelerated diffusion of the technologies associated with low-carbon and renewable energy operations. There is no need to invent these technologies; they all exist. The issue is to diffuse them, and to do so in the fastest possible manner. How, then, can this best be accomplished?

Here is where we must recognize the role of strong state intervention to set the new trajectory in place.

Accelerated Diffusion of Innovations

Depending on the economic and intellectual framework adopted, there are different perspectives on the nature of the barriers to diffusion themselves and on the most efficient means for overcoming them. The contribution of mainstream (neoclassical) economics is to argue that the price differential between renewable energies and fossil fuels and fossil-fueled (thermal) power can be bridged by changing the cost structures with market-based instruments such as taxes (e.g., carbon taxes, fuel taxes), cap-and-trade schemes, or hybrids of the two. The Keynesian wing of neoclassical economics (now in full retreat everywhere after its brief renaissance during the 2008–9 global financial crisis) adds a role for government spending as a means to stimulate demand in certain desired directions, such as in creating markets for clean energy. The alternative neo-Schumpeterian approach (not to be confused with the pure market-oriented Austrian school) focuses on innovation as the real driver of change.[18] It calls for government promotion of the new sector through generic R&D, through government intervention in setting standards and building investment via procurement, and through subsidies and tax breaks for the new sectors (and dismantling existing subsidies for the old sectors). This is pretty much a description of the role that government played in the railroadization of the United States and other Western countries—except that it was not innovation as such, but the promotion of diffusion of innovations developed elsewhere, as well as homegrown innovations such as the union station and the Westinghouse air-brakes system.

In the twentieth century, one would have to say that the East Asian approach, which is by far the most effective approach today in actually building new "clean energy" industries and export sectors, is of this Schumpeterian kind, positioning the state as such, and state agencies, as leading players in mapping out and implementing the new shape of the economy. If global leadership and influence follow from achieving leadership in fundamental energy industries (as happened earlier for Britain,

Germany, and the United States), then one would have to predict a strong future for the East Asian industrial powers in the twenty-first century based on their mastery of the transition to a clean energy economy. This is the foundation of the historical convergence evident in trends in GDP, GDP per capita, and world trade—all discussed earlier. But again it has to be emphasized that it is not innovation as such, but the *diffusion of innovations* that is the central issue.

Building a new industry, particularly one that competes with an existing industry (as renewable and low-carbon technologies compete with fossil-fueled technologies and industries), calls for clear guidance and promotion along multiple dimensions. It is not a simple issue; it is in fact the greatest industrial challenge to be found today.[19] There is basic R&D expenditure along multiple lines of development, which leading countries like the United States and Japan can promote through multiple mechanisms involving technology procurement by both civilian and military authorities, as well as generic R&D funding via universities and national innovation laboratories. Then there is specific early-stage financing of innovation through such institutions as the US Small Business Innovation Research (SBIR) program. The challenge is to create not just new technologies but new systems, business models, and infrastructure.[20] But as fast as the lead countries patent their results and embody them in equipment and systems, they create opportunities for fast followers to license the innovations and purchase the equipment and utilize their own technology transfer and diffusion mechanisms to promote their own development.[21] This also includes multiple pathways, including foreign direct investment by multinational corporations (subject to strict technology transfer and local sourcing conditionality clauses), purchase of equipment, and the attraction of skilled personnel.

This is where the East Asian countries like Japan, Korea, and Taiwan excelled, in sectors such as electronics, memory chips, flat-panel displays, PCs, and IT. They are now utilizing the same approach in the case of clean energy and low-carbon technology industries, with China moving rapidly to a lead position.[22] What we are witnessing is a replication of the East Asian miracle, this time in a new set of green technologies and a new set of countries, with China at the head. If Taiwan's Hsinchu Science and Industrial Park is the exemplary case of such high-tech, fast-follower institutional support, with the public R&D institution the

Industrial Technology Research Institute (ITRI) playing a critical role, then it is being emulated and replicated many times over by China in the case of clean energy—as in the Suzhou Industry Park or the Tianjin Economic-Technological Development Area. In this way China is learning from its own experience and from the collective experience of its East Asian neighbors—and as a group, these countries are clearly proving to be strong competitors for the former leaders in Europe and the United States.

So the real driver of the capacity of emerging industrial giants such as China, India, and Brazil to take up and implement green technologies and systems will be their capacity to build and manage not just individual renewable energy systems and circular economy linkages but also *national systems for technology diffusion*. This means having institutions that scour the world to seek out new and promising technologies, institutional means to secure these technologies and transfer them to the home base, and capacity to diffuse the technology as fast as possible among domestic firms. What we see in China today, as well as in the other East Asian countries and their emulators, is an application to the renewables sector of policies of *fast-followership* that have been tried and tested in earlier experiences with electronics, semiconductors, and IT.[23]

Fast-Follower Strategies

Western think tanks such as the Information Technology and Innovation Foundation (ITIF) in the United States are in the process of developing sets of principles through which they see the United States building its clean energy industries of the future (but so far with scant evidence of success).[24] A better model, grounded in experience, would be the rapid scaling-up of wartime industries in the United States; for example, the automobile industry suspended production of private vehicles in April 1942 until the end of 1944, with wartime investment growing from a mere $1.9 billion in 1940 to $90.9 billion in 1944—equivalent to more than $1 trillion in 2010 dollars.[25]

Using these precedents, we may sketch principles that help to account for and explain the emergence and scaling up of new industrial powers—such as Taiwan's entry into PV solar cells, Korea's entry into the clean-tech sector, or China's entry into many such renewable energy sectors. Catch-up through deployment of fast-follower strategies is the common element. This is key to understanding what they are doing to acquire low-carbon and clean energy technologies and to build new manufacturing industries and value chains around them—and it is key to understanding how other developing countries will also behave as they too understand that the renewable energy revolution is within their grasp.

For example, fast followers look for industries in which there is growth potential and a dominant technology, where mass production can be implemented. Taiwan and Chinese solar PV firms have clearly focused on the dominant technology of crystalline silicon, which is mature, has reached mass production level, and is largely free of intellectual property constraints. Even in second-generation PV there is a new dominant technology led by thin-film semiconductor mixtures, of which CIGS may emerge as dominant.[26] And in the case of concentrating solar power, the molten-salt technology again looks likely to be dominant—and hence to be the target of sustained efforts at new industry construction in countries such as China and India and other fast followers. Similar considerations apply to wind power, where Chinese and Indian firms are introducing their own innovations—Goldwind in China introducing its own turbines equipped with permanent magnet direct drive (PMDD) technology, which eliminates the need for gearing, and Suzlon in India introducing the marketing innovation of providing full customer support along the entire value chain, including financing.

Likewise, fast followers strategize around various means of accessing the dominant technology—from winning contractual links with lead players to licensing technologies, purchasing equipment (even turnkey factories), and acquiring small technology-rich companies. This is an aspect of strategy that is mostly ignored in conventional discussions based on the behavior of established firms—but for latecomers and/or fast followers, strategy revolves around the critical issue of accessing technology in a reliable and rapid fashion. In the solar PV industry, Taiwan firms have accessed the dominant crystalline silicon technology through participating in programs of the national public research institute (ITRI) as well as through licensing and equipment purchase.

As a third example, fast followers cover the value chain as quickly as possible and build a cluster of complementary firms, promoting diffusion of capabilities—frequently clustered geographically such as in Hsinchu in Taiwan or Tianjin in China. The strategic goal is to build a complete industry, together with equipment and materials suppliers, in the shortest possible time.[27] Fast followers seek to reduce their costs through close relations with suppliers, which helps them overcome critical component shortages; supplier relations in particular are used to accelerate such capability enhancement, combined sometimes with a local content rule to force advanced firms into relations with new domestic suppliers. Fast followers in complementary fashion seek to promote local production of equipment as rapidly as possible, again to lower costs and promote complementarities that can grow into clusters.

Of course we can't all be fast followers—there will have to be leaders who take the risks (and rewards) of setting a new trend. But the rewards of leadership and innovation have been greatly exaggerated while the benefits of following closely and in timely fashion have been underrated. There is no need to legislate for innovation; it is a human characteristic to wish to innovate. But fast-followership calls for institutions and policies—as demonstrated clearly by East Asia's newly industrialized countries and now by China.

Supply-Side Acceleration: Logistic Industrial Dynamics

The adoption and diffusion of successive waves of technology follows a distinctive pattern, characterized by the familiar S-shaped curve, characteristic of logistic industrial dynamics. That means that the energy transition is highly likely to follow a similar course. This pattern can be seen in one industrial transition after another, as captured in Figure 7.3.

The chart shows no fewer than seventeen cases of industrial substitution under competitive conditions—exactly as holds now for renewable energy options, and will hold over the next crucial several decades. The pattern of substitution of steel production technologies over the past 150 years, for example, follows this pattern. It is these industrial dynamics that drive the learning curve, or experience curve—as discussed in Chapter 4, on renewable energies. The point is that these are not "natural" phenomena; they are social and economic phenomena that can be shaped and accelerated by sound policy. They enable us to anticipate the industrial dynamics of the supersession of fossil-fueled energy systems by renewable power.

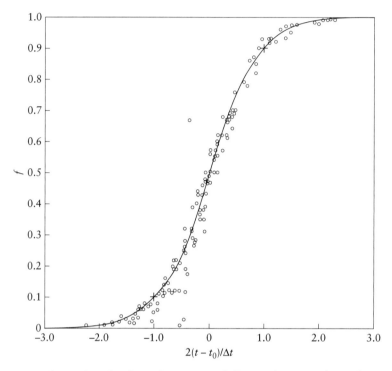

FIGURE **7.3**   Systemic technological transitions following logistic industrial dynamics

SOURCE: Fisher and Pry (1971). Used with permission.

Demand-Side: Accelerating Market Penetration

The fundamental aspect of the transition to new green sectors is that reduced costs drive rapid diffusion—and so cost reduction must be the highest policy priority. Diffusion of renewables and low-carbon, low-waste technologies is held back while their costs exceed fossil-fueled technologies and carbon-intensive products and processes. But as grid parity is approached, fundamental policies are needed to drive diffusion faster—to bring on and accelerate the "rapid adoption" phase of the logistic curve. This is where market mandates and direct support policies such as feed-in tariffs as well as government procurement play a significant role. I propose to call them examples of market-based incentives (MBIs)—in full knowledge of the fact that many economists use this term to indicate carbon taxes and cap-and-trade schemes. But these latter should properly be described as market-based *disincentives*, since they involve penalty payments designed to raise costs of industrial activities utilizing carbon. The only problem is that the evidence supporting the efficacy of such penalty payments is scant. After all, it is a matter of record that railroads came into their own in the nineteenth century without a tax on canals, or PC-based word-processing systems in the twentieth century without a tax on typewriters. It is a peculiar economists' fancy that taxes can drive uptake of a new system.

By contrast, what I am calling market-based incentives act directly on the economic system to provide a (declining) subsidy to users or early adopters of a new technology—in this case, green or clean-tech systems. They are aligned with well-proven economic incentives. Abundant experience indicates how these kinds of policies can work to speed up the process of diffusion of needed innovations.[28] Let me discuss two of them— market mandates and feed-in tariffs.

Market Mandates

Governments can play a powerful role in promoting a new sector simply by stating a target for substitution. This is now widely practiced— as in China's targets for electric power to be generated from renewable sources, Germany's targets announced in 2011 for adoption of renewable energies, and EU targets. Simply by making such a statement, and backing it with policies to make it credible, governments can reduce the risk and uncertainty associated with investing in the new sector. This is a powerful role that governments can and should play in facilitating the new.[29]

In Brazil, for example, market mandates for ethanol in the 1980s ensured that the transport sector became largely independent of imported petroleum; now in the twenty-first century it is moving to almost 100 percent adoption of "flex-fuel vehicles," which can run on any combination of ethanol or petrol. Under the Proalcool Program cane-based ethanol almost completely substituted for gasoline by the mid-1980s; but with falling oil prices, this situation was reversed, and ethanol had been almost completely eliminated by the mid-1990s. Then came flex-fuel vehicles— a Brazilian innovation of the early 2000s utilizing European technology. They had an immediate and dramatic impact on the automotive market in Brazil, rising from a standing start in 2003 to more than 80 percent of new vehicle sales by 2005.[30]

These achievements in Brazil were not the product of mere price manipulation or tax-induced changes; they were the outcome of steady innovation reflected in the learning curve for ethanol production, indicating how petroleum-parity was achieved in the early 2000s, as a result of relentless R&D support in Brazil, corporate R&D provided by the state-owned Petrobras, distribution and logistics supplied by Petrobras, and market mandates. Brazil's exports of sugarcane-based ethanol, which offer the world a ready transition to a post–oil transport sector, have been curtailed (deliberately) by high tariffs imposed on ethanol imports into both the European Union and the United States. Behind the scenes, Brazil was lobbying strongly to have these tariff barriers dismantled, on the grounds that they served the interests of narrow agricultural interests (corn farmers and conglomerates like Archer Daniels Midland) at the expense of millions of potential beneficiaries of lower ethanol prices. The lower prices based on lower costs were driven in Brazil by a relentless focus on R&D to improve efficiencies. In the end these arguments proved persuasive, and the United States announced at the end of 2011 that the subsidies would not be continued in 2012.[31] This was an important step toward the creation of a global free-trade market for sugarcane-based ethanol, complementing the existing free-trade regime that operates for petroleum and its products. All this was achieved because Brazil was prepared to use market mandates as the driving policy.

Market Expansion Through Consumer Support

Experience in Germany and Spain and elsewhere reveals how effective feed-in tariffs can be in promoting the uptake of renewable energies. These work by encouraging independent power producers to invest in REs and connect up to the grid, knowing that they have a guaranteed right to so connect (i.e., reducing the "freedom of contract" of the power producers to require them to accept renewable power) at a guaranteed tariff, or price. The subsidy involved is quite small, and it does not involve the tax system. Feed-in tariffs are actually very efficient policies in driving conversion to renewables when computed according to wattage generated per dollar expended.[32]

Feed-in tariffs have been shown to drive adoption wherever they have been implemented. They are a prime example of what I am calling market-based incentives, in that they work with markets, but on the basis of incentives rather than disincentives (such as taxes or charges). One has to ask, therefore, *why isn't the whole world adopting feed-in tariffs to drive renewables adoption?*[33] The answer must be that the world is aware of the benefits but through "carbon lock-in" is unwilling to let them compete on an equal footing—or in some cases, on any footing at all.

Feed-in tariffs have the advantage that they promote improvements in productivity, because they reward the improver, who continues to receive the mandated tariff. But this highlights at the same time an intrinsic weakness in feed-in tariffs—and that is that they do not build in cost improvements in graduated reductions of the tariff to be paid. The result of such lack of flexibility is that overpayments can be made, leading to declining political support for such policies. The answer is to build a down-escalator clause (also known as tariff degression) into the contracts, requiring the tariffs to decline by a certain amount each year (unless extraordinary circumstances call for change). This has been tried conscientiously in Germany, so far with good results. One might hazard the view that feed-in tariffs are an excellent way of providing graduated subsidy for renewable energy sources, driving their operation to the point of grid parity—and after that they can be withdrawn, having accomplished their purpose. Note that feed-in tariffs operate entirely on the demand side and do not involve in any way the public taxation system.

But good policies at one level can be undermined by poor policies at another, thereby slowing the rate of diffusion. While renewables promotion within Europe at country level through feed-in tariffs (as in Germany, and latterly in Spain and Italy until the policies were phased back) has generally been strong, the same cannot be said for the level of the European Union as a whole. While EU policy documents call for ever-growing contributions to energy supply from renewables (the famous goal of 20 percent by 2020) in practice, the means to achieve this goal turn largely on the creation of a pan-European, harmonized tradable green certificate (TGC) scheme. This would allow energy producers in one part of the European Union to refrain from making investments in renewable energy, to continue to burn coal, and to simply purchase TGCs instead from renewable power generators in Germany, Spain, and elsewhere (while no doubt lobbying to have TGCs distributed free of charge). This was bad enough. But then under pressure, the European Union changed the scheme at the last minute to allow member states to opt out of the pan-European TGC arrangements—thus almost certainly ensuring that some states would opt out and encourage their firms to buy up TGCs and in the process undermine the remaining feed-in tariff schemes. The result promises to be less than encouraging.[34] At the same time that feed-in tariffs are being undermined in the European Union (and not even tried in the United States, apart from isolated state-level initiatives), they are being advanced in China, initially on a small scale in certain key areas such as Tianjin to gain experience, with the clear intention of eventually rolling out the policy nationally.[35]

The Essential Role of Government

The transition to a green economy will not occur without strong state intervention—that much is clear. The point has already been made that if a new green growth capitalism is to be established in the emerging countries of China, India, and Brazil, and then in many other developed and developing countries as its practices prove their superiority in finding a balance between economic growth and environmental sustainability, then it has to be government led. This is necessary to break the carbon lock-in of vested interests and to create a new green growth trajectory. After the new pathway has been established, then the role of government can be allowed to diminish and entrepreneurial initiative allowed to flourish.

While the role of government has frequently been alluded to in Western discussions of climate change mitigation, this is usually taken to mean some draconian intervention such as putting curbs on fossil fuel consumption or imposing unpopular carbon taxes—policies that are frequently (tacitly) regarded as infeasible. This is essentially a defeatist approach to climate change. But in China, and increasingly in other emerging industrial countries, state intervention means, simply and straightforwardly, intervention to change the workings of the economy. It means, in effect, industry strategy—building new industries and allowing unwanted industries to waste away. This is a taboo subject that policy makers in the West associate with "picking winners" and other

supposedly undesirable practices (according to the neoclassical economists' playbook). But China has shown that industry policy is the necessary and feasible core of the approach to greening the economy—with
strong state intervention as its defining strategy.

Government Procurement as a Strategy to Accelerate Diffusion

One of the most powerful instruments ever devised to build markets for new sectors is government procurement, which acts not as a
consumer subsidy but a producer subsidy. And yet paradoxically—despite its widespread recognition as a powerful policy tool—government
procurement appears to have played only a small role (so far) in driving
the transition to a green economy. Indeed, the one time when it was seriously advocated in the United States, in the "turn" to solar power during
the turbulent decade of the 1970s, it was thoroughly dismembered and
dismantled in a way that can be attributed only to powerful fossil fuel
vested interests.

This is what happened. The Federal PV Utilization Program
(FPUP) was a program set up by Congress in 1978 as part of a raft of
support legislation promoting solar energy—and then dismantled, partly
by the Carter administration (despite its symbolic support for solar), and
then eliminated entirely by the incoming Reagan administration in 1981.
The possible scale of market promotion via government procurement was
outlined very clearly in the report of the task force on solar energy commercialization of the Federal Energy Administration (1977b), *Preliminary
analysis of an option for the Federal PV Utilization Program.*[36] Instead
of starting with PV devices and offering calculations based on their presumed capacity utilization improvement, the task force started with an
estimate of the market that could be created by federal procurement, then
estimated the cost reductions that could be anticipated to accrue over
the ensuing five years. This is after all the approach taken to new markets by any competent capitalist firm, which never estimates production
runs and costs on the basis of current market size, but on anticipated
market size, where cost reductions due to experience curves are factored
in. This is also the approach taken by the US military in a variety of procurement programs that have been put in place to create a commercial
market for certain desired products and technologies—such as the way

that government (military) procurement in the fledgling semiconductor industry helped establish firms such as Intel that later proclaimed their entrepreneurial independence. Industrial production of integrated circuits began in the United States in 1962, in response exclusively to Department of Defense (DoD) contracts; by 1968 production had expanded a thousandfold, and costs had reduced twentyfold, from $50 per chip to $2.50. In this way integrated circuits became cost effective in many commercial electronic applications, in addition to their primary military applications. This is a well-honed approach to market creation that has been utilized by the US federal government over and over.[37]

In the case of solar photovoltaics, the approach of the FEA task force was to follow the prior semiconductor example, attempting to promote a market for a specific kind of PV application first through government procurement, with a view to driving down costs so that other applications would then be triggered. The particular segment chosen was generator sets, to be supplied to the DoD to take the place of diesel-fired generators in remote locations, requiring long fuel supply lines that were vulnerable to attack. (It is ironic that this is one of the principal applications being pursued now by the US Armed Forces, three decades later, after suffering increasing casualties in defending oil supply lines in Iraq and Afghanistan.) To this end the task force concluded an interagency agreement with the US Army Mobility Equipment R&D Command to analyze the potential market for such PV generator sets. A preliminary survey indicated that up to one-fifth of the existing diesel-powered generator sets could be replaced by PV units generating 152 MW of power.[38] A twentyfold cost reduction was envisaged over a five-year period, resulting from a "trigger" of a 152 MW government procurement order, designed explicitly to expand the market.[39]

Of course these were wildly ambitious proposals, and the envisaged cost reductions were perhaps unrealistic. But the proposals were never allowed to work or develop their full potential. Instead, the proposals were watered down and killed off. The Federal PV Utilization Program (FPUP) was launched in 1978, but it was not considered part of the National Energy Plan that had been released in 1977, and President Carter himself made a statement to the effect that government procurement would not be considered as a relevant strategy for the US renewable energy program. The purchase plan eventually implemented was budgeted at $98 million (in place of the $400 million envisaged by the task force), and in practice only $25 million of this was actually expended (Hart 1983). The program effectively ran for only two years; it was quickly wound up (down) by the incoming Reagan administration, which saw its energy priorities lying elsewhere.

And so died the most ambitious, farsighted, and potentially most effective program for rapidly building up a solar PV sector that had been developed—up to that point. With hindsight we can see what actually happened to PV cell costs as the learning curve unfolded over the 1980s, 1990s, and 2000s (see Figure 4.3). A more realistic estimate of cost reduction potential might have been a tenfold decline over ten years—but this in itself would have been a major boost to solar PV market prospects and would have triggered technological developments across the electric power sector, both in the United States and abroad. More to the point, had the proposals been acted on they would have had the effect of creating a substantial solar power industry in the United States that would have counteracted the swing back to fossil fuels in the 1980s and the country's increasing dependence on oil imports from Saudi Arabia and the Middle East—and thus lessening the risk of a "9/11 attack" by disaffected Saudi nationals and perhaps the Iraq War. And a stronger US solar industry would have spawned competitors and been able to fully compete with the cost-focused solar industry eventually developed by China. All of this remains speculative because the federal program that would have triggered such a development was stillborn, doubtless because of backroom lobbying by the fossil fuel industry.[40]

Instead, the lead passed to Germany. It was Hermann Scheer and his Social Democrat colleagues working in political cooperation with the Greens in Germany who devised in the late 1980s and 1990s an alternative approach, utilizing feed-in tariffs, culminating in the Renewable Energy Sources Act of 2000.[41] Because of political constraints, the German Social Democratic Party was never able to give serious consideration to the use of government procurement as an industry-building strategy in their own country. This remains the development strategy of choice in the United States, as revealed by impartial studies (e.g., Weiss and Thurbon 2006) of multiple industries, including integrated circuits, aircraft, and many other sectors. But the fossil fuel lobby clearly intervened to ensure that government procurement was never allowed to work its magic in the case of solar PV. Instead, the United States has had to wait another three decades to see PV expand to anything like its potential in a sun-soaked continent, and it is still by no means clear that the United States will ever embrace the full potential of solar PV, as leadership in the industry now passes to China and Germany (and probably Japan). The difference is that China is promoting renewable energy industries (with an eye to their export potential), whereas other countries have promoted renewables markets through consumer subsidies; it is becoming clear which has been the most successful strategy.[42]

Overcoming Olsonian Obstacles

The reason that capturing the transition to a clean-tech economy as a shift in techno-economic paradigm is so important is that it brings the focus onto the process of diffusion (where it belongs) rather than on innovation. The technologies needed for the shift to renewables (wind power, solar PV, concentrating solar) have all been invented, and many are already out of patent protection.[43] The process of diffusion depends on the speed with which new industries producing the new technologies can be built and new markets for utilizing them can be created. There is no other pathway that ensures a fundamental shift in the pattern of technoeconomic supply and demand.

From a political vantage point, the key to seeing the green sector of the economy expand, and to weaken the political opposition from traditional energy and commodities firms, is to build and strengthen the capitalist entrepreneurial sector that sees its future in such a sector. This is precisely what was achieved in the case of the *Renewable Energy Sources Act* in Germany, as the system of feed-in tariffs created new entrepreneurial opportunities for promoters of renewable energy projects—effectively splitting the economic opposition to renewables. Likewise in China, the twin Renewable Energy Law and Circular Economy Promotion Law are achieving a similar result, opening up "economic space" for entrepreneurial opportunities that previous energy orthodoxy had suppressed.[44]

Thus, the transition to a new energy and resource trajectory will not be accomplished simply by applying well-tried strategies of promotion of the new; it will also involve the dismantling of the obstacles and vested interests that stand in the way. Olson (1982) argued that in a

democracy the incumbent interests will always use their political influence to block the emergence of new markets or industries, and the energy
sector certainly shows plenty of examples of this—from subsidies paid
out (even more than a hundred years after their enactment, such as to
support new rig drilling) to the protection of existing infrastructure and
the blocking of policy initiatives to favor the new (e.g., feed-in tariffs,
which are still not operated at the federal level in the United States). Apart
from the huge subsidies that continue to be paid to fossil fuel producers
(dwarfing anything paid to renewable energy producers), there are legal
and administrative hurdles that deliberately protect the status quo. In
the United States, for example, monopolistic centralized power generators are protected not just by tax laws and regulatory barriers but even
by legislative fiat, such as by laws enacted to forbid independent electric
power generators from selling power via the grid or from setting up private transmission systems (e.g., forbidding them from setting up wires
that cross public streets). Whatever flimsy justification there might have
been for such laws in the early years of electric power generation, they are
utilized now as nothing more than a device to block independent power
producers using renewable sources from selling their excess power.[45]

Here we see the point of a public commitment on the part of governments in favor of a new default option in the form of renewables and
resource efficiency, so that such legislative, administrative, and regulatory
barriers can be dismantled without always meeting Olsonian obstacles.

Mandated Renewables Trajectories and State Coordination

Think tanks in the West like ITIF are arguing that no one can stand
up to Chinese mercantilist policies, which promote standardized products
at the expense of innovative new ventures competing in market niches.
Is China really the ogre that is destroying "the global energy innovation
ecosystem"?[46]

There would appear to be some prima facie support for such an
argument when we look at US and EU companies that have been developing innovative new solar PV cells but that succumbed to Chinese competitive pressures in the years 2011-2012. Solyndra in the United States
had to declare bankruptcy, and German Q-Cells had to sell off its CIGS
subsidiary, Solibro—with the Chinese power producer Hanergy snapping

up the firm. These are two cases in which the firms were developing new CIGS thin-film solar cells that would operate at slightly lower efficiencies but with much lower material costs, thereby promising decisive cost advantages. The promise of these kinds of solar cells was undermined by Chinese mass production of first-generation crystalline-silicon solar cells; the Chinese drove down the costs of the standardized products so fast that the newer, lower-cost CIGS cells never had a chance to establish themselves.

Chinese support for renewables is determined, serious, and sustained. This support is being pursued not primarily for reasons to do with climate change but as a national energy security policy, to allow China to build its energy system without impinging on other countries' fossil fuel entitlements and thereby threatening war. It is a smart strategy that suits China. So how, then, should other countries respond?

The United States provides one way forward, by seeking to curb Chinese activities overseas and imposing trade sanctions (penalty tariffs) on Chinese-made imports of solar cells into the United States. The European Union for its part has been threatening even broader sanctions, not just on PV cells but on modules and whole systems as well. Such tariffs are designed to curb sales of China-made products abroad—but the instrument is rather blunt and is already being circumvented by smart Chinese companies that are building their manufacturing base in the United States and that are globalizing their production activities and importing solar cells into the United States from non-mainland Chinese sources (e.g., Taiwan). Moreover, the Chinese are perfectly able to impose countertariffs on US exports of high-value PV components and materials, including pure-grade silicon (for which the United States currently runs a trade surplus with China). These unanticipated consequences are likely to make the trade sanctions relatively ineffective while incurring severe displeasure from China, for which there will be a political price to pay.

The European Union has provided a different competitive strategy, in which the European market for solar PV systems was expanded through consumer subsidies, notably feed-in tariffs—in the expectation that German manufacturing industries would expand to supply the market. As a market expansion strategy it worked extremely well, allowing firms to benefit from cost reductions via the learning curve. But of course it turned out that it was Chinese firms that were the main beneficiaries—

in the absence of specific German industrial policies designed to grow the market in Germany for German-owned and designed PV technologies. Since Germany's swing against nuclear power in 2011–12 there has in fact been a revival of German industrial policies designed to boost what is left of the solar PV cell manufacturing sector—with (so far) positive results.

There is only one effective response to the serious competitive threat posed by China's strong support for renewables—and that is equally strong support for innovation and market expansion by Western countries. While China targets well-established and standardized technologies for rapid scaling up and diffusion (e.g., first-generation crystalline solar PV cells), and does so very effectively, other countries can place reasonable curbs on China's imports (regulating them so that they remain below a certain threshold, in line with WTO stipulations) while actively supporting and building innovative alternatives to China's standardized products.

To continue with the CIGS case (alluded to earlier, involving Solyndra, Q-Cells, and others), it was open—and still is open—to US, EU, and Japanese government policies to rapidly build the market for new, thin-film CIGS solar cells (through producer subsidies and government procurement, both allowable under WTO rules), thereby ensuring that they would achieve cost reductions that would keep them ahead of their first-generation crystalline-silicon alternatives. If the market for CIGS cells grows fast enough, then CIGS technology will become the new dominant technology, with German, US, and Japanese firms already occupying a strong position and able to tweak the technology to drive further improvements. Of course, Chinese firms would then switch to this new, dominant CIGS technology, driving costs and prices down as they do so—and so weaker German, US, and Japanese firms would be driven from the market. But stronger ones would maintain their position, particularly in supplying their domestic market, while they ramp up further innovative variations. And so the process will continue, from one technology generation to another. And eventually, of course, Chinese firms will be innovating as fast as anyone else.

The question, then, has to be asked: Why don't the US, German (EU), or Japanese governments pursue such an obvious counter to the Chinese competitive onslaught? In a word, because they are afraid of any intervention smacking of "industry policy." So powerful has become the neoclassical objection to doing anything connected with promotion of some specific technology (i.e., picking winners) and promotion of market expansion through government procurement (i.e., market interference) that policy makers are now afraid to propose anything along these lines—leaving the field wide open to the Chinese, who suffer from no such inhibitions. This is the great, unanticipated consequence of the West's turn to neoclassical ideologies—pushing privatization, deregulation, and so on, and outlawing anything to do with industry policy. Why this was allowed to happen is another (and very interesting) story.

Think tanks like the Information Technology and Innovation Foundation, based in Washington, DC, valiantly struggle to portray "innovation" as the only way forward and provide support for trade sanctions under the guise that Chinese policies are "mercantilist" (and yet are no more so than those pursued by individual US states like California). In effect, they argue for "stateless innovation" as a counter to China.[47] My argument would lead instead to a full-blooded counter to Chinese targeted industry promotion, through countertargeting of new, innovative technologies and deliberate and determined market expansion via instruments such as public procurement by government. Then we would really see a flourishing of US (and other advanced) renewable energy industries.

There is a clear conclusion to this discussion. *There is no alternative* to the efficacy of state action in setting out the new rules through which energy markets, resources, and commodities markets and markets for finance and capital will have to work. These new rules will establish state-mandated renewables trajectories, and these in turn will liberate entrepreneurial energies to create new firms, and redirect old firms, to achieve the new objectives. It is quite unrealistic to expect new trajectories within capitalism to emerge spontaneously—as seems to be imagined by advocates of free-market environmentalism or "stateless innovation." But once the new trajectories are enforced—mandated, legislated, regulated—then entrepreneurial energies can be allowed to flourish, as indeed they will.

The emergence of a green economy will be systemic, its parts interacting with one another, and it will call for a new "green economics" that is less obsessed with GDP and the costs of transition, and more concerned with the process of moving from one paradigm to another. As alluded to in the introduction to this book, mainstream economics has little to teach concerning a real and important development like the emergence of the green economy because of its intrinsic limitations and blindness—couched as it is in terms of linear rather than circular flow processes, concerned as it is with static equilibrium (even in dynamic models) rather than with evolutionary stable states that can be achieved through eco-industrial initiatives, and avoiding any direct engagement with its ecological setting other than indirectly through notions like market failure and externalities. So we finally turn to the question, what kind of economic analysis would be called for by the transition to a green economy? How will the green economy actually work?

8   From Green Economy to Green Economics

Life sets the rules, Life is more important than our industrial civilization, and Life will continue without us if we drive ourselves to destruction. So what are Life's rules? What are the rules by which a planetary industrial civilization like ours may expect to continue and flourish without irreparably harming itself and its ecological niche?

> —*Ellen LaConte,* Life Rules *(2010)*

When the watermark hits the Plimsoll line, the boat is full, it has reached its carrying capacity. . . . The major task of environmental macroeconomics is to design an economic institution analogous to the Plimsoll mark—to keep the weight, the absolute scale of the economy from sinking our biospheric ark.

> —*Herman Daly and Kenneth Townsend,* Valuing the Earth:
> Ecology, Economics, Ethics *(1992)*

To equate the economic process with a mechanical analogue implies, therefore, the myth that the economic process is a circular merry-go-round which cannot possibly affect the environment of matter and energy in any way. The obvious conclusion is that there is no need for bringing the environment into the analytical picture of that process.

> —*Nicolae Georgescu-Roegen, "Energy and economic myths"*
> *(1975)*

To make sense of the strands of history, it is vital to distinguish between industrialization, capitalism, modern economic growth, *intensive* and *extensive* growth, and economic development.

> —*Eric Jones,* Growth Recurring *(1988)*

Humanity has the ability to make development sustainable—to ensure that it meets the needs of the present without compromising the ability of future generations to meet their own needs.

> —*David W. Pearce,* Blueprint for a Green Economy (1989)

Through concepts like Gaia, we now understand how living systems have shaped the planet that we call home. Living systems survive over millions of years because they are selected out of a bewildering variety of alternatives to do so; the populations that survive over such long evolutionary periods are the ones that are most robust and resilient (as first understood by Darwin). And living systems, it is now understood, utilize the cellular, or modular, organizational principle in preference to all others. They do so, as Herbert Simon was able to explain so well, because it is the organizational principle that is best adapted for accelerating the creation of new life forms, via a pool of intermediate forms or stable subassemblies. Simon captured the impact of these different arrangements in his famous parable of the two watchmakers, Tempus and Horus, with their differing productivities.[1] The point of the story is that complex systems evolve out of simpler systems, where the simple systems themselves are also "wholes" that have evolved out of systems that are even simpler, and so on. This is indeed the way that biological evolution works. It is also the way that the capitalist economy works, when it is allowed to express itself—as firms build networks and clusters with other firms, and as these clusters combine to create industries earning increasing returns.[2]

A revolution in economic thinking is called for to match the revolution in economic practice implied by the new RE^2 default options discussed in the previous chapters. A promising starting point for a sustainable economics is to begin then with the biological features that we call *biomimesis*, or the imitation of nature. Just as Herbert Simon appealed to biological evolution as the testing ground for modular structures, so we may view the same process as a testing ground for powerful models of how an economy must work if it is to be sustainable. This makes sense, because not only are our economic and technological systems part of nature; evolution provides us with a robust set of models that have stood the test of survival over millennia.[3]

My suggestion is that the ideal of the biomimetic economy needs to be brought to the foreground in public debate, in place of notions like natural capital and zero growth. Insisting that economic patterns of behavior mimic those laid down over millions of years by successful life forms, and that the economy coevolve with its ecological setting, would represent a total conceptual rupture with the linear-thinking and extensive-growth-fixated kind of economics that got us into the business-as-usual mess.

Biomimesis provides a theoretical setting within which the notion developed in industrial ecology of interconnections between firms that turn wastes or by-products from one process into inputs for another process makes abundant sense. If this is extended to encompass energy, materials, and water, so that these fundamental constituents are seen as providing the ecological matrix within which the economy develops, then we are well on the way to a "strong" version of sustainability, and thereby to biomimesis.[4] We can generalize these ideas with a notion of *ecological* economics. By this is meant "the science and management of sustainability" (Costanza 1991). It is an approach to economics that abstains from the traditional framework, which treats economic categories as standing apart from ecology, and from the habitual reductionism of economistic thinking in favor of transdisciplinary synthesis.[5] Before we embark on an exploration of green economics, however, there is a "false start" that we need to deal with—and that is the notion of natural capital.

The False Charm of the Concept of Natural Capital

There is a long tradition of biophysical economic reasoning that goes back at least to the physiocrat school that flourished in the eighteenth century in France, prior to the Industrial Revolution, and had a powerful influence on Adam Smith and his 1776 *Wealth of Nations*. Biophysical economics works with a conceptual model that views the economy as connected to, and sustained by, a flow of energy, materials and ecosystem services (Cleveland 1999). Much of the biophysical literature is concerned with the systemic (thermodynamic) influence of energy on the operations of the economy (e.g., building a theory of value grounded in energy), with the evolutionary justification that those communities that learn to economize best on energy throughput are the ones most likely to survive. But much of it is also concerned with the identification and valuation of eco-services provided by nature—conceived as "natural capital."

It is a beguiling idea to construct an argument for better planetary maintenance and eco-efficient economic arrangements in terms of a notion of living within our natural capital. The idea is basically that we have a certain amount of "capital" bequeathed to us by nature (i.e., by the biosphere), and it is our obligation as a species to live within this capital—that is, to live off its "interest" by harvesting energy and resources in a way that does not deplete the capital. As a general principle, no one would disagree with such a proposition; interpreted as a source of ecosystem services, it is consistent with the most sophisticated definition of economic income, provided by Hicks in *Value and Capital* (1939/1946), to the effect that income should be interpreted as the maximum amount that a community can consume over some time period and still be as well off at the end of the period as at the beginning.[6] Every small business owner understands perfectly the need to live within one's capital and to "harvest" it through income derived from activities based on the capital, without depleting it. In the case of a business, the capital is clearly demarcated, in the form of initial capital fund (equity or loan capital) and initial stock; one item can be substituted for another, through the prices attached to various capital items. The whole of business works according to these basic principles.

But as soon as we seek to transfer this model across to the planet and the biosphere, basic problems present themselves. In the first place, the model of substitution, which underpins the idea of capitalization of a business, cannot be extended too far in the case of the biosphere. Some neoclassical economists apply their equilibrium-based models and production functions to the biosphere, by including an item called "natural capital" in the production function; they then simply extend *assumptions* of substitutability to this item. They end up claiming that there is no ecological crisis because manufactured capital can always be substituted for natural capital.[7] Clearly this is not what popularizers of the notion of natural capital like Hawken, Lovins, and Lovins (1999) have in mind.

A more realistic approach is to use the concept of natural capital as a benchmark for maintaining an intact source of *ecosystem services*.[8] Pearce and Turner (1989) pioneered this approach; they insisted that the goal of any environmentally responsible economic analysis should be to keep natural capital intact (which is indeed how they define economic sustainability). How do they define natural capital? Actually, they do not provide a clear definition, but they seem to equate it with the "stock of environmental resources"—leaving the measurement issue unresolved.[9] The fundamental issue, namely that all the resource stocks on which life on our planet depend are so variegated and heterogeneous that they defy summation through any practicable index number (including price), is still left unresolved. As Victor (1991, 203) puts it in an insightful review of these issues: "If the standing stock of timber increases at the same time as the deposits of natural gas decrease, how can it be determined whether the stock of natural capital has risen, fallen or stayed the same?" Indeed—I don't believe that anyone has come up with an answer to this unanswerable question raised by the natural capital approach.

Apart from these kinds of difficulties, raised in an already-extensive critical literature, there are further problems with the idea of natural capital as framing a strategy for building an environmentally responsible economy. In the world constructed by economics, there are producers and consumers. The producers supply factors of production such as capital or labor, and in return for these services, they receive income (wages in the case of labor, interest for capital). These incomes are then distributed and spent by the consumers—creating a (static) circular flow of incomes that reproduces itself in time period after period. So we have to ask, if this is the model being utilized, what is the income received by "natural capital"? The traditional answer would be the income received by the owners of the capital (land), namely landlords. But most natural capital is not privately owned—and there are good reasons for wanting to maintain this situation and not privatize resources held as community assets, such as eco-services from tropical forests. Natural capital *as a concept* simply adds further confusion to this already-confusing landscape—particularly if it is taken to refer to the entire global commons.

A further problem is that the concept of natural capital fits snugly into the traditional production function, purportedly bringing the biosphere into the ambit of neoclassical economic reasoning—but at the cost of imposing the linear "resources in, waste out" mode of thinking on an entity that is clearly cyclical in character. While purporting to bring "nature" into the realm of economic reasoning, the concept of natural capital actually imposes a wholly unrealistic mode of representing economic processes from the econosphere to the biosphere.[10]

All these issues surface with greater urgency in the debates over how to construct a "green GDP" as measure of environmental performance of the economy. I have no wish to diminish these efforts; indeed, they are essential. Green accounting is identified as one of the axioms that would define a green economy (in the final chapter). But it remains the case that a concept of natural capital, with the related notions of ecosystem services and "green GDP," present perhaps insuperable measurement problems—or rather, what is involved is an attempt to measure entities that are inherently immeasurable (such as the eco-services that bees provide in pollinating crops). It would be better to formulate the issue from a different starting point, such as circularity. So the proposal to regard natural capital as a factor of production is unlikely to provide a foundation for a comprehensive ecological economics analysis of sustainability—despite having merit and inspiring much recent analytical work in the search for measures of green GDP. My own preference (and recommendation) is to utilize the notion of *biomimesis* and frame measures of progress in terms of developments toward a *circular economy*. This is a quite different and more direct and fruitful approach.

An Ecological Perspective

While recognition of the disastrous consequences on the planetary environment of the scale of industrial activities (carbon emissions, resource spoliation, waste generation, and dumping) is mounting, this recognition is nevertheless hampered by the conceptual framework utilized in mainstream economics. This is one of the key sources of our inability to clearly recognize the divorce of the economy from its natural or ecological setting. The shift in worldview between the neoclassical approach to economics and the ecological economic view is depicted in Figure 8.1. In Figure 8.1a the neoclassical focus is on the "circular flow" of income, divorced from its ecological matrix.[11]

Figure 8.1a shows the way that mainstream economic analysis envisages the economy: with an inner flow of resources and materials (flowing clockwise) and an outer circular flow of income (shown moving counterclockwise). The income is generated by activities that impinge on natural flows of resources, conceptualized as reduction in natural capital. Through substitution, it is usually assumed that these income flows can be generated indefinitely.

An alternative approach that recognizes the limits that ecological processes place on economic activity, shown in Figure 8.1b, starts with these ecological limits themselves, placing them as a barrier within which economic activities take place. This inversion of the way of conceptualizing

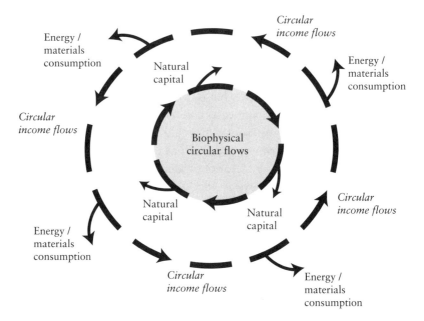

FIGURE **8.1a**   Neoclassical view of the economy in relation to nature
SOURCE: Mathews and Tan.

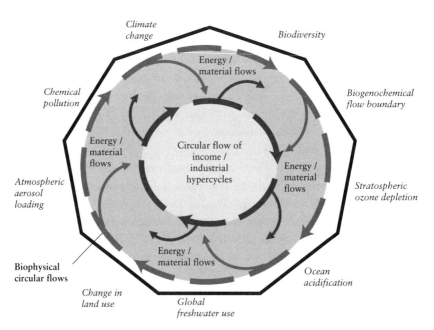

FIGURE **8.1b**   Biomimetic economy, recognizing natural limits
SOURCE: Mathews and Tan.
NOTE: Planetary boundaries based on Rockström et al. (2009).

the economy is all-important in making for practical changes in the rules under which capitalist markets operate. The shift in conception is exhibited in Figure 8.1b, where the *ecological processes are primary* and are depicted as an octagonal set of barriers or limits (following the characterization of the operating space within which the economy may be envisaged, as presented by Rockström and colleagues [2009] in *Nature*). The economy operates within this space—but it is now envisaged not as a static flow of income, but as sequences of value-adding activities, from one firm to another, in value chains. Where these value chains link up with each other, closing the circle, we may describe them as industrial hypercycles.

The point of these two depictions is that the neoclassical view sees natural resources as entering economic analysis only as factors of production (land, or generalized as natural capital) and not exercising any constraint on economic activity, whereas the ecological perspective sees the biospheric cycles as primary and economic activities as being constrained by these cycles. From the latter perspective, economic activities are characterized in terms of the circular flow of income (at the micro level) and *industrial hypercyles* (at the macro level); the energy and material flows into and out from the economy form part of the biophysical circular flows.[12] The most recent scientific view of our breaching the planet's carrying capacity (going beyond the ecological economic Plimsoll line, as Daly [1996] memorably put it) is that provided by Rockström and colleagues (2009).[13] Such an approach, in mapping a safe operating space for humanity, clearly sets the limits beyond which the economy (as a self-contained system) might not be permitted to expand.

Ever since Holling (1973) introduced the idea of resilience of ecosystems, as being a state that could react to unexpected shocks and bounce back to its main dynamics, the focus of ecological studies has been in delineating the contours of such resilience and its sources. Holling himself has gone on to draw implications for other complex systems, notably the economy, and formulated a general adaptive cycle that moves through several phases as complex systems like economies and ecologies respond to shocks.[14] But how does a "steady state" fit with this conception?

The Contested Concept of the Steady State

For more than three decades Herman Daly has been one of the key sources of thinking about how a green economy can work. His main

critique was developed as a young man and was directed at the fool-
ish assumptions that underpin the neoclassical notion of endless growth,
with resource scarcity being circumvented by capital substitution.[15] Out
of this critique came the concept of the steady-state economy (taken over
from the nineteenth-century British political economist John Stuart Mill),
and first clearly formulated in 1973.[16] In his next published paper, presented to the American Agricultural and Applied Economics Association,
"The economics of zero growth," Daly (1972) presented a much more
ambitious assault on the conventional wisdom that foresaw endless exponential growth of the economy against a finite resource base—an evident logical and physical impossibility. Rather than repeat the arguments
in favor of considering a steady-state economy, on this occasion Daly
(1972, 945) set himself the task of demolishing the arguments advanced
by the "growth-maniacs"—or as he put it more delicately, "by those
who remain committed to the orthodox growth paradigm." One source
of confusion is the measure of GDP itself—which as he says, is "a value
index of a quantity produced. It is overwhelmingly an index of physical
throughput." To maximize the throughput flow in and for itself is evidently absurd—and yet this is what mainstream economists were doing
then and *continue to do now.*

This is a body of work that positively cries out for rebuttal from the
economics mainstream. Yet to my knowledge, not a single esteemed member of the economics establishment has ever deigned (or dared) to cross
swords with Daly. The critique remains devastating in its effectiveness—
but spinning in the air, unable to engage with the processes of academic
research and scholarship. Daly has continued to develop this critique, coin-
ing new phrases like the "Plimsoll line" of the economy as characterizing its
carrying capacity, which is not to be exceeded—but basically the critique
stands as it was framed and presented, in the six-year period 1968–74.
Subsequent scholars who argue along similar lines, like Jackson (2009),
can do little more than reiterate Daly's points, albeit in updated form.[17]

It is not my intention to cast doubt on Daly's work, as it is self-
evidently sound in its basic reasoning. There is no getting around the fact
that the economy will have to eventually converge on a material steady
state, in alignment with ecological cycles. The issue is, what is most likely
to move us in that direction and provide the most analytical insight? This
is where I wish to present an alternative perspective.

Daly's approach has not changed much in three decades of exposition (for why change something that is so good?), but it does not seem to have encouraged further analytic work and research. Taken at face value, the steady state is an end point and not a process. But the transition to a green economy cries out for some analytical insight into how the process will be accomplished and what specifically will be the capitalist economic processes that bring us—eventually—to a steady state. And in the meantime, there are the cases of China, and India, and many other countries, now clamoring for their turn to experience growth. How are they to be accommodated in the "steady-state" paradigm, other than by being excluded?

This is why I believe we need a different starting point (but not a different end point) from the steady state. In this book I utilize the notion of the circular economy as such a starting point for an alternative green economics, employing concepts like green growth based on increasing returns—a quintessentially capitalist notion.

The Relevance and Feasibility of Green Growth: Propagating the Green Shoots

For all the lip service paid to growth by economists, its underlying processes are scandalously underresearched and underanalyzed. In mainstream terms growth has conventionally been equated to expansion in gross domestic product (GDP), measured in terms of throughput of resources—and in this form it has quite correctly drawn strong criticism from those economists looking for an alternative.[18] But there have always been heterodox schools of thought on the origins and processes of economic growth—and now the greening of the economy promises to bring these under the spotlight.

Green Growth

The concept of green growth puts two apparently opposed categories together—green, signifying "sustainability," and growth, signifying "expansion" (interpreted as expansion of resource throughput). As such, putting a green complexion on destructive activities creates a paradox. But what if we subverted these terms to give them a fresh interpretation?

What if we interpreted *green* to mean an economy in which RE^2 innovations are creating new business opportunities, driving Schumpeterian creative destruction of the old, fossil fuel economy—as opposed to an economy focused on preservation of a mythical "nature"? And what if we interpreted "growth" not as expansion of resource flows but as increases in income captured through increasing returns generated by manufacturing? This provides a potentially sound and feasible way forward—one that is consistent with a business spirit of entrepreneurial and competitive dynamics and with capitalist processes of business growth that can be maintained on a stable resource foundation.[19]

Let us first take a capitalist or business perspective on the emergence of a green economy. The new "green shoots" can be expected to propagate themselves through the entire economy via interfirm linkages and value chains, particularly in clusters and eco-industrial parks. As one firm seeks advantage through claiming a commitment to reducing its carbon footprint and insists on similar commitments from its suppliers, who in turn will insist on such commitments from their suppliers, so the new green standards will propagate via competitive emulation. A printing firm, for example, may seek competitive advantage as a low-carbon operation, insisting that its paper suppliers adhere to international standards certifying that papers are not sourced from old-growth forests, or certifying that all paper is sourced from recycled materials; and likewise with its suppliers of printing plates, and inks, insisting that they too meet standards of reduced resource impact that will propagate through the economy. This is what Myrdal and Kaldor were referring to when they used the phrase "circular and cumulative causation" to characterize the way a modern sector could be established in a developing economy, for example in a particular region, where each investment builds on previous investments and in turn creates conditions for the next investment. Now we can resort to the same terminology to describe the emergence and propagation of a green sector within the modern capitalist economy. Kaldor was at pains to point to the fact that what drove such propagation was the search for increasing returns, which are achieved as more and firms become interconnected. Again we can therefore pose the search for increasing returns as the driver of firms' green initiatives—and thus as a solution to the problem as to whether the green economy can grow while maintaining a constant resource base.

Circular and Cumulative Causation

The notion of circular and cumulative causation seems to have dropped out of the economics lexicon. It was last used with any seriousness by Kaldor to help explain why some regions developed quickly and effectively while others languished.[20] But the concept is too valuable to allow it to languish in the museum of discarded ideas—alongside the *big push* and other elements of developmental economics of the immediate postwar years. The emergence of the green economy from the womb of the brown, fossil fuel economy is the new, twenty-first-century setting in which these ideas may be applied with vigor—and, one hopes, with rigor as well, when taken up by young scholars skilled in the use of new techniques such as agent-based modeling.

The green economy can be expected to grow and propagate within the womb of the fossil fuel economy, through multiple interfirm connections and their capacity to collectively generate increasing returns (reducing costs and improved productivity). Small islands will start (as in eco-industrial parks), and they will then make connections with other firms and with each other, always through insistence on reducing resource and carbon intensity in their transactions. In this way the islands will link up to form archipelagos and eventually come to dominate the entire economy. Connections will be made between firms that are not necessarily close to each other, forming "virtual" eco-industrial parks and sustainable supply-chain networks.[21] The new system that is emerging can be expected to come to fruition first in China and India and then in the rest of the world by the mid-twenty-first century (i.e., within the next half-century). It is in China that the principle of a circular economy has been adopted as a national development goal, emphasizing multiple eco-linkages between firms as the wastes of one firm become the inputs for another firm.[22] As these linkages propagate, they generate circular flows of resources and materials, in emulation of the great flows of materials through the natural world. Indeed, from the perspective of industrial ecology the two processes are deeply interpenetrated. In this way the green economy will have to become more of a *biomimetic economy*—if it is to survive. A vivid illustration would be provided by the ancient game of Go, in which the players start with isolated stones and build up structures through interconnections (adjacent stones) and then eventually join them up so that they reinforce each other. It is the interconnections that lend strength; for an illustrative sequence, see Figure 8.2.

This is exactly the process we see in the formation of eco-industrial parks and their drive to create interconnections with each other, drawing more and more firms into their ambit and measuring their progress in reducing energy and resource intensity. Take some examples from China. In the eco-industrial park of Suzhou, there are multiple interconnections forming, with firms sharing some inputs and sharing some outputs, thus reducing overall resource intensity.[23] Overall the firms in the park are notching up environmental performance standards that are vastly supe-

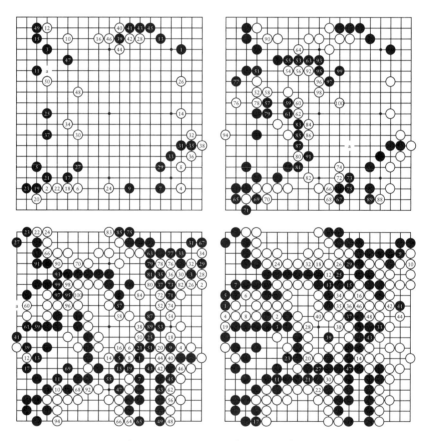

FIGURE **8.2**   Sequences of interconnections in the game of Go
SOURCE: Mathews (2011b). Used with permission.

rior to those found in China generally.[24] In 2008, Suzhou and its sister industrial park, Suzhou New and Hi-Tech Industrial Development Zone, were both recognized as two of the first three approved eco-industrial parks (EIPs) in China. And there are many others moving in the same direction in China, such as Tianjin Economic Development Area, with its ambitious eco-development plans.[25]

These Chinese examples could be multiplied; no doubt there will be many more examples in short order, springing up in India, Brazil, and elsewhere as countries seek latecomer advantages by greening their industrialization processes and strategies. International organizations like the World Bank and the United Nations could add their voice to these transitional dynamics. Agencies including the UN Environment Programme, the UN Development Programme, and the UN Industrial Development Organization (UNEP, UNDP, and UNIDO, respecively) are already formalizing green development strategies. There is a case to be made for the creation of a new UN agency devoted to the measurement, promotion, and defense of the green economy. In the final chapter I outline what role could be played by such a new UN Green Economy Agency—an institution conceived as a civilization-saving measure.

Growth Versus Degrowth

The degrowth proponents state that zero growth will eventually enforce itself and capitalism will have to bow the knee. This line of argument has been developed for three decades now by Herman Daly, one of my erstwhile heroes. (I read him while still a young student at the London School of Economics, in the 1970s.) Daly makes the point consistently that on a planet with finite resources, growth has eventually to stop: there will emerge a "steady state." This is repeated by numerous followers, such as Tim Jackson in the United Kingdom and Brian Czech in the United States.[26]

It all depends, of course, on how one defines "growth." I view the difference between *intensive* and *extensive* growth as fundamental—a point made by Jones (1988) in the epigraph to this chapter. Growth that is measured in increases in GDP is usually extensive growth, associated with increasing flows of materials and energy through the economic system. This is what clearly cannot continue indefinitely—and which indeed must be curbed as a matter of the highest urgency. But *intensive growth* is a different matter entirely. This refers to a growth in value without change in the flow of resources, through increasing levels of recirculation and greater degrees of interfirm exchange intensity. Individual firms, and value chains of firms, will doubtless continue to seek out opportunities to generate increasing returns—just as all capitalist firms before them have done. But increasing returns have until recently been ignored in mainstream economic analysis, which to that extent is a clear departure from capitalist reality. Increasing returns were banished from analysis for reasons solely to do with mathematical tractability of the equations governing supply and demand at equilibrium (no convergence to equilibrium can be demonstrated where increasing returns apply); but in capitalist reality, as opposed to its neoclassical fictions (like constant returns), the search for increasing returns governs strategy. In totality it is increasing returns that create the possibilities for intensive growth. The firms earning increasing returns propagate via interfirm connections through the process of circular and cumulative causation as described by Kaldor and Myrdal. These ideas, which have languished at the margins of economics for so long, should come into their own as the debate between intensive and extensive growth becomes sharper.[27]

It was the American economist Allyn Young, in his 1928 address to the British Association for the Advancement of Science, who boldly posed the issue of increasing returns as the *central question* to be addressed in economic analysis of the modern industrial system. In place of seeing the genesis of increasing returns as a marginal issue, to be dealt with alongside externalities as something quaint and uncommon, Young grasped that increasing returns are central to the way that mass production industries go about building the market for their products. On the strength of the expanded market they are able to invest in specialized capital equipment, and as the market further expands, they are able to make use of specialized value chains of intermediate suppliers, sometimes aggregated altogether in industrial clusters. All this Young saw as the central issue, to be the focus of analysis. If theory could not shed light on these processes, or simply ignored them, then it was theory without point or purpose. Young was comprehensively ignored by his economist colleagues. But now there is a new urgency to this analysis: the framework of increasing returns generated through circular and cumulative causation must be viewed as the means of propagation of the capitalist green economy within the matrix of the old, fossil fuel economy, securing intensive growth within a finite resource base.

Young and other non-orthodox growth theorists like Kaldor and Thirlwall insist that it is not factor questions and supply-side issues that need to be addressed in accounting for increasing returns but growth of markets, that is, growth in demand.[28] This demand-side emphasis is a singular characteristic—an emphasis that mainstream economics has ignored at the risk of making itself irrelevant. Firms in modern mass-production industries first address the market and take active steps to build the market prior to making definitive investments in production. They are prepared to sink large sums into investment in large-scale pro-duction systems that would be completely unwarranted by the current state of demand in the markets concerned. Such investments are made with an eye on growing the market, through cost reduction as fast as possible—and where the cost reductions are based on prior investments in specialized capital equipment provided by specialist suppliers whose existence is made possible by the breadth of the market, as well as in internal efficiencies that are under the firm's direct control. It is clear that this description corresponds almost exactly to the situation of ex-panding mass production systems as they have diffused globally over the past century.

And this is exactly how one may envisage the growth of the green economy within the matrix of the incumbent, fossil fuel economy. It will be *growth in demand for green products*, and the preparedness of capitalist firms to make investments in production systems to meet the anticipated demand, that will enable the green sector to outgrow the old, fossil fuel sector. Indeed, Kaldor coined the happy expression "chain re-action" for such a process—again in a way that is exactly applicable to the growth of firms within the green economy, multiplying the opportu-nities for interaction among themselves as their interconnections grow.

We may also reintroduce into the discussion the notion of the big push as advanced originally by Rosenstein-Rodan and others in the 1940s and 1950s, in the heyday of development economics.[29] I am utilizing this idea because it explicitly makes connections across different economic sectors, seeing each of them operating in systemic, synergistic fashion, mutually supporting each other. This is again how we might envisage—

and model—the growth of the green sector within the womb of the fossil-fueled industrial economy.

So my argument differs from that of zero-growth advocates. I do not see zero growth as a new default option for a green capitalism—provided we understand growth to be intensive and generated by the capture of increasing returns. Under such conditions firms can introduce innovations, and to the extent that they are moving toward RE^2 principles, they will not call for any expansion in resource throughput. There is no magic or sleight of hand here. The generation of increasing returns from a given resource base, improving productivity and hence incomes in a cumulative fashion, has always been the key to capitalist expansion—as demonstrated initially in cities that first developed the elements of capitalist manufacturing.[30] Now as the shift to the green economy gets under way, "green growth" will likewise consist in intensive growth of output from a given resource base without calling for expanded resource throughput.[31]

Dynamics of Eco-Industrial Initiatives

In the interests of taking the study of eco-industrial initiatives further, and placing them within an economic and evolutionary setting, I pose two criteria to be utilized in examining the success of each such initiative: that (1) it must improve the eco-efficiency of the group of firms as a whole while (2) improving the profit position of at least one firm without damaging the profit position of the others. The first criterion has been intensively discussed in the literature already (e.g., Ehrenfeld 2005); a number of measurements for eco-efficiency have been developed and applied in previous studies, such as a tangible reduction in material throughput, in energy released, in carbon dioxide released, or in some biological measure like basic oxygen demand of watercourses. But there also needs to be an economic dimension to such initiatives—to bring them within the ambit of "ecological economics." That is why the second criterion is proposed. This approach has an analogue with the definition of Pareto efficiency in mainstream economics, which states that an allocation of goods is subject to a Pareto improvement if a new allocation makes at least one person better off without making anyone else worse off. Let us agree to call initiatives that satisfy both conditions as being "Pareto eco-efficient."[32]

Pareto Eco-Efficiency

Leading circular economy initiatives such as those made in China may be measured against those two criteria; they seem to have made clear Pareto improvements in an eco-industrial sense, leading to the formation of an eco-industrial area or region. In this setting, we are interested in whether the group as a whole can evolve, though a series of eco-industrial initiatives, to the point at which the firms in the group can reach a (temporary) steady state in the sense that no further eco-improvements are feasible, given the technology employed. The key idea is that it is the eco-efficiency of the group of firms that improves, through their increasingly close interaction and trade (e.g., along value chains)—rather than within individual firms themselves. Collectively, such firms generate increasing returns, which we recognize as green growth.

Evolutionary Stable State

The analytical goal of this kind of approach would be to prove an analogue of the central theorem of neoclassical economics, which states that under certain assumptions (e.g., convexity) the existence and uniqueness of a competitive equilibrium may be demonstrated and that it is Pareto efficient. This is a purely comparative static result, and the equilibrium obtained is a purely ideal phenomenon that has never been demonstrated in any real economy. By contrast, in the eco-industrial setting we are interested in real activity sets that link firms together through their resource and energy flows, and in real developmental changes to the configuration of these activities; these could encompass eco-industrial initiatives that would evolve over time and thereby change the shape of the activity networks (e.g., through the creation of industrial hypercycles). The point of interest lies in securing theorems that describe the development of an "evolutionary stable state" achieved by the application of "evolutionary stable strategies" (ESS) in such a setting, which can be empirically demonstrated in terms of real connections between firms and creation of real superstructures such as clusters and industrial hypercycles. An analogue of the central theorem in economics would be a theorem (or theorems) demonstrating the existence and uniqueness of an evolutionary stable state between a set of firms generated through their making dynamic eco-linkages with each other, where the stable state is characterized as being Pareto eco-efficient. I pose this as a challenge for young industrial ecologists and economists.

Path Dependence

A final analytical challenge is posed by the issue of path dependence—another heterodox topic that promises to come into its own as a green economics develops. Paul David, the former student of Alexander Gerschenkron, created something of a sensation with his 1985 paper read to the American Economic Association on the iron grip that QWERTY exercised on typewriter keyboard design, even extending to the design of computer keyboard layouts—long after the reasons for the initial design had been forgotten and when far more efficient alternatives were available. David advanced this story as a way of illustrating the significance of history for economics and for the far-reaching consequences of seemingly trivial design choices. The implicit challenge to the timeless world of mainstream economics was quickly sensed, and many tried to decry the example and David's characterization.[33] The related notion of lock-in was at the same time developed by Brian Arthur (1989, 1994); both notions, path dependence and lock-in, depend ultimately on the workings of increasing returns in a growing economic system.

It hardly needs to be emphasized that "carbon lock-in," by which is implied the entire set of institutions, practices, standards, and infrastructure created by the fossil fuel economy, is the ultimate example of path dependence. The interest here lies not so much in accounting for the lock-in or on how the fossil-fueled pathway was chosen over others—but on how to *break* the lock-in and path dependence that now exercises such a grip on the global economy, and *create* a new lock-in along green development trajectories. The issue is whether the analytical preconditions identified by David (and Arthur) to account for lock-in and path dependence can be untangled to indicate a way out of the morass. David focuses most strongly on micro-level irreversibilities (e.g., sunk costs that cannot be undone) and the sequence of actions that result in *path-constrained amelioration*. His approach provides compelling evidence of the need for strong state intervention to change the pathway that is dependent on fossil fuels to an alternative that works on renewable energies and resource efficiency. In the absence of such intervention, the forces making for path dependence are simply allowed to operate without hindrance—further "locking in" the system to its current carbon dependence.

The economy that operates in real time (via path dependence) and subject to real ecological cycles and pressures is the setting in which a green economics can come into its own and offer real insights into the workings of a genuinely sustainable system. I have offered examples of the kind of economic analysis needed in which closed-loop, economic interfirm relations are seen as the norm rather than the exception. Linear economic analysis remains the overwhelming (and unthinking) preference in formal economic modeling—driven by an assumption that economic activities can be thought of as "single production" activities rather than as "joint activities" which is actually the case in reality—as argued convincingly by Kurz (2006). Timeless economic analysis concerned only with the conditions in which a (fictional) equilibrium might be established has little to offer of real value. Path dependence, following David, will come to be seen as the norm rather than the exception—and will be used in a positive sense in the building of new RE^2 pathways as well as in the negative sense of breaking with the fossil-fueled path—as is already evident in Chinese scholarship. We may look forward to a renaissance in economic thought and analysis emanating from China, that parallels the rise of eco-industrial initiatives on a large scale and that takes the circular economy as its inspiration and guide.

Toward the Biomimetic Economy

An economy that imitates the great cycles of nature in biomimetic fashion is the goal of the transformations discussed in this book—and unlike the transient character of fossil-fueled innovations such as fracking for coal seam gas, the biomimetic goal will remain the standard for centuries, even millennia. The biomimetic economy points to industrial solutions that live off renewable income—such as renewable energy sources, circular economy initiatives and resource recycling, and eco-financing. It has the appeal of finding common ground between East and West, in the sense that it is attuned to both Western notions of thermodynamic stability and Pareto eco-efficiency and Eastern, Confucian, and neo-Confucian notions. Indeed, none of the core streams of Chinese thought (Daoism, Buddhism, and Confucianism) has an exploitative attitude to nature—all see it as coevolving with human activity.[34]

In this way, economic circularity and biomimesis has the appeal of finding common ground between East and West, and between North and South, in the sense that it generates a framework for developing countries (building renewable energy and recycling industries) and for countries that are already developed (new industries to take over from the obsolete fossil fuel sectors). The idea of the biomimetic economy promotes practical solutions like renewable energy sources as the default option while casting doubt on pseudosolutions such as carbon capture and storage and carbon markets with their inflated expectations. Above all, such a conception provides a far-reaching and powerful ideal that can generate effective policies to curb global warming while offering ethically satisfying business opportunities for young entrepreneurs.

So, there is an alternative framework for analyzing the economics of the green economy, emphasizing its capitalist characteristics and its convergence toward ecological alignment. It is the linkages between firms that enable them to earn increasing returns, away from equilibrium, without increasing the resource base. This is green growth. So it is feasible to analyze the prospects of China, India, and others as "growing" their economies through increasing returns, on the basis of interfirm linkages and externalities (Marshall's external economies as opposed to the internal economies earned inside the firm), without necessarily growing their resource base, that is, their resource throughput. Of course, they will continue to grow their resource demands, as well as their energy demands, while steadily improving their energy efficiency and resource efficiency. They will make material progress in this endeavor as they shift to renewable energies and to circular economy interfirm linkages—based on turning "wastes" into inputs and making recycling the default option.

The analysis of this greening of capitalism would draw little of value from the bankrupt neoclassical economic paradigm with its obsession with equilibrium-based comparative static analysis conducted on an economy that has no financial sector and which operates without reference to its ecological setting. Instead, a green economics is emerging that is what we might call (in a mischievous spirit) decidedly "Schinskyan" in scope and character. This Schinskyan approach is shorthand for a synthesis that is fundamentally Minskyan, blended with a flavor of Schumpeter, of Keynes, of Young, and of Holling. It will be Minskyan in its emphasis on the need to control the financial character of capitalist dynamics, and the necessity to closely regulate the green financial sector to ensure that it stays within "hedge funding" operations that can repay both interest and principal out of earnings. There will need to be a control (or steering) mechanism that can intervene quickly and effectively if the green finance sector strays into "speculative territory" where earnings can cover interest payments only and the principal needs to be periodically rolled over; it will have to call out the financial cavalry if the sector ever lapses into "Ponzi" territory where earnings can cover neither interest nor principal and depend on asset inflation, or bubbles, for their sustenance.[35]

A green economics will be Minskyan with a Schumpeterian flavor because it will recognize the role of technological change, of creative destruction, of entrepreneurial initiative funded by credit creation as drivers of green growth. It will also be Schumpeterian in its recognition of the cycles of growth that allow the economy to be restructured, weeding out the old and inefficient and making way for the new—particularly the new green firms that will oust the old fossils. A green economics will have a Keynesian flavor in that it will be based not just on real flows of energy and materials but also on expectations, without simplistic assumptions of self-correcting equilibrium processes. It will have a Youngian flavor because it will recognize the role of demand in growing the economy, enabling specialization and multifirm connections to work their magic through increasing returns, the basis of sustainable growth. And it will be firmly grounded in the ecological insights of Holling—fragility versus resilience of ecosystems—and thereby never lose sight of the fact that the economy is a human "technology" constructed within the great cycles of the biosphere.[36] The paradigm of a circular economy and renewable energy system—or what I am calling a system running on RE^2 principles—will act as a guide and driver of the appropriate policies, in the firm expectation that the end point will indeed be a steady-state economy that is resilient, both financially and ecologically. This provides a radical new starting point not just for the real economy but for economics itself.

9   The Greening of Capitalism

The crisis consists precisely in the fact that the old is dying and the new cannot be born; in this interregnum a great variety of morbid symptoms appear.

—*Antonio Gramsci,* Selections from Prison Notebooks
    (1930/1971)

We are now in the middle of a long process of transition in the nature of the image which man has of himself and his environment. Primitive men, and to a large extent also men of the early civilizations, imagined themselves to be living on a virtually illimitable plane. There was almost always somewhere beyond the known limits of human habitation . . . a frontier. That is, there was always someplace else to go when things got too difficult. . . . The image of the frontier is probably one of the oldest images of mankind, and it is not surprising that we find it hard to get rid of. Gradually, however, man has been accustoming himself to the notion of the spherical earth and a closed sphere of human activity.

—*Kenneth E. Boulding, "The economics of the coming*
    Spaceship Earth" (1966)

[The environmental crisis] is not the product of man's biological capabilities, which could not change in time to save us, but of his social actions—which are subject to much more rapid change. . . . Here we can learn a basic lesson from nature: that nothing can survive on the planet unless it is a cooperative part of a larger, global whole.

—*Barry Commoner,* The Closing Circle *(1971)*

In his prison cell in 1930, while the world was about to plunge into the Great Depression, the Italian revolutionary Antonio Gramsci had his eyes firmly on the process of transition, from the old to the new. In his view, the old represented Western capitalism (albeit one that had only just appeared in its industrial form in Italy) and the new, the Soviet

Union.[1] But his insight transcends these particular choices of oppositional categories; his dictum applies with equal, if not stronger, force to the present global situation, in which an industrial civilization based on and powered by fossil fuels is dying but will not cede the stage to its successor, the green civilization based on a circular economy, renewable energies, and eco-finance. This is the great challenge faced by our industrial civilization—and it is the reason it is likely that the new, green development model will emerge first from China, the industrial latecomer, and then be diffused around the world through competitive emulation and industrial dynamics. But the outcome is anything but certain.

We owe the image of Spaceship Earth as defining a new view of the economy, aligned with its ecological limits, to the English polymath and inspirational economist, Kenneth Boulding. In a seminal essay, penned in 1966, Boulding contrasted the image of the frontier, as an open system beyond which there was always room for further expansion, with that of the closed system that constitutes a spaceship—a closed system in which "the outputs of all parts of the system are linked to the inputs of other parts." Indeed, as he put it so clearly: "There are no inputs from outside and no outputs to the outside; indeed there is no outside at all" (Boulding 1966, 1).

The Perennial Image of Spaceship Earth

Boulding's (1966) essay stands the test of time because he advances the image of the economy of Spaceship Earth as a defining image for an epoch—a transitional epoch that was moving from an economy in which there really was a frontier, an open economy, to one in which there was no longer a frontier, and the closed system of the earth was pressing in on all sides. Boulding strove for an image that captured the moment of transition and would express the essence of the goal.[2] Spaceship Earth is certainly that image. And it is still the most relevant image for our time—with the difference that now we are realizing that time is perhaps running out and the dangerous image of the frontier needs to be put well and truly behind us.

For his part, Barry Commoner (1971) ended his great work, *The Closing Circle*, with a rousing appeal to the wisdom of life in circulating everything—as in the epigraph to this chapter. Commoner, the accomplished biologist, was concerned above all to see the cycles that drove biological success incorporated into industrial and economic processes.

The power of images, or metaphors, is that they provide us with visual means to resolve complex problems. And the 1970s witnessed a fierce battle between images or metaphors, with Boulding on one side with his Spaceship Earth (flanked by Commoner with his closing circle and Daly with his steady state) and Hardin on the other, with his lifeboat ethic and tragedy of the commons (flanked by Paul and Anne Ehrlich with their population bomb). In many ways, we are still living through this battle of images, or debate in the academy of ideas—with extremely serious consequences if we get it wrong.[3]

Let us give Boulding the floor first. In deducing economic principles for Spaceship Earth, Boulding contrasted the economics of the open economy as a "cowboy economy"—associated with "reckless, exploitative, romantic and violent behavior," that is, characteristic of the open society. By contrast the spaceship economy is one in which "the earth has become a single spaceship, without unlimited reservoirs of anything, either for extraction or for pollution, and in which, therefore, man must find his place in a cyclical ecological system which is capable of continuous reproduction of material form even though it cannot escape having inputs of energy."[4]

Boulding highlighted the difference between the two kinds of economy, for example, in the process of consumption. In the cowboy economy, he argues that "consumption is regarded as a good thing and production likewise; and the success of the economy is measured by the amount of the throughput from the factors of production, a part of which, at any rate, is extracted from the reservoirs of raw materials and noneconomic objects, and another part of which is output into the reservoirs of pollution." Gross national product (GNP) is a rough measure of this throughput—and so he characterizes GNP as a rough measure of the success of an open economy. But in the closed-system Spaceship Earth economy, it is necessary to differentiate GNP into parts—that which "is derived from reproducible resources" and that which consumes virgin resources and generates waste.

By contrast, Boulding argues, in the Spaceship Earth economy, "throughput is by no means a desideratum, and is indeed to be regarded as something to be minimized rather than maximized." From this follows the entire edifice of work on resource throughput taxation, taking the emphasis of taxation away from productive use of capital and labor, placing it instead on use of exhaustible (non-renewable) resources—as in carbon and fuel taxes.

Forty years on, we have a name for this emulation of natural cycles, *biomimesis*, and a name for the closing of the circle, the *circular economy*. We have the disciplines of ecological economics, of industrial ecology and industrial symbiosis. We are on the cusp of the total conversion of our energy systems to a renewable basis, eliminating the cancer of fossil fuels and their products of combustion. Some advanced countries are promoting these solutions, in the form of renewable energies, circular economy industrial linkages and cycles, and eco-finance to drive it all, *as if their life depended on it*. So forty years on from Commoner's groundbreaking analysis, and Boulding's wonderful metaphor of Spaceship Earth, one might say that humanity is closer to resolving the contradictions they laid bare.

We are also forty years on in terms of industrialization via the business-as-usual (BAU) trajectory, now diffusing to encompass China and India and many other countries coming after them. The environmental degradation, the expropriation of nature, the waste and irrelevance of so much economic activity, is now so much worse. The problems are now so much more serious—culminating in the greatest problem of all, the planetary catastrophe represented by climate change (not even mentioned in Commoner's book, so slight was the issue viewed at the time).

Now we give the floor to Hardin. He is a distinguished biologist, but he certainly set the cat among the pigeons when he formulated his twin notions of the tragedy of the commons (1968) and then his lifeboat ethic (1974)—the latter crafted specifically as a response and "refutation" of Boulding's image of Spaceship Earth. Hardin (1974, 561) acknowledges the efficacy of the spaceship metaphor in justifying pollution control measures; but he insisted that a spaceship has to have a captain, or someone in control: "A true ship always has a captain. It is conceivable that a ship be run by a committee. But it could not possibly survive if its course were determined by bickering tribes that claimed rights without responsibilities." Thus Hardin's first major point is that the spaceship metaphor is used to justify demands on common resources without acknowledging

corresponding spaceship responsibilities. If this is what Boulding was saying, it certainly escaped me—and many others. But Hardin's substantive
point is that if people are in a lifeboat (as he characterized the US population in 1974, in the midst of a large and hostile poorer world population),
then they commit collective suicide by taking in other survivors. This is
clearly an argument directed against immigration (in a narrow sense) and
against the exercise of global responsibilities in a wider sense.

Hardin argued that the most "toxic freedom" is the freedom to
breed, so that only through coercive restriction of population would the
global ecological problem be solved. Hardin (1974) thus coined a second
parable for industrial society in the form of the lifeboat ethic, by which the
rich nations maintain barriers against immigration by the poor, using the
argument that there are not sufficient resources for all. Hardin no doubt
simply made explicit what many people were thinking—but the emphasis
on population as the source of problems rather than changes to the industrial system is still (in my view) a fundamentally misguided approach.[5]

Since Hardin and Commoner and Boulding and others engaged
in their polemic in the 1970s, the world population has continued to
expand (it doubled in the three decades from 1970 to 2000, from around
3.5 billion to 6.5 billion), with by far the greater part of the increase
coming from the developing (poor) world. China has expanded in that
time but has moderated its growth with a draconian population policy
limiting couples to one child per family (or two in exceptional circumstances, with payment of a fee). While this policy might be considered
supportive of Hardin's position, it was in fact imposed as an interim step
by a government that realized that unrestrained population growth would
destroy China's advance in material welfare; the government concluded
that a rational policy of restraint (as opposed to an irrational policy
implemented via war or famine) would actually serve the country well.
China also had the state power giving it the authority to implement such
a policy—a policy that has lain beyond the capacity of the Indian government to implement, with disastrous results for India.

As China grows wealthier, so the emphasis on its one-child policy
is relaxing; the anticipated reductions in population resulting from industrialization and urbanization are being allowed to exert their effects.
Let's face it: people are basically rational. If they are living in poverty in
a village on an agrarian basis, then having large families makes sense as a

means of providing labor and for social security in old age. But as people move off the land and inhabit cities, where industrial jobs are the magnet, then having children becomes less attractive—*much* less attractive.[6] Where women have some modicum of rights and are admitted to literacy programs, they quickly register their own wishes as to having children (by reducing the numbers). As the world industrializes and urbanizes, it will no doubt solve the population problem as formulated by Hardin, by Paul Ehrlich and Anne Ehrlich, and others. And it will solve it through recognizing the need for a new model of an industrial economy, for a greening of capitalism. In this fundamental sense, Boulding and Commoner won the battle of ideas, and Boulding has given us an image in his Spaceship Earth that is worthy of its celebrated status.

Three Kinds of Economy

The principal task we face today is to navigate this Spaceship Earth in a way that enables a population of eventually nine or even ten billion to aspire to a reasonable income without destroying the material basis of the economy. The world's largest uncontrolled experiment is under way—and we have no idea of the outcome.

But we do have some guidelines, as I have sought to demonstrate in this book. I have utilized three kinds of economic "models" or sets of axioms—those covering the agrarian economy; the fossil-fueled industrial economy; and the renewable, circular economy. Let me summarize the main features of these three axiomatic representations.

Agrarian Economy

The agrarian economy (Malthusian, preindustrial) was one that worked within its organic sources of energy and local produce. Trade was not a major factor and land rents ate away at the agricultural surplus. Increasing returns were available, but only in city-based manufacturing (originating in Italian city-states like Florence, Venice, and Genoa).[7] In the agrarian economy the limiting factor is the *price of food*— specifically, the price of grain. Enormously complex economic systems were built on this basis, some lasting for thousands of years (as in China), with a recurring feature of famines resulting from misalignment of food supplies, demand, and prices. And some clearly outlasted their ecological base; they collapsed, through soil degradation, water shortages, crop failure, deforestation, and associated calamities such as plagues. Malthus captured the essence of this economy in his "law" that resource use would always outrun population—with calamitous results. It appears to have been no accident that the only country to break out of this Malthusian straitjacket was the country that happened to be induced to substitute a fossil fuel (coal) for its traditional organic sources of energy; this is what set Britain on a new trajectory and propelled it to world supremacy as the first industrial nation.

Fossil-Fueled Industrial Economy

The industrial economy powered by fossil fuels unleashed astonishing improvements in productivity—unheard of in the agrarian economy. These were translated into increases in per capita income, without the Malthusian consequences—that is, escaping from the Malthusian trap. But it is not so easy to escape, after all. Now the system has expanded globally, and the "trap" is the whole planet (*only one Earth*). The promise was great—but now it cannot be redeemed for billions of people who are clamoring to have their turn to experience the comforts of industrialization. In the fossil-fueled industrial economy, the limiting factor is the *price of energy* (i.e., oil)—and indeed, a convincing case can be made that economic crises of the past several decades have all been triggered by increases in the price of oil. It is not really surprising that the price of oil, the dominant commodity of the fossil fuel industrial era, should be related so profoundly to economic upturns and downturns. Nevertheless this fact is not widely known; it takes a courageous analyst to bring it into focus.[8]

The axioms of the fossil-fueled industrial economy include its propensity to grow without limit, and the assumption that capital can always be substituted for resources as they reach their peak in supply. Firms are modeled as always seeking growth (as their raison d'être) and consumers as being insatiable.[9] But in a finite world, this idealist creation of an ever-expanding economy cannot be substantiated; its promise cannot be redeemed. Increasingly in the industrial economy the financial sector grows through the creation of more and more complex debt instruments, spinning webs of credit that can keep growing at compound interest rates without regard to the material economy's ability to discharge the debts. This results in financial crises of increasing magnitude and the system comes to be untethered from its grounding in the real world of production. Polanyi was close to the mark with his claim that the central categories of the new capitalist order—land, labor, and money—were essentially fictitious.

Let us call this second model a "discharge" industrial system—in the sense that it lives off its capital and discharges this (as in a battery)—as well as discharging its wastes into a sewer it calls nature.[10] By contrast, we can call a third model, emerging now, a "recharge" industrial system— because it is continuously recharging itself—with renewable energy, with recirculated resources, and with targeted eco-finance. Such a recharging system is inherently sustainable.

Biomimetic, Green Growth Economy

This third, and emergent model, is the economy powered by re-newable energies, recirculation of resources, and targeted eco-finance. It is one that has a set of rules that can deliver both rising incomes and a sustainable pattern of industrial activity. It is everywhere seeking to be born, yet is blocked by the carbon lock-in prevalent in the West and emerging with force in the industrializing world. My argument is that an alternative growth and development model is emerging most clearly in the East, particularly in China. While the terms *green development* and *green growth* are subject to various interpretations, the key ideas are that an industrial system based on something other than fossil fuels and extensive resource throughput is being constructed—with small initial steps but always aimed at minimizing the fossil-fueled industrial footprint.[11] The goal of such an approach is to build energy systems that can increasingly live off their renewable energy income and materials processing industries that tend to minimize virgin resource inputs. Both aspects have profound implications for countries' development prospects.

It might be helpful to specify just what is meant by this emer-gent green growth economy, if only to anticipate the policy measures that would be needed to help bring it into existence and to derive the forms of economic behavior that will be generated. I shall develop a "model" of a green growth economy in the form of a set of ten principles, or axioms, that can be viewed as driving the process, shaping decisions at the point where they are being made.[12]

Principles of a Green Economy

The biggest failing of mainstream economics is that it has no real theory of the firm. The so-called theory of the firm really treats these complex entities as no more than sole traders, responding like automata to price signals. So let us begin a summary account of the green growth economy by acknowledging that its protagonists will be capitalist firms, with all their sources of internal and external organizational complexity that enable them to generate increasing returns.[13] They will formulate business plans and execute them with a view to making a profit—subject to the rules and regulations prevailing at the time, together with any extra regulation imposed to maintain the sustainability of the green economy. Stringent regulations will catalyze these competitive responses, as argued by leading strategy theorists.[14] The economy consists, then, of a series of value-adding steps undertaken by firms, in which the inputs are resources, energy, and finance, together with labor, and the outputs are products (where services are a particular form of product); energy and resources circulate in one direction, and money (fees, taxes, royalties) circulates in the other direction. Corporations are to be recognized as the central players in this economy, acting independently in the pursuit of profit (but not necessarily with limited liability). Firms in such a green economy will be required to provide full and audited data on the ways in which their activities impinge on the environment, that is, on the ecological setting in which the firms and economy operate.

Now let us specify the forces impinging on the kinds of decisions these firms will be making as the economy grows its green shoots.

Renewables and Clean Tech as the Preferred Option

The fossil-fueled industrial economy lived off its common resource base, ignoring the replenishing flow of energy that comes from the sun every day. The green economy will reverse this emphasis and live off its solar input—rather like agriculture has done for ten thousand years (albeit with fossil fuels making increasing inroads, through mechanization, fertilizers, pesticides, and herbicides). Just as a complex series of choices were made in Britain in the eighteenth century to introduce new fossil-fueled energy sources in place of organic practices (e.g., coal in place of charcoal in iron smelting), so in the twenty-first century a new cycle of such choices present themselves in greening one industrial sector after another—starting with generation of power itself. As against the fossil-fueled and centralized energy systems of the mass production paradigm, carried over into the fifth (IT) epoch, where energy insecurity prevailed because of geopolitics and endless conflict over access to oil supplies, in the green economy energy security will be the ideal, achieved through manufacturing of energy devices tapping into a variety of renewable energy supplies. The marginal cost of generating renewable electrical power will come to approach zero, so that costs of constructing renewable energy systems will be governed by capital charges priced by eco-targeted financial instruments. At the margin, choices in favor of renewables will come to be the norm.

Resource Circulation (Circular Economy) as Preferred Option

A complementary shift away from the linear resource flows of the fossil-fueled economy is also under way. A fundamental feature of the clean-tech shift is reducing the flow of resources to curb the prevalent linear model where virgin resources are extracted at one end (from nature) and waste resources are dumped at the other end (again into a sink called nature). In Germany and some European countries an alternative approach to resource management known as "cradle to cradle" (C2C) has been developed, and in China an even more radical process of linking industrial waste flows to alternative uses as industrial inputs is actively promoted under the rubric of the circular economy and its promotion law. Improving resource efficiency through recirculation is just as important a feature of the new paradigm as energy renewal and efficiency, secured again by choices made by firms to reduce resource throughput in settings shaped by price signals.

Eco-Finance to Drive the Transition

Firms will build the green economy through investment, financed by eco-finance instruments. No great transformation is feasible without the participation of the finance sector: any notion that it can be engineered by public finance alone is a fantasy. And the heart of finance is the system of bonds—the capitalist instrument of credit par excellence. What is needed are new financial instruments that can channel investments *at scale* toward clean-tech and renewable projects, involving choices made by institutional investors. As they purchase green bonds, they will liberate finance to flow to new RE^2 investments.[15]

Eco-finance that is carefully regulated will provide the most efficient catalyst for the emergence of the green economy, through differential loan charges that favor green investments over generic investments upholding the old "brown" economy. In this way investment will be able to create a new economic order without the obstruction of vested interests that will always delay and frustrate policies that are implemented after the fact (such as carbon taxes), when plant and equipment have been installed and production systems are in operation.

Global Free Trade in Renewable Power and Clean-Tech Products

Products produced by firms that are greening will need to have existing hindrances to trade dismantled. The basic resource of the industrial economy has been oil, which is traded globally in a market that is unencumbered by tariffs and legal restrictions (but subject to strict standards). No such favorable circumstance exists as yet for the basic carrier of the new paradigm, which is renewable electric power, nor for the products produced under green conditions. There are proposals for international carriage and interconnection of renewable electric power, such as the Desertec proposal linking North Africa with Europe, or the Asian Super Grid proposal, which would link wind and solar farms in Mongolia with energy-consuming industries in China, Japan, and Korea in the first instance and further afield in South Asia in the longer term.[16] Adopting the perspective of emergence of a sixth techno-economic paradigm (TEP) shift would facilitate the dismantling of trade barriers holding up such international power interconnections.[17]

Indeed, global free trade in renewable power and clean-tech goods will be a fundamental feature of the emergent green economy. Unhindered trade will enhance prospects for developing countries to export renewable power and sustainable fuels while maximizing opportunities for developed countries to export advanced green technologies—thereby accelerating the diffusion and expansion of green economic sectors. Just as expansion of IT industries was driven by a trade agreement known as the Information Technology Trade Agreement (ITA), endorsed by a group of countries in 1996 and then adopted by the World Trade Organization (WTO) (reducing tariffs on IT products and underwriting their global expansion), so a similar trade agreement for clean-tech products and services is needed—as called for by think tanks such as the Information Technology and Innovation Foundation (ITIF) in Washington DC and the International Centre for Trade and Sustainable Development (ICTSD) in Geneva.[18] An important step toward such an agreement was the adoption by APEC countries in 2012 of a commitment to reduce tariffs on a range of clean-tech goods ("environmental goods") to less than 5 percent within five years.[19]

Green Infrastructure: Smart Grid and Smart Economy

The green economy will be an intelligent economy (or "smart economy"), utilizing a smart power grid that is IT enhanced. In this way adjustments will be made that render the green infrastructure resilient and adaptable and able to accommodate fluctuating renewable inputs. While the fossil-fueled energy systems were laid down as part of the fossil fuel era, the emergence of the fifth paradigm opened the way for IT-based systems, which have been encompassing the globe for the past three decades. *But IT applications stopped short of energy systems.* It is only with the rise of smart grids, designed to accommodate a rising proportion of renewable energy generation, that IT has come to be applied directly to the energy system and thereby complete the IT revolution begun earlier. This creates enormous opportunities for investment in green infrastructure, by both government and private players.[20] The application of IT to the energy and resource flow systems would be expected to have wider ramifications, culminating in the capacity to trace the flow of every product and commodity that circulates in the global economic system. This would amount to what is coming to be called the Internet of things, and specifically in energy terms as the Internet of energy.[21] If governments make explicit commitments to promote renewables, and in particular to promote standards for IT enhancement of electric power grids, then they are paving the way for successful emergence of the new paradigm, and indeed the emergence of a smart (IT-enhanced) economy—with enhanced possibilities for decentralized production and power generation systems to emerge.

Creative Destruction to Be Allowed to Work, Contra "Carbon Lock-In"

The essence of Schumpeter's view of the workings of capitalism is that it is uniquely characterized by creative destruction, by which the old is destroyed to make way for the new. But in practice the incumbents do everything in their power to block the process; it is frequently allowed to operate only through forceful intervention by the state, which has the task of upholding processes of fair competition and correcting for subsidies enjoyed by incumbents. The fossil fuels sector has a "lock" on industry structures and pricing, backed by widespread subsidies (such as exploration and drilling tax breaks) creating an overarching path dependence that is well expressed as "carbon lock-in." The first policy implication of adopting the perspective of an emergent sixth TEP shift is to insist that creative destruction be allowed to proceed, through unraveling the subsidies applied to fossil fuels and giving new renewable and clean-tech firms the tax concessions and support they need to break the existing carbon lock-in. The governments that adopt such a perspective are the ones that can expect to see firms advancing the new paradigm most effectively. Market-based incentives can be anticipated as driving the transition.

Taxes to Be Levied on Pollution and Virgin Resources

Market-based disincentives, such as taxes and charges, will also have a role to play. Taxes are generally levied in ways that reflect the reigning orthodoxy. Prior to the rise of industrialization, taxes tended to be levied on trade (customs and excise) and on manufacturing (such as various imposts on materials). Tax systems in earlier industrial techno-economic paradigms have been based on labor and capital as well as trade (in the form of tariffs, excise, and duties). Now in the green economy the opportunity to fundamentally rethink the source (and purpose) of taxes can be taken. To facilitate the transition to a new green paradigm, the burden of taxation needs to shift to sources of pollution, such as carbon-intensive industries and fossil-fuel-consuming sectors.[22] Such a transition is already under way, with Germany applying considerable gasoline taxes (along with other countries in Europe) and now swinging toward what is called "environmental taxation," and China likewise taking steps to shift the burden of taxation away from labor and capital toward activities that lead to pollution (Chen 2013). These trends can only be expected to continue and strengthen—their effects compounding with those induced by reforms to commodity markets requiring commodities traded to carry electronic histories. While I have decried the impact that such taxation measures can be expected to have (see my earlier discussion of market-based incentives versus market-based disincentives), I also recognize that a fully functioning green economy will dispense with the lop-sided taxation systems inherited from the fossil fuel era. A system that taxes labor and capital while giving tax breaks—enormous tax breaks—to fossil fuel activities like drilling for new oil wells, will clearly have to give way to one in which carbon-intensive activities are penalized and carbon-light activities are promoted. My point is that these trends toward green taxation can be expected to flourish once the world is embarked on a new trajectory—but on their own they will be unable to effect the shift in trajectory needed in the absence of strong state action.

Public Expenditure to Catalyze Green Shoots

Taxes that are collected are then spent as public investment and transfers. The transfers are designed to make up for market inefficiencies and the provision of basic goods—health care, infant and aged care, education—that are needed to uphold civilized values. Investment is designed to provide basic infrastructure that is needed to ensure that the economy works—and to correct for biases introduced during the reign of fossil fuels. So public expenditure can catalyze the creation of energy- and water-efficient urban systems for power supply, water, drainage, and sewerage, creating twenty-first-century systems that will underwrite the anticipated urbanization of the Chinese, Indian, and then global economies. Green industrialization thus will extend to encompass the production of green energy, water, and food in ways that reinforce and build on one another.[23] State expenditure at multiple levels, such as public procurement strategies, can act to catalyze the emergence of green shoots that would otherwise wither and die.

Green Accounting, in Place of GDP

The green economy needs a new system for measuring its own economic performance, as successor and alternative to the linear throughput accounting system of conventional GDP. Circularity will be central to the transition and will call for new measurement systems. Measurement is important because it creates a focus for public discussion; analysis of economic issues has been framed by GDP growth as virtually the only response to a range of problems that in fact could be tackled by alternative approaches, if the measures supporting these approaches were available. While the value of the GDP as a single statistical measure of economic activity is widely acknowledged, the need for a broader "dashboard" of economic, social, and environmental indicators is also widely recognized.[24] Amartya Sen (1981) proposed a broad measure of welfare—the Human Development Index—which has now been estimated and published for two decades, while Herman Daly with John Cobb (1989) proposed the Genuine Progress Indicator (GPI), which has also had some impact. Most progress has been achieved in formulating a green GDP that adds (subtracts) the value of ecosystem services from conventional GDP—and in China it is under active discussion.[25] None of these measures truly breaks with GDP as a measure of linear throughput (as discussed in the previous chapter); something quite different is needed to capture progress in achieving a circular economy. It is likely to be in China or Germany that such an alternative series of measures emerges.[26]

Finance to Be Treated as Utility

The green finance sector will come to be viewed through Minskyan lenses, as being inherently unstable and prone to speculative bubbles. These are simply part of the operation of the capitalist system; there is no point in wishing them away. But if they are endemic, then it makes sense to regulate the system stringently to capture and quash such bubbles before they do damage and contaminate the rest of the economy. It is the absence of such Minskyan skepticism, and the consequent absence of stringent regulation, that has allowed for the shocking wealth polarization and failure to regulate banks and financial institutions of the past three decades, culminating in the global financial crisis of 2008.

Such an approach is akin to treating finance as just another utility—putting the supply of credit on the same footing as supply of water, or gas or electric power, where there is little argument over the need for stringent regulation to ensure that monopolies and quasi monopolies behave in the public interest. Finance is of course different, in that it involves an artificial creation—credit, money—and an economy-wide function.[27] But there is no doubt that treating it like a utility in at least the green development sector will make this sector less prone to bubbles, or better able to deal with and crush bubbles before they expand through their own positive feedback processes. This in turn will make the green development sector capable of generating superior returns, in that the risks and uncertainty of investing in green products and technologies will be reduced.

Once a green development sector with a well-regulated finance system supporting it is created, it is likely to have powerful spillover effects on the wider finance system of "wild capitalism." This could result in meaningful structural reform of finance generally—a matter that has been widely discussed in forums like the G-20 but where little real action has been taken for the past decade and a half at least, since the Asian financial crisis of 1997–98. I am not saying that green finance is going to solve all the problems of the wider financial system and its need for structural reform—but well-regulated green finance could solve its own problems and generate superior returns, and in that sense demonstrate the advantages of stringent regulation to the wider financial system. Of course this battle will doubtless be just as difficult and vexatious as the battles engaged so far between renewable energies and fossil fuels.

All these features are brought out to emphasize the new organizational logic that promises to underpin the emergence of the new green economy or techno-economic paradigm—a logic based on renewability, resilience, decentralization, open competition, and resource husbandry. This is a logic opposed to resource profligacy, overcentralization, and oligopoly—the hallmarks of the fossil fuel and nuclear era. The point of bringing out these principles, or axioms is to emphasize the main lines of development where entrepreneurial initiative can be expected to reap rewards and policy can facilitate the process of transition, as opposed to upholding the status quo.[28] So what kind of economy would these axioms produce?

Is the Green Economy a Capitalist Economy?

I offer these principles, or axioms, as the defining features of what will doubtless come to be called the *green capitalist economy*—or the spaceship economy, the closed-loop economy, the circular economy, the green growth economy, the clean-tech economy. It is the successor to the "wild" capitalism that expanded to fill the planet (and is still expanding, if we include the last few remaining frontiers, such as the Amazon region in Brazil).[29] The point of spelling out the axioms, or set of principles, is to use them to derive the features or patterns of behavior that we would associate with a green economy.[30] Would an economy characterized by these axioms produce rising incomes? Yes, because firms would be looking to make profits from economizing on energy and material inputs, for which they would receive favorable tax treatment—and their resultant competitive advantages would then translate into higher incomes. Would such an economy allow for growth and innovation? Yes, because it would build on lock-in and path dependence to create a new green trajectory in which competitive dynamics would sort out the most desirable and efficient forms of tapping into renewable energy sources and making links between industrial activities to create a circular economy. Growth in such an economy would be grounded in the generation of increasing returns, with a constant resource base, rather than on expanding resource throughput. Would such an economy produce sufficient taxation to provide acceptable levels of collective protection and service? Yes, because taxation would yield income from nondesirable activities, and as those diminish, the level of taxation would be fixed by collective (political) means, and periodically adjusted, in accordance with the meeting of such a social goal.

Most significant, would such an economy be expected to keep within the boundaries of its ecological limits? Yes, because its default position of working off renewable energies and recirculating resources would trend toward the economy working within ecological cycles—

calling for direct observation of deviations (by a body established for the purpose, such as a UN Green Economy Agency), with corrective actions (taxes, limits or penalties) being implemented.

My claim is that this set of axioms is sufficient to produce a green economy, or economy of sustainable enterprise. Let me illustrate. We do not need a specific axiom for labor, since in such an economy, labor will be a highly valued input, with an emphasis on up-skilling (particularly in relation to ecological demands). A firm that sought competitive advantage by driving down the cost of labor through refusing to provide career paths and up-skilling, would be seeking to substitute machinery for labor and would be subject to heavy tax penalties, and so would be induced to shift its focus. There would also be positive inducements (market-based incentives) as well as negative incentives created by taxation.

Nor do we need an axiom on the distribution of income, since in this economy all income would be earned through work, other than small amounts through the use of personal property and royalties earned through generation of intellectual property; it is only when an economy allows propertied wealth to become obtrusive that incomes are skewed and rational collective decisions are no longer possible. Neither do we need an axiom for consumer behavior, because consumers who are also producers of, say, energy or who are paying taxes based on resource utilization will have an inbuilt limit to their consumption, operating in the same way as satiety reduces appetite. Thus the implicit (and sometimes explicit) mainstream economics axiom that consumers will increase demand forever (i.e., nonsatiety, or insatiability, subject only to an income constraint)—albeit subject to diminishing marginal effect—will be superseded. In the green growth economy consumers-cum-producers would become aware of their actions and the impact of their choices, and thus would impose their own limits on their propensities.

The green growth economy is visibly and transparently capitalist in that it allows for and favors private ownership of material production systems; it has a well-developed system for allocation of finance and credit creation, to be utilized by entrepreneurs; and taxation ensures that firms do not grow too large to be able to compete unfairly through price gauging or other forms of unfair trade practices. It is not a socialist economy because it does not recognize collective ownership of resources—although collective management and control of renewable resources

would probably be necessary and would be implemented to avoid tragedies of the commons.

Yet, as emphasized repeatedly, the role of the state in bringing this
green economy into existence and in regulating its activities in a sustainable manner, is to be recognized as a key principle.[31] Initially policies
such as market mandates and differential borrowing rates at state-funded
development banks can be expected to exert primary influence in shifting
the economy onto a new, green trajectory. Market-based incentives such
as policy loans, local investment subsidies, and market-creation efforts
can be expected to work more effectively than market-based disincentives
such as taxes and charges. Yet as the green sector grows and matures,
carbon taxes can be expected to provide discriminatory power to enable
entrepreneurs to choose between different investment options.

Once launched on its new trajectory where the economy is powered by renewable energy and recirculates almost all resources, the full
power of capitalist tools—property rights, markets, and creative destruction—can be expected to work and produce the expected results
of rising incomes and wealth. This is the position of the "free market
environmentalists" with whom I agree—subject to the very important
caveat that the new trajectory that breaks with a business-as-usual pathway cannot be expected to be reached through capitalist entrepreneurship alone. It will require strong state intervention. The significance of
the green growth strategies being pursued in China and Korea lies in
this—that these countries are utilizing state intervention to create a new
growth trajectory in which capitalist entrepreneurial dynamics can be unleashed to generate new products, lower costs, new jobs, and new export
platforms for the future. So—can free-market environmentalism save the
planet?[32] Yes—but only if it is allowed to work on a new trajectory, created expressly as a break with the conventional pathway through state
intervention.

This "model" of a green growth economy is offered as an ideal
type—in the sense of Weber, who worked with "ideal types" as the key
elements of his economic sociology, rather than with positivist notions
that adhere to some statistical regularity. Ideal types in this sense belong
to the world of ideas rather than to demonstrated regularities. Nevertheless, they aid thinking and argument.[33] And this is precisely the sense in

which this model of a green economy is offered—to aid thinking about how such an entity is likely to emerge and how it is likely to work. It is not meant to apply to any existing, real economy—although it is clear that it draws from some of the existing initiatives and programs that have been initiated by real economies, particularly China and Germany.

Most significant, an economy characterized by the organizational principles of the green techno-economic paradigm and associated policies would be expected to keep within the boundaries of its ecological limits. It would call for direct monitoring and intervention to keep activities within their ecological boundaries. Thus, the green growth economy may be viewed as an important step toward the reconciliation of ecological and economic principles.

Governance of the Green Economy

In the end, the green economy is to be recognized as a subsystem of wider planetary processes—and as such, its impact on these wider processes needs to be directly measured and controlled. There is a world of meaning in these two words—*measured* and *controlled*. The point I am making here is that "economic regulation" expressed *indirectly* through prices or interest rates engaged in reciprocal causation—as in conventional economic analysis—in the end falls short. The era in which we could institute measures to control prices or interest rates in the economy conceived as an autonomous system, without regard to the impact of this system on its ecological setting that ultimately sustains it, is assuredly past. Thus, some *direct measurement* of humankind's impact on the planet is increasingly urgent; some framework within which issues may be raised and acted on legitimately is likewise becoming urgent— particularly after the failure of the fifteen-year Kyoto effort under the UN Framework Convention on Climate Change (UNFCCC). Now the way is clear for a fresh approach.

The need for some form of collective control is inescapable if the global economy is to keep within its ecological limits—and sanctions are going to be needed to back up this control. There is no point in imagining that "goodwill" would be sufficient to keep the economic activities of nine billion people aligned with ecological limits. Some form of global monitoring and control apparatus is eventually going to be needed—to firmly anchor the economy in its ecological setting.

Take as an example the satellite monitoring of global carbon emissions. Here is a case in which the technology for such global monitoring has become available. What is needed is the institutional initiative to create a body that would conduct and make public the results of such monitoring. Rather than expecting countries to monitor carbon emissions from their own industries by satellite, it would make sense to perform this task globally, on behalf of all countries. (This is not to say that individual countries could not monitor greenhouse gas emissions if they wish, and many would no doubt want to do so, such as the United States.) The data acquired by such satellite surveillance would be fed to an independent global authority to publicize the data and pass the identities of recalcitrant companies, sectors, and countries to the United Nations, the WTO, and the World Bank so that they can be publicly identified.[34]

This is where we reencounter Hardin's tragedy of the commons. How is it to be avoided? Is there an alternative to the need for a global authority with coercive powers? The case of the need for direct measures to control the spread of antibiotic-resistant bacteria in hospitals provides a clear counterexample: each hospital can implement its own more or less efficient procedures, but the problem resides in the population at large and in the ways that these hospital-level interventions interact. The point about antibiotic-resistant bacteria is that they can build up in hospital settings, in spite of the hospitals' best endeavors to restrain them.

This is a case of an *intractable collective action problem*, where nothing short of a "direct control" solution is called for. Its implications when carried over to the case of global warming—and all the other ills besetting a planet under siege—is that economists' market-based proposals such as carbon taxes and cap-and-trade schemes offer weak support for policies favoring low-carbon technologies. I have argued that both market-based incentives (as opposed to disincentives like taxes and charges) and direct state intervention are actions needed to shift the system onto a new trajectory.

At the same time, the emergent green economy will call for higher levels of responsibility on the part of corporations—and certainly higher than the license granted under the official doctrine of limited liability. This doctrine is barely more than 150 years old, having been brought in as a means to stimulate investment by allowing investors to evade personal liability for subsequent bad business decisions. It has worked extremely well in its aim of promoting investment—but it is now ill suited to an environment in which corporations can tip the balance between survival and its opposite. Clearly, some public debate is needed on this issue—and some courageous steps forward in restoring personal liability where it is needed, particularly in the finance sector.[35]

The Emergent Green Growth Economy—Releasing Eco-Imagination

With few exceptions, the debate over the future of our industrial civilization fails to capture its capitalist reality. The debate remains locked in a conception of the economy shorn of its industrial *capitalist* characteristics and their effects. Books and reports are published, calling urgently for action and for new policies, such as in setting national or even global targets for reducing carbon emissions. But in the absence of changes to the underlying *rules* and *institutions* that drive the industrial capitalist economy, these calls remain merely rhetorical. Some exceptions have recently appeared.[36] These are interesting departures, which I build on in this study of the underpinnings that drive growth, expansion, and destructiveness of the system we call industrial capitalism. My concern is to sketch how this system may be tamed, or "naturalized," in the sense of bringing it into conformity with its natural limits while still allowing the driver of the system—the capitalist corporation—relative freedom of contract and, at the same time, enabling a majority of the world's population to achieve a decent standard of living. Is there a "spirit of capitalism" that is inherently destructive, that will continue to destroy the planet and its resources until, as Weber famously put it, "the last ton of fossilized coal is burnt"? We may call this emergent system a form of "naturalized capitalism"—or, in deference to Kaletsky and his capitalism 4.0, a new capitalism 5.0. Whatever we call it, this is clearly the *next* Great Transformation—one that, if it succeeds, will enable global capitalism to coexist with its natural biospheric limits; and if it fails, will in all probability mean the end of our global industrial civilization.[37]

Global warming remains the preeminent environmental issue, trumping all others in its seriousness. So the capacity of any revamped or redesigned system of industrial capitalism has to be able to demonstrate that it can deal with global warming—indeed, neutralize it as an issue, even if its containment calls for constant vigilance.

Michael Mann, whose *Sources of Social Power* has been highly influential in explicating the foundations of the trajectory of industrial civilization, has recently advanced the view that all four of his "sources"— military, economic, political, and ideological—have now turned from advancing our industrial civilization to bringing about its potential destruction. As Mann frames the argument, economic power has driven the uptake and expansion of fossil fuels in a "treadmill of profit"; political power has worked hand in glove with economic interests, viewing the expansion of industrial capitalism as bringing in more state revenues and expanding power abroad (think of the US State Department as America's Ministry of Oil); military power has driven the displacement of coal by oil and gas in the twentieth century and making the US Armed Forces the world's largest consumer of fossil fuels (albeit now turning to renewables, as noted earlier)—all buttressed by a "powerful ideology of modernization in which nature is explicitly subordinated to culture" (Mann 2013, 364–65). Nothing less than a change in our system of capitalism, he concludes, would prove adequate to the task of dealing with global warming, which he sees as a systemic (or existential) challenge.[38] Mann advances this view in a pessimistic (perhaps he would say realistic) vein, seeing full well the enormity of the challenge of changing an entire industrial system—and one that has shown itself to be so productive. One way forward, he notes, involves "a split among capitalists, with low-emitters turning against high ones" (Mann 2013, 383). I concur that this does seem to be a chink in the otherwise impenetrable armor of "carbon lock-in."[39]

Likewise, Gus Speth (2009), an influential environmental advocate in the United States, has come out with a swinging critique of his own and others' previous positions, with the statement that nothing short of a fundamental change to the capitalist order is needed to deal with the current range of problems, among which global warming again takes precedence. He calls for radical changes including a constraint on capitalist firms' freedom of contract, constraints on their limited liability, and constraints on market operations. He acknowledges that this would be a major change in the system of American capitalism. Michael Mann comments that it would be a major change in *any* system of industrial capitalism.

In the United Kingdom, Jonathan Porritt (2005), former head of Friends of the Earth and long an articulate advocate of environmental concerns, has in his tract *Capitalism as if the World Matters* asserted that his own and others' previous positions were never going to do anything more than alleviate some symptoms, and never looked like grappling with the fundamental sources of the problems—by which, again, he means the current capitalist order. Thus, Porritt advocates positions that go to the heart of the functioning of the global financial system—on the sound rationale that if that system is indeed the source of the problems, then it must be viewed as the site of the solutions. The investment required is huge—but consider the vast sums that have been "wasted" (or appropriated) as transfer payments to the Wall Street bankers who gave the world the global financial crisis—estimated as upward of US\$5 trillion.[40]

This is my starting point, and the starting point for the analysis presented in this book. It is time to move on from the critique of *effects* to examine the *causes*—and to locate the causes in the *rules* and *procedures* by which the firms and markets of the capitalist industrial civilization work.

This is also where I part company with many of the advocates of a fresh approach to the specific issues raised by global warming. It is now widely acknowledged that the global community grappled with the issue of anthropogenic climate change, over the fifteen years from 1994 to 2009, with a flawed model of what needed to be done and what could be done.[41] The way that the issue was "framed" (to use the suggestive terminology of Hulme) was as a pollution problem that called for a specific "solution" in terms of controls over the pollutant.[42] Whereas this approach might have worked with localized pollutants like sulfur dioxide emissions from power plants causing "acid rain" and destroying forests, in the case of a systemic effect like global warming it would never prove to be sufficient, nor would it be able to summon the needed political will. Hulme characterizes the issue as not so much an environmental or pollution problem—that is, one with a clear solution—but rather as more of a problem like abortion, with its conflicts between political positions such as a woman's right to choose, on the one hand, and defense of the fetus on the other. This "reframes" the issue—but of course it leaves unanswered the question of what is to be done.

Or take the case of Prins and Rayner (2007b), who gave the world such a startlingly original analysis of the flawed Kyoto process in their paper "The wrong trousers" (a title with wonderfully comic Wallace and Gromit connotations). After the disappointments of Copenhagen, the authors joined with others to call for a fresh approach to dealing with the problem of global warming. They called for an approach that would dispense entirely with the thinking that underpinned the Kyoto Protocol—obsessed as it was with national commitments to reduce carbon emissions that were not tied in any way to practical proposals like promotion of renewable energy sources or recycling initiatives. This group of forward-thinking political scientists and political economists issued a fresh analysis in 2010 that is rich in its analysis of why the Kyoto approach failed, but then offers *just one specific proposal*, namely a call for a "mild" tax on carbon emissions to raise funds for R&D on energy alternatives.[43] No doubt this is a worthy proposal. But they have not a word to say on the capitalist markets and institutions that got us into the mess, and not a word on how to refashion them. One could make the same comment about other prominent advocates of "more R&D" who remain silent on the refashioning of capitalist rules and institutions that are needed.[44]

The Oxford energy economist Dieter Helm has added his voice to the debate, calling too for a new approach to international regulation and leaving behind the flawed Kyoto process. He advocates a balancing of taxes on carbon production with carbon consumption, arguing for a regime of border carbon adjustments (BCAs), which would translate into import duties and export bounties to the extent that a country's carbon taxes were out of line with the rest of the world's. Such external adjustments are certainly more sensible that unilaterally imposed single-country carbon taxes, but the practicalities of achieving reciprocal implementation remain just as elusive.[45] Helm backs up this proposal with a call to follow energy prices and allow coal seam gas to substitute for coal (better in terms of greenhouse gas emissions but disastrous in terms of an overall strategy) and, again, calling for greater commitment to R&D on energy alternatives.[46] Again, nothing on how to reframe the rules of capitalism to bend it as a system toward greater alignment with the ecological systems within which it is embedded.

The time for such reticence is surely past. Social scientists everywhere now face the challenge of putting their shoulders to the wheel and engaging with the most thoroughgoing critique that the capitalist system has ever had, and to engage with the demands of proposing specific, far-reaching, and entirely practical proposals for its fundamental reform. I hesitate to use the word *revolution* because of all the baggage the word carries—and because I am not calling for the "overthrow" of capitalism in the sense that Lenin, Trotsky, or Mao might have interpreted the term. Rather, my starting point is to acknowledge the extraordinary productivity achievements notched up by industrial capitalism over the past two centuries, and its potential in raising hundreds of millions of people—indeed, billions—out of poverty in forthcoming decades. But having acknowledged this, the next step is to also acknowledge that the system as currently formulated and operating—in its business-as-usual format—is causing irreparable harm, and may be committing us all to ecological suicide.

Scholars and commentators are coming to see the possibility of a genuine alternative to "wild capitalism" (Nolan 2009) emerging in China and in Asia generally, as the realization grows that the Western model of industrial capitalism, based on endless growth in resources, materials, and consumption, is actually a fiction and cannot realistically hold out promise for the rising populations of China, India, and Brazil, as well as the many countries lining up behind them looking to enjoy the benefits of industrialization. These countries, led by China, are starting to move in the direction of resource constraint, reliance on renewable energies, and financial market responsibility. Michael Spence, winner of the 2001 Bank of Sweden Prize in Economics (also known as the Nobel Memorial Prize in Economic Sciences), calls this the "next convergence" (in the sense of China and India closing the gap between the West and the "rest") and describes the new pattern of development as "Asia's new growth model."[47] I agree with Spence that this turn toward the internalization of sustainability criteria in China's new pattern of growth is a development of "enormous significance" both for China and the world. China's current Twelfth Five-Year Plan could well provide the "blueprint" for an emergent green economy.

My argument, then, is that the world can keep the attractive features of industrial capitalism—its restlessness, its drive for innovation, its entrepreneurship and capacity to sustain individual initiative—while re-channeling the insatiable acquisitiveness of capitalist firms to make them not only less destructive but actually a source of sound systemic behavior. The key is to understand the dynamics that are driving change and to comprehend them as something that adds up to a new totality, a new kind of economic system. We may call what emerges a "naturalized" industrial capitalist economy, by contrast with the denaturalized system that grew and expanded for the past two and a half centuries and which now threatens our industrial civilization with collapse. It is fundamentally a system that can deliver truly sustainable green growth.

This, then, is the essence of the *next* Great Transformation—it will create an economy that can anticipate and evaluate the changes involved, at a planetary level. It promises to be a conscious transformation—one in which there is a clear limit of the trillionth tonne of carbon emissions.[48] It will create an economy of genuinely sustainable enterprise—in which sustainability is not some piece of corporate rhetoric, issued for public consumption and not acted on but an outcome of fundamental changes in the rules by which industrial capitalism works.

Of course the transformation will not be limited to the changes in energy markets, materials, and finance markets that I have focused on in this text. There will be complementary changes in agriculture (shifting to greater reliance on perennials and soil conservation, for example, and new modes of storing carbon in the soil).[49] There will be changes in water supply, featuring conservation, recycling, and organizing controlled access to virtually limitless sources of seawater, such as through desalination utilizing renewable energies; again China is building new desalination industries designed for its own uses and for export to a water-hungry world, utilizing the same strategies of catch-up and fast-follower innovation as in renewable energies.[50] The production of water, energy, and food will come to be interlinked and placed on a sustainable footing of dependence on manufacturing systems (e.g., controlled environment greenhouses, solar thermal systems, desalination plants), generating the familiar increasing returns—as opposed to the diminishing returns found in traditional agriculture and extractive industries. There will be complementary and equally fundamental changes in architecture, city design, and green building, and in many other features of the consumptionist, fossil-fueled civilization that became the norm in the twentieth century.[51] I have elected not to enter these topics, partly to keep the present text to a manageable length, and partly because changes in the fundamental markets of capitalism will have clear spillover impact in all other aspects of our industrial civilization.

We need to dispense with the simplistic parables from the past. Adam Smith's hidden hand justified a self-regulating economy that minimized state interference—but it loses salience as we fill the planet and there is no longer a frontier. Garrett Hardin's tragedy of the commons steps in with a story that makes resolving collective action problems seem to be insoluble absent draconian state ownership and control—and paves the way to a nasty lifeboat ethic that absolves the wealthy of their social responsibility. Instead, we need a new story that fits the emerging requirements of a biomimetic economy managed within known and measured ecological limits. The image of the garden and our role as gardener comes to mind—a story that sees humanity cultivating the biomimetic economy within planetary boundaries, intervening to enable the earth to be fruitful but responsible in respecting ecological limits and balances.[52] The gardener is an appropriate image that fosters care and responsibility while counteracting the swagger of "technofixes" such as launching planetary shields to reduce solar flux and thereby "fix" global warming—at vast and unknown risk.

The building of the green growth economy as successor to the fossil fuel economy promises to be the *next Great Transformation*. Like the first Great Transformation, it will involve fundamental changes to the operation of energy markets, resources and commodity markets, and markets for finance, as well as for product markets generally, making them ecologically aligned through their eco-tagging and eco-audit trails. This next Great Transformation is emerging first in China, at the behest of the Chinese Communist Party, which sees its future survival and legitimacy tied to delivering further growth in incomes and wealth for the Chinese people, a promise that the Chinese leadership recognizes can be delivered only with a new model of growth. To the extent that we can anticipate a "new convergence," it could be from West to East as Europe and the United States are compelled to take heed of the Chinese growth experience and other developing countries use it as their model. This could turn out to be the best hope for the planet.

In retrospect, we may view the insatiable performance of industrial capitalism as the product of its expansive phase, as it "filled" the earth and occupied every niche. But it cannot be allowed to continue as the operating system of an industrial capitalism that has reached the finite limits of the planet, where there are no more frontiers to exploit. Something has to be done to change the operating system of the global capitalist order from a "wild," frontier economy to a responsible gardening economy—and it has to be done quickly. The alternatives of resource wars and climate change on a ruinous scale, that wipes out not only our civilization but a large swath of the earth's other inhabitants as well, is unthinkable.

Neo-Schumpeterian, Neo-Gerschenkronian, and Neo-Olsonian Perspectives

The argument developed in this book, as flagged in the introduction, has essentially been grounded in the great contributions of Schumpeter, Gerschenkron, and Olson. It is *neo-Schumpeterian* in that it takes Schumpeter's insights into the dynamic, entrepreneurial character of capitalism as the defining feature of the emerging green growth capitalism. I have stressed that the new green sectors can be expected to emerge in life-and-death struggle with the incumbent, fossil-fuel-based industries— with perhaps some surprising developments as elements of the fossil fuel sector break away and "green" their own activities, in partnership with green start-ups, as in the case of oil and gas companies promoting biofuels and eventually renewable energy systems. The neo-Schumpeterian character of the analysis presented can be found in the insistence that creative destruction will be the hallmark of an emergent green capitalism, and that the new green energy and resource circulation sectors will be competitive and dynamic and innovative in a way that the giant firms of the fossil fuel era never have been.

The argument has also been that the new green growth capitalism will emerge first in China and then in other developing countries, where aspirations to industrialize and build healthy, growing economies are frustrated by shortages of fossil fuels and other resources and rising political (and ultimately military) tensions associated with the peaking of such resources. The emergent countries are free to adopt the latest in clean technologies developed elsewhere and to capture latecomer advantages through doing so. This is essentially a *neo-Gerschenkronian* argument, in that potential advantages of being a latecomer are identified by the countries' leaderships and strategies are framed as a means of capturing these advantages. It is clear that there is a wealth of experience in formulating and executing latecomer strategies in East Asia, which China is exploiting in its green development model, and which other newly developed and emerging countries can be expected to adopt as well.

Finally, the argument has emphasized all along that the barriers to the successful emergence of a green growth capitalism will be formidable and that vested interests will not give way. This means that reason alone is not enough to effect the transition. There needs to be political calculation, the forging of alliances, the building of entrepreneurial coalitions, and the marginalization of the most obdurate of the forces of resistance. This is to enter the world of *neo-Olsonian* calculation, where the sway of vested interests obstructs change and new coalitions need to be formed to drive through the barriers that these vested interests create. We have seen that these forces sustaining the fossil fuel status quo run deep; they include not just the still-enormous subsidies that are channeled toward these interests, but more fundamentally the vast infrastructure that the oil and coal and gas companies have created, and that they will seek to retain tenaciously, and more fundamentally still, the vast fossil fuel reserves that such companies have amassed and on which they pin their stock market valuations. This "unburnable carbon" could prove to be perhaps the most fundamental barrier to the shift to a low-carbon economy, which will call for clever policies to enable the companies concerned to find ways to extricate themselves from such stranded assets.[53] The death agonies of the fossil fuel system will be savage and long, and they will threaten the world with destruction. The building of a new green growth capitalism will hence provide a fresh round of challenges where neo-Olsonian strategies will be needed to meet them.

We do not have to know that global warming is taking place to support a green economy—or to support measures taken by governments to facilitate the emergence of such a green economy.[54] In fact there are any number of reasons for wanting to get economies off their dependence on fossil fuels, quite apart from the contested issue of global warming. There are the geopolitical tensions associated with the random distribution of oil supplies (and supplies of other fossil fuels, including shale oil and coal seam gas). Turning off the oil tap means turning off the financial sources of petro-regimes' power. Second, oil-dependent economies are at the mercy of cartels like OPEC and the arbitrary pricing of oil—thus condemning developing countries to pay exaggerated rents to oil producers. Then there are developing countries. Do they stand to gain more from developing their own energy industries—or importing energy in the form of oil and gas supplies? For reasons best known to itself, the World Bank has consistently evaded policies that would impinge directly on energy choices, nor viewed the building of renewable energy industries as a passport to industrial wealth. But the mega-industrializers of the early twenty-first century, led by China and India, are taking matters into their own hands and framing their own industrial development strategies around renewable energies and circular economy initiatives.[55]

J. C. Spender has a nice line in arguing that we can never "know" exactly how our industrial activities impinge on the earth's climate. As he puts it, we didn't create the ecosphere, and so we can never hope to fully understand it (by contrast with our ability to understand the workings of the machines that we create ourselves—even very complex machines like electric power grids, or the Internet).[56] Yes, it's true that we can never know—*really know*—what the effects of our actions will be; but we can assuredly have a good idea, allowing us to take evasive action that is feasible. And the principle of no regrets is surely an excellent principle to appeal to in such matters.[57] A no-regrets approach means taking actions that do not have potentially catastrophic consequences. The issue of nuclear power is a case in point. For all the arguments in favor of nuclear power—that it is relatively carbon clean, that it is safer than coal mining when measured in terms of known fatalities over a particular operating period, and so on—these all fail against the powerful argument that a failure of a nuclear reactor can have potentially disastrous consequences. This has been learnt in Japan with the Fukushima reactors that were rendered inoperable by the combined impact of an earthquake and tsunami—natural disasters known to occur in Japan.

Now a policy of developing an energy system based on renewables is an excellent example of a no-regrets policy at work. The only risk associated with renewable energy sources is the "risk" that they will not be able to provide baseload power. But it is clear that as electric power companies upgrade the grids, to make them "strong and smart" (as in China) then this risk is diminishing rapidly. Otherwise the risks of going with renewable energies are no greater than the risks associated with any industrial activity. Yes, there can be fatalities due to accidents; there can be toxic effects from some of the more exotic materials put to use (like the arsenides in CIGS solar panels). But there is surely enough experience by now in dealing with such "regular" or common industrial risks that they cannot be seriously raised as a reason for not proceeding with the renewables option.

In contrast, the advantages of going with renewables and low-carbon technologies—once the cost differential has been overcome—are compelling. As discussed in Chapter 4, renewables offer overwhelming advantages in being available almost everywhere, free of charge, and without any legally sanctioned limits. The availability of energy from the sun is pervasive and free—which is doubtless one of the factors that has contributed to the hostility expressed by conventional and traditional power producers. But the Chinese (and Germans and others) are demonstrating how capitalist calculation can be applied to such a free resource and profits can be generated—without any attempt being made by anyone to privatize, or "own" the sun. The profits come from the application of sophisticated technology to the harvesting of solar energy to produce usable power. Capitalist dynamics can operate at every step of this process—from the development of the needed technologies and the protection of the ideas embodied in these technologies via patenting, to the building of electric power infrastructure and concentrating solar power stations.[58] All this can be accomplished with perfectly understandable capitalist conventions, including conventions for distinguishing between investments that deliver benefits today and those that are targeted at the future.[59]

So—even if it turns out that the dangers of global warming have been exaggerated, and carbon dioxide turns out not to be the major source of pollution that it appears to be (and even if the dangers of excessive carbon dioxide emissions have been stoked by nuclear scientists anxious to deflect attention from the radioactive hazards of their own industry), there is still little future for a world bound to fossil fuels because of their imminent scarcity. And even if the exploitation of unconventional fossil fuels delays the onset of peak fuel concerns, the dangers of international tensions over access to dwindling resources, and the geopolitical threat they represent, would still loom large. The inescapable fact is that renewables represent a genuine escape from these traps—and the only one that we can count on. They offer genuine energy security as well as economic security. As a civilization we escaped from the Malthusian trap by utilizing fossil fuels, first in the seventeenth century and on an increasing scale ever after—but we have now reached effectively the end of that road. A renewable and ecologically benign alternative in the form of renewable energies and circular economy initiatives now offers a comparable escape from the resource-strained world created by industrialization. It stands as the *inevitable option* for humanity, and for our civilization based on industrial capitalism.[60]

Ultimately, we cannot know whether the changes advocated in this book will occur fast enough to save our industrial civilization. Carbon lock-in may prevail, and vested interests may place endless blockages in the way of the coming greening of capitalism through renewables and circular economy initiatives. Our kind of industrial civilization may end up by committing ecological suicide, in the manner of an Easter Island. The only force standing in the way of climate obscurantism and vested interest is capitalism itself—in the sense that capitalist entrepreneurs can see where profits can be made through introducing the renewables and circular economy initiatives; they will themselves strive to dismantle the barriers placed in their way. Capitalists can be very persuasive when they see barriers erected between themselves and realizable profit.

This is why I insist that if global warming and all the other ills of our industrial civilization are the creation of capitalism, then it is to capitalism that we must look to find a solution. It cannot be the kind of capitalism that created this present system. It will have to be a green growth capitalism based on renewables and circular economy principles—with sustainability built into the DNA of institutions, organizations, and industrial processes. Nothing else would be acceptable—for us or for the planet. It is to capitalist dynamics that we entrust the future of our industrial civilization.

Reference Matter

Notes

Chapter 1

1. See the Organization for Economic Cooperation and Development's *Global Perspectives on Development* reports, particularly the first one, published by the OECD Development Centre in 2010.

2. See Pomeranz (2000) on the Great Divergence. On the more recent Great Convergence, see, for example, Martin Wolf, "In the grip of a great convergence," *Financial Times*, January 4, 2011, http://www.ft.com/cms/s/0/072c87e6-1841-11e0-88c9-00144feab49a.html#axzz1edU6FbyK.

3. See Michael Spence (2011a, 2011b), who argues that the Great Convergence is bringing billions of new participants into the industrial arena. The changing industrial geography of the world, emphasizing the rise of China and India, is analyzed by Shahid Yusuf and Kaoru Nabeshima (2010).

4. Polanyi's study of the capitalist industrial transformation was written during his years of exile in London and published in 1944 in his final years of exile in the United States. Block (2003) provides a useful introduction.

5. See Hu (2006a, 2006b, 2011, 2014). On a similar theme, see Nair (2011) and Walz (2010); for comparisons with earlier industrial transitions, see Yuval Atsmon et al., "Winning the $30 trillion decathlon: Going for gold in emerging markets," *McKinsey Quarterly*, August 2012, http://www.mckinsey.com/insights/strategy/winning_the_30_trillion_decathlon_going_for_gold_in_emerging_markets.

6. For an informed discussion, see Bowen and Frankhauser (2011); for an example of a negative view, see Resnick et al. (2012) on green initiatives in southern Africa. Walz (2010), Rifkin (2011), Zysman and Huberty (2011, 2013), and Hallegatte et al. (2012) further nuance the issue.

7. On carbon lock-in, see Unruh (2000) and, most recently, Unruh and del Rio (2012).

8. For a robust advocacy of free-market environmentalism, see Anderson and Leal (2001), who are associated with the Property and Environment Research Center; a succinct account is provided by Jeffreys (1994). A stimulating debate pro and contra free-market environmentalism was provided by Smith (1995) and Narveson (1995) in the same issue of *Journal of Agricultural and Environmental Ethics*. On the financial meltdown and its roots in sweeping deregulatory reforms that created leviathan financial institutions and a shadow banking system, see, e.g., the analysis by former International Monetary Fund economist Simon Johnson (2009).

9. On the use of common law procedures for resolving environmental property rights disputes, see Adler (2000, 2012); for a popular exposition of the same, see Adler (2011).

10. Economists point to the possibility of state interventions themselves being motivated by rent seeking. Smart governments minimize this possibility with their emphasis on what Amsden (2001) calls "reciprocal control mechanisms" to counteract cronyism—as well as strong anti-corruption enforcement, as practiced, for example, by Singapore.

11. As noted in the Preface, I see my arguments for the greening of capitalism as complementing the work of Deidre McCloskey and her endorsement of free-market environmentalism. McCloskey is in the process of writing and publishing the four-volume treatise *The Bourgeois Era*, in which she provides a strong defense of capitalism and its virtues. Two volumes have been published (McCloskey 2006, 2010), and a third has been available on the Internet for comment and feedback (McCloskey 2013).

12. One such climate scientist has been Dr. James Hansen, who has cast doubt on China's renewables prospects in congressional and Senate testimony (e.g., http://www.columbia.edu/~jeh1/mailings/2014/20140313_SenateTestimony .pdf). For a response from Dr. Hao Tan and myself, defending our characterization of China's renewables revolution, see "Jousting with James Hansen: China building a renewables powerhouse," March 26, 2014, http://www.japanfocus .org/events/view/214.

13. This has been the pattern in other important industrial initiatives, such as reliance on industrial clusters and special economic zones, where India has emulated Chinese initiatives.

14. See the statement from the US Energy Information Administration, "China consumes nearly as much coal as the rest of the world combined," January 29, 2012, http://www.eia.gov/todayinenergy/detail.cfm?id=9751.

15. Dr. Hao Tan and I discussed China's 2013 additions of power capacity and electric energy generation, seeing them as pointing the way toward future

trends, in our editorial in *Carbon Management* (Mathews and Tan 2014b), in our letter to *Nature* (Mathews and Tan 2014a), and in our post "China's continuing renewable energy revolution: Global implications," at *Asia-Pacific Journal: Japan Focus*, March 24, 2014, http://www.japanfocus.org/-John_A_-Mathews/4098.

16. While the Twelfth Five-Year Plan set this target of 30 percent by nonfossil sources as being reached by 2020, it was brought forward to 2015 in the 2012 Energy White Paper (see Mathews and Tan 2013).

17. The same contrast between green and black in China's development is made by Christina Larson, "The great paradox of China: Green energy and black skies," August 17, 2009, *Yale Environment 360*, http://e360.yale.edu/content/print.msp?id=2180.

18. See the text with this title by Zysman and Huberty (2011); see also Zysman and Huberty (2013).

19. It's rather like the Kyoto Protocol, with its unworkable distinctions between Annex I and Annex II countries.

20. The first text to use the term *green economy* as implying one in which growth is viewed as feasible and desirable in resolving environmental problems (as opposed to zero growth) appears to be *Blueprint for a Green Economy*, by the British scholar David W. Pearce (1989). He went on to produce a series of such "Blueprint" books, including for the World Bank, before his untimely death in 2005, at the age of sixty-three.

21. I make repeated appeal in this book to increasing returns as the means through which growth can be continued without expanding the resource base. The concept of increasing returns has disappeared from the economics lexicon because of the difficulties involved in demonstrating the existence of an equilibrium with anything other than constant returns; for an elaboration, see Buchanan and Yoon (1994). Of course, increasing returns are the engines of firm growth—whether recognized in neoclassical economics or not.

22. This argument is elaborated in the paper published by Dr. Erik Reinert and myself in *Futures* (Mathews and Reinert 2014).

23. See my exposition in *Futures* (Mathews 2012b), and presentations by Soogil Young, former chair of the Korean Presidential Committee on Green Growth.

24. A spate of reports from international agencies attests to this. The United Nations issued the Report of the Secretary-General's High-Level Panel on Global Sustainability in early 2012: *Resilient People, Resilient Planet: A Future Worth Choosing* (United Nations 2012); the World Bank (2012) issued its long-anticipated report *Inclusive Green Growth: The Pathway to Sustainable Development* some months later, in May, at the Seoul Green Growth Summit, with a whole chapter devoted to "green innovation and industrial policies"; the UN Environment Program (2011) has issued its own treatment of the issues in

Towards a Green Economy: Pathways to Sustainable Development and Poverty Eradication; the UN Industrial Development Organization has also been active, with a series reports such as *A Greener Footprint for Industry* (UNIDO 2010); and the UN Economic and Social Commission for Asia and the Pacific has a long-standing interest in furthering discussion on green growth issues in Asia and the Pacific, such as through the *Low Carbon Green Growth Roadmap for Asia and the Pacific* (UNESCAP and Korea International Cooperation Agency 2012); and UNESCAP (2012) has combined with the Asian Development Bank and UN Environment Program to produce *Green Growth, Resources and Resilience: Environmental Sustainability in Asia and the Pacific*. Together, these documents provide a comprehensive set of policies and programs for shifting toward green growth and, in many cases, endorse green industrial policies as a means of doing so. A new international organization, the Global Green Growth Institute (GGGI) has now been formed, at the instigation of Korea; and a new knowledge platform created, the Green Growth Knowledge Platform (GGKP) (created by the GGGI, OECD, UNEP, and the World Bank), to drive the diffusion and adoption of green growth strategies; see for example the review of country experiences in GGBP (2014).

25. I am using the term *business as usual* as shorthand for the fossil-fueled, resource-inefficient system that is currently dominant, as contrasted with the alternative based on renewables and resource recirculation. This is the terminology adopted by the International Energy Agency and the Intergovernmental Panel on Climate Change and other official bodies; for an exploration of the term, see Samans (2009).

Chapter 2

1. According to estimates by the British economist N. F. R. Crafts (1985), income per person (in 1970 US dollars) in England doubled over the century 1760 to 1860, rising from about $400 in 1760 to $430 in 1800, $500 in 1830, and then $800 in 1860.

2. On China's population shifts, see the estimates by the US demographer J. S. Durand (1977).

3. See, for example, Crafts (1985). The most authoritative treatment of the Industrial Revolution in Britain is now Allen (2009).

4. Karl Polanyi (1886–1964) was a Hungarian Jewish intellectual, a product of the social and political ferment in pre- and postwar Central Europe. As a young man in Budapest, he engaged with other intellectual notables such as Karl Mannheim and Györgi Lukács, and he was involved in supporting the Hungarian republic and its social-democratic Károlyi regime. When it fell in 1924, he fled to Vienna, where he worked as a journalist and editor; then in 1933, under the

impact of Nazism, he had to flee Vienna and arrived in London, where he eked out a living lecturing with the Workers' Education Association. Polanyi finally ended up in the United States, where he penned *The Great Transformation*— a reflection on the wars of the twentieth century and their origins in the nineteenth-century social and economic transformations that had started centuries earlier in Britain.

5. In the real, organic, socially bonded society out of which the market society was wrenched, the need to restore some sense of cohesiveness was expressed through what Polanyi called a "double movement," or feedback loop, resulting in the formation of trade unions, credit unions, cooperatives and social democracy, and ultimately the whole political apparatus of corporatism, and its deadly outgrowths in the twentieth century: fascism and Nazism.

6. Polanyi's 1944 book has gone through numerous editions, most recently reissued by Beacon Press in Boston, with an introduction by Fred Block and a foreword by Joseph Stiglitz. For insightful treatments of Polanyi's contribution to Western political economic thought and on the writing of *The Great Transformation*, see Block (2003); on Polanyi's conceptual innovations and intellectual affiliations, see Dale (2010).

7. The closest exponent of such a perspective in the current period of globalization is arguably John Gray (2000/2009), who argues that the neoliberal project to create a global market order is as utopian as the nineteenth-century version critiqued by Polanyi, and will in the long run prove just as devastating as communism and fascism in the twentieth century. Polanyi developed a critique of the market order from the Left, while Gray does so from the Right (if such labels now have any meaning).

8. See in particular the work of Deidre McCloskey, and especially her running critique of Polanyi contained in the web-based draft of the forthcoming third volume of her series Bourgeois Virtues: *The Treasured Bourgeoisie: How Markets and Innovation Became Virtuous, 1600–1848*, available at http://www.deirdremccloskey.com/weblog/2011/01/06/contents-of-the-bourgeois-revaluation-draft-jan-2011/.

9. In this text I am taking Robert Allen's (2009) study of the Industrial Revolution, and his arguments as to how and why it happened as it did in Britain, as guide. Daron Acemoglu and James Robinson (2012) also provide an insightful analysis of the institutional and political changes that led to the Industrial Revolution, and account for its thoroughgoing character. But oddly enough, they make little mention of fossil fuels—which is like describing a steam locomotive without mentioning that it runs on coal, or a car on petrol.

10. The term *industrial revolution* is actually quite recent. It was introduced by French scholars in the early nineteenth century, largely referring to what was going on in Britain. Then the term was picked up and popularized in lectures by the brilliant young scholar Arnold Toynbee at Oxford in 1884. Toynbee was only

thirty years old, and he died of overwork shortly after. See Arnold Toynbee, "Lectures on the Industrial Revolution in England," 1884, available at http://socserv .mcmaster.ca/econ/ugcm/3ll3/toynbee/indrev. Nef (1943) provides a scholarly discussion of the origins of the term and antecedents.

11. This clarity is thanks to pioneering studies by American scholars such as Nef (1977) and Chandler (1972); German scholars such as Sieferle (1982/2001); and British scholars including Wrigley (1962, 1988), Cameron (1985), Church (1994), Flinn (1984), Thomas (1980, 1985), as well as the interpreters of this transition for its impact on world history by scholars such as Kenneth Pomeranz, Robert Allen, and Ian Morris. Smil (1994) provides an authoritative account of the significance played by energy in world history, while McNeill and McNeill (2003) attribute the role of energy (and fossil fuels) their correct historic significance. This body of work stands in stark contrast to mainstream economic history, which continues to ignore the role played by coal in effecting the Industrial Revolution—or is deliberately downplayed by scholars such as Clark and Jacks (2008).

12. Sieferle (1982/2001) remains the most striking of the studies of the arduous transition that constituted the Industrial Revolution, particularly the century of changes that preceded the breakthrough in 1750 that saw one sector after another find ways to utilize coal.

13. By far the most significant of these innovations was the steam engine (known at the time as an atmospheric engine, because the steam played a role in creating a vacuum that was filled by air driven by atmospheric pressure). For insightful accounts of the technological evolution that spawned these innovations, see works by Crump (2010) and Rosen (2010). Rosen develops the argument that steam, together with industry and invention, constitutes the "most powerful idea in the world," which by the end of the book is revealed (spoiler!) as the creation of the patent system. The argument is compelling.

14. I take the year 1712 as definitively marking the onset of the industrial era, which has thus been developing now for more than three hundred years. The more usual starting date of 1750 or 1760 coincides with observable changes in major industries like textiles but misses the prior essential changes in substitution of sources of energy. Steffen and colleagues (2011) date the onset of the Anthropocene epoch to the year 1750.

15. See Allen (2009, 2011) for an excellent summary account in all its global richness.

16. There is now a flourishing school of economic historical enquiry into these processes of energy-material transformation informed by modern concepts of energy and exergy (available energy). See Sieferle (1982/2001) and Krausmann, Schandl, and Sieferle (2008) as representative examples.

17. See Smith (2010), chap. 1. For an accessible review, see John Gray, "The intensifying struggle for natural resources," *New Statesman*, 31 March 2011, http://www.newstatesman.com/books/2011/03/natural-resources-world-global. Michael Klare (2012) provides an arresting account of impending resource conflicts in his most recent book.

18. Al Gore's *An Inconvenient Truth* (2006) frames the issue, of course, as one in which the entire industrial civilization faces ruin if alternatives cannot be found: this is his "inconvenient truth." But Gore remained tied to the science and steered clear of the technology. In his more recent book, *Our Choice: How to Deal with the Climate Crisis* (2009), Gore deals (finally) explicitly with renewable energies and makes a persuasive case that they must take priority in any action plan.

19. For a succinct overview of this history, see Fulcher (2004).

20. On the Eastern origins of many of the innovations made in the West, where it was the openness of European societies that enabled them to take advantage of these innovations, see, for example, Hobson (2004). The rise and fall of these great powers is vividly described by Kennedy (1987).

21. On the rise of the financial system, see, for example, Ferguson (2008).

22. See Kaminker and Stewart (2012), where sustained attention is given to the barriers standing in the way of the deployment of such funds at scale in accelerating the uptake of renewable energies around the world.

23. The German sociologists and economic historians Max Weber and Werner Sombart, writing at the turn of the nineteenth and twentieth centuries, respectively, have provided the most penetrating critique of the rationalist underpinnings of capitalism; see Parsons (1928) for a sympathetic and clear account of their contributions.

24. Here I draw on my paper published in *Futures* (Mathews 2011b).

25. Maddison (2001) provides definitive quantitative estimates of national GDP over the two millennia, from AD 1 to 2001. Figure 2.6 is derived directly from Maddison's table 8b, "Share of world GDP, 20 countries and regional totals, AD 1–2001." He elaborates on the rise of China in Maddison (2006). For an interesting discussion of the various approaches to depicting two thousand years of economic change in a single chart, see the article "More 2,000 years in a single graphic," *The Economist*, 12 June 2012, http://www.economist.com/blogs/graphicdetail/2012/06/mis-charting-economic-history.

26. Acemoglu and Robinson (2012) have transformed the debate over why some nations are rich and others poor, tracing the origins to politics and property rights. They make a convincing case that these were the most important institutions accounting for the Great Divergence in the first place—but they are on shakier ground when they discuss China of the past three decades. On this aspect of their work, see the review by Gideon Haigh, "West complacent over why

nations fail," *Financial Times*, 25 February 2013, http://www.ft.com/intl/cms/s/0/fdb95588-7f3e-11e2-89ed-00144feabdc0.html.

27. The swing by China behind a "new economic policy" in 1979 is one of those world-historic events, comparable in effect to the Industrial Revolution and the French Revolution. The role in this turn after Mao's death, by party leaders Deng Xiaoping (Naughton 1993) and Hua Guofeng (Tiewes and Sun 2011), cannot be underestimated. For a recent and thorough account of the Chinese Communist Party and its role in micromanaging the entire Chinese renaissance, see McGregor (2010).

28. In the year 2010 China displaced the United States as the world's top manufacturing nation, ending the US reign of 110 years. See Peter Marsh, "China noses ahead as top goods producer," *Financial Times*, 13 March 2011, http://www.ft.com/intl/cms/s/0/002fd8f0-4d96-11e0-85e4-00144feab49a.html#axzz1cRvmsynP.

29. On China's ecological modernization, see Mol (2006). For sympathetic treatments of China's rise and the issues raised, not least for China itself, see texts such as Martin Jacques's (2009) *When China Rules the World*; Odd Arne Westad's (2012) *Restless Empire: China and the World since 1750*, and James Fallows's *China Airborne* (2013). The World Bank (2013) has combined with the influential Development Research Center of the State Council to produce a comprehensive treatise on China's modernization: *China 2030: Building a Modern, Harmonious, and Creative Society*.

30. See the 2010 *Global Perspectives on Development* report (OECD Development Centre 2010).

31. See Martin Wolf, "In the grip of a Great Convergence," *Financial Times*, 4 January 2011, http://www.ft.com/intl/cms/s/0/072c87e6-1841-11e0-88c9-00144feab49a.html#axzz1wGtoT2YI.

32. See Ed Crooks and Lucy Hornby, "The new gas guzzler," *Financial Times*, 9 October 2013, http://www.ft.com/intl/cms/s/0/01ba1a04-2c24-11e3-acf4-00144feab7de.html.

33. Similar long-term (decadal) price increases can be found for uranium oxide (nuclear fuel), aluminum, copper, and other minerals, as verified by long-term price charts published by Infomine, at http://www.infomine.com/investment/metal-prices/copper/.

34. Julian Simon (1932–98) was a prolific and influential opponent of resource pessimism, taking on the "population bomb" advocate Paul Ehrlich in particular. Arguing that more people should be seen as a boon rather than a disaster, he called his best-selling book *The Ultimate Resource*, referring to people as such a positive resource. I am engaging here with this book (1981/1998) and with his article on the same theme published in 1994 in *Economic Affairs*.

35. On "tipping point" in its general sense, when a small perturbation can lead to a large change, see Gladwell (2000).

36. Structural change in these emerging economies, with consequent shifts in demand, will also play a significant role in future patterns of resource use. On these processes and their catch-up dynamic, in Asia and Africa generally, see Oyelaran-Oyeyinka and Rasiah (2009).

37. In her writings on the virtues of capitalism, Deidre McCloskey (2006, 2010, forthcoming) singles out Julian Simon for special endorsement. The critique advanced here, that Simon's trends could be understood as applying to a version of industrial capitalism that was still expanding and was not having to accommodate the demands of China in a world that is increasingly "full," serves also as a response to McCloskey—in the spirit of an "imaginary dialogue" with her. It is of interest that in 2013 McCloskey received the Julian L. Simon Memorial Award from the Competitive Enterprise Institute.

38. Hu (2006a, 2006b) outlined his arguments in an influential pair of papers on why green development was "an inevitable choice for China." He has followed up with a book issued in 2011 by the Brookings Institution, *China in 2020: A Different Kind of Superpower*, which likewise devotes a chapter to the green development model; and in 2014 by a new book, *China: Innovative Green Development*, which lays out an argument similar to the one developed in this text, and written contemporaneously. An argument for an alternative "Asian growth model" is provided by Nair (2011), while the United Nations Environment Program (UNEP 2011) has come out strongly in favor of a green development model.

39. I am deliberately introducing my own acronym, BICs, in place of the usual BRICs because I regard Russia as a special case, with a development strategy couched almost exclusively in terms of fossil fuels.

40. See the paper on this theme published by Erik Reinert and myself in the journal *Futures* (Mathews and Reinert 2014) and our post "US energy security—beware false comfort," *The Globalist*, March 20, 2014, http://www .theglobalist.com/energy-security-beware-false-comfort/.

41. In 1662 or thereabouts, the French philosopher and polymath Blaise Pascal penned his famous "wager" that it made sense even for a nonbeliever to credit the existence of God, since the gains were immeasurable and the penalties nonexistent. The same logical structure attends China's (and the world's) approach to the issues of creation of circular economy and renewable energies systems, as argued by many, and notably by Irish American publisher Tim O'Reilly: "Pascal's wager and climate change," 19 January 2009, *The Edge*, http://radar .oreilly.com/2009/01/pascals-wager-and-climate-change.html.

42. The twentieth century was a century of oil wars, with the United States as the century's leading "oil power" being closely involved with many of them, along

with Britain and France (Klare 2012). Think of the US oil blockade of Japan that triggered the Pacific War, the US overthrow of the Mossadegh government in Iran in 1953, numerous interventions in oil-rich South American countries such as Venezuela and Bolivia—not to mention the Gulf War and Iraq War. The link between oil and war has been well studied—see the books by Michael Klare (2002, 2012) as representative, as well as the geostrategic visions based on oil developed by contributors to US foreign policy, such as Brzezinski (1997). As China has become a major industrial player in the twenty-first century, with its own oil supply lines to defend, the risks increase of stumbling into a military confrontation with the United States; see Klare and Volman (2006) on the United States, China, and the scramble for Africa's oil.

43. With my collaborator Dr. Hao Tan I have been emphasizing that China is becoming a renewables powerhouse in numerous publications (Mathews and Tan 2013, 2014a, 2014b) and in the post "China's continuing energy revolution: Global implications," *Asia-Pacific Journal: Japan Focus*, March 24, 2014, http:// www.japanfocus.org/-John_A_-Mathews/4098, and the 2012 posts "China's industrial energy revolution (part 1)," http://www.japanfocus.org/-Hao-Tan/3874, and "China's industrial energy revolution (part 2)," http://www.japanfocus.org/ -Hao-Tan/3881. On the resource implications of the renewable energy shift, see Mathews and Tan (2014c).

44. China is becoming one of the world's most significant users of power generation technologies that minimize carbon emissions from coal, such as fluidized bed combustion—collectively known as "clean coal" technologies.

45. Ho (2006, 3) takes up this point, arguing that "China is showing clear signs of greening as new institutions and regulations are created, environmental awareness increases and green technologies are implemented. However, the question remains whether this is sufficient to effectuate long-term sustainable development."

46. Actually, the United States did eliminate its external tariff targeted at Brazilian imports of ethanol at the beginning of 2012, by allowing the tariff and complementary production tax credit to lapse. The European Union has yet to follow the US lead, and it retains high tariff barriers against imports of biofuels— "justified" in terms of sustainability criteria. For a discussion, see my posting to *The Globalist*, "The end of the U.S. ethanol tariff," 6 January 2012, http://www .theglobalist.com/StoryId.aspx?StoryId=9505.

47. See Davidson (2012) and Morris and Pehnt (2012) for accounts of the German *Energiewende*; it promises to provide a lead for the rest of the world in how to build renewable energy industries, comparable to that already instigated by China. The United States, by contrast, has been stuck with its "carbon lock-in" and is now driving the coal seam gas and shale oil revolution, locking the country into further fossil fuel dependence.

48. The geopolitics of oil is a topic that is attracting increased attention: Renner (2006) offers the argument that new oil finds lock the Western world more firmly into the fossil fuel paradigm, while Graetz (2011) sees energy policy in the United States as reaching a new low. By contrast, Yergin (2011), like Maugeri (2009), paints an essentially optimistic view regarding global oil supplies.

49. Immanuel Kant published his essay "Perpetual Peace: A Philosophical View" in 1795, in the glow of the first years of the French Revolution.

50. In striking contrast with the US Congress and executive administration, the US military is under no illusions as to the long-term costs of its overdependence on oil, and it is taking active steps to reduce that dependence while also planning for a world in which security issues are defined by global warming effects. On the Pentagon's search for energy alternatives, see Elisabeth Rosenthal, "U.S. Military orders less dependence on fossil fuels," *New York Times*, 4 October 2010, http://www.nytimes.com/2010/10/05/science/earth/05fossil.html. On the security implications of global warming as viewed from the Pentagon, see the report from the Defense Science Board Task Force (2011), "Trends and implications of climate change for national and international security."

Chapter 3

1. Crutzen (2002, 23) put it as follows: "It seems appropriate to assign the term 'Anthropocene' to the present, in many ways human-dominated, geological epoch, supplementing the Holocene—the warm period of the past 10–12 millennia. The Anthropocene could be said to have started in the latter part of the eighteenth century, when analyses of air trapped in polar ice showed the beginning of growing global concentrations of carbon dioxide and methane. This date also happens to coincide with James Watt's design of the steam engine in 1784."

2. See Crutzen (2002, 23).

3. See Steffen, Persson et al. (2011); Steffen, Grinevald et al. (2011). McNeill (2000) poses the advent of the fossil fuel era graphically as representing "something new under sun."

4. A group of scientists writing in the journal *Conservation Biology* (Caro et al. 2011) argued that the term *Anthropocene* is misleading because it implies that nowhere on the earth is natural. This has been countered by another group of scientists writing in the *New York Times*, arguing that the term is appropriate because it is consistent with centuries of human fashioning of the environment; it frames debate as ensuring that this fashioning itself is to be guided by sound ecological insight rather than preservation of a mythical "nature." See Emma Marris, Peter Kareiva, Joseph Mascaro, and Erle C. Ellis, "Hope in the Age of Man," *New York Times*, 7 December 2011, http://www.nytimes.com/2011/12/08/opinion/the-age-of-man-is-not-a-disaster.html?_r=1&src=tp.

5. Nobel laureate Paul Krugman uses the graphic expression "cooking" the planet through fossil fuel combustion—which we might extend to "swallowing" the planet through excessive resource usage (to continue Krugman's metaphor). See Paul Krugman, "Who cooked the planet?" *New York Times*, 25 July 2010, http://www.nytimes.com/2010/07/26/opinion/26krugman.html?_r=1. Nolan (2009) refers graphically to unrestrained capitalism as "wild"—meaning untamed.

6. See "China's environment minister: Pollution, environmental destruction 'grave impediments' to nation's development," *New York Times*, 3 January 2011.

7. See Economy (2005); and in particular on China's devastating water issues, see Economy (2013). An equally pessimistic account is provided by Grumbine (2010).

8. Victor Mallet, "Dirty business," review, *Financial Times*, June 26, 2004, http://www.ft.com/intl/cms/s/0/436248b6-c70f-11d8-a07a-00000e2511c8.html?siteedition=intl#axzz2mRQqJ01l.

9. Greenberg (2010) provides a comprehensive review of depletion of fisheries stocks by our industrial civilization.

10. I discuss Hardin's notion of the tragedy of the commons later in this chapter.

11. Randers (2008)—one of the authors of the *Limits to Growth* publication of 1972—has spent a professional career studying the phenomenon of overshoot and collapse. In his 2008 review, he notes some examples to drive home the reality of the concept. Well-known examples are the overfishing of the Newfoundland cod fishery and the overharvesting of wood on Easter Island, which led to the collapse of the prosperous way of life of the islanders prior to the arrival of Europeans in 1722.

12. An editorial in the *New York Times* puts the matter well:
What makes Chile different isn't just the scale of its aquaculture. Its basic means of forestalling the salmon virus is tragic in itself: salmon-farming companies move their pens from polluted water to pristine water, edging their way steadily south down the fjords that define the Chilean coast. This is the equivalent of moving industrial hog farms onto virgin prairie. . . . Salmon farming everywhere has repeated too many of the mistakes of industrial farming—including the shrinking of genetic diversity, a disregard for conservation, and the global spread of intensive farming methods before their consequences are completely understood. The death of millions of farmed salmon in Chilean waters was a warning sign that must be heeded.

See "About that salmon," editorial, *New York Times*, 31 July 2011, http://www.nytimes.com/2011/08/01/opinion/about-that-salmon.html.

13. Highlights include the books by Ponting (1991), McNeill (2000, 2007), and Diamond (2005), with Radkau (2008) providing a skeptical edge.

14. Tainter (1998, 2006) provides a critique of the overshoot-and-collapse school of thought—but these are really arguments about how a society accommodates an impending resource shortage, with loss of complexity one of the mediating processes.

15. The earlier date of around AD 300 used by Diamond is now hotly contested by specialists such as Hunt and Lipo (2006). These authors dispute Diamond's argument that deforestation was the original cause of the sequence of events that culminated in collapse on Easter Island and lay much more emphasis on degradation following European contact (including repeated raids by slave traders in the eighteenth century), and query much of the chronology; but there is no getting around the fact that this island's resources were destroyed by humans, and not by natural causes. Diamond (2007) responded.

16. See O'Sullivan (2008) for an even-handed overview of the topic, with a plea for a socially sophisticated, "anthropological" approach to analyzing cases of collapse. Radkau (2008) brings the argument closest to this text, in his emphasis on the scale of the activity being the key to the damage it causes.

17. See Hubbert (1956) for the first account of "peak oil"; Hubbert elaborated on his insights twenty years later (Hubbert 1976). Heinberg (2007) has extended the phrase to "peak everything."

18. Charts showing the peaking of oil production in the United States are widely available, such as at ASPO (http://www.peakoil.net), The Oil Drum (2005–13) (http://www.theoildrum.com), and other public domain sources.

19. Campbell and Lahererre's (1998) was the key text that announced a new cause for concern—and was elaborated on by Deffeyes (2001) and Aleklett and colleagues (2010). The key text rebutting the thesis is that by Yergin (2011), based on the widespread availability of nonconventional fossil fuels. But this misses the peak oil argument that the nonconventional fuels become economically feasible only after the peaking of conventional fuels.

20. A senior executive at the Italian oil corporation Eni, Leonardo Maugeri, in an article in the *Wall Street Journal*, declared that the coming century would "overflow with petroleum"; see "The crude truth about oil reserves," 4 November 2009, http://online.wsj.com/article/SB10001424052748704107204574470700973579402.html#printMode. For a more measured by no less optimistic view, see Maugeri (2009).

21. The first "modern" mention of peak oil was made in 2002, at a conference organized by petroleum geologist Colin Campbell. A newspaper report in the *Florida Times Union* quoted Matt Simmons: "'There is no factual data to support

the general sense that the world will be awash in cheap oil forever,' said Matthew Simmons, an investment banker who helped advise President Bush's campaign on energy policy. 'We desperately need to find a new form of energy'": Bruce Stanley, "Experts say crude supplies waning," *Florida Times Union*, May 25, 2002, http://jacksonville.com/tu-online/stories/052502/bus_9499294.html. See Simmons's book *Twilight in the Desert* (2005), plus recent peak oil publications from Uppsala, such as Höök, Hirsch, and Aleklett (2009). Matt Simmons died in September 2010.

22. For regular updates, see the ASPO website (http://www.peakoil.net).

23. See Klare (2012) for a penetrating analysis of the fossil fuels (and particularly oil) industry and its culture of conflict; earlier works include Klare (2002, 2004). A specific analysis focused on China and the United States and the scramble for oil in Africa is found in Klare and Volman (2006).

24. An article in *National Geographic* in 2009 put the matter succinctly:

Nowhere on Earth is more earth being moved these days than in the Athabasca Valley. To extract each barrel of oil from a surface mine, the industry must first cut down the forest, then remove an average two tons of peat and dirt that lie above the oil sands layer, then two tons of the sand itself. It must heat several barrels of water to strip the bitumen from the sand and upgrade it, and afterward it discharges contaminated water into tailings ponds. . . . The oil sands are still a tiny part of the world's carbon problem—they account for less than a tenth of one percent of global CO_2 emissions—but to many environmentalists they are the thin end of the wedge, the first step along a path that could lead to other, even dirtier sources of oil producing it from oil shale or coal.

See Robert Kunzig, "Scraping bottom," *National Geographic*, March 2009, http://ngm.nationalgeographic.com/2009/03/canadian-oil-sands/kunzig-text.

25. A major leak occurred in March 2013 in the Pegasus oil pipeline operated by ExxonMobil. But it was barely reported in the US media. See my analysis of this incident, and the possible reasons for the media's reluctance to report bad tidings concerning oil coming from Canadian tar sands, in "Exxon's Pegasus oil spill—and the myth of US 'energy independence,'" *The Globalist*, May 9, 2013, http://www.theglobalist.com/exxons-pegasus-oil-spill-and-the-myth-of-u-s-energy-independence/.

26. See the "Ethical Oil" campaign website (http://www.ethicaloil.org).

27. The report states: "Over two thirds of currently planned expansions of U.S. oil refining capacity are designed and intended to accommodate heavier, dirtier crude oil from Canadian 'tar sands,' according to data on U.S. oil refinery permitting activity under the Clean Air Act, recently compiled and analyzed by the Environmental Integrity Project." See Environmental Integrity Project, "Feeding U.S. refinery expansions with dirty oil," June 2008, http://environmentaldefence.ca/sites/default/files/report_files/EIPTar%20Sand%20Report_FINAL.pdf.

28. See "Energy discoveries reshape politics and economics worldwide," *International Herald Tribune*, 27 October 2011.

29. See "Fracking could have caused East Coast earthquake," *RT Online*, 24 August 2011, http://rt.com/usa/news/fracking-earthquake-virginia-dc-817-061/.

30. For a comprehensive critique of the case for expanding the coal seam gas and "tight" oil supply industry, see the report to the Post-Carbon Institute by J. David Hughes (2013a), *Drill Baby, Drill*, where he shows that optimistic predictions of these alternative fossil fuels evading the "peak oil" constraints are misplaced; for a summary article published in *Nature*, see Hughes (2013b).

31. See Tom Levitt, "China-Canada tar sands deal gets final approval," *China-Dialogue*, 12 February 2013, http://www.chinadialogue.net/blog/5700-China-Canada-tar-sands-deal-gets-final-approval/en.

32. See Lord Stern's (2007) *The Review of the Economics of Climate Change*, a report that has been highly influential in shaping public discussion of the issue.

33. I put the word *facts* in quotes only to emphasize the contested nature of the whole field of climate studies and global warming. But the reports from the IPCC make for sobering reading—as do the even more vociferous calls from leading climate scientists like James Hansen (2009) and other scientists such as Tim Flannery (2001, 2009) and political scientists like Dryzek (2007/2012). For a sample of the doggedly "denialist" literature, much of which reduces to a sense that investments in renewables are a waste of resources, see Lawson (2009). For an excellent short summary exposition, see Maslin (2009); for a more substantial review, see Dryzek, Norgaard, and Shlosberg (2011).

34. The chart showing temperature fluctuations over the past thousand years (Mann, Bradley, and Hughes 1999) became celebrated when it was chosen to head the 2001 report of the Intergovernmental Panel on Climate Change. At the time it was also disparaged as the "hockey stick graph." Despite the public controversy, the data shown in the chart by Michael E. Mann and colleagues remains the mainstream scientific view, as validated by a 2006 report from the US National Research Council. An excellent account of the controversy is to be found at the Wikipedia entry "Hockey stick controversy," at http://en.wikipedia.org/wiki/Hockey_stick_controversy, as well as the exposition in M. E. Mann (2012).

35. See the paper in *Nature* that describes such an "aerosol cooling" effect, where the authors, Andreae, Jones, and Cox (2005, 1187), state: "Atmospheric aerosols counteract the warming effects of anthropogenic greenhouse gases by an uncertain, but potentially large, amount."

36. The Swedish scientist Svante Arrhenius is credited with the first clear formulation of the greenhouse effect, in 1902. Arrhenius was seeking to explain the ice ages and formulated the "law" that "if the quantity of carbonic acid increases

in geometric progression, the augmentation of the temperature will increase nearly in arithmetic progression." Arrhenius was awarded the Nobel Prize for unrelated work in ionic chemistry—and he was also involved in railway electrification in Sweden from hydroelectric sources. See the tribute to him from the Royal Swedish Academy of Engineering Sciences, at http://www.iva.se/upload/Verksamhet/Högtidssammankomst/Minnesskrift%202008.pdf. An illuminating account of the early greenhouse effect speculations was provided by the Australian polymath Murray Sayle (2006), just prior to his death. For an account of the contribution by the British nineteenth-century scientist John Tyndall, see Hulme (2009a).

37. See T. J. Blasing, "Recent greenhouse gas concentrations," February 2014, Carbon Dioxide Information and Analysis Center, http://cdiac.ornl.gov/pns/current_ghg.html. For the estimate of the cumulative carbon emissions over the 250 years from 1750 to 2000 with reference to the "trillionth tonne," see Allen and colleagues (2009).

38. This is the point that is persuasively argued by Ehrenfeld and Hoffman (2013). Christoff and Eckersley (2013) argue that globalization provides a further complication in formulating environmentally sustainable strategies.

39. For a comprehensive review, see Stern, Common, and Barbier (1996, 1151), who begin their exposition with these words: "The environmental Kuznets curve (EKC) hypothesis is that environmental damage first increases with income, then declines. This might be taken to suggest that economic growth is not a threat to global sustainability, and that there are no environmental limits to growth. In the last five years there have been several empirical investigations of the EKC hypothesis. The results have been mixed."

40. China continues the trend of rising energy intensity followed by falling intensity, telescoped into a very few years. Its goals for reducing energy intensity were actually embodied in its Eleventh Five-Year Plan, calling for a reduction in energy intensity of 20 percent over the five years from 2006 to 2010 (very nearly attained) and a further reduction over the years 2011 to 2015.

41. One prominent contributor was Wilfred Beckerman (1992, 482), who delivered himself of the verdict: "there is clear evidence that, although economic growth usually leads to environmental degradation in the early stages of the process, in the end the best—and probably the only—way to attain a decent environment in most countries is to become rich."

42. The idea seems to have been floated first by Dales (1968/2002, 107), in a single paragraph: "The solution recommended . . . in this essay [is that] transferable property rights be established for the disposal of wastes. The government can choose any level of pollution it wishes by setting the number of . . . Pollution Rights it issues—the number to be subject to change at five-year or ten-year intervals. Because transferable (or full) property rights always command an explicit

price, the establishment of such Rights makes it easy to establish a market in them. In turn, the buying and selling of the Rights in an open market . . . results in a theoretically efficient allocation of "anti-pollution effort" as between different dischargers."

43. See Wara (2007) on the dangers and unintended consequences in the emergent carbon markets. Authors such as Newell and Paterson (2010) seem to base most of their discussion of "climate capitalism" on the presumed operation of carbon markets; I prefer to focus on fundamental changes to energy, resources, and finance.

44. Examples would be the "green" indexes on the Brazilian commodities and futures exchange, targeted at index-traded funds.

45. On this point, see the debate between Paterson and Newell (2012), defending their book, and Lohmann (2011, 2012), criticizing their premises in seeing carbon markets as effective; Lohmann seems to have the better of the argument. Recent papers by Sovacool (2010, 2011) probe these issues.

46. See the points made by the *Economist* moderator Emma Duncan in the 2008 online debate on the topic "this house believes that carbon offsets undermine the effort to tackle climate change." Michael Wara of Stanford and Kevin Smith of Carbon Trade Watch and Platform and others spoke for the motion, and Henry Derwent of the International Emissions Trading Association, businessman Mark Trexler, and others spoke against. The motion was carried by 55 percent of online voters. The results are available at the website "Post-debate," http://www.economist.com/debate/overview/136.

47. Other kinds of "carbon capture" that involve not inert storage but utilization of CO_2 as an industrial raw material are by contrast a very promising line of development. The most encouraging are various proposals for the greening of cement through absorption of carbon dioxide as it sets; this has been termed *eco-cement* by the Australian entrepreneur John Harrison—as outlined on his website TecEco (http://www.tececo.com.au).

48. On corporate sustainability and corporate interaction with the natural environment, see, for example, Dunphy (2003) and Aragón-Correa (1998); on business alliances for sustainability, see Grayson and Nelson (2013). Esty and Winston (2006) provide numerous examples of firms that turn "green to gold" through such initiatives. On the empirical evidence backing greater profits being associated with compliance with more stringent environmental standards, see Porter and van der Linde (1995); as well as Porter and Reinhardt (2007).

49. The literature on corporate environmental responsibility approaches this issue, sometimes in an indirect manner; see Rivera and DeLeon (2008) for a more robust engagement with voluntary environmental programs and their shortcomings if pursued as an end in themselves.

50. The ICO2 Index is traded on the Brazilian Commodities Exchange; it consists of shares of companies that have agreed to adopt transparent practices with respect to their greenhouse gas emissions.

51. The idea of unburnable carbon has been developed by the Carbon Tracker Institute; see the institute's 2013 report "Unburnable Carbon 2013: Wasted capital and stranded assets," at http://www.carbontracker.org/wastedcapital.

52. The idea of the green paradox has already attracted a scholarly debate. The argument is formalized by van der Ploeg and Withagen (2012) through analysis of monopolistic competition, and in the absence of political support for the steep taxes advocated by Sinn, they argue for second-best policies based on R&D subsidies for renewables. This is unfortunately a rather unimaginative end point for the debate.

53. Aristotle, *The Politics*, book 11, chapter 3; see also the epigraph to this chapter.

54. The Nobel laureate Elinor Ostrom (recently deceased) spent her career examining these "common pool resources" problems and the variety of means utilized to resolve them—in opposition to the stark conclusions of the tragedy of the commons. But she is the first to admit that such solutions have little traction in a global setting, such as in the case of global warming (Basurto and Ostrom 2009), while insisting that action can be taken at multiple "nested" levels (Ostrom 2010).

55. Commentators on Hardin, in particular Ostrom (1990, 2010) and Wade (1987), have advanced "common ownership" and institutional innovations as a means of dealing with collective action problems and avoiding the tragic outcome. Wade, for example, discusses South Indian villages where cooperatives were formed to regulate the supply of irrigation water. The collective action problem (CAP) here is that each village has an interest in raising the level of irrigation water (to enhance agricultural yields) and preventing individual villagers from cheating or free riding on the good behavior of others. Their solution often took the form of a village cooperative, which was able to enforce a set of rules for regulating water flow (such as a rule requiring the villager with land closest to the source to take water only after the villager with the most distant land has been able to water his land).

56. Nevertheless, there have been proposals to place the atmosphere in some kind of "trust" arrangement, on the analogy with private property solutions to common pool resources (CPR) problems of a more contained character; see, for example, Barnes (2006), in which a "capitalism 3.0" is proposed based on such a reclaiming of the atmospheric commons (for a sympathetic review, see Costanza [2007]). It suffices to ask how China would react to such proposals to see why they would face insuperable obstacles.

57. See Bennett (2008) for an ecological assessment of China's Sloping Lands Conversion Program.

58. See, for example, the successive public interventions of the Danish polemicist Bjørn Lomborg (2007, 2010). Despite the sophistication of his arguments, his policy prescriptions usually boil down to "more R&D," whereas proposals from others to build industrial momentum for renewables through expanding markets and driving down prices are met with scorn.

59. Barry Commoner (1917–2012) was a biologist and celebrated author who also sought to put his ideas for a convergence between economic and ecological processes into practical effect, through mounting a presidential campaign in the United States on behalf of the Citizens' Party. His 1971 book *The Closing Circle* had an enormous impact and generated a lively debate in the pages of the *Bulletin of the Atomic Scientists*; it was followed by books on the energy choices facing America (Commoner 1976, 1979). In 1990, at the age of seventy-three, he published his last book, *Making Peace with the Planet*.

60. In the chapters to come, I draw on my published works that take a strategic perspective on renewable energy systems, resource recirculation, green finance, and the greening of capitalism (Mathews 2007a, 2007b, 2008a, 2008b, 2010, 2011a, 2011b, 2011c, 2012a, 2012b, 2013a, 2013b, 2013c, 2014), as well as the collaborative works Mathews and Baroni (2013); Mathews, Hu, and Wu (2011); Mathews and Kidney (2010, 2012); Mathews et al. (2010); Mathews and Reinert (2014); Mathews and Tan (2009, 2011, 2013, 2014a, 2014b, 2014c); and Mathews, Tang, and Tan (2011).

Chapter 4

1. Thomas Edison is the famed inventor of the phonograph, telegraph, and incandescent lightbulb, as well as direct current (DC) electric power. Nikola Tesla is not nearly as well known, but he had just as much an impact through his invention of alternating current (AC) generated from his rotating magnetic field oscillator. AC versus DC was the first great standards war of the modern era, pitting Edison and General Electric against Tesla and Westinghouse.

2. There is of course already a vast literature on renewable energies, and several journals devoted to their technological, industrial, and financial features. A very useful primer on the whole subject is provided by David MacKay (2009), with his celebrated text *Sustainable Energy—Without the Hot Air*; for an equally authoritative approach, without any bias toward nuclear power, see Makhijani (2007) and Leggett (2013) for a comprehensive perspective on the dawning of a new age of renewables.

3. On China's buildup of momentum in renewable energy industries, see, for example, Martinot (2010). Lin and colleagues (2008) document the impact that

these renewable energies are having on China's carbon emissions. Urban, Benders, and Moll (2009) capture the role that renewable energies and low-carbon technologies are playing in China's modernization.

4. The logistic function describes the familiar S-shaped curve that best captures the process of substitution of one industrial technology by another, and one product by another; see Fisher and Pry (1971) for an early exposition. My paper with Italian collaborator Paolo Baroni (2013) links the logistic curve with the cost curve (or experience curve), thereby creating what we call an industrial logistic surface in three dimensions; this provides a means to link policies to expand the market directly with the cost reductions and accelerated uptake achieved.

5. On China's astonishing growth rates, see recent studies such as those by Rasiah, Zhang, and Kong (2013) and Lin (2012). On China's energy industrial revolution, see, for example, Martinot (2010). China's strategies are now starting to attract the interest of legal scholars, such as Eisen (2011).

6. China consumed 3.4 billion tonnes of coal in 2010, doubling its consumption over just six years—and it burnt 1.5 billion tonnes of this coal in power stations (46 percent). In the face of predictions of coal's falling away as an energy source, China's rise has put it back at the center of the world energy industry. The steep upward curve in coal consumption and energy production since 2001 is clearly evident. See the two-part contribution to *Asia-Pacific Journal: Japan Focus*, by Hao Tan and myself, in December 2012 (http://japanfocus .org/-Hao-Tan/3881).

7. SGCC has committed a 4 trillion yuan investment over the course of the Twelfth and Thirteenth Five-Year Plans (i.e., up to 2020)—or around US$642 billion, far more than is projected by any other country.

8. According to the State Grid Corporation, China will have 1.7 TW of generating capacity by 2020, 59 percent of which will come from coal-based (thermal) sources. Our projections shown in Figure 4.2 are consistent with this prediction.

9. This curve shows renewable sources as contributing 685 GW by 2020 (out of a total of 1785 GW) (or 38 percent, as mentioned earlier), rising to 1600 GW out of a total of 2000 GW by 2030—or 80 percent, and 1890 GW out of 2100 GW by 2040.

10. To make the conversion between emissions of carbon and of carbon dioxide, multiply level of CO_2 by 12/44 to get the level of carbon; or the level of carbon by 44/12 to get the level of carbon dioxide. The approximate 1.5 Gt of coal thus produces around 0.84 Gt carbon emissions, or 3.1 Gt CO_2.

11. On this shift in the green sectors in both China and India, see Lema and Lema (2012).

12. See Juan Forero, "In Brazil, the wind is blowing in a new era of renewable energy," *Washington Post*, 31 October 2013, http://www.washingtonpost.com/world/

in-brazil-the-wind-is-blowing-in-a-new-era-of-renewable-energy/2013/10/
30/8111b7e8-2ae0-11e3-b141-298f46539716_story.html.

13. See my blog posting, "Renewable energy and the real Clash of Civilizations," *The Globalist*, 3 February 2013, http://www.theglobalist.com/storyid
.aspx?StoryId=9890.

14. On the German *Energiewende*, see, for example, Davidson (2012); the term was first used by Krause (1982).

15. "Europe's dirty secret: The unwelcome renaissance," *The Economist*, 5 January 2013, http://www.economist.com/news/briefing/21569039-europes-energy
-policy-delivers-worst-all-possible-worlds-unwelcome-renaissance/print.

16. Note that the German levels of investment are well below those committed by the SGCC in China. Dagmar Dehmer, "The German Energiewende—the first year," *Electricity Journal*, January–February 2013, 71–78, http://www.science
direct.com/science/article/pii/S104061901200317X.

17. "Germany's energy transformation," *The Economist*, 28 July 2012, http://
www.economist.com/node/21559667.

18. See Anna Leidreiter, "Hamburg citizens vote to buy back energy grid," World Future Council, 25 September 2013, http://power-to-the-people.net/2013/
09/hamburg-citizens-vote-to-buy-back-energy-grid/.

19. Erik Gawel, Sebastian Strunz, and Paul Lehmann, "The German *Energiewende* under attack—is there an irrational Sonderweg?" UFZ Discussion Paper No. 15/2012, http://www.econstor.eu/handle/10419/64555.

20. See Elisabeth Rosenthal, "U.S. Military orders less dependence on fossil fuels," *New York Times*, 4 October 2010, http://www.nytimes.com/2010/10/05/
science/earth/05fossil.html.

21. See the official project website at Sandia Laboratories (http://energy
.sandia.gov/?page_id=2781) and a useful description by Tina Casey, "In first test, U.S. Military's SPIDERS microgrid uses 90% renewable energy," *Clean Technia*, 12 February 2013, http://cleantechnica.com/2013/02/12/u-s-militarys-new
-spiders-renewable-energy-microgrid/. Andrew DeWit provides an insightful overview of the project and the wider US military push to create its own renewable energy revolution in "The U.S. military, green energy and the SPIDERS at Pearl Harbor," *Asia-Pacific Journal*, 11 (March 2013), http://japanfocus.org/
-Andrew-DeWit/3909.

22. See John Lyons, Richard Chait, and James Valdes, "Assessing the army power and energy efforts for the warfighter," Center for Technology and National Security Policy, National Defense University, March 2011.

23. For a review of programs and thinking on the issue, see the Department of Defense (2011) statement of its "operational energy strategy" and the report "Integration and penetration opportunities of alternative energy, fuels, and

technologies within military systems, logistics and operations," M. L. Perez project leader, Document No. D-4026, Institute for Defense Analysis, January 2010.

24. See Andrew DeWit's articles in *Asia Pacific Journal: JapanFocus*, such as "Japan's new green political innovators respond to government attempts to restart nuclear power," 13 June 2012, http://www.japanfocus.org/events/view/152; and "Japan's remarkable renewable energy drive—after Fukushima," 11 March 2012, http://www.japanfocus.org/-Andrew-DeWit/3721.

25. The proposal to link solar and wind farms in Mongolia with the rest of Asia is also known under the name Gobitec; see Cooper and Sovacool (2013) for a sober assessment.

26. See Mitsuro Obe, "First the iPhone; now renewables," *Wall Street Journal*, 18 June 2012, http://online.wsj.com/article/SB10001424052702304371504577 404343259051300.html.

27. Zhengrong Shi, founder of Suntech, is a strong proponent of global free trade in clean technology. As he puts it: "It is time for us to embrace a global free trade zone in clean power technology—and start to break down the walls of global trade instead of putting them up." See Zhengrong Shi, "Solar energy trade wars—Enough is enough," *Financial Times*, 11 September 2012, http://blogs.ft.com/beyond-brics/2012/09/11/guest-post-solar-energy-wars-enough-is-enough/#axzz2NNAI6r2B.

28. This plant is operated by a joint venture involving Masdar from Abu Dhabi and SENER, the Spanish engineering and construction firm. See Sara Hamdan, "Energy plant makes a leap in solar power," *New York Times*, 25 October 2011, http://www.nytimes.com/2011/10/26/business/energy-environment/energy-plant-makes-a-leap-in-solar-power.html.

29. This land intensity of 2.5 hectares per MW generated by the Shams 1 CSP plant is now the standard for the emerging industry; the Solana generating station in the United States is rated at 280 MW and requires 770 hectares—or 2.75 hectares per MW.

30. Just four countries of the Maghreb (Morocco, Tunisia, Algeria, and Libya) have between them 4.8 million square kilometers. So a total installation of 1 TW of CSP could fit into a small box just 2 percent of the total available land area—land that is not being used for any other purpose.

31. See Battaglini and colleagues (2009) and Trieb and colleagues (2012) for scholarly evaluations of the Desertec proposal, reaching positive conclusions, particularly on the development potential arising for the Middle Eastern and North African countries.

32. A total of 17.5 GW of CSP projects were under development worldwide, according to GTM Research, in 2011; the United States led with about 8.7 GW. Spain ranked second with 4.5 GW in development, followed by China

with 2.5 GW. See Ucilia Wang, "The rise of concentrating solar thermal power," *Renewable Energy World*, 6 June 2011, http://www.renewableenergyworld.com/rea/news/article/2011/06/the-rise-of-concentrating-solar-thermal-power.

33. The Indian Ministry of New and Renewable Energy (itself a major latecomer institutional innovation) has a goal that India should be producing 20 GW of grid-connected solar power by 2022, of which 50 percent would be produced from CSP.

34. The development of CSP facilities is one of the most promising of the renewable energy pathways for emerging and developing countries. Early examples of successful recent projects in Spain, such as the world's first commercial power tower with molten-salt technology to allow for continuous power generation at the 20 MW Gemasolar plant, provide the outlines of a trajectory that could be followed in southern Africa and elsewhere (Dunn, Hearps, and Wright 2012).

35. The 100 GW global projection by 2025 is made by AT Kearney and the European Solar Thermal industry association, in their investment report "Solar Thermal Electricity 2025," http://www.estelasolar.eu/fileadmin/ESTELAdocs/documents/Cost_Roadmap/2010-06%20-%20Solar%20Thermal%20Electricity%202025%20-%20ENG.pdf. Upward of 1,500 GW will be needed in a genuine "10 TW Big Push" for a global transition. This gives a feel for the scale of the transition that is under way (Mathews and Tan 2014c).

36. *Dispatchable* is the term used in energy studies to indicate power that is available upon demand.

37. For such a critique, see, for example, Ausubel (2007), who has been a long-standing critic of renewable energy options, on grounds that are now largely obsolete—as discussed in the section "Real men don't do renewables."

38. There is, of course, a vast literature on the energy options facing humankind. Studies like those of Jacobson and Delucchi (2009, 2010) pave the way for future sustained work on a world powered exclusively by renewables. In individual countries strong efforts are under way; the case of Australia is reviewed by Falk and Settle (2011).

39. I take Ausubel (2007) simply as representative of a body of literature that argues against renewables, sometimes in the most specious of terms. For another sample of the genre, see Morriss and colleagues (2011), *The False Promise of Green Energy*, issued by the Cato Institute, where again the usual arguments—cost, reliability, scalability, resource intensity—are rolled out.

40. The energy and automotive worlds were shaken out of their complacency in February 2014 when the US company Tesla Motors announced its intention of building a GW-scale battery factory in California, the GIGA project. This certainly puts paid to any Ausubel-inspired notion that batteries count for nothing in the global energy market. Tesla's view of the future of EVs sees them as crossing

boundaries, to become an important source of energy storage (e.g., vehicle to grid V2G); on this aspect, see the study by myself and Danish colleagues Poul Andersen and Morten Rask (2009). On Tesla Motors' boundary-breaking strategies, see Chet Lyons, "Tesla's GIGA battery factory threatens the auto, utility and buildings control markets," 3 March 2014, http://www.greentechmedia.com/articles/read/Teslas-Giga-Battery-Factory-Threatens-the-Auto-Utility-and-Building-Contr.

41. The Deutsche Bank has lent its name to such a prediction; see Becky Beetz, "Deutsche Bank—Sustainable solar market expected in 2014," *pv-magazine*, 28 February 2013, http://www.pv-magazine.com/news/details/beitrag/deutsche-bank—sustainable-solar-market-expected-in-2014_100010338/#axzz2NJVDi3wr.

42. See UBS Investment Research, "The unsubsidised solar revolution," 15 January 2013, which explains the reasoning: http://qualenergia.it/sites/default/files/articolo-doc/UBS.pdf.

43. Technological innovations such as permanent magnet direct drive (PMDD), being taken up and propagated by Chinese and German giants such as Goldwind and Enercon, eliminate the need for gearing and drastically reduce maintenance costs, especially for offshore wind power farms. In this way technological innovation works with the experience curve to drive down costs.

44. Lund University's International Institute for Industrial Environmental Economics has been a prominent base for such studies; see Neij (2008) for a summary of the work on experience curves in energy systems. Wind turbines are viewed as decreasing in cost by 10 percent for every doubling of cumulative installed power between now and 2050, while for solar PVs the cost reduction should be even steeper (from a higher base).

45. See the 2009 presentation by Griffith, "Climate change recalculated," at http://fora.tv/2009/01/16/Saul_Griffith_Climate_Change_Recalculated.

46. If each can is 25 centimeters deep with a radius of 10 centimeters, then the extended cylindrical surface is 750 square centimeters, and 200 billion such surfaces aggregate to 15,000 square kilometers of aluminum surface in one year. That's twice the target for production of parabolic mirrors over ten years.

47. For the material requirements for producing CSP installations, see Pihl and colleagues (2012); for comparable calculations regarding wind turbines, see Martínez and colleagues (2009). On the resource implications of a total shift to renewables, see Mathews and Tan (2014c).

48. Lund (2010) provides a valuable discussion of the obstacles that stand in the way of 100 percent renewables through twelve case studies demonstrating how radical alternatives only come from companies new to the industries, in what the author calls "choice awareness" theory. Likewise, Ayres and Ayres

(2010) provide a comprehensive analysis of the issues involved in making the total transition.

49. Victor and Yanosek (2011, 112) may be taken as representative scholars endorsing this view; while they claim that there is a "crisis in clean energy" (mainly because of overreliance on short-term subsidies in the West, particularly the United States), they state the case firmly for "the adoption of rules mandating that an increasing share of energy be derived from clean sources."

50. It is certainly odd that proponents of "free-market environmentalism" seem to be so uniformly opposed to renewable energy in all its forms. See, for example, Andrew Morriss, "The green energy mirage," 2011, http://www.perc.org/articles/article1365.php; Andrew Morriss, "U.S. can't afford to scrap nuclear power," 2011, http://www.perc.org/articles/article1370.php. This pro–fossil fuels and pro-nuclear stance puts the Property and Environment Research Center in a most unfavorable light, as taking a stand in support of big oil and centralized power generators and against the emergence of a genuine free market for renewables.

51. Artificial photosynthesis would extract carbon from the atmosphere and use it with solar energy and water to produce zero-carbon fuels and other raw materials; see Faunce (2012) for a succinct summary of the possibilities. Ammonia production via the Bosch-Haber process is now a century old and arguably still the most important technology invented in the past hundred years, because of its significance for agriculture. An alternative "solid-state ammonia synthesis" likewise utilizes nitrogen from the atmosphere but fixes it with drastically lower carbon intensity, opening up possibilities for "clean" nitrogenous fertilizers but also for widespread use of ammonia as a safe alternative to hydrogen as fuel. The process is promoted by the NH3 Fuel Association (http://nh3fuelassociation.org/ongoing-projects/); see Leighty and Holbrook (2012) for a discussion. Note that these two prospective energy technologies would be zero carbon and constitute the last word in carbon sequestration, making maximum positive use of the most abundant gas in the atmosphere (N_2) and the most troublesome (CO_2).

52. The Australian entrepreneurial initiative Sundrop Farms captures such a triple dividend, in the otherwise barren landscape of Port Augusta in South Australia. See the interview with founder and CEO Philipp Saumweber in *Future Directions International*, 19 September 2013; and my own comments at *The Conversation*, "Tomatoes watered by the sea: Sprouting a new way of farming," http://theconversation.com/tomatoes-watered-by-the-sea-sprouting-a-new-way-of-farming-23119.

53. See the works on international tensions related to fossil fuels by authors such as Klare (2012).

Chapter 5

1. See Michele Field, "Cradle to cradle: No harder to understand than 'recycling,'" *Food Ethics* 4, no. 3: 21–22, http://www.foodethicscouncil.org/system/files/Cradletocradle.pdf.

2. The late Ed Cohen-Rosenthal was a visionary promoter of industrial ecology initiatives from his base at Cornell University. I counted him as a friend and colleague.

3. The discipline of industrial ecology has many founding figures, among whom have to be counted Ayres, Kneese, Stahel, Simonis, Ehrenfeld, Graedel, Allenby, Cooper, and Lifset. Lifset and Graedel (2002) and Ayres (2008) provide comprehensive overviews, while Erkman (2002) probes the historical roots of the subject. Ehrenfeld and Hoffman (2013) offer a discussion of the issues, pointing to the vastly increased complexity of present challenges and the inadequacy of the social and economic models being utilized to tackle them.

4. For an overview, see OECD (2008). Preston (2012) provides an updated list of companies that are already engaging in resource recirculation activities, such as the Dutch carpet company Desso and the Japanese electronics company Kyocera.

5. The World Business Council for Sustainable Development coined the concept of eco-efficiency in its 1992 publication *Changing Course*—based on the notion of producing more goods and services while using fewer resources and generating less waste and pollution. Out of these ideas comes the idea of reducing resource throughput "from cradle to grave"—meaning at every step of the life cycle of products.

6. The English political economist William Stanley Jevons, in his treatise on the British coal industry (1865), formulated the proposition that improvements in fuel efficiency led to broader applications and so higher levels of consumption. This is now known as the Jevons paradox, or the "rebound effect." From the perspective developed in this book, the Jevons paradox underlines the necessity for state action to shift the economy onto a new energy trajectory rather than relying on market forces alone (even if corrected with a carbon tax).

7. Braungart and McDonough see cradle-to-cradle as an expression of eco-effectiveness, as opposed to eco-efficiency and its "cradle-to-grave" thinking. *Cradle to Cradle: Remaking the Way We Make Things* is the title of their bestselling book, published in 2002, based on the 1998 article, and it has remained their expression of choice over the subsequent decade of very active promotion of this idea.

8. For an expression of these principles, see Steve Bolton, "Design in harmony with natural cycles: The cradle to cradle framework," *CHEManager Europe*, 29 January 2010, http://www.chemanager-online.com/en/topics/chemicals-distribution/design-harmony-natural-cycles.

9. This initiative of trademarking the term *cradle to cradle* might have made the authors wealthy, but it has done a disservice to the wider dissemination of the principles. In this text, we leave C2C thinking to one side and concentrate instead on the more fundamental ideas of circular flows in the economy—or circular economy thinking.

10. The idea of the circular economy seems to have been expressed first by Pearce and Turner in their 1989 book *Economics of Natural Resources and the Environment*. But of course the concept goes back to cycles as they occur in nature, and to ideas like Commoner's "closing of the circle" (1971).

11. See Joss Bleriot, "'Europe needs to embrace the closed loop model,' says Belgian EU Presidency," 7 September 2010, http://www.ellenmacarthurfoundation .org/about/circular-economy/europe-needs-to-embrace-the-closed-loop-model -says-belgian-eu-presidency.

12. This foundation, created as a not-for-profit initiative designed to stimulate fresh thinking by the solo yachtswoman Ellen Macarthur, has since been promoting the idea of the circular economy heavily on the foundation's website (http:// www.ellenmacarthurfoundation.org/about/circular-economy). In 2012 the foundation commissioned its first major report, *Towards the Circular Economy*, available at http://www.ellenmacarthurfoundation.org/business/reports/ce2012.

13. On the Rhineland-Palatinate circular economy initiative, see the report *The Circular Economy State of Rhineland-Palatinate*, available at http://www .stoffstrom.org/fileadmin/userdaten/dokumente/Veroeffentlichungen/Kreislauf wirtschaft_RLP-UK_web.pdf.

14. For example, German recycling levels in 2006 reached 77 percent in packaging, while for batteries the level was 72 percent and for paper 87 percent. These data come from the report to the World Bank by Peter Heck, of the German Institute for Applied Material Flow Analysis, "Circular economy related international practices and policy trends, 2006," http://siteresources.worldbank .org/INTEAPREGTOPENVIRONMENT/Resources/CircularEconomy_Policy _FinalDraft_EN.pdf.

15. Likewise, local initiatives such as the Zero Emission Village at Weilerbach, a project dating from 2001, entails optimization of regional material flows, in partnership with the Institute for Applied Material Flow Management.

16. For further elaboration, see Jofre and Morioka (2005); for this insight I am indebted to Amanda Parker's unpublished master's thesis "Open economy industrial policy: A new orientation for a former developmental state—The case of eco-energy-industry policies in Japan" (Department of Government and International Relations, University of Sydney).

17. Examples of these synergistic arrangements in the developed world are referred to as "combined heat and power" (CHP) initiatives, and there are hundreds

of such examples, particularly in Northern Europe. China is drawing inspiration from these initiatives and making CHP a principle of industrial design throughout the economy.

18. There is a growing literature on China's circular economy initiatives. Chinese scholars were publishing articles in Chinese in the 1990s and then in English in the 2000s, such as Zhu and Côté (2004); Fang, Côté, and Qin (2007); Geng and Doberstein (2008); Zhu (2008); and Shi, Chertow, and Song (2010). For recent Chinese innovations, see Li and Yu (2011), Ding and Hua (2012), and Su and colleagues (2013). Hao Tan and I published a comprehensive overview in the *Journal of Industrial Ecology* (Mathews and Tan 2011) and developed the argument that China is incorporating the circular economy into its development strategy, in *Asian Business and Management* (Mathews, Tang, and Tan 2011).

19. The concept of ecological modernization is also relevant here, by which is meant a modernization of the economy that takes into account environmental or ecological pressures. See Mol and Sonnenfeld (2000) for a succinct summary; and Mol (2006) for an application of this way of thinking to China.

20. This second batch of eco-industrial parks counted thirty-one enterprises from eleven key industries, seventeen areas or enterprises engaging in four key activities, twenty industrial parks, and seventeen provinces and cities were listed. A program established by the Ministry of Environment Protection in conjunction with two other ministries designated a total of thirty eco-industrial parks (EIPs) across the country up to December 2008.

21. Economy (2013) provides an overview of China's manifold water problems and the regional as well as global implications of short-term solutions adopted.

22. On Kalundborg in Denmark, see Jacobsen (2006); on Kwinana and Gladstone in Australia, see Van Beers and colleagues (2007). On cases in China, see the paper by Hao Tan and myself in *Journal of Industrial Ecology* (Mathews and Tan 2011), as well as recent reviews, like that by Ding and Hua (2012).

23. The literature on industrial ecology utilizes several terms to indicate the essentially "ecological" nature of industrial linkages that tend to close industrial loops—such as *industrial symbiosis, industrial ecosystem, eco-industrial development, eco-industrial park*, and so on (see, e.g., Chertow 2007; Gibbs et al. 2005). I choose to use the term *eco-industrial initiative* because this seems to capture the flavor of the various approaches and coincides with the introduction of the concept of Pareto eco-efficiency, to be discussed later.

24. Eigen and Schuster (1979) created a sensation with their discovery that complex molecules could form sequences of reactions that would eventually close the loop, creating a material demonstration for the possibility of self-reproducing molecular forms—and hence, life. In the industrial setting it is a biomimetic form

of hypercycle that is of interest—an industrial counterpart to a biological form that evolved as part of the processes that created a living planet.

25. On Kwinana and Gladstone, see Van Beers and colleagues (2007); on Kawasaki, see Van Berkel and colleagues (2009); on Ulsan in Korea, see Park and colleagues (2008); for a comparative overview, see Van Berkel (2009). This kind of field research is one of the most important contributions that the new field of industrial ecology is offering. For a general treatment of climate change and the contribution of eco-design, see Ryan (2008).

26. In my 2008 article in *Energy Policy* (Mathews 2008b), I discussed a simple extension of existing futures contracts traded on commodities markets—in particular, a certifiably sustainable biofuels futures contract that would bring together the ideas of traceability and certification and embed them in the contractual details governing the trade in the commodity. My proposal was that the Certification of Analysis and Classification that forms part of the existing bioethanol futures contract offered by the Brazilian Mercantile and Futures Exchange be extended to provide proof of origin of the feedstock and the ethanol, in addition to the technical specifications currently required. Thus a new "sustainable" ethanol futures contract would call for provision by the seller of a certificate of analysis, classification, *and* proof of origin, where the proof of origin would supply data concerning the plantation where the feedstock was grown and the biorefinery where the fuel was produced, and subsequent blendings of the fuel, carried in bar-code form. If the commodity were to be blended with ethanol from other sources, and onsold through another exchange (e.g., in Europe), then the blended ethanol would likewise carry a bar-code proof of origin, reflecting the sources of the blended product and the exchanges through which it had passed. A multiply blended and multiply on-sold commodity would carry the entire history of its blending and sales in its barcoded proof of origin (backed by a web-based inventory). In this way, the proposal demonstrates its compatibility with the blending practices of global commodity traders such as ADM, Cargill, and Bunge. It had been the incompatibility of existing certification schemes with these blending practices that constituted an insuperable barrier to practical certification of sustainability so far.

27. This is brought out as one of features (or axioms) of the green economy, as discussed in Chapter 9.

28. The "Internet of things" was proposed by Gershenfeld and Krikorian (2004) in a *Scientific American* article. The idea has caught on and is the subject of an expanding literature; see Atzori, Iera, and Morabito (2010) for a recent survey. The Internet of things is mentioned in China's Twelfth Five-Year Plan.

29. I am introducing this terminology as counterpart to the IT-enabled "smart grid." Both concepts derive their force from the application of information technology to traditional activities, which thus gives them a capacity of memory and

intelligent decision-making that was previously unavailable—indeed, unthinkable. My argument is that the IT-enabled "smart economy" will provide the setting for the universal tracing of materials and resources, which in turn will drive recirculation, thus bringing industrial activities' footprint to approach zero as the economy becomes circular.

Chapter 6

1. See the website of Climate Bonds Initiative, at http://climatebonds.net/wp-content/uploads/2010/06/4-pager_climatebonds.pdf.

2. The Swedish bank Skandinavska Enskilda Banken (SEB) has been a pioneer of green bonds since 2008, when it was involved in the first World Bank issuance. The SEB's Christopher Flensborg, head of sustainable products and development at the bank, was closely involved with Kexim in framing the design of the Korean green bond—hence his comments in the epigraph to this chapter. See Mark Nicholls, "Painting the bond markets green," *Institutional Investor*, June 2013, https://yoursri.com/responsible-investing/newsletter/Topic%20of%20the%20month%20June%202013.

3. The pricing of the bond opened at 100 basis points above US Treasury bonds, but tightened to 95 basis points above as a result of high demand; existing five-year Korean government bonds are trading at 104 basis points above US Treasury bonds.

4. Interview by the author with Kexim bank officials in Seoul, April 2014.

5. On the OECD studies, see, for example, Kaminker and Stewart (2012), cited in the epigraph to this chapter.

6. For an accessible and authoritative account of this financial evolutionary process, see Ferguson (2008).

7. On the Japanese long-term credit banking system, see Aoki and Patrick (1994).

8. Kingston (2013) provides the definitive discussion. See also my own article on this point, "No limited liability for speculative financial transactions," at the website of the Network for Sustainable Financial Markets (http://www.sustainablefinancialmarkets.net/2011/06/14/no-limited-liability-for-speculative-financial-market-transactions/).

9. The Carbon Tracker Initiative (http://www.carbontracker.org), for example, is tracking issues of new securities by the world's stock exchanges and drawing attention to the carbon risk exposure they entail. The 2013 report carries an explanation of the concept of stranded assets: see "Unburnable carbon 2013: Wasted capital and stranded assets," http://www.carbontracker.org/wastedcapital.

10. On these eco-securities, here termed *climate bonds*, see, for example, Mathews and colleagues (2010) and Mathews and Kidney (2012); on discussions regarding the establishment of a green investment bank in the United Kingdom, see, for example, Holmes and Mabey (2010). The Climate Bonds Initiative is

a voluntary grouping of finance professionals and academic advisers (including myself), based in London, and organized by eco-entrepreneur Sean Kidney; its website is found at http://climatebonds.net.

11. A step toward such a situation was taken in November 2011, when four major European banks adopted a charter that would prevent their offering finance to dirty coal-fired power station projects. The banks are HSBC, Standard Chartered, BNP Paribas, and Credit Agricole, together with F&C Asset Management. See "Banks draw up code for lending on power plants," *Financial Times*, 23 October 2011, http://www.ft.com/cms/s/0/93505a16-fbfa-11e0-989c-00144feab49a .html#axzz2kPK85vmE.

12. Of the $100 trillion bonds market, $47 trillion is accounted for by government bonds, $42 trillion by financial-sector bonds, and $11 trillion by corporate bonds. See the report from McKinsey Global Institute, "Financial globalization: Retreat or reset?" March 2013, http://www.mckinsey.com/insights/ global_capital_markets/financial_globalization.

13. The OECD is actively contributing to these debates. In a 2011 report the role of pension funds in investing in new vehicles or instruments targeted at green projects was canvassed (Della Croce, Kaminker, and Stewart 2011). Corfee-Morlot and colleagues (2012) focused on a green investment policy framework, targeted at low-carbon, climate-resilient infrastructure.

14. The high cost of capital is a principal deterrent that is holding back investors in infrastructure projects in developing countries, as emphasized in a report issued in 2014 by Climate Policy Initiative: David Nelson and Gireesh Shrimali, "Finance mechanisms for lowering the cost of renewable energy in rapidly developing countries," January 2014, http://climatepolicyinitiative.org/wp-content/ uploads/2014/01/Finance-Mechanisms-for-Lowering-the-Cost-of-Clean-Energy -in-Rapidly-Developing-Countries.pdf.

15. See Sonia Kolesnikov-Jessop, "A change of heart on investing in the climate," *New York Times*, 27 November 2011, http://www.nytimes.com/2011/ 11/28/business/global/28iht-RBOG-BONDS28.html. For the latest on climate bonds standards, see the dedicated website Climate Bond Certified (http://stan dards.climatebonds.net).

16. Indeed, *chain reaction* is the term utilized by the Cambridge heterodox economist Nicholas Kaldor, to describe the process in general terms, as he put it in his 1970 address on Regional economic policy to the Scottish Economic Society. I return to this theme in Part 3.

17. See Sanderson and Forsythe (2013) for an illuminating account of the role of the CDB in both extending China's fossil fuel supply lines and underpinning the internationalization of renewable energy companies.

18. In January 2014 the BNDES raised €650 million on international markets, with demand exceeding the offer by three times and returns to investors being set

at 3.783 percent per year. This demonstrates the experience and competence of the BNDES in issuing bonds; the next step would be to issue green bonds.

19. This section is based on interviews conducted with Mr. Sergio Weguelin, then at the BNDES in mid-2012 and mid-2014.

20. A more general version of this idea might be called the differential principle, in that it identifies the point of change of a system as the point at which it is most susceptible to effective intervention in moving the system to a new trajectory.

21. See the CBRC's "Green Credit Guidelines" at http://www.cbrc.gov.cn/EngdocView.do?docID=3CE646AB629B46B9B533B1D8D9FF8C4A. For illuminating commentary, see the Climate Bonds website at http://www.climatebonds.net/2013/10/chinas-finance-sector-regulators-are-pushing-green/.

22. The study by Carmen Reinhart and Kenneth Rogoff (2009), *This Time It's Different: Eight Centuries of Financial Folly*, supplies a range of cases of financial bubbles and crashes over centuries of capitalist development.

23. Minsky's financial instability hypothesis is outlined in his major publication, *Stabilizing an Unstable Economy* (1986/2008), and in papers devoted to the topic, including Minsky (1995, 1996). In the words of the *Wall Street Journal*: "Hyman Minsky . . . spent much of his career advancing the idea that financial systems are inherently susceptible to bouts of speculation that, if they last long enough, end in crises. At a time when many economists were coming to believe in the efficiency of markets, Mr. Minsky was considered somewhat of a radical for his stress on their tendency toward excess and upheaval. . . . Today, his views are reverberating from New York to Hong Kong as economists and traders try to understand what's happening in the markets. . . . Indeed the "Minsky moment" has become a fashionable phrase on Wall Street"; Justin Lahart, "In time of tumult, obscure economist gains currency," *Wall Street Journal*, 18 August 2007, http://online.wsj.com/article/SB118736585456901047.html.

24. Minsky's financial instability hypothesis turns on three processes or modes of credit creation that may always be observed in the finance sector. There is first credit creation via "hedge borrowing," in which the debt can be serviced through cash flow arising from the investment project; then there is "speculative borrowing," in which cash flow can service interest repayments but not the principal, which must be periodically rolled over; and third, there is "Ponzi borrowing," in which the cash flow can service neither principal nor interest, and it is only appreciation in the value of the underlying asset that can prolong the process. The first process is stable; the second shows signs of instability; the third is an outright bubble that can only burst, with widespread destruction. Clearly the goal in green finance would be to regulate the sector so as to ensure that it stays within the ambit of hedge borrowing (in Minsky's sense)—as discussed further later in this chapter, in the section "Green economics."

25. Here I am making fleeting reference to an enormous and growing literature on the issues associated with the "financialization" of the world economy and the problems generated by this. See Dore (2008) for an early analysis, prior to the great financial crisis of 2008–9; and Lazonick (2011) for a more recent analysis that links financialization to corporate pursuit of "shareholder value."

26. See the discussion paper on green National Appropriate Mitigation Action (NAMA) bonds, under the Kyoto Protocol, issued by the IETA, at http://www.ieta.org/index.php?option=com_content&view=article&id=423: green-nama-bonds-summary-note&catid=24:position-papers&Itemid=91.

27. See my (somewhat negative) comments on the IETA draft discussion paper, "Why, I've believed as many as six impossible things before breakfast," at the Climate Bonds Initiative website, at http://climatebonds.net/2010/06/why-sometimes-i%e2%80%99ve-believed-as-many-as-6-impossible-things-before-breakfast%e2%80%a6/.

28. For a classic statement of the issues involved, see the 2003 report "Unwanted, unproductive and unbalanced: Six arguments against an investment agreement at the WTO," Public Citizen, http://www.citizen.org/documents/MIA@WTO.pdf.

29. It might be argued that some investors see the green bond as riskier and so demand a premium—but it is unlikely that such an approach would be sustainable. The case for green bonds is grounded firmly in their capacity to offer institutional investors superior, safer investments for their funds under management, at comparable or lower cost.

Chapter 7

1. The Illinois Central was chartered in 1851 and constructed the longest railroad in the world (at the time) connecting Chicago to the Midwest. The financing of these US railroads through government-mandated bonds, and Abraham Lincoln's role as the lawyer representing the interests of the Illinois Central, were central to the success of US railroadization. For a Schumpeterian analysis, see Andersen (2002).

2. Acemoglu and Robinson (2000) outlined their basic distinction between political and economic losers from change in their article "Political losers as a barrier to economic development"; they cite with approval Mokyr's telling phrase, in the epigraph to this chapter. Acemoglu and Robinson have since expounded a comprehensive account of why some nations succeed and others fail, in their magisterial *Why Nations Fail* (2012).

3. The phrase "carbon lock-in" was coined by Unruh (2000, 2002); the phenomenon has been explored by many others in the energy literature such as

Sovacool (2009). Of the writers on renewable energy, none has captured the political dimensions of the transition better than Scheer (2002, 2005, 2007, 2011).

4. Schumpeter's massive work *Business Cycles*, published in two large volumes in 1939, remains the most ambitious of the explorations of industrial economic history and the phenomena of business cycles. While long on insightful description, it was short on rigorous statistical analysis, for which he was excoriated in a review published in 1940 by Simon Kuznets, a fellow scholar of the upswing-downswing phenomenon (but who refused to recognize it as cyclical) and who made his name as founder of national income accounting and the concept of gross national product. Others have contributed more recently, notably Freeman and Perez (1988), who introduced the influential notion of the techno-economic paradigm to describe each successive era, associated with sweeping change from some new general technology. The world economic historian Angus Maddison provided a balanced summing up in his 1991 book *Dynamic Forces in Capitalist Development*. My fellow "critical Schumpeterian" at Trinity College, Dublin, Professor Bill Kingston (2006), has developed an innovative critique of Schumpeter's long waves theory by focusing on new forms of intellectual property as driving each wave, in place of physical technologies.

5. One of the first and most enduring of these contributions was that by Freeman and Perez (1988)—and in subsequent elaborations by Perez (2002) and by Freeman and Louçã (2001). Note that the periodization of the first wave ignores the earlier energy transition in Britain, discussed in Chapter 2; this is defensible on the grounds that the changes had not yet had economy-wide effects.

6. Actually, these dates are not "generally accepted," but they provide a starting point for further analysis. While legions of economists have over the years occupied themselves with market trivia, these most fundamental aspects of capitalist industrial dynamics have languished for want of scholarship. The Russian polymath Andrey Korotayev together with his collaborator Sergey Tsirel has recently revived the study of long waves (or K-waves, after Kondratiev [Kondratieff]) by subjecting the time series to spectral analysis—thereby providing solid proof that these waves exist (Korotayev and Tsirel 2010).

7. The Allianz research report, *The sixth Kondratieff—long waves of prosperity*, provides a comprehensive exposition, drawing on the work of the German scholar Leo Nefiodow. For commentary, see my analysis in Mathews (2013c).

8. The original work on long waves was conducted by the Russian political economist Nikolai Kondratieff (see his basic exposition that appeared in English in 1935). The subsequent work on technoeconomic paradigm shifts was carried forward in the 1980s. There were in fact two strands of this framework. There is Freeman (1983, 1986) and Perez (1983, 1985, 2010) together with Perez and Soete (1988), and what emerged as a joint vision in Freeman and Perez (1988),

where the emphasis is on the triggering of new long waves by clusters of innovations, and upswings and downswings reflecting the struggles of the new to be born and the old to refuse to die. Freeman and Perez identify five such shifts or technology surges—the latest being the surge associated since the 1970s with the introduction of information and communication technologies (ICT). Then there is a second strand initiated by Perez (2002, 2011) herself, where she links the technology narrative with financial investment, speculation, and bubbles.

9. New reports from significant market players such as Deutsche Bank and the Macquarie Group were claiming in early 2013 that grid parity was already achieved in India and parts of Italy and would be widespread by 2014. See "Deutsche Bank: Sustainable solar market expected in 2014," *pv-magazine*, 20 February 2013, http://www.pv-magazine.com/news/details/beitrag/deutsche-bank—sustainable-solar-market-expected-in-2014_100010338/#axzz2N09qbbf7.

10. The costs of manufactured systems such as solar PV cells are falling dramatically (Bazilian et al. 2013). Costs of coal seam gas (secured through hydraulic fracture) are lower than for conventional gas—but these too can be expected to rise as the difficulties surrounding their capture are confronted. Foreign policy realists in the United States are moving away from analysis based on two stark extremes—worldwide hegemony or narrow isolation—and are arguing for a middle position that calls for an alternative "concert balancing" approach among a plurality of fossil fuel powers (Porter 2013).

11. Many of these identified changes reinforce each other, as when electric vehicles start to serve as distributed systems of energy storage—as anticipated by the Silicon Valley entrepreneur Elon Musk and his Tesla Motors start-up, where energy storage is to be provided by the proposed GIGA battery plant as well as the fleet of vehicles themselves.

12. On carbon lock-in, see Unruh (2000, 2002); on its role in slowing diffusion of renewables, see Sovacool (2009) as well as Negro, Alkemade, and Hekkert (2012).

13. Investments in renewable energies reached US$257 billion in 2011—more than a quarter of a trillion dollars—and they have stayed there, more or less, in 2012 and 2013, according to Bloomberg New Energy Finance (see "Clean Energy Investment," http://about.bnef.com/presentations/clean-energy-investment-q4-2013-fact-pack/). Large as this seems, it is still small compared to the trillions that bodies such as the International Energy Agency assert will be needed.

14. Spectral analysis examines wave formations from the frequency domain (looking for repeated wave patterns) rather than the time domain; it is known as Fourier analysis, after the French founder of the approach. Spectral analysis is fundamental to the vast array of innovations in the twentieth-century electronics,

IT, and telecom industries. The analysis reported here is by Korotayev and Tsirel (2010).

15. For the 2008 Merrill Lynch report, see Steven Milunovich and José Rasco, "The sixth revolution: The coming of cleantech," 17 November 2008, http://www.responsible-investor.com/images/uploads/resources/research/21228316156Merril_Lynch-_the_coming_of_clean_tech.pdf. For the 2012 Allianz Global Investors report, see Hans-Joerg Naumer, Dennis Nacken, and Stefan Scheurer, "The 'green' Kondratieff—or why crises can be a good thing: A new cycle of prosperity, driven by 'symbiotic' growth," June 2012, https://www.allianzglobalinvestors.de/cms-out/kapitalmarktanalyse/docs/pdf-eng/analysis-and-trends-the-green-kondratieff.pdf.

16. See, for example, Jacobson and Delucchi (2011); Scheer (2011).

17. Ayres and Ayres (2010) emphasize this aspect of the transition.

18. See Dosi and Nelson (2010) for a synoptic overview. On the need for a fresh approach to managing the diffusion to green technologies, see Mowery, Nelson, and Martin (2010). For an evolutionary perspective, focused on "survival of the greenest," see van den Bergh and colleagues (2006).

19. See my earlier work on the East Asian approach to innovation via diffusion management: Mathews (2001, 2002, 2005, 2006, 2007b, 2009) as well as Mathews and Cho (2000). Shahid Yusuf (2003) has written extensively on the rise of East Asia, emphasizing its innovative features.

20. See the exposition of the model developed by the Defense Advanced Research Projects Agency (DARPA) applied to energy innovation, by Bonvillian and Van Atta (2011). Hargadon and Kenney (2012) make the interesting argument that venture capital in the United States is not leading to strong green industry development.

21. Fast-follower strategies as developed in East Asia are the subject of growing literature (but still small, given their importance). See Mytelka (2004), Ho (2005), and Oyelara-Oyeyinka and Rasiah (2009) for treatments from various perspectives, as well as my own work and collaborative efforts.

22. See the reports of the China Greentech Initiative (with consulting group PricewaterhouseCoopers as strategic partner) such as the *2012 China Greentech Report*, at http://www.pwc.com.au/consulting/publications/china-greentech-report.htm. Scholarly work on China's adoption and rapid diffusion of green technologies continues to grow, with notable recent additions from Lewis (2013), Andreozzi (2012), Petti (2012), and Martinot (2010).

23. In our paper on the accelerated uptake of PV solar cell manufacture in Taiwan, my coauthors Hu Mei-Chih and Wu Ching-Yan and I outlined several steps involved in developing a fast follower strategy; these would seem to be just as

important as the familiar emphasis on innovation (Mathews, Hu, and Wu 2011). See also my studies conducted with Keun Lee (Lee and Mathews 2010, 2012).

24. Recent publications from the Information Technology and Innovation Foundation tend to favor strategies based on innovation over all else. While this may make some sense in the US setting, in opposition to "do nothing" policies from the energy industry, such strategies ignore the power of government support for diffusion, such as through the proposed Clean Energy Deployment Administration (CEDA); for a useful discussion in the context of the growing trade skirmish between the United States and China over solar PV cells, see Hauser (2013). The 2009 ITIF report by Stephen Ezell and Rob Atkinson, "The good, the bad and the ugly of innovation policy," is particularly critical of China (http://www.itif.org/publications/good-bad-and-ugly-innovation-policy), while the earlier 2009 report "Rising tigers, sleeping giant" (http://archive.itif.org/index.php?id=315) cast the same strategies in a favorable light.

25. See Delina and Diesendorf (2013) for an insightful discussion of wartime mobilization as model for rapid national buildup of renewables systems.

26. CIGS stands for copper, indium, gallium, and selenide, the semiconductor materials used in thin-film solar cells (as contrasted with crystalline silicon).

27. The building of intermediate suppliers—and particularly equipment suppliers—is key to the success of new industry creation efforts. It is the absence of such focus on the role of intermediates and equipment suppliers that accounts for the weakness of renewable energy promotion schemes utilizing only tradable green certificates, as in Europe and the United States; see Bergek and Jacobsson (2010) and Jacobsson and colleagues (2009). De la Tour, Glachant, and Ménière (2011) provide an illuminating account of Chinese firms' strategies in entering the PV sector, with their concentration on seeking to build technological capacity in the upper parts of the value chain, involving silicon wafer supply. On Taiwan's fast follower strategy in entering the solar PV industry, see my study conducted with Taiwan collaborators Mei-Chih Hu and Ching-Yan Wu (Mathews, Hu, and Wu 2011).

28. The key point I am making here is that market-based incentives provide positive financial incentives, as opposed to the negative incentives (disincentives) embodied in carbon taxes or pollution taxes generally. Apart from the examples discussed in the following section, there are other cases that one could refer to, such as China's Sloping Lands Conversion program, discussed in Chapter 3.

29. The role that facilitating state institutions can play in fostering new green industries is the subject of a burgeoning literature; see Wong (2005, 2006) for representative cases from East Asia. The fast-follower strategies developed in East Asia and the transition to innovation are the subject of insightful papers by Kim (2010, 2011) on the case of telecommunications in Korea, and by Lee (2013).

30. See the presentation by Henry Joseph to the Brazilian Automotive Association (ANFAVEA) in March 2013, "Flex fuel vehicles in Brazil," at http://www.globalbioenergy.org/fileadmin/user_upload/gbep/docs/2013_events/GBEP_Bioenergy_Week_Brasilia_18-23_March_2013/4.5_JOSEPH.pdf.

31. But not (yet) the European Union. See my analysis of these developments in *The Globalist* post "The end of the U.S. ethanol tariff," http://www.theglobalist.com/StoryId.aspx?StoryId=9505.

32. Studies of German experience with feed-in tariffs are now widely available; see Jacobsson and Lauber (2006) for a useful historical overview. Fischer and Preonas (2010) provide a comparative analysis of all known market expansion policies, noting that conflicts between the policy goals mean effectively that the whole can be construed as less than the sum of the parts.

33. Deutsche Bank has been a strong proponent of the German feed-in tariff system, issuing report after report, culminating in what it calls the "Get FiT Program," which involves global diffusion of feed-in tariff systems; see http://www.dbadvisors.com/content/_media/GET_FIT_-_042610_FINAL.pdf.

34. The argument is presented forcefully in Jacobsson and colleagues (2009); while Bergek and Jacobsson (2010) pose the critical question, whether tradable green certificates constitute cost-efficient policy driving technical change or a rent-generating machine? The literature on the superiority of feed-in tariff schemes over TGC schemes is considerable—as reviewed by Fischer and Preonas (2010).

35. This is a characteristic East Asian, and now Chinese, practice in innovation diffusion. On China's feed-in tariffs experimentation, see Coco Liu, "China uses feed-in tariff to build domestic solar market," *New York Times*, 14 September 2011, http://www.nytimes.com/cwire/2011/09/14/14climatewire-china-uses-feed-in-tariff-to-build-domestic-25559.html?pagewanted=all.

36. The report itself is no longer available and has not yet (apparently) been uploaded to the web—itself a gross oversight. For an overview of the program, I am indebted to the discussion provided by Commoner (1979) and in more conventionally academic mode by Hart (1983). Yergin (2011), in a book that otherwise cheers on the American fracking revolution, nevertheless has an interesting chapter on the stillborn solar revolution ushered in under the Carter administration.

37. On the role of government procurement in the US semiconductor program, see the report *DoD PV energy conversion systems market inventory and analysis* (FEA 1977a). On the strategy of government procurement generally, as practiced very successfully by the US federal government, see Mowery and Rosenberg (1991) for a treatment from the perspective of innovation, and Weiss and Thurbon (2006) from the perspective of political economy. On the role of the US state generally as a powerful driver of innovation (as opposed to the generally

propagated view of the United States as a "liberal market economy"), see the book edited by Fred Block (2011) and the pioneering study by Weiss (2014). The role that the DARPA model could play in energy innovation is discussed by Bonvillian and Van Atta (2011).

38. Cost considerations indicated that PV units could substitute for a conventional 1.5 MW diesel-fueled generator at around $10 per watt, and for a larger 5 MW generator at around $3.70 per watt. (By 1985 the cost of PV-generated power had in fact reduced to $6.50 per watt—and by 2010 it had reduced to $1.50 per watt.) On the basis of these cost data, the task force estimated the impact of a government procurement order for 152 MW of PV generator sets over a five-year period. The estimated costs were expected to fall from $10 per watt at the start to $2 to $3 per watt after the first year, to around $1 per watt after the second year, and to $0.50 per watt after the fifth year.

39. In practice, the cost has reduced from $60 per watt in 1976, to around $5 per watt after 1000 MW had been installed (1994–95), and to $1.50 per watt by 2010 after more than 10,000 MW (10 GW) had been installed. This is a fortyfold cost reduction over thirty-five years. On the theoretical link between cost reduction and market uptake of new energy technologies, see my paper with Paolo Baroni on our construction of a three-dimensional industrial logistic surface (Mathews and Baroni 2013).

40. A similar story can be told for the case of wind power, where state-level incentives had created a strong wind power industry in California that by the early 1980s claimed more than 90 percent of the world's installed capacity. But again the incentives were dismantled and the United States frittered away its lead, with the stop-start character of the federal production tax credit playing a key role in the decline. See Lewis and Wiser (2007) for a comparative overview.

41. This was the Erneuerbare Energien Gesetz (EEG), best translated as the Renewable Energy Sources Act. On its significance, see Scheer (2011).

42. The Georgetown University scholar Joanne Lewis (2011, 2013) has emphasized this point in her work on China's wind power; she compares China favorably with India and Korea. For an insightful discussion of the interactions (and conflicts) between various kinds of policies used in promoting renewables, see Fischer and Preonas (2010).

43. Nemet (2009) shows definitively that there is no connection between diffusion of a new energy technology (in his case, Californian wind power, with its high levels of early penetration) and innovation; all the patents for wind power were created before the miniboom and faded away once the boom was in full swing.

44. Hermann Scheer (2007, 276) himself put the matter very clearly: "This [building of renewable energy opportunities] opens the way for a split in the "economy," a fracture in the business community that is a necessary precondition

for any breakthrough to renewable energy. It is a fracture between those business interests that are or feel themselves to be dependent (for better or worse) on the traditional energy business and those that recognize or pursue their future opportunities in the shift to renewable energy. . . . These interest conflicts come to light through the creation of a 'critical mass,' in other words, through a growing number of renewable energy businesses inside Germany that are already earning annual sales of more than 10 billion Euros."

45. See Ayres and Ayres (2010) for an investigation into the extent of legislative and regulatory protection of existing centralized electric power producers. This "electric lock-in" complements the "carbon lock-in" investigated in the case of fossil fuel protection (Unruh 2000); both forms of vested interest act to block the emergence of the new renewable energy and resource efficiency techno-economic paradigm.

46. See Matthew Stepp, *The Globalist*, 6 February 2013, http://www.theglo balist.com/storyid.aspx?storyid=9894. My response can be found at the same blog: "The Globalist debate: How to compete with China in renewables," 26 April 2013,   http://www.theglobalist.com/the-globalist-debate-how-to-compete-with -china-in-renewables/.

47. Polemicists like Lomborg (2010) maintain a similar stance, always emphasizing innovation with its vague, future-focused payoff over market expansion with its immediate, proven cost-reduction potential. Yet as noted earlier, Nemet (2009) has already demonstrated clearly that uptake of a new energy technology is not linked with innovation in terms of patenting rates—and must therefore be associated with other forms of promotion.

Chapter 8

1. According to the parable, Tempus built his watches from separate parts; every time he was disturbed, the half-built watch fell apart, and he had to start again. Tempus built very few watches. Horus instead created subassemblies and built his watches out of these. When he was disturbed, all he lost was a subassembly that could be replaced. Horus built lots of watches and prospered (see Simon 1962).

2. Scholars such as Reap, Baumeister, and Bras (2005) outline an approach to the design of the industrial system as a whole, along biomimetic lines, in what they call "holistic biomimesis"—an approach that moves beyond design of individual products and processes along biomimetic lines to consider the systemic and eco-systemic levels that are normally left out of such practices. They build on others to formulate "conditions conducive to life"—having been tested by several billion years of evolutionary development—that can be applied in an economic setting.

3. On biomimesis, see Benyus (1997); for further elucidation, see Benyus and Baumeister (2004).

4. On the philosophical foundations of the concept of biomimesis, see the study from my sister, Freya Mathews (2011). She has made major contributions to explicating the notion of biomimesis as a novel socioeconomic goal that breaks with the conventional fossil-fueled wisdom.

5. For an elaboration on these themes, see the influential texts by Martinez-Alier (1987, 2000) and Costanza (1991)—founding texts of the discipline. Cavalcanti (2010) provides an overview of the development of ecological economic thinking. Barbier and Markandya (2012) provide an updated treatment of a "blueprint for a green economy," thereby paying their dues to the original work under this name published by Pearce (1989).

6. Hicks was working here with a static concept of the conditions that produce potential output; but of course they are themselves produced by earlier output, in an endless sequence of backward regression. This is why a dynamic approach to these matters is essential.

7. See, for example, the treatment of natural capital in Dasgupta and Heal (1979), and in the papers by Solow (1974, 1991/2005). Solow's work has been very influential in promoting the view that capital substitution provides a ready means of avoiding resource collapse.

8. For ecosystem services, think of bees providing pollination services for crops, without which modern farming would be impossible. For a discussion, see Kremen (2005). More generally, environmental or ecological economics examines environmental issues from the viewpoint of (mainstream) economics, introducing such questions as the valuation of resources and ecosystem services. In addition to founding texts already mentioned, see Thampapillai (1991); Pearce (1998); Söderbaum (2000).

9. Pearce and Turner (1989) provide four possibilities for measuring natural capital—as physical quantities, as the total value of resource stocks (imputed by their prices), as the unit value of the eco-services provided by the resource stocks, and as the value of the resource flows emanating from the resource stocks (where resource flow is computed as the product of price by quantity).

10. Neumayer (2003) captures this argument neatly in the idea that the neoclassical production function, with its absorption in notions of substitutability, can provide only a weak concept of sustainability and that real sustainability calls for a different and deeper approach.

11. These charts as well as others were drawn in collaboration with my collaborator, Dr. Hao Tan.

12. I referred to and defined industrial hypercycles in Chapter 5, when discussing the circular economy as a new industrial ecology paradigm.

13. The planetary boundaries, as proposed by Johan Rockström and colleagues (2009), are defined by nine variables that are key to maintain Earth's system to be the safe operating space for humanity, including climate change; rate of biodiversity loss (terrestrial and marine); interference with the nitrogen and phosphorus cycles; stratospheric ozone depletion; ocean acidification; global freshwater use; change in land use; chemical pollution; and atmospheric aerosol loading. The idea has been elaborated on in the report to the Club of Rome: *Bankrupting Nature: Denying Our Planetary Boundaries* (Wijkman and Rockström 2012).

14. Holling (1973) remains an essential point of reference for such studies. Holling (1986, 2001) himself has further clarified his conceptual framework and notion of adaptive cycle. A comprehensive overview of resilience and sustainability is provided by Folke (2006); while Gunderson and Holling (2002) bring the insights together in an overarching concept of panarchy.

15. The notion of capital substitution as solution to the problem of resource scarcity was put forward forcefully by Robert Solow in a series of papers, most famously in his Ely Address to the American Economic Association at the end of 1973 (Solow 1974) and elaborated on later (Solow 1991/2005). This intervention delivered a fatal blow to the arguments of the limits to growth and other approaches labeled (pejoratively) "neo-Malthusian"; they are only now being queried and revisited, in studies such as those by Victor (2008).

16. Daly was a young academic economist at Louisiana State University in the late 1960s when he burst on the economics scene with a series of fundamental papers developing the idea of the steady-state economy. He started with an essay accepted for publication in the premier *Journal of Political Economy* (flagship of the Chicago School) on the deep analogies between the biological and economic sciences, where both were focused on the life process (Daly 1968, 392). Drawing on Bates, Georgescu-Roegen, and Boulding (whom I revisit in the final chapter), Daly sketched a parallel between *biological metabolism*, which takes in matter and energy and processes it, producing degraded matter and energy as waste, and *economic metabolism*, or processing, which performs the same feat, with the flow in both cases governed by the laws of thermodynamics. See Daly (1972, 1973, 1974a, 1974b, 2005).

17. There is by now a substantial literature on the critique developed by Daly. There is also the Center for the Advancement of the Steady State Economy and its associated blog, *Daly News* (http://steadystate.org/learn/blog/).

18. For a comprehensive overview of the issues, see the report of the Stiglitz-Sen-Fitoussi Commission, "Measurement of economic performance and social progress." The Commission was established by then-president Nicolas Sarkozy of France in 2008 and reported in 2009 (Stiglitz, Sen, and Fitoussi 2009).

19. This conception of green growth can be traced to the 1989 text *Blueprint for a Green Economy*, by the British economics scholar David W. Pearce (with Anil Markandya and Edward Barbier).

20. Kaldor (1970, 340) put the matter thus, in his address to the Scottish Political Economy Association:

To explain why certain regions have become highly industrialised, while others have not we must introduce quite different kinds of considerations—what Myrdal called the principle of "circular and cumulative causation." . . . As Allyn Young pointed out in a famous paper, Adam Smith's principle of the "division of labor" operates through the constant sub-division of industries, the emergence of new kinds of specialized firms, of steadily increasing differentiation—more than through the expansion in the size of the individual plant or the individual firm.

21. See Winkler (2011) for an exposition of the greening of supply-chain systems, viewed as the necessary complement to greening at the individual company level.

22. Terminological confusion is possible here. By "circular economy" I mean an economy based on circular flows of materials and resources, in conscious imitation of the great cycles (carbon, nitrogen, phosphorus) of the biosphere. This is to be contrasted with the neoclassical economic conception of the "circular flow" economy, which is merely a flow of income unconnected to ecological limits. The use of the term *circular* in "circular and cumulative causation" refers, by contrast, to feedback loops that "close the circle." See Mathews and Tan (2011) for a recent account of the emergence of the circular economy in China, where it is now embodied in the Twelfth Five-Year Plan as a central goal of national development.

23. The Suzhou eco-industrial park was opened in 1994 as a cooperative development between Singapore and China. After a rocky start it is now flourishing, having attracted more than 2,400 foreign-invested firms, as well as local entrepreneurial firms, in sectors encompassing electronics, semiconductors, biotechnology, IT, biopharmaceutical, and health care. The park's managers deliberately follow a "value chain completion" strategy in attracting new firms, identifying gaps in the existing value chains and seeking to fill them with new firms.

24. For example, firms in Suzhou achieve levels of chemical oxygen demand and sulfur dioxide emissions that are one-eighteenth and one-fortieth of China's national averages, and its energy consumption levels to only 0.36 tonnes of standard coal equivalent per 10,000 RMB. See the official Suzhou website at http://www.sipac.gov.cn/english/zhuanti/jg60n/gjlnbtsj/.

25. My collaborator Dr. Hao Tan and I discussed these in Mathews and Tan (2011); see also Shi, Chertow, and Song (2010).

26. On this point, see Czech (2008), as well as Victor (2008) for a book-length treatment of macroeconomic modeling of a steady state, and Victor (2010) for an exposition in *Nature*; Heinberg (2011) adds his arguments, and Jackson (2009) draws on Victor in making the case for prosperity without growth. Stoll (2010) provides a vivid picture of the "specter" of a no-growth world; he also cites Solow

to the effect that capitalism and nongrowth in (extensive) resource throughput is perfectly feasible. This is richly ironic, given Solow's role in providing intellectual support for the notion of endless growth based on resource substitution, in the 1970s.

27. See Toner (2000, 2001) for a discussion of circular and cumulative causation (C&CC) and why it disappeared from economic analysis; on this theme, see also Berger (2009). Myrdal employed the term as a means of explaining the intensification of the gap between developing and developed economies; the concept was linked with his notion of backwash effects (1957); for an elaboration, see Fujita (2004). Kaldor (1970) used the concept in his address to the Scottish Economic Society at the University of Aberdeen and in subsequent critical writings (Kaldor 1972, 1975). For a treatment that reconciles Myrdal's and Kaldor's approaches to C&CC, see O'Hara (2008).

28. The heterodox schools of thought on the origins of economic growth, and the centrality in the process of manufacturing with its increasing returns, support a lively scholarly interchange. Key players are the Hungarian-British economist Nicholas Kaldor (1967), with his empirically based "laws of growth," and his intellectual successor Anthony Thirlwall (2002), together with Cambridge growth economists like Cripps and Tarling (1973). Reinert and I link increasing returns and manufacturing to renewables and green development, thereby creating a new platform for the expansion of renewables industries (Mathews and Reinert 2014).

29. See Rosenstein-Rodan (1943), whose "big push" idea sparked a stream of work in development economics.

30. Erik Reinert (1999, 2007) has explored these themes and provides illuminating discussions of early contributors to political economy (such as Antonio Serra), prior to Adam Smith, reflecting on the role of increasing returns from manufacturing generated in Renaissance Italian city-states; see also Mathews and Reinert (2014).

31. As part of an expanding literature on green growth, see the OECD's 2011 report as well as contributions from Hallegatte and colleagues (2012) and Jänicke (2012). Bowen and Frankhauser (2011) adopt a skeptical viewpoint.

32. The lowercase version is also commonly utilized in economic analysis. Dr. Hao Tan and I introduced the concept of Pareto eco-efficiency in our paper on China's advances in industrial ecology associated with the development of a circular economy (Mathews and Tan 2011).

33. See David (1985) for the original exposition, where David advances three arguments as to why QWERTY became locked in as the keyboard design—technical interrelatedness, economies of scale, and quasi-irreversibility of investment. He was challenged largely by Liebowitz and Margolis (1995). David then produced many papers advancing the argument, particularly David (2007), in

which path dependence is viewed as a "foundational concept for historical social science."

34. Jenkins (2002, 43) notes that for Daoism, "the natural world is not an external utilitarian resource to be controlled and exploited, but a dynamic process within which harmonisation is a liberating abstraction from the competitive striving of everyday human existence."

35. For the clearest statement by Minsky himself of his financial instability hypothesis, where capitalist financial processes are analyzed in terms of the three-fold categorization as hedge based, speculative, or Ponzi-like, see Minsky (1995), as well as his book-length treatment, Minsky (1986).

36. Holling's insights are discussed earlier. His principal contribution, dating back to Holling (1973), was to set ecological concepts within a framework of complex system dynamics. An obvious challenge therefore presents itself: why not adapt Minsky, with his explicit usage of terms like *resilience* and *stability* of the financial system, to Holling, with his application of such terms to complex economic and ecological processes?

Chapter 9

1. See Gramsci's (1930/1971) *Selections from Prison Notebooks*, edited and translated by Quintin Hoare. Wollen (1991) provides an insightful discussion of this phrase from Gramsci.

2. Actually, Boulding was an accomplished coiner of metaphors and devoted considerable thought to the question of "images" in the human psyche. As he put it: "Behavior, whether of the amoeba, the rat, the man, the group, the state, the firm, or the Federal Reserve Board is determined not by any immediate stimulus, but by the Image—the view of the universe which the organism or organization possesses at the moment. Every Image is endowed with a value structure, and behavior always consists in moving into the most highly valued part of the Image. Thus the Image is a kind of capital-structure of information: it is built up out of Messages, but these messages are themselves filtered through the value system of the image." Boulding (1956), as quoted in his sympathetic biography *Creative Tension: The Life and Thought of Kenneth Boulding* (Kerman 1974, 55).

3. Of course Boulding didn't invent the image of Spaceship Earth. The phrase probably goes back to Henry George, in his best-known work *Progress and Poverty* (1879, book 4, chapter 2), where he states: "It is a well-provisioned ship, this on which we sail through space."

4. This and the following citations come from the online version of Boulding's celebrated 1966 paper, available at http://www.panarchy.org/boulding/spaceship.1966.html.

5. Naess (2004) provides a powerful critique of the lifeboat ethic, calling it "the tragedy of Hardin's Social Darwinism."

6. The issue can be posed in the following neat formulation: "Is economic development the best contraceptive? Or is voluntary contraception the best form of development?" Clearly both have a role to play. See Joel Cohen, "How to deal with 7 billion people?" *International Herald Tribune*, 24 October 2011.

7. The origins of increasing returns as a concept may be traced to Italian theorists of the urban manufacturing economy. Italian scholars who anticipated these ideas and elaborated on the role of urban clusters must certainly include Antonio Serra in 1613 (*Breve Trattato delle cause che possono far abbondare li regni d'oro e d'argento dove non sono minere*, or Brief treatise on the causes that can increase wealth in terms of gold and silver where there are no mines) and before him Giovanni Botero in 1590 (*Delle cause della grandezza delle citta*, or Causes of the greatness of cities). On the significance of their ideas for a long-lost tradition of political economy, but one that is highly relevant to the study of clusters, see Reinert (1999).

8. See Jeff Rubin's paper for CIBC World Markets, "Just how big is Cleveland?" 31 October 2008, http://research.cibcwm.com/economic_public/down load/soct08.pdf. His argument is that it was implausible that the bursting of the housing bubble in the United States (e.g., in Cleveland) could have precipitated a global recession; more plausible, he says, is that housing market bubbles were bursting at the same time as oil prices were rising. This argument is elaborated in his book-length exposition *Oil and the End of Globalization* (Rubin 2009). Rubin's analysis linking oil price spikes to recessions finds support in such mainstream sources as the Federal Reserve (e.g., Federal Reserve Board of San Francisco, *Economic Letter*, 18 November 2005).

9. In mainstream economics (reflecting fossil-fueled industrial reality) the constraints on consumption stem from income, not from the environment or ecological limits. This is anomalous, since the universal rule throughout the biological world is that organisms eat (consume) only up to a point recognized as satiety.

10. An Austrian school of social ecology, centered on the Institute of Social Ecology at Klagenfurt University, Vienna, has been developing sophisticated industrial metabolic measures of this kind of industrial system—what Fischer-Kowalski and colleagues (2010) describe as a transformation from an agrarian, biomass-based to an industrial, fossil-fuel-based social metabolism.

11. Recent contributions to the debate over "green growth" or "green development" express a caution that needs to be added to the more optimistic reports from the UN Development Program and other agencies. They include those by Schmalensee (2012), who focuses on the long-term costs of such a strategy with little regard to the benefits; van der Ploeg and Withagen (2012), where they note

the difficulties of launching green growth strategies at a time of economic crisis; and Barbier (2012), who notes the failure of the G-20 summit in Mexico in late 2012 to pay any more than lip service to policies favoring green growth.

12. In Chapter 7 I argued that the world was moving inexorably to a new techno-economic paradigm—the sixth such shift since the first Industrial Revolution. I shall use the terms *green economy* and *new (sixth) techno-economic paradigm* interchangeably.

13. For an informed critique, see Joffe (2011); from an evolutionary perspective, see Nelson (2011).

14. In a 1995 paper coauthored with Claas van der Linde, Michael Porter argues that the conflict between economy and ecology grows out of a static conception of environmental regulation, where technology and rules are fixed and firms are forced to work within these rules, which are viewed as raising costs. A more dynamic view, by contrast, would see firms profiting from strict regulation by becoming more innovative and *lowering* their costs as a result of such innovativeness. This work has been extended by Porter and Reinhardt (2007) into an approach to dealing with climate change; again the gist is that progressive firms will find innovative ways to reduce their carbon emissions, and by so doing they will also find new ways to compete and excel. My comment is that such firm-level innovations in corporate and social responsibility (CSR) will always be constrained while the system remains locked to its business-as-usual trajectory.

15. The World Bank and International Finance Corporation have pioneered such instruments in the form of green bonds, which have provided a way of testing the waters. In early 2013 the first national bank stepped forward to issue a US$500 million green bond; this was the Korean Export-Import Bank. The bond issue was oversubscribed nearly fourfold, at US$1.8 billion. This points to unsatisfied demand on the part of institutional investors for safe, medium-term clean-tech bonds, which will tap into the tens of trillions of dollars controlled by institutional investors (Kaminker and Stewart 2012) and ensure a successful transition away from a fossil-fuel-dominated paradigm. The Korean Export-Import Bank bond is discussed in Chapter 6.

16. See my 2012 posting "The Asian Super Grid," *Asia Pacific Journal: Japan Focus*, http://www.japanfocus.org/-John_A_-Mathews/3858.

17. In complementary terms, the *price of renewable electric power*, traded in competitive markets across national boundaries, can be expected to emerge as the regulator of the new green-tech economy—just as the price of food was the regulator of the agrarian economy and the price of oil has been (and still is) the regulator of the fossil-fueled industrial economy. In competitive markets the price of renewable electric power will continue to fall, driven by learning-curve dynamics and the free availability of the renewable resources which are tapped

(e.g., sun, wind, tides). Its marginal price will eventually approach zero, forcing existing power generation companies to radically revise their business plans (as is already happening). Rifkin (2013) has made this phenomenon of zero marginal cost the core of a sweeping argument; my own view is that Rifkin misses the even more fundamental point that all renewables are the products of manufacturing, and as such are capable of generating increasing returns.

18. See the 2012 ITIF policy call, "WTO should create a clean technology agreement modelled on the ITA," http://www.itif.org/content/wto-should -create-clean-technology-agreement-modeled-ita-combat-green-mercantilism; and see the 2011 ICTSD position paper, "Fostering low-carbon growth: The case for a Sustainable Energy Trade Agreement," as well as an analysis of the prospects for China signing such an agreement (Meléndez-Ortiz, Monkelbaan, and Riddell 2012). My own take can be found at http://www.theglobalist.com/time-new -global-trade-deal-focused-green-growth/.

19. The APEC countries signing up for this commitment include China, the United States, Japan, and Australia.

20. See Zenghelis (2012) for an insightful account of engaging in green infrastructure investment, as well as *The Green Investment Report* of the World Economic Forum (2013).

21. I illustrated the idea in an article published a few years ago in *Energy Policy* on the tracing of biofuel flows through attaching electronic identifiers to futures contracts traded on commodities exchanges (Mathews 2008b). The same idea can carry over to almost all commodity flows, making their origins transparent to consumers and to producers who utilize the commodities, and specifically allowing governments to tax virgin flows while favoring those that are recirculated. See Gershenfeld and Krikorian (2004) for the Internet of things (as elaborated by Atzori, Iera, and Morabito 2010); it is referred to explicitly in China's Twelfth Five-Year Plan.

22. On green taxes, and on environmental taxes more generally, see the 2013 OECD survey report and contributions from scholars such as Bosquet (2000), Nordhaus (2008), and Speck and Ekins (2011).

23. See my posting on this theme to *The Conversation*, describing the interesting initiative of Sundrop Farms: "Tomatoes watered by the sea: Sprouting a new way of farming," 17 February 2014, https://theconversation.com/ tomatoes-watered-by-the-sea-sprouting-a-new-way-of-farming-23119.

24. This idea was advanced by the Stiglitz-Sen-Fitoussi Commission on the "Measurement of Economic Performance and Social Progress," established by President Sarkozy in France in 2008 and which reported in 2009. See the final report from the commission chaired by Joseph Stiglitz and consisting also of Amartya Sen and Jean-Paul Fitoussi, released in September 2009, at http://www

.stiglitz-sen-fitoussi.fr/en/index.htm. For a useful introduction to the issues, see Jon Gertner, "The rise and fall of the GDP," *New York Times*, 13 May 2010, http://www.nytimes.com/2010/05/16/magazine/16GDP-t.html?pagewanted=all.

25. See Daly and Cobb (1989/1994) for the Genuine Progress Indicator. On the green GDP, see Boyd (2007) for a useful conceptual discussion, as well as Lawn (2003). China's attempts to launch a green GDP are discussed in Li and Lang (2010). On Chinese experiments with different local versions of a green GDP, see, for example, Xu, Yu, and Yue (2010), reporting on green GDP measurement for the city of Wuyishan.

26. See Geng (2011) and Geng and colleagues (2012) for a review of the progress China has made in measuring its convergence on a circular economy.

27. The noted economist Robert Shiller (2012) argues something similar in his book, *Finance and the Good Society*: namely that finance should be viewed not simply as the manipulation of money or the management of risk but as the stewardship of a society's assets. The financial crash of 2007/8, he argues, underlines the point that good finance should serve a wide social purpose. Viewing finance as a utility takes this argument a step further.

28. Zysman and Huberty (2011, 2013) make a similar point in arguing that green growth considerations need to develop beyond religion to reality—meaning that they must engage with the world as it is.

29. The Brazilian federal government is battling what seem to be intractable problems involved in trying to preserve the Amazonian rain forest—by far the largest on the planet—and open it up in a controlled fashion for economic activity. An important initiative is the Amazon Fund, launched in December 2008 at the fifteenth Conference of the Parties (under the Kyoto Protocol) staged in Nairobi, Kenya, with a $1 billion donation from Norway. The fund, managed by the Brazilian Development Bank, is seeking to drive initiatives in Amazonia that offer incentives both for preservation and for sustainable development of the already-deforested area.

30. We may contrast these axioms with those offered by McDonough and Braungart (2002) in what they describe as "cradle to cradle" (C2C) thinking.

31. On the essential role of the state in driving innovation in the United States, see Weiss (2014).

32. This was the question asked by Jeffreys (1994). As noted earlier, Narveson (1995) and then Anderson and Leal (2001) have provided a statement of the free-market environmentalist position, while Adler (2001, 2009) has elaborated on its legal ramifications. Stroup (2008) argues that "3-D" property rights are needed to ensure favorable environmental outcomes—clearly defined, easily defensible, and capable of smooth divestiture. Of course these are characteristics that are exceedingly difficult to achieve in practice.

33. Weber's (1922/1947) own exegesis can be found in his *The Theory of Social and Economic Organization*; Swedberg (2000) provides a scholarly account of the significance of his thought.

34. See discussions of the use of satellite remote-sensing technology to collect data needed for verification purposes by such international treaties as the Kyoto Protocol, by Rosenqvist and colleagues (2003)—although these authors are more concerned with monitoring vegetation cover on the earth than with point emissions of greenhouse gases.

35. See Kingston (2013) for an illuminating discussion.

36. There are studies that call for a redesign of the institutions of property and ownership to take resources out of the commons. See Newell and Paterson (2010) and Lovins and Cohen (2011) for accounts that discuss the operating rules of a capitalism geared to keep within its ecological limits, and see Barnes (2006) for an account of "capitalism 3.0," by which he means a capitalism with new property rights that place ownership of common resources in trusts. While these proposals are of interest, I see little prospect of their being acted on until there have been the more immediate changes in energy markets, resources and commodity markets and financial markets discussed in this text. Hamilton (2010) provides a sobering assessment of our civilization's prospects under the impact of climate change. Kaletsky (2010) provides an account of what he calls capitalism 4.0, but he does not include discussion of ecological issues.

37. See Garnaut (2008), Stern (2009), Flannery (2001, 2009, 2011), Speth (2009), Moriarty and Honery (2011), and Martenson (2011) for representative discussions of the ecological limits to present patterns of industrial production. Discussion of the end of industrial civilization or even extinction of the human race has been canvassed by Morgan (2009). Gray (2007), in *Al Qaeda and What It Means to Be Modern*, provides a stimulating critique of the neoliberal globalization project and argues that the twenty-first century will see devastating resource wars in the absence of a change in direction.

38. See Mann's *Sources of Social Power* quartet, a work of scholarship spanning nearly three decades; the most recent volume contains a discussion of global warming in its chapter 12 (Mann 1986, 1993, 2012, 2013).

39. See Mann (2013, 361–99). Mann's discussion, which starts by demonstrating how fossil-fueled industrial capitalism has turned all four sources of social power against itself, stands out as the most politically sophisticated of the critiques of global warming, informed as it is by decades of intense social science research and explication. When he writes that the resolution of global warming, if it is to be achieved at all, will involve a coming (global) political struggle, he cannot be far off the mark. But in technological terms he is, I have argued in Chapter 4, unnecessarily defeatist.

40. A 2011 estimate by Nassim Nicholas Taleb (of "black swan" fame) and Mark Spitznagel (a hedge fund manager) states that filings with the US Securities and Exchange Commission reveal that sums paid to bankers over the previous five years amounted to $2,200 billion—or $2.2 trillion. "Extrapolating over the coming decade," they write, "the numbers would approach $5 trillion." See Nassim Nicholas Taleb and Mark Spitznagel, "The great bank robbery," *Project Syndicate*, 2 September 2011, http://www.project-syndicate.org/commentary/taleb1/English.

41. The year 1994 saw the staging of the first conference of the UNFCCC, and 2009 witnessed the fifteenth Conference of the Parties in Copenhagen, under the Kyoto Protocol.

42. See Hulme (2009b) for a discussion of the various "framings" of the global warming problem that make it so difficult to arrive at consensus as to what are its sources and what needs to be done.

43. See Prins and colleagues (2010), "The Hartwell Paper: A new direction for climate policy after the crash of 2009," and the earlier papers by Prins and Rayner (2007a, 2007b).

44. I am thinking here of contributors to the debate over global warming such as Lomborg (2007, 2010) and his many public statements since these books appeared, always with the same call for "more R&D"; and the scholars associated with the Information Technology and Innovation Foundation (ITIF) in the United States, such as Matthew Stepp and Jesse Jenkins (2012), with their emphasis on clean energy innovation. My own approach, by contrast, emphasizes the process of market expansion as priority in order to drive down costs.

45. The problem is that border carbon adjustment transfers to the international realm all the difficulties involved in introducing carbon taxes and takes on a decidedly protectionist air—particularly if targeted at China by the European Union. See Weitzel and Peterson (2012) for a fair—and negative—assessment.

46. See Helm (2012a) for a book-length treatment, and Helm (2012b) for a summary exposition published in *Nature*.

47. An argument along these lines is developed by Michael Spence, "Asia's new growth model," *Project Syndicate*, 1 June 2011, http://www.project-syndicate.org/commentary/spence23/English.

48. I am referring here to the argument that carbon emissions need to be kept below a threshold of 1 trillion tonnes to avoid a temperature increase exceeding 2°C (Allen et al. 2009), as discussed earlier. Scientists like Calvin (2011) continue to insist on technological fixes to achieve such a goal.

49. On the shift from annuals to perennials as the basis of a sustainable agriculture (undoing the ill effects of an industrialized version of the first agricultural

revolution of ten thousand years ago), see some of the interesting contributions such as that by Wes Jackson and the Land Institute (e.g., Jackson 2011) and the emerging debate over the addition of biochar to soil, both to enhance its power to support agriculture and as a store of carbon (e.g., Lehmann 2006, 2007).

50. See, for example, the insightful article by Michael Wines, "China takes a loss to get ahead in the business of fresh water," *New York Times*, 25 October 2011, http://www.nytimes.com/2011/10/26/world/asia/china-takes-loss-to-get -ahead-in-desalination-industry.html?pagewanted=all.

51. In connection with green building, see, for example, the designs for Chinese cities emerging from the studio of William McDonough (of cradle-to-cradle thinking) and described in his interview "From products to cities," at http:// sustainablecities.dk/en/actions/interviews/william-mcdonough-from-prod ucts-to-cities. Other green building designs of note include the Vanke Center in Shenzhen, China, characterized by the architect Steven Holl as a "horizontal sky-scraper" that is based entirely on renewable energy and recycled water (http:// www.stevenholl.com/project-detail.php?id=60&type). For overviews of such initiatives, see Droege (2006); as well as Newman, Beatley, and Boyer (2009).

52. *The Constant Gardener* is the title of a 2001 novel by John LeCarre, which was translated into a successful film in 2005 starring Rachel Weisz and Ralph Fiennes. I am borrowing this title to stand for a broader story—but one that is consistent with the novel's message of reining in the power of large corporations. Sustainability as gardening is also consistent with *Flourishing*, in which John Ehrenfeld and Andrew Hoffman (2013) develop the theme of gardening of the earth.

53. See the reports from the Carbon Tracker Initiative (CTI), which have led the way in formulating the notion that fossil fuel reserves constitute stranded assets of "unburnable carbon." See CTI, "Unburnable carbon 2013: Wasted capital and stranded assets," http://www.carbontracker.org/wastedcapital.

54. A telling argument along these lines was formulated by publisher Tim O'Reilly in response to a question posed at the beginning of 2012 by *The Edge*: "What is your favorite deep, elegant or beautiful explanation?" (http:// edge.org/response-detail/2942/what-is-your-favorite-deep-elegant-or-beautiful -explanation).

55. For an elaboration of this perspective, see my papers on developing countries and renewable energy (Mathews 2007a, 2007b) and later on the greening of development strategies (Mathews 2013a). The World Bank (2012) has belatedly changed its voice and now argues for green growth strategies as development policy.

56. See Spender (2011, 141).

57. A related approach is the precautionary principle as utilized in industrial medicine, indicating that substances or processes should be regarded as dangerous

or toxic until shown to be otherwise—not always reliable, but a better principle that "anything goes." For an explication, see Grandjean and colleagues (2004).

58. There is a strong parallel here between drawing (profitably) from a common resource like the sun and drawing (profitably) from an open-source technology like software systems. There is widespread agreement that open-source software is poised to become the largest element in the global software industry. See Mike Volpi, "A 'perfect storm' moment for multibillion dollar open source companies," 25 March 2014, http://recode.net/2014/03/25/a-perfect-storm-moment-for-multi billion-dollar-open-source-companies/.

59. Some might argue that "real options" theory would be useful in this context, in quantifying investment options—but the transfer of such methods from the realm of financial analysis to the realm of public policy would be fraught.

60. *Inevitable*—unable to be avoided, evaded, or escaped. A fitting word to describe the shift that must occur to take the world off its "business as usual" trajectory.

Bibliography

Acemoglu, D., and Robinson, J. 2000. Political losers as a barrier to economic development, *American Economic Review*, 90 (2): 126–130.

Acemoglu, D., and Robinson, J. 2012. *Why Nations Fail: The Origins of Power, Prosperity and Poverty*. New York: Crown Business.

Adler, J. H. 2001. Free & green: A new approach to environmental protection, *Harvard Journal of Law and Public Policy*, 24 (2): 653–694.

Adler, J. H. 2009. Taking property rights seriously: The case of climate change, *Social Philosophy and Policy*, 26 (2): 296–316.

Aleklett, K., Höök, M., Jakobsson, K., Lardelli, M., Snowden, S., and Söderbergh, B. 2010. The peak of the oil age: Analyzing the world oil production reference scenario in *World Energy Outlook 2008*, *Energy Policy*, 38: 1398–1414.

Allen, M. R., Frame, D. J., Huntingford, C., Jones, C. D., Lowe, J. A., Meinshausen, M., and Meinshausen, N. 2009. Warming caused by cumulative carbon emissions: Towards the trillionth tonne, *Nature*, 458: 1163–1166.

Allen, R. C. 2009. *The British Industrial Revolution in Global Perspective*. Cambridge: Cambridge University Press.

Allen, R. C. 2011. *Global Economic History: A Very Short Introduction*. Oxford: Oxford University Press.

Amsden, A. 2001. *The Rise of "The Rest": Challenges to the West from Late-Industrializing Economies*. New York: Oxford University Press.

Andersen, E. S. 2002. Railroadization as Schumpeter's standard case: An evolutionary-ecological account, *Industry and Innovation*, 9 (1–2): 41–78.

Andersen, P. H., Mathews, J. A., and Rask, M. 2009. Integrating private transport into renewable energy policy: The strategy of creating intelligent recharging grids for electric vehicles, *Energy Policy*, 37: 2481–2486.

Anderson, T. L., and Leal, D. R. 2001. *Free Market Environmentalism*. New York: Palgrave.

Andreae, M. O., Jones, C. D., and Cox, P. M. 2005. Strong present-day aerosol cooling implies a hot future, *Nature*, 435: 1187–1190.

Andreozzi, M. 2012. Solar photovoltaic industry development from the early 1990s to world leadership. In *Technological Entrepreneurship in China: How Does It Work?*, edited by C. Petti and M. Ederer, 86–102. Cheltenham, UK: Edward Elgar.

Aoki, M., and Patrick, H. 1994. *The Japanese Main Bank System*. Oxford: Oxford University Press.

Aragón-Correa, J. A. 1998. Strategic proactivity and firm approach to the natural environment, *Academy of Management Journal*, 41 (5): 556–567.

Arthur, W. B. 1989. Competing technologies and lock-in by historical small events, *Economic Journal*, 99 (1): 116–131.

Arthur, W. B. 1994. *Increasing Returns and Path Dependence in the Economy*. Ann Arbor, MI: University of Michigan Press.

Atzori, L., Iera, A., and Morabito, G. 2010. The Internet of things: A survey, *Computer Networks*, 54 (15): 2787–2805.

Ausubel, J. H. 2007. Renewable and nuclear heresies, *International Journal of Nuclear Governance, Economy and Ecology*, 1 (3): 229–243.

Ayres, R. U. 2008. Sustainability economics: Where do we stand? *Ecological Economics*, 67: 281–310.

Ayres, R. U., and Ayres, E. H. 2010. *Crossing the Energy Divide: Moving from Fossil Fuel Dependence to a Clean-Energy Future*. Upper Saddle River, NJ: Wharton School Publishing.

Barbier, E. B. 2012. The green economy post Rio+20, *Science*, 338: 887–888.

Barbier, E. B., and Markandya, A. 2012. *A New Blueprint for a Green Economy*. London: Routledge/Taylor & Francis.

Barnes, P. 2006. *Capitalism 3.0: A Guide to Reclaiming the Commons*. San Francisco: Berrett-Koehler.

Barnes, W., and Gilman, N. 2011. Green social democracy or barbarism: Climate change and the end of high modernism. In *The Deepening Crisis: Governance Challenges After Neoliberalism*, edited by C. Calhoun and G. Derluguian, 43–66. New York: New York University Press.

Basurto, X., and Ostrom, E. 2009. The core challenges of moving beyond Garrett Hardin, *Journal of Natural Resources Policy Research*, 1 (3): 255–259.

Battaglini, A., Lilliestam, J., Haas, A., and Patt, A. 2009. Development of SuperSmart grids for a more efficient utilisation of electricity from renewable sources, *Journal of Cleaner Production*, 17 (10): 911–918.

Bazilian, M., Onyeji, I., Liebreich, M., MacGill, I., Chase, J., Shah, J., Gielen, D., Arent, D., Landfear, D., and Zhengrong, S. 2013. Re-considering the economics of photovoltaic power, *Renewable Energy*, 53: 329–338.

Beckerman, W. 1992. Economic growth and the environment: whose growth? Whose environment? *World Development*, 20: 481–496.

Bennett, M. T. 2008. China's Sloping Land Conversion program: Institutional innovation or business as usual? *Ecological Economics*, 65 (4): 699–711.

Benyus, J. M. 1997. *Biomimicry: Innovation Inspired by Nature*. New York: William Morrow.

Benyus, J., and Baumeister, D. 2004. *Principles of Life*. Helena, MT: Biomimicry Guild.

Bergek, A., and Jacobsson, S. 2010. Are tradable green certificates a cost-efficient policy driving technical change or a rent-generating machine? Lessons from Sweden 2003–2008, *Energy Policy*, 38: 1255–1271.

Berger, S., ed. 2009. *The Foundations of Non-Equilibrium Economics: The Principle of Circular and Cumulative Causation*. London: Routledge.

Block, F. 2003. Karl Polanyi and the writing of *The Great Transformation*, *Theory and Society*, 32: 275–306.

Block, F., ed. 2011. *State of Innovation: The U.S. Government's Role in Technology Development*. New York: Paradigm Publishers.

Bonvillian, W. B., and Van Atta, R. 2011. ARPA-E and DARPA: Applying the DARPA model to energy innovation, *Journal of Technology Transfer*, 36: 469–513.

Bosquet, B. 2000. Environmental tax reform: does it work? A survey of the empirical evidence, *Ecological Economics*, 34: 19–32.

Boulding, K. E. 1956. *The Image: Knowledge in Life and Society*. Ann Arbor: University of Michigan Press.

Boulding, K. E. 1966. The economics of the coming Spaceship Earth. In *Environmental Quality in a Growing Economy*, edited by H. E. Jarrett, 3–14. Baltimore, MD: Johns Hopkins University Press.

Bowen, A., and Frankhauser, S. 2011. The green growth narrative: Paradigm shift or just spin? *Global Environmental Change*, 21: 1157–1159.

Boyd, J. 2007. Non-market benefits of nature: What should be counted in green GDP? *Ecological Economics*, 61 (4): 716–723.

Buchanan, J. M., and Yoon, Y. J., eds. 1994. *The Return to Increasing Returns*. Ann Arbor, MI: University of Michigan Press.

Calvin, W. H. 2011. *The Great CO_2 Cleanup: "Clean Up Your Own Mess" Is Now Urgent*. Available at williamcalvin.org.

Cameron, R. 1985. A new view of European industrialization, *Economic History Review*, 38 (1): 1–23.

Campbell, C., and Lahererre, J. 1998. The end of cheap oil, *Scientific American*, (March): 78–83.

Caro, T., Darwin, J., Forrester, T., Ledoux-Bloom, C., and Wells, C. 2011. Conservation in the Anthropocene, *Conservation Biology*, 26 (1): 185–188.

Cavalcanti, C. 2010. Conceptions of ecological economics: Its relationship with mainstream and environmental economics, *Estudos Avançados*, 24 (68): 53–67.

Chandler, A. D. 1972. Anthracite coal and the beginnings of the Industrial Revolution in the United States, *Business History Review*, 46 (2): 141–181.

Chen, S. 2013. What is the potential impact of a taxation system reform on carbon abatement and industrial growth in China? *Economic Systems*, 37: 369–386.

Chertow, M. R. 2007. "Uncovering" industrial symbiosis, *Journal of Industrial Ecology*, 11 (1): 11–30.

Christoff, P., and Eckersley, R. 2013. *Globalization and the Environment*. Lanham, MD: Rowman & Littlefield.

Church, R. A. 1994. Introduction to *The Coal and Iron Industries*, edited by R. A. Church. Vol. 10 of *The Industrial Revolutions*, edited by R. A. Church and E. A. Wrigley. Oxford, UK: Economic History Society and Blackwell.

Clark, G. 2007. *A Farewell to Alms: A Brief Economic History of the World*. Princeton, NJ: Princeton University Press.

Clark, G., and Jacks, D. 2008. Coal and the Industrial Revolution, 1700–1869, *European Review of Economic History*, 11: 39–72.

Cleveland, C. J. 1999. Biophysical economics: From physiocracy to ecological economics and industrial ecology. In *Bioeconomics and Sustainability: Essays in Honor of Nicholas Georgescu-Roegen*, edited by J. Gowdy and K. Mayumi. Cheltenham, UK: Edward Elgar.

Cohen-Rosenthal, E. 2000. A walk on the human side of industrial ecology, *American Behavioral Scientist*, 44 (2): 245–264.

Commoner, B. 1971. *The Closing Circle: Nature, Man and Technology*. New York: Alfred A. Knopf.

Commoner, B. 1976. *The Poverty of Power: Energy and the Economic Crisis*. New York: Random House.

Commoner, B. 1979. *The Politics of Energy*. New York: Alfred A. Knopf.

Commoner, B. 1990. *Making Peace with the Planet*. New York: Pantheon Books.

Cooper, C., and Sovacool, B. K. 2013. Miracle or mirage? The promise and peril of desert energy (parts 1 and 2), *Energy Policy*, 50: 628–636, 820–825.

Corfee-Morlot, J., Marchal, V., Kauffmann, C., Kennedy, C., Stewart, F., Kaminker, C., and Ang, G. 2012. Towards a green investment policy framework: The case of low-carbon, climate-resilient infrastructure. Environment Working Paper No. 48, Organisation for Economic Co-operation and Development, Paris.

Costanza, R., ed. 1991. *Ecological Economics: The Science and Management of Sustainability*. New York: Columbia University Press.

Costanza, R. 2007. Avoiding system of failure: An upgraded version of capitalism is needed to protect the world's resources, *Nature*, 446: 613–614.

Crafts, N. F. R. 1985. *British Economic Growth During the Industrial Revolution*. Oxford: Clarendon Press.

Cripps, T. F., and Tarling, R. J. 1973. Growth in advanced capitalist economies, 1950–1970. Department of Applied Economics Occasional Paper 40, Cambridge University Press.

Crump, T. 2010. *A Brief History of How the Industrial Revolution Changed the World*. London: Constable & Robinson.

Crutzen, P. J. 2002. Geology of mankind, *Nature*, 415: 23.

Czech, B. 2008. Prospects for reconciling the conflict between economic growth and biodiversity conservation with technological progress, *Conservation Biology*, 22 (6): 1389–1398.

Dale, G. 2010. Social democracy, embeddedness and decommodification: On the conceptual innovations and intellectual affiliations of Karl Polanyi, *New Political Economy*, 15 (3): 369–393.

Dales, J. H. 1968/2002. *Pollution, Property and Prices*. Toronto: University of Toronto Press; Edward Elgar.

Daly, H. E. 1972. In defense of a steady state economy, *American Journal of Agricultural Economics*, 54: 945–954.

Daly, H. E., ed. 1973. *Toward a Steady State Economy*. San Francisco: W. H. Freeman.

Daly, H. E. 1974a. The economics of the steady state, *American Economic Review*, 64 (2): 15–21.

Daly, H. E. 1974b. Steady state economics versus growth-mania: A critique of the orthodox conceptions of growth, wants, scarcity and efficiency, *Policy Science*, 5 (2): 149–167.

Daly, H. E. 2005. Economics in a full world, *Scientific American*, 293 (3): 100–107.

Daly, H. E., and Cobb, J. B., Jr. 1989. *For the Common Good: Redirecting the Economy toward Community, the Environment, and a Sustainable Future*. Boston: Beacon Press.

Daly, H. E., and Townsend, K. N. 1992. *Valuing the Earth: Ecology, Economics, Ethics.* Cambridge, MA: MIT Press.

Dasgupta, P., and Heal, D. 1979. *Economic Theory and Exhaustible Resources.* Cambridge: Cambridge University Press.

David, P. 1985. Clio and the economics of QWERTY, *American Economic Review*, 75 (2): 332–337.

David, P. 2007. Path dependence: A foundational concept for historical social science, *Cliometrica*, 1: 91–114.

Davidson, O. G. 2012. *Clean Break: The Story of Germany's Energy Transformation and What Americans Can Learn from It.* Brooklyn, NY: InsideClimate News.

Deffeyes, K. 2001. *Hubbert's Peak: The Impending World Oil Shortage.* Princeton, NJ: Princeton University Press.

De la Tour, A., Glachant, M., and Ménière, Y. 2011. Innovation and international technology transfer: The case of the Chinese photovoltaic industry, *Energy Policy*, 39: 761–770.

Delina, L. L., and Diesendorf, M. 2013. Is wartime mobilisation a suitable policy model for rapid national climate mitigation? *Energy Policy*, 58: 371–380.

Della Croce, R., Kaminker, C., and Stewart, F. (2011), The role of pension funds in financing green growth initiatives. Working Papers on Finance, Insurance and Private Pensions No. 10, OECD, Paris.

Department of Defense. 2011. "Energy for the warfighter: Operational Energy Strategy." Washington, DC: Department of Defense.

Diamond, J. 2005. *Collapse: How Societies Choose to Fail or Survive.* London: Allen Lane.

Diamond, J. 2007. Easter Island revisited, *Science*, 317: 1692–1694.

Diesendorf, M. 2011. Redesigning energy systems. In *Climate Change and Society*, edited by J. S. Dryzek, R. B. Norgaard, and D. Schlosberg, 561–580. Oxford: Oxford University Press.

Ding, J., and Hua, W. 2012. Featured chemical industrial parks in China: History, current status and outlook, *Resources, Conservation and Recycling*, 63: 43–53.

Dore, R. 2008. Financialization of the global economy, *Industrial and Corporate Change*, 17 (6): 1097–1112.

Dosi, G., and Nelson, R. 2010. Technical change and industrial dynamics as evolutionary processes. In *Handbook of Innovation*, edited by B. Hall and N. Rosenberg. Amsterdam: Elsevier. (Early version available as LEM Working Paper, Sant'Anna School of Advanced Studies, Pisa, http://www.sssup.it/UploadDocs/5580_2009_07.pdf.)

Drechsler, W., Kattel, R., and Reinert, E. 2009. *Techno-Economic Paradigms: Essays in Honour of Carlota Perez.* London: Anthem Press.

Droege, Peter. 2006. *Renewable City: A Comprehensive Guide to an Urban Revolution.* Chichester, UK: Wiley-Academy.

Dryzek, J. S. 2007/2012. *The Politics of the Earth: Environmental Discourses.* Oxford: Oxford University Press.

Dryzek, J. S., Norgaard, R. B., and Schlosberg, D., eds. 2011. *The Oxford Handbook of Climate Change and Society.* Oxford: Oxford University Press.

Dunn, R. I., Hearps, P. J., and Wright, M. N. 2012. Molten-salt power towers: Newly commercial concentrating solar storage, *Proceedings of the IEEE,* 100 (2): 504–515.

Dunphy, D. 2003. Corporate sustainability: Challenge to managerial orthodoxies, *Journal of Management and Organization,* 9 (1): 2–11.

Durand, J. S. 1977. Historical estimates of world population: An evaluation, *Population and Development Review,* 3 (3): 253–296.

Economy, E. 2004. *The River Runs Black: The Environmental Challenges to China's Future.* Ithaca, NY: Cornell University Press.

Economy, E. 2013. China's water challenge: Implications for the U.S. rebalance to Asia, Statement before Senate Foreign Relations Committee on East Asian and Pacific Affairs, 24 July 2013, http://www.cfr.org/china/chinas-water-challenge-implications-us-rebalance-asia/p31147.

Ehrenfeld, J. R. 2005. Eco-efficiency: Philosophy, theory and tools, *Journal of Industrial Ecology,* 9 (4): 6–8.

Ehrenfeld, J. R., and Hoffman, A. J. 2013. *Flourishing: A Frank Conversation About Sustainability.* Redwood City, CA: Stanford University Press.

Ehrlich, P. R., and Ehrlich, A. H. 1968. *The Population Bomb.* New York: Ballantine Books.

Eigen, M., and Schuster, P. 1979. *The Hypercycle: A Principle of Natural Self-Organization.* Stuttgart, Germany: Springer.

Eisen, J. B. 2011. China's greentech programs and the USTR investigation, *Sustainable Development Law and Policy,* 11 (2), 3–8, 70–74.

Erkman, S. 2002. The recent history of industrial ecology. In *A Handbook of Industrial Ecology,* edited by R. U. Ayres and L. W. Ayres, 27–35. Cheltenham, UK: Edward Elgar.

Esty, D. C., and Winston, A. 2006. *Green to Gold: How Smart Companies Use Environmental Strategy to Innovate, Create Value and Build Competitive Advantage.* New Haven, CT: Yale University Press.

Falk, J., and Settle, D. 2011. Australia: Approaching an energy crossroads, *Energy Policy,* 39 (11): 6804–6813.

Fallows, J. 2013. *China Airborne: The Test of China's Future*. New York: Vintage.

Fang, Y., Cote, R. P., and Qin, R. 2007. Industrial sustainability in China: Practice and prospects for eco-industrial development, *Journal of Environment Management*, 83: 315–328.

Faunce, T. A. 2012. *Nanotechnology for a Sustainable World: Artificial Photosynthesis as the Moral Culmination of Nanotechnology*. Cheltenham, UK: Edward Elgar.

Federal Energy Administration. 1977a. *DoD photovoltaic energy conversion systems market inventory and analysis* (lead authors R. M. Terry, C. P. Carter, J. Israel, O. H. Merrill, and M. G. Semmans), 2 vols. Washington, DC: Federal Energy Administration.

Federal Energy Administration. 1977b. Preliminary analysis of an option for the Federal Photovoltaic Utilization Program (lead authors O. H. Merrill, J. C. Belote, M. R. Hamilton, J. S. Hauger, and J. Israel). Washington, DC: Federal Energy Administration.

Ferguson, N. 2008. *The Ascent of Money: A Financial History of the World*. London: Allen Lane.

Fischer, C., and Preonas, L. 2010. Combining policies for renewable energy: Is the whole less than the sum of its parts? *International Review of Environmental and Resource Economics*, 4: 51–92.

Fischer-Kowalski, M., Krausmann, F., Steinberger, J. K., and Ayres, R. U. 2010. Towards a low-carbon society: Setting targets for a reduction of global resource use. IFF Social Ecology Working Paper No. 115, Institute of Social Ecology, Vienna.

Fisher, J., and Pry, R. 1971. A simple substitution model of technological change, *Technological Forecasting and Social Change*, 3: 75–88.

Flannery, T. 2001. *The Weather Makers: How Man Is Changing the Climate and What It Means for Life on Earth*. New York: Atlantic Monthly Press.

Flannery, T. 2009. *Now or Never: Why We Must Act Now to End Climate Change and Create a Sustainable Future*. New York: Atlantic Monthly Press.

Flannery, T. 2011. *Here on Earth: A Natural History of the Planet*. New York: Atlantic Monthly Press.

Flinn, M. W. 1984. *The History of the British Coal Industry, Vol. 2*. Oxford, UK: Clarendon Press.

Folke, C. 2006. Resilience: The emergence of a perspective for social-ecological systems analyses, *Global Environmental Change*, 16 (3): 253–267.

Freeman, C., ed. 1983. *Long Waves in the World Economy*. London: Butterworth.

Freeman, C., ed. 1986. *Design, Innovation and Long Cycles in Economic Development*. London: Frances Pinter.

Freeman, C., and Louçã, F. 2001. *As Time Goes By: From the Industrial Revolutions to the Information Revolution*. Oxford: Oxford University Press.

Freeman, C., and Perez, C. 1988. Structural crises of adjustment: Business cycles and investment behaviour. In *Technical Change and Economic Theory*, edited by G. Dosi, C. Freeman, R. Nelson, G. Silverberg, and L. Soete, 38–61. London: Pinter Publishers.

Friedrichs, J. 2011. Peak energy and climate change: The double bind of post-normal science, *Futures*, 43: 469–477.

Fulcher, J. 2004. *Capitalism: A Very Short Introduction*. Oxford: Oxford University Press.

Fujita, N. 2004. Gunnar Myrdal's theory of circular and cumulative causation revisited. Economic Research Center Discussion Paper No. 147. Nagoya University, Nagoya, Japan.

Garnaut, R. 2008. *The Garnaut Climate Change Review: Final Report*. Cambridge: Cambridge University Press.

Geng, Y. 2011. Eco-indicators: Improve China's sustainability targets, *Nature*, 477: 162.

Geng, Y., and Doberstein, B. 2008. Developing the circular economy in China: Challenges and opportunities for achieving "leapfrog development." *International Journal of Sustainable Development and World Ecology*, 15: 231–239.

Geng, Y., Fu, J., Sarkis, J., and Xue, B. 2012. Towards a national circular economy indicator system in China: An evaluation and critical analysis, *Journal of Cleaner Production*, 23: 216–224.

Georgescu-Roegen, N. 1971. *The Entropy Law and the Economic Process*. Cambridge, MA: Harvard University Press.

Georgescu-Roegen, N. 1975. Energy and economic myths, *Southern Economic Journal*, 41 (3): 347–381.

Gerschenkron, A. 1962. *Economic Backwardness in Historical Perspective*. Cambridge, MA: Harvard University Press.

Gershenfeld, N., and Krikorian, R. 2004. The Internet of things, *Scientific American*, 291 (4): 76–81.

GGBP (Green Growth Best Practice). 2014. *Green Growth in Practice: Lessons from Country Experiences*. Available at http://www.greengrowthknowledge.org/resource/green-growth-practice-lessons-country-experiences.

Gibbs, D., Deuz, P., and Procter, A. 2005. Industrial ecology and eco-industrial development, *Regional Studies*, 39 (2): 171–183.

Gilding, P. 2011. *The Great Disruption*. London: Bloomsbury Publishing.

Gore, A. 2006. *An Inconvenient Truth: The Planetary Emergency of Global Warming and What We Can Do About It.* New York: Rodale Books.

Gore, A. 2009. *Our Choice: A Plan to Solve the Climate Crisis.* New York: Rodale Books.

Graetz, M. J. 2011. *The End of Energy: The Unmaking of America's Environment, Security, and Independence.* Boston: MIT Press.

Gramsci, A. 1930/1971. *Selections from Prison Notebooks*, edited and translated by Quintin Hoare. London: New Left Books.

Grandjean, P., Bailar, J. C., Gee, D., Needleman, H. L., Ozonoff, D. M., Richter, E., Sofritti, M., and Soskolne, C. L. 2004. Implications of the precautionary principle in research and policy-making, *American Journal of Industrial Medicine*, 45 (4): 382–385.

Gray, J. 2000/2009. *False Dawn: The Delusions of Global Capitalism.* London: Granta.

Gray, J. 2007. *Al Qaeda and What It Means to Be Modern.* London: Faber & Faber.

Grayson, D., and Nelson, J. 2013. *Corporate Responsibility Coalitions: The Past, Present and Future of Alliances for Sustainable Capitalism.* Redwood City, CA: Stanford University Press.

Greenberg, P. 2010. *Four Fish: The Future of the Last Wild Food.* London: Penguin Press.

Grossman, G. M., and Krueger, A. B. 1995. Economic growth and the environment, *Quarterly Journal of Economics*, 112: 353–378.

Grübler, A., Nakićenović, N., and Victor, D. 1999. Dynamics of energy technologies and global change, *Energy Policy*, 27: 247–280.

Grumbine, R. E. 2007. China's emergence and the prospects for global sustainability, *Bioscience*, 57 (3): 249–255.

Grumbine, R. E. 2010. *Where the Dragon Meets the Angry River: Nature and Power in the People's Republic of China.* Washington, DC: Island Press.

Gunderson, L., and Holling, C. S., eds. 2002. *Panarchy: Understanding Transformations in Human and Natural Systems.* Washington, DC: Island Press.

Hallegatte, S., Heal, G., Fay, M., and Treguer, D. 2012. From growth to green growth. Working Paper No. 17841, National Bureau of Economic Research, Washington, DC, http://www.nber.org/papers/w17841.

Hamilton, C. 2010. *Requiem for a Species: Why We Resist the Truth About Climate Change*, London: Earthscan.

Hansen, J. 2009. *Storms of My Grandchildren: The Truth About the Coming Climate Catastrophe and Our Last Chance to Save Humanity.* London: Bloomsbury.

Hardin, G. 1968. The tragedy of the commons, *Science*, 162 (3859): 1243–1248.

Hardin, G. 1974. Living on a lifeboat. *BioScience*, 24 (10): 561–568.

Hargadon, A., and Kenney, M. 2012. Misguided policy? Following venture capital into clean technology, *California Management Review*, 54 (2): 118–139.

Hart, S. L. 1983. The Federal Photovoltaics Utilization Program: An evaluation and learning framework, *Policy Sciences*, 15 (4): 325–343.

Hauser, J. 2013. From sleeping giant to friendly giant: Rethinking the United States solar energy trade war with China, *North Carolina Journal of International Law and Commercial Regulation*, 38: 1061–1090.

Hawken, P., Lovins, A., and Lovins, L. H. 1999. *Natural Capitalism: Creating the Next Industrial Revolution*. Boston: Little, Brown.

Heinberg, R. 2007. *Peak Everything: Waking up to the Century of Declines*. Gabriola Island, BC: New Society Publishers.

Heinberg, R. 2011. *The End of Growth: Adapting to our New Economic Reality*. Gabriola Island, BC: New Society Publishers.

Helm, D. 2012a. *The Carbon Crunch: How We're Getting Climate Change Wrong—And How to Fix It*. New Haven, CT: Yale University Press.

Helm, D. 2012b. Climate policy: The Kyoto approach has failed, *Nature*, 491: 663–665.

Hicks, J. R. 1939/1946. *Value and Capital*. Oxford, UK: Clarendon Press.

Ho, P. 2005. Greening industries in newly-industrialising countries: Asian-style leapfrogging? *International Journal of Environment and Sustainable Development*, 4 (3): 209–226.

Hobson, J. M. 2004. *The Eastern Origins of Western Civilisation*. Cambridge: Cambridge University Press.

Holling, C. S. 1973. Resilience and stability of ecological systems, *Annual Review of Ecology and Systematics*, 4: 1–24.

Holling, C. S. 1986. The resilience of terrestrial ecosystems: Local surprise and global change. In *Sustainable Development of the Biosphere*, edited by W. C. Clark and R. E. Munn, 292–317. Cambridge: Cambridge University Press.

Holling, C. S. 2001. Understanding the complexity of economic, ecological and social systems, *Ecosystems*, 4: 390–405.

Holmes, I., and Mabey, N. 2010. Accelerating the transition to a low-carbon economy: The case for a Green Infrastructure Bank. London: E3G.

Höök, M., Hirsch, R., and Aleklett, K. 2009. Giant oil field decline rates and their influence on world oil production, *Energy Policy*, 37: 2262–2272.

Hu, A. 2006a. Green development: The inevitable choice for China (part 1), *China Dialogue*, http://www.chinadialogue.net/article/show/single/en/134.

Hu, A. 2006b. Green development: The inevitable choice for China (part 2), *China Dialogue*, http://www.chinadialogue.net/article/show/single/en/135 -Green-development-the-inevitable-choice-for-China-part-two-.

Hu, A. 2011. *China in 2020: A New Type of Superpower*. Washington, DC: Brookings Institution.

Hu, A. 2014. *China: Innovative Green Development*. Heidelberg, Germany: Springer.

Hubbert M. K. 1956. Nuclear energy and the fossil fuel (Drilling and production practice). Washington, DC: American Petroleum Institute.

Hubbert, M. K. 1976. Exponential growth as a transient phenomenon in human history. Paper presented before World Wildlife Trust, 4th International Congress, San Francisco, http://www.hubbertpeak.com/hubbert/wwf1976/.

Hughes, J. D. 2013a. Drill, baby, drill: Can unconventional fuels usher in a new era of energy abundance? Post-Carbon Institute, http://shalebubble.org/drill-baby-drill/.

Hughes, J. D. 2013b. A reality check on the shale revolution, *Nature*, 494: 37–38.

Hulme, M. 2009a. On the origin of "the greenhouse effect": John Tyndall's 1859 interrogation of nature, *Weather*, 64 (5): 121–123.

Hulme, M. 2009b. *Why We Disagree About Climate Change: Understanding Controversy, Inaction and Controversy*. Cambridge: Cambridge University Press.

Hunt, T. L., and Lipo, C. P. 2006. Late colonization of Easter Island, *Science*, 311 (5767): 1603–1606.

Intergovernmental Panel on Climate Change. 2011. *Renewable Energy Sources and Climate Change Mitigation: Special Report of the Intergovernmental Panel on Climate Change*, edited by O. Edenhofer, R. P. Madruga, and Y. Sokona. Cambridge: Cambridge University Press.

Intergovernmental Panel on Climate Change. 2013. *Fifth Assessment Report. Climate Change 2013: The Physical Science Basis*. Geneva: IPCC.

International Centre for Trade and Sustainable Development. 2011. Fostering low-carbon growth: The case for a Sustainable Energy Trade Agreement. Geneva: ICTSD.

International Energy Agency. 2013. *Tracking Clean Energy Progress 2013: IEA Input to the Clean Energy Ministerial*. Paris: IEA.

Jackson, T. 2009. *Prosperity Without Growth: Economics for a Finite Planet*. London: Earthscan.

Jackson, W. 2011. *Nature as Measure: The Selected Essays of Wes Jackson*. Berkeley, CA: Counterpoint Press.

Jacobsen, N. B. 2006. Industrial symbiosis in Kalundborg, Denmark: A quantitative assessment of economic and environmental aspects, *Journal of Industrial Ecology*, 10 (1–2): 239–255.

Jacobson, M. Z., and Delucchi, M. A. 2009. A path to sustainable energy by 2030, *Scientific American*, (November): 57–65.

Jacobson, M. Z., and Delucchi, M. A. 2011. Providing all global energy with wind, water and solar power, Pt 1: Technologies, energy resources, quantities and areas of infrastructure, and materials, *Energy Policy*, 39 (3): 1154–1169.

Jacobsson, S., Bergek, A., Finon, D., Lauber, V., Mitchell, C., Toke, D., and Verbruggen, A. 2009. EU renewable energy support policy: Faith or facts? *Energy Policy*, 37: 2143–2146.

Jacobsson, S., and Lauber, V. 2006. The politics and policy of energy system transformation—explaining the German diffusion of renewable energy technology, *Energy Policy*, 34: 256–276.

Jacques, M. 2009. *When China Rules the World: the Rise of the Middle Kingdom and the End of the Western World*. London: Allen Lane.

Jänicke, M. 2012. "Green growth": From a growing eco-industry to economic sustainability, *Energy Policy*, 48: 13–21.

Jeffreys, K. 1994. Free-market environmentalism: Can it save the planet? *Economic Affairs*, (April): 6–9.

Jenkins, T. N. 2002. Chinese traditional thought and practice: Lessons for an ecological economics worldview, *Ecological Economics*, 40: 39–52.

Jevons, W. S. 1865. *The Coal Question: An Inquiry Concerning the Progress of the Nation, and the Probable Exhaustion of our Coal-Mines*. London: Macmillan.

Joffe, M. 2011. The root cause of economic growth under capitalism, *Cambridge Journal of Economics*, 35 (5): 873–896.

Jofre, S., and Morioka, T. 2005. Waste management of electric and electronic equipment: Comparative analysis of end-of-life strategies, *Journal of Material Cycles and Waste Management*, 7 (1): 24–32.

Johnson, S. 2009. The quiet coup, *Atlantic*, (May 2009), http://www.theatlantic .com/doc/print/200905/imf-advice.

Jones, E. L. 1988. *Growth Recurring: Economic Change in World History*. Oxford, UK: Clarendon Press.

Kaldor, N. 1967. *Strategic Factors in Economic Development*. Frank W. Pierce Memorial Lectures, October 1966. Ithaca, NY: Cornell University.

Kaldor, N. 1970. The case for regional policies, *Scottish Journal of Political Economy*, 17: 337–348.

Kaldor, N. 1972. The irrelevance of equilibrium economics, *Economic Journal*, 82: 1237–1255.

Kaldor, N. 1975. What is wrong with economic theory, *Quarterly Journal of Economics*, 89: 347–357.

Kaletsky, A. 2010. *Capitalism 4.0: The Birth of a New Economy*. London: Bloomsbury.

Kaminker, C., and Stewart, F. 2012. The role of institutional investors in financing clean energy. OECD Working Papers on Finance, Insurance and Private Pensions, No. 23, OECD, Paris.

Kennedy, P. 1987. *The Rise and Fall of the Great Powers: Economic Change and Military Conflict from 1500 to 2000.* New York: Random House.

Kerman, C. E. 1974. *Creative Tension: The Life and Thought of Kenneth Boulding.* Ann Arbor: University of Michigan Press.

Kim, S.-Y. 2010. Transitioning from fast-follower to innovator: The institutional foundations of the Korean telecommunications sector, *Review of International Political Economy*, iFirst: 1–29.

Kim, S.-Y. 2011. The politics of technological upgrading in South Korea: How government and business challenged the might of Qualcomm, *New Political Economy*, 17 (3): 293–312.

Kingston, W. 2006. Schumpeter, *Business Cycles* and co-evolution, *Industry and Innovation*, 13 (1): 97–106.

Kingston, W. 2013. Schumpeter and the end of Western capitalism, *Journal of Evolutionary Economics*. doi: 10.1007/s00191-013-0312-x.

Klare, M. T. 2002. *Resource Wars: The New Landscape of Global Conflict.* New York: Metropolitan Books.

Klare, M. T. 2004. *Blood and Oil: The Dangers and Consequences of America's Growing Petroleum Dependency.* New York: Metropolitan Books.

Klare, M. T. 2012. *The Race for What's Left: The Global Scramble for the World's Last Resources.* New York: Metropolitan Books.

Klare, M., and Volman, D. 2006. America, China, and the scramble for Africa's oil, *Review of African Political Economy*, 33 (108): 297–309.

Kondratieff, N. D. 1935. The long waves in economic life, *Review of Economic Statistics*, 17 (6): 105–115.

Korotayev, A. V., and Tsirel, S. V. 2010. A spectral analysis of world GDP dynamics: Kondratieff waves, Kuznets swings, Juglar and Kitchin cycles in global economic development, and the 2008–2009 economic crisis, *Structure and Dynamics*, 4 (1), http://escholarship.org/uc/item/9jv108xp.

Krause, F. 1982. *Energy Transition [Energiewende]: Growth and Prosperity Without Oil or Uranium.* Freiburg, Germany: Institute for Applied Ecology.

Krausmann, F., Schandl, H., and Sieferle, R. 2008. Socio-ecological regime transitions in Austria and the United Kingdom, *Ecological Economics*, 65 (1): 187–201.

Kremen, C. 2005. Managing ecosystem services: What do we need to know about their ecology? *Ecology Letters*, 8 (5): 468–479.

Kurz, H. D. 2006. Goods and bads: Sundry observations on joint production, waste disposal, and renewable and exhaustible resources, *Progress in Industrial Ecology*, 3 (4): 280–301.

LaConte, E. 2010/2012. *Life Rules: Nature's Blueprint for Surviving Economic and Environmental Collapse.* Gabriola Island, BC: New Society Publishers.

Lawn, P. 2003. A theoretical foundation to support the index of sustainable economic welfare (ISEW), genuine progress indicator (GPI), and other related indexes, *Ecological Economics*, 44: 105–118.

Lawson, N. 2009. *An Appeal to Reason: A Cool Look at Global Warming.* London: Duckworth.

Lazonick, W. 2011. From innovation to financialization: How shareholder value ideology is destroying the U.S. economy. In *The Handbook of the Political Economy of Financial Crises*, edited by M. H. Wolfson and G. Epstein, chap. 24. New York: Oxford University Press.

Lee, K. 2013. *Schumpeterian Analysis of Economic Catch-up: Knowledge, Path-Creation and the Middle-Income Trap.* Cambridge: Cambridge University Press.

Lee, K., and Mathews, J. A. 2010. From the Washington Consensus to the BeST Consensus for world development, *Asian Pacific Economic Literature*, 24 (1): 86–103.

Lee, K., and Mathews, J. A. 2012. South Korea and Taiwan. In *Innovative Firms in Emerging Market Countries*, edited by E. Amann and J. Cantwell, 223–245. New York: Oxford University Press.

Leggett, J. K. 2013. *The Energy of Nations: Risk Blindness and the Road to Renaissance.* London: Earthscan.

Lehmann, J. 2006. Black is the new green, *Nature*, 442: 624–626.

Lehmann, J. 2007. Bioenergy in the black, *Frontiers in Ecology and the Environment*, 5 (7): 381–387.

Leighty, W. C., and Holbrook, J. H. 2012. Alternatives to electricity for transmission, firming storage, and supply integration for diverse, stranded, renewable energy sources: Gaseous hydrogen and anhydrous ammonia fuels via underground pipelines, *Energy Procedia*, 29: 332–346.

Lema, R., and Lema, A. 2012. Technology transfer? The rise of China and India in green technology sectors, *Innovation and Development*, 2 (1): 23–44.

Lewis, J. I. 2011. Building a national wind turbine industry: Experiences from China, India and South Korea, *International Journal of Technology and Globalisation*, 5 (3–4): 281–305.

Lewis, J. I. 2013. *Green Innovation in China: China's Wind Power Industry and the Global Transition to a Low-Carbon Economy.* New York: Columbia University Press.

Lewis, J. I., and Wiser, R. H. 2007. Fostering a renewable energy technology industry: An international comparison of wind industry policy support mechanisms, *Energy Policy*, 35: 1844–1857.

Li, J., and Yu, K. 2011. A study on legislative and policy tools for promoting the circular economic model for waste management in China, *Journal of Material Cycles and Waste Management,* 13 (2): 103–112.

Li, V., and Lang, G. 2010. China's "green GDP" experiment and the struggle for ecological modernisation, *Journal of Contemporary Asia,* 40 (1): 44–62.

Liebowitz, S. J., and Margolis, S. E. 1995. Path dependence, lock-in, and history, *Journal of Law and Economic Organization,* 11 (1): 205–226.

Lifset, R., and Graedel, T. E. 2002. Industrial ecology: Goals and definitions. In *A Handbook of Industrial Ecology,* edited by R. U. Ayres and L. W. Ayres, 3–15. Cheltenham, UK: Edward Elgar.

Lin, J., Zhou, N., Levine, M., and Fridley, D., 2008. Taking out 1 billion tons of CO_2: The magic of China's 11th Five-Year Plan, *Energy Policy,* 36: 954–970.

Lin, J. Y. 2012. *The Quest for Prosperity: How Developing Economies Can Take Off.* Princeton, NJ: Princeton University Press.

Lohmann, L. 2011. Capital and climate change, *Development and Change,* 42 (2): 649–668.

Lohmann, L. 2012. A rejoinder to Matthew Paterson and Peter Newell, *Development and Change,* 43 (5): 1177–1184.

Lomborg, B. 2007. *Cool It: The Skeptical Environmentalist's Guide to Global Warming.* New York: Knopf.

Lomborg, B. 2010. *Smart Solutions to Climate Change: Comparing Costs and Benefits.* Cambridge: Cambridge University Press.

Lovins, L. H., and Cohen, B. 2011. *Climate Capitalism: Capitalism in the Age of Climate Change.* New York: Hill and Wang.

Lowe, E. A. 1997. Creating by-product resource exchanges: Strategies for eco-industrial parks, *Journal of Cleaner Production,* 5(1–2): 57–65.

Lund, H. 2010. *Renewable Energy Systems: The Choice and Modeling of 100% Renewable Solutions.* London: Elsevier and Academic Press.

MacKay, D. J. C. 2009. *Sustainable Energy—Without the Hot Air.* Cambridge, UK: UIT Cambridge.

Maddison, A. 1991. *Dynamic Forces in Capitalist Development.* New York: Oxford University Press.

Maddison, A. 2001. *The World Economy: A Millennial Perspective.* Paris: OECD.

Maddison, A. 2006. Asia in the world economy, 1500–2030 AD, *Asia-Pacific Economic Literature,* 20 (2): 1–37.

Makhijani, M. 2007. *Carbon-Free and Nuclear-Free: A Roadmap for U.S. Energy Policy.* Tacoma Park, MD: IEER Press.

Malthus, T. 1798/1826. *An Essay on the Principle of Population.* London: John Murray. http://www.econlib.org/library/Malthus/malPlong.html.

Mann, M. 1986. *Sources of Social Power, Volume I: A History of Power from the Beginning to AD 1760*. Cambridge: Cambridge University Press.

Mann, M. 1993. *Sources of Social Power, Volume II: The Rise of Classes and Nation States, 1760–1914*. Cambridge: Cambridge University Press.

Mann, M. 2012. *Sources of Social Power, Volume III: Global Empires and Revolution, 1890–1945*. Cambridge: Cambridge University Press.

Mann, M. 2013. *Sources of Social Power, Volume IV: Globalizations, 1945–2011*. Cambridge: Cambridge University Press.

Mann, M. E. 2012. *The Hockey Stick and the Climate Wars: Dispatches from the Front Lines*. New York: Columbia University Press.

Mann, M. E., Bradley, R. S., and Hughes, M. K. 1999. Northern hemisphere temperatures during the past millennium: Inferences, uncertainties, and limitations, *Geophysical Research Letters*, 26 (6): 759–762.

Martenson, C. 2011. *The Crash Course: The Unsustainable Future of Our Economy, Energy and Environment*. New York: Wiley.

Martínez, E., Sanz, F., Pellegrini, S., Jiménez, E., and Blanco, J. 2009. Life cycle assessment of a multi-megawatt wind turbine, *Renewable Energy*, 34: 667–673.

Martinez-Alier, J. 1987. *Ecological Economics*. Oxford, UK: Basil Blackwell.

Martinez-Alier, J. 2000. Ecological economics. In *International Encyclopedia of the Social and Behavioral Sciences*, 4016–4023. Philadelphia, PA: Elsevier.

Martinot, E., 2010. Renewable power for China: Past, present, and future, *Frontiers of Energy and Power Engineering in China*, 4 (3): 287–294.

Maslin, M. 2009. *Global Warming: A Very Short Introduction*. Oxford: Oxford University Press.

Mathews, F. 2011. Towards a deeper philosophy of biomimicry, *Organization and Environment*, 24 (4): 364–387.

Mathews, J. A. 2001. National systems of economic learning: The case of technology diffusion management in East Asia, *International Journal of Technology Management*, 22 (5–6): 455–479.

Mathews, J. A. 2002. The origins and dynamics of Taiwan's R&D consortia, *Research Policy*, 31 (4): 633–651.

Mathews, J. A. 2005. The intellectual roots of latecomer industrial development, *International Journal of Technology and Globalisation*, 1 (3–4): 433–450.

Mathews, J. A. 2006. *Strategizing, Disequilibrium and Profit*. Redwood City, CA: Stanford University Press.

Mathews, J. A. 2007a. Can renewable energies be turned to a source of advantage by developing countries? *Revue de l'Energie*, 576 (March–April): 96–105.

Mathews, J. A. 2007b. Latecomer strategies for catching-up: The cases of renewable energies and the LED programme, *International Journal of Technological Learning, Innovation and Development*, 1 (1): 34–42.

Mathews, J. A. 2008a. Energizing industrial development, *Transnational Corporations*, 17 (3): 59–84.

Mathews, J. A. 2008b. Towards a sustainably certifiable futures contract for biofuels, *Energy Policy*, 36: 1577–1583.

Mathews, J. A. 2009. China, India and Brazil: Tiger technologies, dragon multinationals and the building of national systems of economic learning, *Asian Business and Management*, 8 (1): 5–32.

Mathews, J. A. 2010. Designing energy industries for the next industrial revolution, *Organizational Dynamics*, 39 (2): 155–164.

Mathews, J. A. 2011a. China's energy industrial revolution, *l'Industria*, 32 (2): 309–328.

Mathews, J. A. 2011b. Naturalizing capitalism: The next Great Transformation, *Futures*, 43: 868–879.

Mathews, J. A. 2011c. Reforming the international patent system, *Review of International Political Economy*, 19 (1): 169–180.

Mathews, J. A. 2012a. Design of industrial and supra-firm architectures: Growth and sustainability, *Journal of Organizational Design*, 1 (2), http://ojs.statsbiblioteket.dk/index.php/jod/article/view/6454/6050.

Mathews, J. A. 2012b. Green growth strategies: Korea's initiatives, *Futures*, 44: 761–769.

Mathews, J. A. 2013a. The greening of capitalism. In *The Handbook of Global Companies*, edited by J. Mikler, 421–436. Cambridge, UK: Wiley-Blackwell.

Mathews, J. A. 2013b. Greening of development strategies, *Seoul Journal of Economics*, 26 (2): 147–172.

Mathews, J. A. 2013c. The renewable energies technology surge: A new techno-economic paradigm in the making? *Futures*, 46: 10–22.

Mathews, J. A. 2014. Twelve theses on the greening of capitalism. Paper presented at DRUID Society conference, Copenhagen Business School, June 16.

Mathews, J. A., and Baroni, P. 2013. The industrial logistic surface: Displaying the impact of energy policy on uptake of new technologies, *Energy*, 57 (1): 733–740.

Mathews, J. A., and Cho, D.-S. 2000. *Tiger Technology: The Creation of a Semiconductor Industry in East Asia*. Cambridge: Cambridge University Press.

Mathews, J. A., Hu, M.-C., and Wu, C.-W. 2011. Fast-follower industrial dynamics: The case of Taiwan's Solar PV industry, *Industry and Innovation*, 18 (2): 177–202.

Mathews, J. A., and Kidney, S. 2010. Climate bonds: Mobilizing private financing for carbon management, *Carbon Management*, 1 (1): 9–13.

Mathews, J. A., and Kidney, S. 2012. Debate: Financing climate-friendly energy development through bonds, *Development Southern Africa*, 29 (2): 337–349.

Mathews, J. A., Kidney, S., Mallon, K., and Hughes, M. 2010. Mobilizing private finance to drive an energy industrial revolution, *Energy Policy*, 38: 3263–3265.

Mathews, J. A., and Reinert, E. S. 2014. Renewables, manufacturing and green growth: Energy strategies based on capturing increasing returns, *Futures*, 61 (Sep): 13–22.

Mathews, J. A., and Tan, H. 2009. Biofuels and indirect land use change effects: The debate continues, *Biofuels, Bioproducts and Biorefining*, 3 (3): 305–317.

Mathews, J. A., and Tan, H. 2011. Progress towards a circular economy in China: Drivers (and inhibitors) of eco-industrial initiative, *Journal of Industrial Ecology*, 15 (3): 435–457.

Mathews, J. A., and Tan, H. 2013. The transformation of the electric power sector in China, *Energy Policy*, 52: 170–180.

Mathews, J. A., and Tan, H. 2014a. China leads the way on renewables, *Nature*, 508 (2014): 319.

Mathews, J. A., and Tan, H. 2014b. China's energy industrial revolution, *Carbon Management*, 5 (1): 1–3.

Mathews, J. A., and Tan, H. 2014c. A 10 trillion watt "Big Push" to decarbonize the world's electric power, *Journal of Sustainable Energy Engineering* (forthcoming).

Mathews, J. A., Tang, Y., and Tan, H. 2011. China's move to a circular economy as a development strategy, *Asian Business and Management*, 10: 463–484.

Maugeri, L. 2009. Squeezing more oil from the ground, *Scientific American*, 301 (4): 56–63.

McCloskey, D. N. 2006. *The Bourgeois Virtues: Ethics for an Age of Commerce*. Chicago: University of Chicago Press.

McCloskey, D. N. 2010. *Bourgeois Dignity: Why Economics Can't Explain the Modern World*. Chicago: University of Chicago Press.

McCloskey, D. N. Forthcoming. *The Treasured Bourgeoisie: How Markets and Innovation Became Virtuous, 1600–1848, and Then Suspect*. http://www.deirdremccloskey.com/weblog/2010/01/09/the-bourgeois-revaluation-table-of-contents/.

McDonough, W., and Braungart, M. 1998. The NEXT industrial revolution, *Atlantic* (October): http://www.theatlantic.com/magazine/print/1998/10/the-next-industrial-revolution/4695/.

McDonough, W., and Braungart, M. 2002. *Cradle to Cradle: Remaking the Way We Make Things*. New York: North Point Press.

McGregor, R. 2010. *The Party: The Secret World of China's Communist Rulers*. London: Allen Lane and Penguin Press.

McNeill, J. R. 2000. *Something New Under the Sun: An Environmental History of the 20th-Century World*. New York: W. W. Norton.

McNeill, J. R. 2007. World environmental history: The first 100,000 years, *Historically Speaking*, 8 (6): 6–8.

McNeill, J. R., and McNeill, W. H. 2003. *The Human Web: A Bird's-Eye View of World History*. New York: W. W. Norton.

Meléndez-Ortiz, R., Monkelbaan, J., and Riddell, G. 2012. China's global and domestic governance of climate change, trade and sustainable energy: Exploring China's interests in a global massive scale-up of renewable energies. Working Paper No. 24, March, Research Center for Chinese Politics and Business, Indiana University, http://www.indiana.edu/~rccpb/pdf/MMR%20RCCPB%2024%20SETA%20Mar%202012.pdf.

Minsky, H. P. 1986/2008. *Stabilizing an Unstable Economy*. New York: McGraw-Hill Professional.

Minsky, H. P. 1995. Sources of financial fragility: Financial factors in the economics of capitalism. Hyman Minsky archive, Paper No. 69, http://digitalcommons.bard.edu/hm_archive/69/.

Minsky, H. P. 1996. Uncertainty and the institutional structure of capitalist economies, *Journal of Economic Issues*, 30 (2): 357–368.

Mokyr, J. 1990. *The Lever of Riches: Technological Creativity and Economic Progress*. New York: Oxford University Press.

Mol, A. P. J. 2006. Environment and modernity in transitional China: Frontiers of ecological modernization, *Development and Change*, 37 (1): 29–56.

Mol, A. P. J., and Sonnenfeld, D. A., eds. 2000. *Ecological Modernisation around the World: Perspectives and Critical Debates*. London: Frank Cass.

Morgan, D. R. 2009. World on fire: Two scenarios of the destruction of human civilization and possible extinction of the human race, *Futures*, 41: 683–693.

Moriarty, P., and Honnery, D. 2011. *Rise and Fall of the Carbon Civilisation: Resolving Global Environmental and Resource Problems*. Green Energy and Technology. Heidelberg, Germany: Springer.

Morris, C., and Pehnt, M. 2012. *Energy Transition: The German Energiewende*. Berlin: Heinrich Böll Foundation. http://www.energytransition.de.

Morriss, A. P., Bogart, W. T., Meiners, R. E., and Dorchak, A. D. 2011. *The False Promise of Green Energy*. Washington, DC: Cato Institute.

Mowery, D. C., Nelson, R. R., and Martin, B. R. 2010. Technology policy and global warming: Why new policy models are needed (or why putting new wine in old bottles won't work), *Research Policy*, 39 (8): 1011–1023.

Mowery, D. C., and Rosenberg, N. 1991. *Technology and the Pursuit of Economic Growth*. Cambridge: Cambridge University Press.

Myrdal, G. 1957. *Economic Theory and Underdeveloped Regions*. London: University Paperbacks, Methuen.

Mytelka, L. 2004. Catching up in new wave technologies, *Oxford Development Studies*, 32 (3): 389–405.

Naess, P. 2004. Live and let die: The tragedy of Hardin's social Darwinism, *Journal of Environmental Policy and Planning*, 6 (1): 19–34.

Nair, C. 2011. *Consumptionomics: Asia's Role in Reshaping Capitalism and Saving the Planet*, Oxford, UK: Infinite Ideas.

Narveson, J. 1995. The case for free market environmentalism, *Journal of Agricultural and Environmental Ethics*, 8 (2): 145–156.

Naughton, B. 1993. Deng Xioaping: The economist, *China Quarterly*, 155: 492–497.

Nef, J. U. 1943. The industrial revolution reconsidered, *Journal of Economic History*, 3 (1): 1–31.

Nef, J. U. 1977. An early energy crisis and its consequences, *Scientific American*, 237 (5): 140–152.

Negro, S., Alkemade, F., and Hekkert, M. P. 2012. Why does renewable energy diffuse so slowly? A review of innovation system problems, *Renewable and Sustainable Energy Reviews*, 16: 3836–3846.

Neij, L. 2008. Cost development of future technologies for power generation: A study based on experience curves and complementary bottom-up assessments, *Energy Policy*, 36: 2200–2211.

Nelson, R. R. 2011. The complex economic organization of capitalist economies, *Capitalism and Society*, 6 (1): article 2, http://www.bepress.com/cas/vol6/iss1/art2.

Nemet, G. F. 2009. Demand-pull, technology-push, and government-led incentives for non-incremental technical change, *Research Policy*, 38: 700–709.

Neumayer, E. 2003. *Weak versus Strong Sustainability: Exploring the Limits of Two Opposing Paradigms*, 2nd ed. Cheltenham, UK: Edward Elgar.

Newell, P., and Paterson, M. 2010. *Climate Capitalism: Global Warming and the Transformation of the Global Economy*. Cambridge: Cambridge University Press.

Newman, P., Beatley, T., and Boyer, H. 2009. *Resilient Cities: Responding to Peak Oil and Climate Change*. Washington, DC: Island Press.

Newton, J. 1987. *Uncommon Friends: Life with Thomas Edison, Henry Ford, Harvey Firestone, Alexis Carrel & Charles Lindbergh*. New York: Harcourt Brace.

Nolan, P. 2009. *Crossroads: The End of Wild Capitalism*. London: Marshall Cavendish.

Nordhaus, W. D. 2008. *A Question of Balance: Weighing the Options on Global Warming Policies*. New Haven, CT: Yale University Press.

O'Hara, P. A. 2008. Principle of circular and cumulative causation: fusing Myrdalian and Kaldorian growth and development dynamics, *Journal of Economic Issues*, 42 (2): 375–387.

Olson, M. 1982. *The Rise and Decline of Nations*. New Haven, CT: Yale University Press.

Organisation for Economic Co-operation and Development. 2008. *Measuring Material Flows and Resource Productivity*. Paris: OECD.

Organisation for Economic Co-operation and Development. 2011. *Towards Green Growth*. Paris: OECD.

Organisation for Economic Co-operation and Development. 2013. *Climate and Carbon: Aligning Prices and Policies*. OECD Environment Policy Paper No. 1, October, OECD, Paris.

Organisation for Economic Co-operation and Development, Development Centre. 2010. *Perspectives on Global Development 2010. Shifting Wealth*. Paris: OECD.

Ostrom, E. 1990. *Governing the Commons: The Evolution of Institutions for Collective Action*. Cambridge: Cambridge University Press.

Ostrom, E. 2010. Polycentric systems for coping with collective action and global environmental change, *Global Environmental Change*, 20: 550–557.

O'Sullivan, P. 2008. The "collapse" of civilizations: What paleoenvironmental reconstruction cannot tell us, but anthropology can, *Holocene*, 18 (1): 45–55.

Oyelaran-Oyeyinka, B., and Rasiah, R. 2009. *Uneven Paths of Development: Innovation and Learning in Asia and Africa*. Cheltenham, UK: Edward Elgar.

Park, H.-S., Rene, E. R., Choi, S.-M., and Chiu, A. S. F. 2008. Strategies for sustainable development of industrial park in Ulsan, South Korea: From spontaneous evolution to systematic expansion of industrial symbiosis, *Journal of Environmental Management*, 87: 1–13.

Parsons, T. 1928. "Capitalism" in recent German literature: Sombart and Weber, *Journal of Political Economy*, 36 (6): 641–661.

Paterson, M., and Newell, P. 2012. Of heroes, villains and climate capitalism: A response to Larry Lohmann, *Development and Change*, 43 (5): 1171–1175.

Pearce, D. W. 1998. *Economics and Environment: Essays on Ecological Economics and Sustainable Development*. Cheltenham, UK: Edward Elgar.

Pearce, D. W., with Markandya, A., and Barbier, E. 1989. *Blueprint for a Green Economy*. London: Earthscan.

Pearce, D. W., and Turner, R. 1989. *Economics of Natural Resources and the Environment*. Baltimore, MD: Johns Hopkins University Press.

Pearce, D. W., and Warford, J. J. 1993. *World Without End: Economics, Environment, and Sustainable Development*. Washington, DC: World Bank.

Perez, C. 1983. Structural change and assimilation of new technologies in the economic and social systems, *Futures*, 1983 (10): 357–375.

Perez, C. 1985. Microelectronics, long waves and world structural change: New perspectives for developing countries, *World Development*, 13 (3): 441–463.

Perez, C. 2002. *Technological Revolutions and Financial Capital: The Dynamics of Bubbles and Golden Ages*. Cheltenham, UK: Edward Elgar.

Perez, C. 2010. Technological revolutions and techno-economic paradigms, *Cambridge Journal of Economics*, 34: 185–202.

Perez, C. 2011. Finance and technical change: A long-term view, *African Journal of Science, Technology, Innovation and Development*, 3 (1): 10–35.

Perez, C., and Soete, L. (1988). Catching up in technology: Entry barriers and windows of opportunity. In *Technical Change and Economic Theory*, edited by G. Dosi, C. Freeman, R. R. Nelson, G. Silverberg, and L. Soete, 458–479. London: Pinter.

Pernick, R., and Wilder, C. 2007. *The Clean Tech Revolution: The Next Big Growth and Investment Opportunity*. New York: HarperCollins.

Petti, C., ed. 2012. *Technological Entrepreneurship in China: How Does It Work?* Cheltenham, UK: Edward Elgar.

Pihl, E., Kushnir D., Sandén, B., and Johnsson, F. 2012. Material constraints for concentrating solar thermal power. *Energy*, 44, 944–954.

Piore, M., and Sabel, C. 1984. *The Second Industrial Divide: Possibilities for Prosperity*. New York: Basic Books.

Ploeg, F. van der. 2011. Macroeconomics of sustainability transitions: Second-best climate policy, green paradox, and renewables subsidies, *Environmental Innovation and Societal Transitions*, 1: 130–134.

Ploeg, F. van der, and Withagen, C. 2012. Is there really a green paradox? *Journal of Environmental Economics and Management*, 64: 342–363.

Polanyi, K. 1944 (1957/2001). *The Great Transformation: The political and economic origins of our time*, foreword by Joseph E. Stiglitz and introduction by Fred Block). Boston: Beacon Press.

Pomeranz, K. 2000. *The Great Divergence: China, Europe and the Making of the Modern World Economy*. Princeton, NJ: Princeton University Press.

Ponting, C. 1991. *A Green History of the World*. London: Penguin.

Porritt, J. 2005. *Capitalism as if the World Matters*. London: Earthscan.

Porter, M. E., and Reinhardt, F. L. 2007. Grist: A strategic approach to climate, *Harvard Business Review*, (October): 1–3.

Porter, M. E., and van der Linde, C. 1995. Toward a new conception of the competitiveness-environment relationship, *Journal of Economic Perspectives*, 9 (4): 97–118.

Porter, P. 2013. Sharing power? Prospects for a U.S. concert-balance strategy. Carlisle, PA: Strategic Studies Institute. http://www.strategicstudiesinstitute.army.mil/pubs/display.cfm?pubID=1149.

Preston, F. 2012. A global redesign? Shaping the circular economy. Briefing Paper BP 2012/02, Chatham House, London, http://www.chathamhouse.org/publications/papers/view/182376.

Prins, G., and Rayner, S. 2007a. Time to ditch Kyoto, *Nature*, 449 (25 October): 973–975.

Prins, G., and Rayner, S. 2007b. The wrong trousers: Radically rethinking climate policy, Joint Discussion Paper of James Martin Institute of Science and Civilization (University of Oxford) and MacKinder Centre for the Study of Long-Wave Events (London School of Economics).

Prins, G., Rayner, S., et al. 2010. The Hartwell Paper: A new direction for climate policy after the crash of 2009. Oxford, UK: Institute for Science, Innovation and Society; London: London School of Economics, MacKinder Programme for the Study of Long Wave Events. http://eprints.lse.ac.uk/27939/.

Radkau, J. 2008. *Nature and Power: A Global History of the Environment* (translated from German). Cambridge: Cambridge University Press.

Randers, J. 2008. Global collapse—Fact or fiction? *Futures*, 40: 853–864.

Rasiah, R., Zhang, M., and Kong, X. 2013. Can China's miraculous growth continue? *Journal of Contemporary Asia*, 43 (2): 295–313.

Reap, J., Baumeister, D., and Bras, B. 2005. Holism, biomimicry and sustainable engineering, Paper No. IMECE2005-8134. In *Proceedings of the International Mechanical Engineering Conference (IMECE2005)*, American Society of Mechanical Engineering. https://fenix.tecnico.ulisboa.pt/downloadFile/3779573621557/Support_10_Reap_2005.pdf.

Reinert, E. S. 1999. The role of the state in economic growth, *Journal of Economic Studies*, 26 (4–5): 268–326.

Reinert, E. S. 2007. *How Rich Countries Got Rich . . . and Why Poor Countries Stay Poor*. New York: Carroll & Graf.

Reinhart, C., and Rogoff, K. 2009. *This Time It's Different: Eight Centuries of Financial Folly*. Princeton, NJ: Princeton University Press.

Renner, M. 2006. The new geopolitics of oil, *Development*, 49: 56–63.

Rifkin, J. 2011. *The Third Industrial Revolution: How Lateral Power Is Transforming Energy, the Economy, and the World*. London: Palgrave Macmillan.

Rifkin, J. 2013. *The Zero Marginal Cost Society: The Internet of Things, the Collaborative Commons, and the Eclipse of Capitalism*. London: Palgrave Macmillan.

Rivera, J. E., and DeLeon, P. 2008. Voluntary environmental programs: Are carrots without sticks enough? *Policy Studies Journal*, 36 (1): 61–63.

Rockström, J., et al. 2009. A safe operating space for humanity, *Nature*, 461: 472–475.

Rosen, W. 2010. *The Most Powerful Idea in the World: A Story of Steam, Industry and Invention*. New York: Random House.

Rosenqvist, Å., Milne, A., Lucas, R., Imhoff, M., and Dobson, C. 2003. A review of remote sensing technology in support of the Kyoto Protocol, *Environmental Science and Policy*, 6 (5): 441–455.

Rosenstein-Rodan, P. N. 1943. Problems of industrialisation in Eastern and South-Eastern Europe, *Economic Journal*, 53 (210–211): 202–211.

Rubin, J. 2009. *Why Your World Is About To Get a Whole Lot Smaller: Oil and the End of Globalization*. Toronto: Random House.

Ryan, C. 2008. Climate change and ecodesign, Part I: The focus shifts to systems, *Journal of Industrial Ecology*, 12 (2): 140–143.

Samans, R. 2009. *Beyond Business as Usual: G20 Leaders and Post-Crisis Reconstitution of the International Economic Order*. Washington, DC: Center for American Progress.

Sanderson, H., and Forsythe, M. 2013. *China's Superbank: Debt, Oil and Influence—How China Development Bank Is Rewriting the Rules of Finance*. Hoboken, NJ: Bloomberg Press and Wiley.

Sayle, M. 2006. Overloading Emoh Ruo: The rise and rise of hydrocarbon civilisation, *Griffith Review*, (Winter): 11–115.

Scheer, H. 2002. *The Solar Economy: Renewable Energy for a Sustainable Global Future* (translated from the German *Solare Weltwirtschaft*, 1999). London: Earthscan.

Scheer, H. 2005. *A Solar Manifesto*, 2nd ed. London: Earthscan.

Scheer, H. 2007. *Energy Autonomy: The Economic, Social and Technological Case for Renewable Energy* (translated from the German *Energieautonomie: Eine Neue Politik fur Erneuerbare Energien*, 2005). London: Earthscan.

Scheer, H. 2011. *The Energy Imperative: 100 Percent Renewable Now*. Abingdon, UK: Earthscan and Routledge.

Schmalensee, R. 2012. From "green growth" to sound policies: An overview, *Energy Economics*, 34: 52–56.

Schumacher, E. F. 1973. *Small Is Beautiful: A Study of Economics as If People Mattered*. London: Blond and Briggs.

Schumpeter, J. A. 1912/1934. *The Theory of Economic Development: An Inquiry into Profits, Capital, Credit, Interest and the Business Cycle*. Cambridge, MA: Harvard University Press.

Schumpeter, J. A. 1939. *Business Cycles: A Theoretical, Historical and Statistical Analysis of the Capitalist Process*, vols. 1 and 2. New York: McGraw-Hill.

Sen, A. 1981. Public action and the quality of life in developing countries, *Oxford Bulletin of Economics and Statistics*, 43 (4): 287–319.

Shi, H., Chertow, M., and Song, Y. 2010. Developing country experience with eco-industrial parks: A case study of the Tianjin Economic-Technological Development Area in China, *Journal of Cleaner Production*, 18: 191–199.

Shiller, R. J. 2012. *Finance and the Good Society*. Princeton, NJ: Princeton University Press.

Sieferle, R.-P. 1982/2001. *The Subterranean Forest: Energy Systems and Industrial Revolution*, translated by Michael Osmann. Isle of Harris, UK: White Horse Press.

Simmons, M. 2005. *Twilight in the Desert: The Coming Saudi Oil Shock and the World Economy*. New York: Wiley.

Simon, H. 1962. The architecture of complexity, *Proceedings of the American Philosophical Society*, 106 (6): 467–482.

Simon, J. L. 1981/1998. *The Ultimate Resource*. Princeton, NJ: Princeton University Press.

Simon, J. L. 1994. More people, greater wealth, more resources, healthier environment, *Economic Affairs*, (April): 22–29.

Sinn, H.-W. 2012. *The Green Paradox: A Supply-Side Approach to Global Warming*. Cambridge, MA: MIT Press.

Smil, V. 1994. *Energy in World History*. Boulder, CO: Westview Press.

Smith, L. C. 2010. *The World in 2050: Four Forces Shaping Civilization's Northern Future*. New York: Dutton/Penguin.

Söderbaum. P. 2000. *Ecological Economics: A Political Economics Approach to Environment and Development*. London: Earthscan.

Solow, R. M. 1974. The economics of resources or the resources of economics, *American Economic Review*, 64 (2): 1–14.

Solow, R. M. 1991/2005. Sustainability: An economist's perspective (lecture delivered at Woods Hole, MA, 1991). In *Economics of the Environment: Selected Readings*, edited by R. Stavins, 179–187. New York: W. W. Norton.

Sovacool, B. 2009. Rejecting renewables: The socio-technical impediments to renewable electricity in the United States, *Energy Policy*, 37 (11): 4500–4513.

Sovacool, B. K. 2010. Building umbrellas or arks? Three alternatives to carbon credits and offsets, *Electricity Journal*, 23 (2): 29–40.

Sovacool, B. K. 2011. Four problems with global carbon markets: A critical review, *Energy and Environment*, 22 (6): 681–694.

Speck, S., and Ekins, P., eds. 2011. *Environmental Tax Reform*. Oxford, UK: Oxford Scholarship Online Monographs.

Spence, M. 2011a. Asia's new growth model, Project Syndicate (1 June 2011), http://www.project-syndicate.org/commentary/spence23/English.

Spence, M. 2011b. *The Next Convergence: The Future of Economic Growth in a Multispeed World*. New York: Farrar, Straus, and Giroux.

Spender, J. S. 2011. Considering green business and green values. In *Green Business, Green Values, and Sustainability*, edited by C. N. Pitelis, J. Keenan, and V. Pryce, 141–154. London: Routledge.

Speth, G. 2009. *The Bridge at the Edge of the World: Capitalism, the Environment, and Crossing from Crisis to Sustainability*. New Haven, CT: Yale University Press.

Steffen, W., Crutzen, P. J., and McNeill, J. R. 2007. The Anthropocene: Are humans now overwhelming the great forces of Nature? *Ambio*, 36: 614–621.

Steffen, W., Grinevald, J., Crutzen, P., and McNeill, J. 2011. The Anthropocene: Conceptual and historical perspectives, *Philosophical Transactions of the Royal Society (A)*, 369: 842–867.

Steffen, W., Persson, A., et al. 2011. The Anthropocene: From global change to planetary stewardship, *Ambio*, 40: 739–761.

Stepp, M., and Jenkins, J. 2012. The future of global climate policy. Washington, DC: Information Technology and Innovation Foundation. http://www.itif.org/publications/future-global-climate-policy.

Stern, D. I., Common, M. S., and Barbier, E. B. 1996. Economic growth and environmental degradation: The environmental Kuznets curve and sustainable development, *World Development*, 24 (7): 1151–1160.

Stern, N. 2007. *The Stern Review of the Economics of Climate Change*. London: H. M. Treasury.

Stern, N. 2009. *A Blueprint for a Safer Planet: How to Manage Climate Change and Create a New Era of Progress and Prosperity*. London: Bodley Head.

Stiglitz, J. E., Sen, A., and Fitoussi, J.-P. 2009. *Report by the Commission on the Measurement of Economic Performance and Social Progress*. http://www.stiglitz-sen-fitoussi.fr/en/index.htm.

Stoll, S. 2010. Fear of fallowing: The specter of a no-growth world, *Harper's*, (March): 88–94.

Stroup, R. 2008. Free market environmentalism. *Library of Economics and Liberty*, http://www.nesgeorgia.org/files/free_market_environmentalism.pdf.

Su, B., Heshmati, A., Geng, Y., and Yu, X. 2013. A review of the circular economy in China: Moving from rhetoric to implementation, *Journal of Cleaner Production*, 42: 215–227.

Swedberg, R. 2000. *Max Weber and the Idea of Economic Sociology*. Princeton, NJ: Princeton University Press.

Tainter, J. A. 1988. *The Collapse of Complex Societies*. Cambridge: Cambridge University Press.

Tainter, J. A. 2006. Archaeology of overshoot and collapse, *Annual Review of Anthropology*, 35: 59–74.

Tesla, N. 1900/2011. *My Inventions and Other Writings*, introduced by Samantha Hunt. New York: Penguin.

Thampapillai, D. 1991. *Environmental Economics*. Melbourne: Oxford University Press.

Thirlwall, A. P. 2002. *The Nature of Economic Growth: An Alternative Framework for Understanding the Performance of Nations*. Cheltenham, UK: Edward Elgar.

Thomas, B. 1980. Towards an energy interpretation of the industrial revolution, *Atlantic Economic Journal*, 8 (1): 1–16.

Thomas, B. 1985. Escaping from constraints: The Industrial Revolution in a Malthusian context, *Journal of Interdisciplinary History*, 15: 729–753.

Tiewes, F., and Sun, 2011. China's new economic policy under Hua Guofeng: Party consensus and party myths, *China Journal*, 66 (July): 1–23.

Toner, P. 2000. *Main Currents in Cumulative Causation: The Dynamics of Growth and Development*. London: Palgrave Macmillan.

Toner, P. 2001. "History versus equilibrium" and the theory of economic growth, by Mark Setterfield: A comment, *Cambridge Journal of Economics*, 25 (1): 97–102.

Toynbee, A. 1884. Lectures on the Industrial Revolution in England, http://socserv.mcmaster.ca/econ/ugcm/3113/toynbee/indrev.

Trieb, F., Schillings, C., Pregger, T., and O'Sullivan, M. 2012. Solar electricity imports from the Middle East and North Africa to Europe, *Energy Policy*, 42: 341–353.

UN Economic and Social Commission for Asia and the Pacific. 2010. *Green Growth: Resources and Resilience*. Bangkok: UNESCAP.

UN Economic and Social Commission for Asia and the Pacific. 2011. *What is green growth?* Bangkok: UNESCAP.

UN Economic and Social Commission for Asia and the Pacific. 2012. *Low-carbon green growth roadmap for Asia and the Pacific: Turning resource constraints and the climate crisis into economic growth opportunities*. Bangkok: UNESCAP.

UN Environment Programme. 2011. *Towards a Green Economy: Pathways to sustainable development and poverty eradication*. Nairobi: UNEP.

UN Industrial Development Organization. 2010. *A Greener Footprint for Industry: Opportunities and Challenges of Sustainable industrial development*. Vienna: UNIDO.

United Nations. 2012. *Resilient People, Resilient Planet: A future worth choosing*. Report of high-level panel on global sustainability to the UN Secretary-General. New York: United Nations. http://www.un.org/gsp/report.

Unruh, G. C. 2000. Understanding carbon lock-in, *Energy Policy*, 28 (12): 817–830.

Unruh, G. C. 2002. Escaping carbon lock-in, *Energy Policy*, 30 (4): 317–325.

Urban, F., Benders, R. M. J., Moll, H. C., 2009. Renewable and low-carbon energies as mitigation options of climate change for China, *Climate Change*, 94: 169–188.

Van Beers, D., Corder, G., Bossilkov, A., and Van Berkel, R. 2007. Industrial symbiosis in the Australian minerals mining industry, *Journal of Industrial Ecology*, 11 (1): 55–72.

Van Berkel, R. 2009. Comparability of industrial symbiosis. *Journal of Industrial Ecology,* 13(4): 483–486.

Van Berkel, R., Fujita, T., Hashimoto, S., and Fujii, M. 2009. Quantitative assessment of urban and industrial symbiosis at Kawasaki, Japan, *Environmental Science and Technology*, 43 (5): 1271–1281.

Van den Bergh, J. C. J. M., Faber, A., Idenburg, A. M., and Oosterhuis, F. H. 2006. Survival of the greenest: Evolutionary economics and policies for energy innovation, *Environmental Sciences*, 3 (1): 57–71.

Van der Ploeg, F., and Withagen, C. 2012. Is there really a green paradox? *Journal of Environmental Economics and Management*, 64 (3): 342–363.

Vazquez-Brust, D. A., and Sarkis, J., eds. 2012. *Green Growth: Managing the Transition to a Green Economy*. Heidelberg, Germany: Springer.

Victor, D. G., and Yanosek, K. 2011. The crisis in clean energy: Stark realities of the renewables craze, *Foreign Affairs*, 90 (July–August): 112–120.

Victor, P. A. 1991. Indicators of sustainable development: Some lessons from capital theory, *Ecological Economics*, 4 (3): 191–213.

Victor, P. A. 2008. *Managing Without Growth: Slower by Design, Not Disaster*. Cheltenham, UK: Edward Elgar.

Victor, P. A. 2010. Questioning economic growth, *Nature*, 468 (18 November): 370–371.

Wade, R. 1987. The management of common property resources: Collective action as an alternative to privatisation or state regulation, *Cambridge Journal of Economics*, 11: 95–106.

Walz, R. 2010. Competences for green development and leapfrogging in newly industrializing countries, *International Economics and Economic Policy*, 7: 245–265.

Wara, M. 2007. Is the global carbon market working? *Nature*, 445: 595–596.

Weber, M. 1922/1947. *The Theory of Social and Economic Organization*, translated by A. M. Henderson and Talcott Parsons. New York: Free Press.

Weiss, L. 2014. *America Inc.? Innovation and Enterprise in the National Security State*. Ithaca, NY: Cornell University Press.

Weiss, L., and Thurbon, E. 2006. The business of buying American: Public procurement as trade strategy in the USA, *Review of International Political Economy*, 13 (5): 701–724.

Weitzel, M., and Peterson, S. 2012. Border carbon adjustment: Not a very promising climate policy instrument, Kiel Policy Brief No. 55, Kiel Institute for the World Economy, Kiel, Germany.

Westad, O. A. 2012. *Restless Empire: China and the World Since 1750*. New York: Basic Books.

Wijkman, A., and Rockström, J. 2012. *Bankrupting Nature: Denying Our Planetary Boundaries* (Report to the Club of Rome). London: Earthscan and Routledge.

Winkler, H. 2011. Closed-loop production systems: A sustainable supply chain approach, *CIRP Journal of Manufacturing Science and Technology*, 4: 243–246.

Wollen, P. 1991. Scenes from the future: Komar & Melamid, *New Left Review*, 181 (January–February): 69–80.

Wong, S.-F. 2005. Obliging institutions and industry evolution: A comparative study of the German and UK wind energy industries, *Industry and Innovation*, 12 (1): 117–145.

Wong, S.-F. 2006. *Environmental Technology Development in Liberal and Coordinated Market Economies: Tweaking Institutions*. London: Palgrave Macmillan.

World Bank. 1992. *World Development Report 1992*. Washington, DC: World Bank.

World Bank. 2012. *Inclusive Green Growth: The Pathway to Sustainable Development*. Washington, DC: World Bank.

World Bank and Development Research Center. 2013. *China 2030: Building a Modern, Harmonious, and Creative Society*. Washington, DC: World Bank.

World Economic Forum. 2013. *The Green Investment Report: The Ways and Means to Unlock Private Finance for Green Growth*. Geneva: World Economic Forum.

Wrigley, E. A. 1962. The supply of raw materials in the Industrial Revolution, *Economic History Review*, 15 (1): 1–16.

Wrigley, E. A. 1988. *Continuity, Chance and Change: The Character of the Industrial Revolution in England*. Cambridge: Cambridge University Press.

Xu, L., Yu, B., and Yue, W. 2010. A method of green GDP accounting based on eco-service and a case study of Wuyishan, China, *Procedia Environmental Sciences*, 2: 1865–1872.

Yergin, D. 2011. *The Quest: Energy, Security and the Remaking of the Modern World*. New York: Penguin Press.

Young, A. 1928. Increasing returns and economic progress, *Economic Journal*, 38 (152): 527–542.

Yusuf, S., ed. 2003. *Innovative East Asia: The Future of Growth*. Washington, DC: World Bank.

Yusuf, S., and Nabeshima, K., eds. 2010. *Changing the Industrial Geography in Asia: The Impact of China and India*. Washington, DC: World Bank.

Zenghelis, D. 2012. A strategy for restoring confidence and economic growth through green investment and innovation. Policy brief, Grantham Research Institute, London School of Economics, Centre for Climate Change Economics and Policy, University of Leeds, United Kingdom.

Zhu, D. 2008. Background, pattern and policy of China for developing circular economy. *Chinese Journal of Population, Resources and Environment*, 6 (4): 1–6.

Zhu, Q., and Côté, R. P. 2004. Integrating green supply chain management into an embryonic eco-industrial development: A case study of the Guitang Group. *Journal of Cleaner Production*, 12: 1025–1035.

Zysman, J., and Huberty, M. 2011. *Green Growth: From Religion to Reality*. Berkeley, CA: Berkeley Roundtable on the International Economy. http:// brie.berkeley.edu/publications/From-Religion-to-Reality.pdf.

Zysman, J., and Huberty. 2013. *Can Green Sustain Growth? From the Religion to the Reality of Sustainable Prosperity*. Redwood City, CA: Stanford University Press.

Index

Page numbers followed by "f" or "t" indicate material in figures or tables.

Abu Dhabi, and CSP, 97, 99
accelerated diffusion of innovations, 163–165
Acemoglu, Daron, 154, 243n9, 245n26, 271n2
aerosol cooling effect, 62
aggregation, of financial capital, 136, 140
agrarian economy, 209–210
Allen, Miles R., 66
Allen, Robert, 26, 243n9
Allianz Global Investors, 155, 156t, 162
Al Qaeda and What It Means to Be Modern (Gray), 288n37
Amazon Fund, 287n29
ammonia, as zero-carbon fuel, 112, 263n51
Amsden, Alice, 240n10
Anasazi (Pueblo) culture collapse, 54–55
Anthropocene epoch, 50–51, 244n14, 249nn1, 4

anthropogenic climate change, 37, 60, 227. *See also* global climate change
antibiotic-resistant bacteria, as example of collective action problem, 224
APEC (Asia-Pacific Economic Cooperation) countries, and clean-tech trade agreement, 215, 286n19
Arctic sea-ice cover, 63–64 (63f)
Aristotle, 49, 73
Arrhenius, Svante (and greenhouse effect), 63, 253–254n36
Arthur, Brian, 200
ASG (Asian Super Grid) proposal, 92–96 (93f), 99, 214
Asian financial crisis (1997–98), 219
Asia-Pacific Economic Cooperation (APEC), 215, 286n19
ASPO (Association for the Study of Peak Oil), 56
Athabasca Valley, and tar sands, 252n24
atmospheric commons, 256n56

atmospheric steam engine, 26, 244n13
Australia, 122, 126, 263n52, 286n19
Ausubel, Jesse, 102–104, 261nn37, 40
Ayres, Robert U., 278n45

banking. *See* finance
Barbier, Edward B., 254n39, 284–285n11
Barnes, Peter, 256n56, 288n36
Barnes, William, 109–110
Basic Law for Promoting the Creation of a Recycling-Oriented Society 2000, Japan, 119
batteries: cadmium-telluride, 103–104; for electric cars, 107–108; experience curve for, 107–108; lithium-ion, 108; recycling of, 265n14; Tesla Motors, 261–262n40, 273n11; US Battery Consortium, 103
BAU. *See* "business as usual" (BAU) approach
Baumeister, Dayna, 278n2
BCAs (border carbon adjustments), 228, 289n45
bees, and climate change, 73, 187, 279n8
Beijing model of green development, 42–48
Bergek, Anna, 276n34
best-practice benchmarks, 144
BICs (Brazil, India, China), 43–44, 86, 247n39
"big push" (Rosenstein-Rodan), 197, 282n29
bilateral investment treaties, and impact on carbon reduction policies, 147–148
biochar, 289–290n49
biomimetic economy: as biological and economic metabolism, 280n16;

and circular economy, 183, 187, 207; as common ground between East and West, 201–202; as ecological matrix, 184; and game of Go, 193–194 (194f); moving toward, 201–203; recognizing natural limits, 188f; as rupture with linear thinking, 183. *See also* circular economy; green economy
black energy, 59, 90. *See also* fossil fuels; green and black model
black revolution (China), 51–52
Blueprint for a Green Economy (Pearce), 182, 241n20
"blueprint for a green economy" (China's Twelfth Five-Year Plan), 279n5
BNDES (Brazilian Development Bank), 10, 143–145, 269–270n18, 287n29
bond markets, 132–136, 138–139 (139f), 140–142. *See also* green banks
border carbon adjustments (BCAs), 228, 289n45
Bosch-Haber process, 263n51
Botero, Giovanni (and Italian Renaissance economic theorists), 284n7
Botswana, 99
Boulding, Kenneth E., 204–209, 283n2. *See also* Spaceship Earth metaphor
Braungart, Michael, 114, 115–117, 264n7, 265n9
Brazil: Amazonian rain forest, 287n29; bioenergy, 46; bioethanol futures contracts, 267n26; Brazilian Development Bank (BNDES), 10, 143–145, 269–270n18, 287n29; ethanol mandates, 169; as "farm of the world," 35; long-term economic

fluctuations, 37; wind and hydro initiatives, 86–87. *See also* BICs (Brazil, India, China)

BRICs, 37. *See also* BICs (Brazil, India, China)

Britain: colonialism, 29–32, 37; energy revolution (1650–1750), 25–26, 35; Industrial Revolution, 3, 21–22 (22f), 24, 210

bubbles, financial, 146, 160–162, 218, 284n8

Bush, George H. W., and Gulf War, 40

Bush, George W., and Iraq War, 40

"business as usual" (BAU) approach, 7, 242n25; assumption of unlimited resources, 31, 34; blunting free market forces, 9; and climate change, 207; costs of, 5; getting beyond, 7; unsustainability of, 52

business cycles, 154–156 (156t). *See also* TEP (techno-economic paradigms)

Business Cycles (Schumpeter), 21, 153, 272n4

C2C/"cradle-to-cradle" thinking, 116–118, 213, 264n7, 265n9

cadmium-telluride cells, 103–104. *See also* batteries

Calvin, William H., 289n48

Campbell, Colin, 56

cap-and-trade, 72, 169, 224

capitalism: achievements of, 4–5; always seeking growth, 210–211; "capitalism 3.0," 256n56, 288n36; "capitalism 4.0," 288n36; "capitalism 5.0," 225; green growth economy as, 220–223; land, labor, money categories, 23, 211; limits of "wild" version, 42, 67–72; need for

new rules for, 7–8, 67, 227, 229–230; up- and downswings in, 154–155, 156t, 161, 272n4, 273n8; viewed as core problem, 2, 225–227. *See also* finance; industrial capitalism

Capitalism as If the World Matters (Porritt), 227

capital substitution, 280n15

carbon capture and storage (CC&S), 67, 71, 75

carbon dioxide: carbon capture, 67, 71, 75, 255n47; carbon markets and, 69–70, 134; carbon offsets, 71, 147; carbon particulate pollution, 45; China as largest emitter of, 37; China's projected emissions of, 65–66 (66f), 86; conversion factor for carbon emissions, 258n10; corporate and social responsibility for, 71–72; emission targets, 289n48; global carbon emission limits, 64–67; levels of historically, 60, 61f; technical fixes and, 70–71

Carbon Efficient Index (ICO2), 72

carbon lock-in, 6–8, 105, 145, 149, 160, 171–172, 200, 211, 216, 226, 236, 240n7, 248n47, 271n3, 273n12, 278n45; at 4TEP level, 160; countering with creative destruction, 216; countering with point of investment incentives, 145; defined, 6, 154; as example of path dependence, 200; at "gut level," 105; leading to split among capitalists, 226; origin of phrase, 271n3; working against market forces, 7

carbon markets, 14–15, 67, 69–70, 75, 134, 147, 202, 255nn43, 45; and speculation, 70, 160

carbon taxes, 7, 14–15, 72, 163, 169, 172, 214, 222–228, 275. *See also* market-based disincentives
Carbon Tracker Initiative (CTI), 72, 268n9, 290n53
Carter, Jimmy, 173–174, 276n36
causation, circular and cumulative (C&CC), 192–195
CBRC (China Banking Regulatory Commission), 145
CC&S (carbon capture and storage), 67, 71, 75
CDB (China Development Bank), 143, 145, 269n17
CDM (Clean Development Mechanism), 69–70, 147
CEDA (Clean Energy Deployment Administration), 275n24
cellular/modular organizational principle, 183
Center for International Climate and Environmental Research in Oslo (CICERO), 133, 142
"chain reactions," in green economy, 197, 269n16
Chandler, Alfred D., 27
Chilean salmon farms, 53, 250n12
China: air pollution, 5, 45; Beijing model of green development, 42–48; black revolution, 51–52; changes in tax policy, 217; circular economy initiatives, 122, 266n18; coal consumption by, 258n6; energy industrial revolution, 80–87; energy security concerns, 38–42 (39f), 44–45, 80, 178; fast-follower strategies, 165–167, 230; green and black model, 9–14 (12f–14f); green and black paradox, 120; having motive and means, 9; income trends, 3; joining WTO, 81; and

"last straw" industrialization, 64; as leader in renewables, 5–6; as leader of sixth TEP, 160; long-term economic fluctuations, 36–37 (36f); and Malthusian trap, 22–23; McDonough city designs for, 290n51; "new economic policy" (1979), 246n27; nuclear power generation, 12, 82f; post-1979 GDP rise, 80–81; projected carbon emissions, 65–66 (66f); recycling initiatives, 119–120; "smart and strong" grid, 82, 83f, 101, 234; thermal power, 12f; as top manufacturing nation, 246n28; wind power, 12 (13f), 81–82 (82f); as "workshop of the world," 35. *See also* BICs (Brazil, India, China); Eleventh Five-Year Plan (China); Twelfth Five-Year Plan (China)
China Banking Regulatory Commission (CBRC), 145
China Development Bank (CDB) 143, 145, 269n17
China National Offshore Oil Corporation (CNOOC), 59
"choice awareness" theory, 262n48
CHP (combined heat and power), 265–266n17
Christoff, Peter, 254n38
CICERO (Center for International Climate and Environmental Research in Oslo), 133, 142
CIGS (copper, indium, gallium, selenide), 177–179, 275n26
circular and cumulative causation (C&CC), 149, 192–197, 281n20
circular economy, 10–11, 43–44, 47–48, 70, 76, 113, 149, 158, 165, 176, 187, 191, 193, 199, 201, 207, 213, 218, 220, 234, 236, 247n41,

265nn9–12, 266n18, 279n12, 281n22, 287n26; as alternative green economics, 191; biomimesis and, 187; China and, 10–11, 48, 117–122, 176, 193; and closed loops, 122–127 (124f–127f), 266–267n24; and commodity markets, 128; Germany and, 118; as inevitable option for humanity, 236; inter-firm linkages in, 202; investors for, 149; Japan and, 47, 119; levels of, 122; as measure of progress, 187; need for policies supporting, 70; and Pareto eco-efficiency, 199; Pascal's wager and, 44; pioneers in, 115–116; as preferred option, 213; reducing resource flows, 43; as rupture in linear economy, 129–130; as starting point for green economics, 191
circular flow parity, 129
circular production system, 120
clean coal technologies, 248n44
Clean Development Mechanism (CDM), 69–70, 147
Clean Energy Deployment Administration (CEDA), 275n24
"cleaner production," 122
clean-tech, and trade agreement, 214–215
Climate Bonds Initiative, 131, 140, 142, 268–269n10. *See also* green/climate bonds
climate change. *See* global climate change
closed-cycle planet/economy, 115, 118, 122
closed loops, 122–125, 266–267n24. *See also* industrial hypercycles
The Closing Circle (Commoner), 76, 204–206, 257n59

CNOOC (China National Offshore Oil Corporation), 59
coal: Age of, 2; clean coal technologies, 248n44; coal-fired electric power, 11, 12f, 81; coal seam gas (CSG), 57–59, 111, 228, 248n47, 253n30, 273n10; colonialism and acquisition of, 30–32; current emissions from, 64; and dip in global warming, 62; German phasing out of, 88; and Malthusian trap, 23; objections to shift of, 35; replacing wood and charcoal, 27–29; and rise of industrialization, 25–27, 28f; Ruhr Valley deposits, 34
The Coal Question (Jevons), 21
Cobb, John, 218
Cohen-Rosenthal, Edward, 114, 115, 264n2
coke iron furnaces, 26
Collapse (Diamond), 54
collapses, preindustrial, 54–55
collective action problem (CAP), 256n55; intractable versions, 224
colonialism and industrialization, 29–32, 37, 42
commodities markets, 127–129, 217
Common, Michael S., 254n39
Commoner, Barry, 49, 76, 204–209, 257n59
common law, problems of time and scale in, 8
common pool resources (CPRs), 256nn54, 56
concentrating solar power (CSP). *See* CSP (concentrating solar power)
"concert balancing," approach in international relations, 273n10
The Constant Gardener (novel, film), 290n52

consumer behavior in green economy, 221

control apparatus for green economy, 223–225

conversion factor for carbon emissions, 258n10

Corfee-Morlot, Jan, 269n13

Cornucopians, 53

corporate and social responsibility (CSR), as corporate response to environmental pressure, 71–72, 285n14, 309n14

corporations and doctrine of limited liability, 224–225

Costanza, Robert, 184

cost reduction, 87, 107–108, 159, 168, 173–175, 179, 197, 258n4, 262n44, 277n39, 278n47; and solar PV, 106; and wind power, 106. *See also* learning curves

counter-greenhouse effect, 62

covered bonds, 136. *See also* green / climate bonds

"cowboy economy" (Boulding) 206. *See also* "wild capitalism"

Cox, P. M., 253n35

Cradle to Cradle (Braungart and McDonough), 264n7, 265n9

"cradle-to-cradle"/C2C thinking, 116–118, 213, 264n7, 265n9

Crafts, N. F. R., 242n1

creative destruction, 6, 8, 16, 94, 130, 154, 158, 192, 203, 216, 222, 232

credit and debt instruments, 32–34, 69

Crédit Mobilier bank, 135–136

Crutzen, Paul, 50–51, 249n1

CSG (coal seam gas), 57–59, 111, 228, 248n47, 253n30, 273n10

CSP (concentrating solar power), 96–100; China and, 81, 99; countries showing interest in, 99, 101–102, 260–261nn32–34; fast followers' interest in, 166; land required for, 103, 260nn29, 30; and molten salt storage technology, 97, 99–100, 104; pairing with water desalinization, 112; possibly self-sustaining, 100; projecting requirements for, 110–111

CTI (Carbon Tracker Initiative), 72, 268n9, 290n53

cumulative (and circular) causation (C&CC), 192–195

Czech, Brian, 195

Dales, J. H., 254–255n42

Daly, Herman, 182, 189–191, 195, 206, 218, 280n16

Daoism, 283n34

Darby, Abraham, 26

David, Paul A., 200, 282–283n33

debt and credit instruments, 32–34, 69

decentralized power generation, 89, 96

Deepwater Horizon drilling disaster, 111

default options, for renewable energy and resource efficiency, 8, 107, 111–112, 129–130, 148–150, 177, 183, 202, 220

degrowth, 15, 195–198. *See also* zero growth

DeLeon, Peter, 255n49

demand-side policy to promote market adoption, acceleration, 168–172, 197

democratization of economic power, 89

Deng Xiaoping, 246n27

desalination, 230

Desertec Foundation, 92; proposal, 98f, 217n33

Deutsche Bank, 135–136, 276n33

developing countries, 2–5; "circular and cumulative causation" in, 192, 282n27; climate bonds as default option for, 148–149; CSP projects for, 261n34; and Desertec proposal, 98–99; diffuseness of renewables a boon to, 104–105; fast-follower strategies for, 166; global free trade and, 214–215; green development "inevitable choice" for, 4, 10; green leapfrogging and, 141–142; loan risk premiums on, 148–149; and "new convergence," 231; population growth in, 208; shifting wealth and, 38; solar PV costs and, 106–107; World Bank and, 234

Diamond, Jared, 54–55, 251n15

Diesendorf, Mark, 97

differential principle, 270n20

diffusion of innovations, acceleration, 162–165, 173–176

diminishing returns, and extractive industries, 16, 43, 230

direct measurement, planetary impact, 223

"discharge" industrial system, 211

dispatchable power supplies, defined, 261n36

doctrine of limited liability, 224–225

double movement/feedback loops, 24, 243n5

down-escalator clauses (feed-in tariffs), 171

Dreaming with BRICs (Goldman Sachs report), 35–36

Drechsler, Wolfgang, 158

Dubos, Rene, 1

DuPont (RRR), 116

East Asian strategies to promote diffusion of innovations, 163–165. See also fast-follower strategies

Easter Island, 54–55, 67, 251n15

Eastern thought/philosophy, 201–202

Eckersley, Robin, 254n38

eco-cement, 255n47

eco-efficiency, 116, 264n5

eco-finance, 148–149, 205, 207, 211, 213–214

eco-imagination, 225–232

eco-industrial: initiatives, dynamics of, 198–201; linkages forming circular economy, 121–127, 194; parks, 121, 122, 194; use of term, 266n23; virtual parks, 193

ecological economics, 184, 187–189 (188f)

economic and biological metabolisms, 280n16

economic downturn of 2008/2009. See global financial crisis (2008/2009)

economic growth and environment, 68–69, 210–211

Economics of Natural Resources and the Environment (Pearce and Turner), 265n10

Economy, Elizabeth, 52

"eco-securities," 138

ecosystem services, 185–187, 279n8

eco-tagging, 127–129, 231; and futures contracts, 267n26, 286n21

eco-worthiness, 136–137, 142

Edison, Thomas, 79, 80, 257n1

Ehrenfeld, John R., 254n38, 264n3

Ehrlich, Paul and Anne, 41, 206, 209

Eigen, M., 123, 266n24

EKC (environmental Kuznets curve), 67–69, 75, 254n39

Electrical and Electronic Equipment Act (2006, Germany), 118
Electricity Business Act (Japan), 95
electricity trading (renewable), 94
"electric lock-in," 278n45
electric power generation capacity in China, 84–85 (84f)
electric vehicles (EVs), 108, 159, 262n40, 273n11
electronic identifiers on futures contracts, 286n21. *See also* eco-tagging
Eleventh Five-Year Plan (China), 10, 45, 254n40
Ellen Macarthur Foundation, 118. *See also* circular economy
Energiewende (energy transformation, Germany), 7, 87–90
energy: as driver of Great Transformation, 25–29; and industrial revolution, 25–26, 244n14; oil dependency and energy insecurity, 38–42 (39f); security from renewables, 80, 87, 105, 178, 213, 236; WTE (waste-to-energy) initiative, 92. *See also* fossil fuels; nuclear energy; renewables; wind energy
energy industrial revolution, 158; in China, 80–87; in Germany, 87–90
energy security, through manufacturing of renewables, 80, 87, 105, 178, 213, 236
energy storage. *See* batteries
Engels, Friedrich, 1
England. *See* Britain
environmental Kuznets curve (EKC), 67–69, 75, 254n39
environmental taxation, 217. *See also* market-based disincentives
equipment suppliers, 275n27. *See also* value chains

equity markets, 134. *See also* stranded assets
ESS (evolutionary stable strategies), 199–200
Essay on the Principle of Population (Malthus), 22
Esty, Daniel C., 255n48
ethanol, as biofuel, 169–170, 267n26
"ethical oil," as PR campaign, 58
European Union (EU), 171–172, 178–179
evolution, biological, 183; technological, 244n13
evolutionary stable strategies (ESS), 199–200
EVs (electric vehicles), 108, 159, 262n40, 273n11
experience curves, 106–107 (106f), 159, 167, 173. *See also* learning curves
extractive vs. manufacturing industries (and diminishing returns), 43
extreme resources, 57–59. *See also* CSG (coal seam gas); shale oil
ExxonMobil, and maintenance of carbon lock-in, 252n25

Fable of the Bees (Mandeville), 73
fabrication facilities for renewables, 104
famine, 22–23, 209–210
"farm of the world," Brazil as, 35
fast-follower strategies, 165–167, 274nn21, 23
Federal Energy Administration (US), 173
Federal PV Utilization Program (FPUP), 173–175
feedback loops/double movement (Polanyi), 24, 243n5

feed-in tariff systems, 47, 86, 88–90, 92, 96, 106, 168–172, 175–178, 276nn32–35; effect on costs, 106; European Union, 171–172; Germany, 88–89, 170, 175, 176; Italy, 171; Japan, 92, 96; Spain, 170–171

fertilizer consumption, 31f

fictitious commodities (Polanyi), 23–24

fifth techno-economic paradigm, 155, 157–158, 213, 215

finance: aggregating financial capital, 136, 140; banking regulation, 218–219; bubbles, 146, 160–162, 218, 284n8; crises, 211; eco-finance, 148–149, 214; financial instability hypothesis, 283n35; "financialization," 271n25; "Ponzi scheme" financing, 146; as a utility, 219, 287n27. *See also* finance; global financial crisis (2008/2009); green/climate bonds

Finance and the Good Society (Shiller), 287n27

firm(s): and doctrine of limited liability, 224–225; growth as perpetual goal of, 210–211; theory of the, 212

First Solar, 107

Fischer, Carolyn, 276n32

Fischer-Kowalski, Marina, 284n10

Fitoussi, Jean-Paul, 286–287n24

Five-Year Plans (China), 10, 45, 254n40. *See* Twelfth Five-Year Plan (China)

Flensborg, Christopher, 131, 268n2

flex-fuel vehicles (in Brazil), 169

fluctuating demand, and renewables, 94–96

fluctuating power sources, 88

fluidized bed combustion, 248n44

Ford Motor Company, and mass production, 120

foreign direct investment, 31f

fossil fuels: as cause of war, 112–113; China's use of, 11, 45; as driver of economy, 139; economic limiting factors for, 210–211; exhibiting overshoot, 55–59; financial market support for, 137; geopolitical issues of, 233–234; global uptake of, 28–29 (29f); pace of replacement of, 108–111; territorial disputes over, 96; as "unlimited" power, 23; and US industrialization, 27, 28f

FPUP (Federal PV Utilization Program), 173–175

"fracking" (hydraulic fracturing), 58–59, 88, 273n10

Freeman, Christopher, 156–158, 272nn4, 8

free market environmentalism (FME), 7–8, 130, 180, 222, 240n8, 263n50

Friedrichs, Jörg, 53

Friends of the Earth, 48, 227

frontier, end of, 41, 204. *See also* "wild capitalism"

Fukushima disaster, 47, 81, 87, 92, 111, 234

FutureGen project, 71

futures contracts, and eco-tagging, 267n26, 286n21

Gaia concept, 183

garbage (waste) to energy, 92

gardener image, 231

GATS (General Agreement on Trade in Services), 147–148

GDP: and energy use, 69; growth in as economic goal, 31, 129–130; as index of physical throughput, 190; total real, 31f

generator sets, market creation for (under FPUP), 174

Genuine Progress Indicator (GPI), 218
geo-engineering solutions for global warming, 70–71
George, Henry, 283n3
Georgescu-Roegen, Nicolae, 114, 182
Germany: about-turn on nuclear power, 47, 87–88, 179; circular economy (*Kreislaufwirtschaft*), 118; competition with China, 178–179; *Energiewende* (energy transformation), 7, 47, 87–89; environmental taxation, 217; recycling levels, 265n14; tariff degression, 171
Gerschenkron, Alexander, 136
GIGA battery plant (Tesla Motors), 273n11
Giga Solar, 81
Gilman, Nils, 109–110
Gladstone, Australia, 122, 126
global climate change/global warming, 59–64 (61f–63f); anthropogenic, 37, 60, 227; compared to abortion issue, 227; "denialism" literature on, 253n33; framings of, 289n42; and "hockey stick graph," 253n34; as intractable collective action problem, 224; requiring change in capitalism to address, 225–226; threat of, 51. *See also* carbon dioxide
global dimming, 62
global financial assets, 139f
global financial crisis (2008/2009), 136–137; amount lost in, 227; causes of, 284n8; K-waves and, 155, 161 (161f); and need for safer investments, 148–149; showing need for regulation/good finance, 218–219, 287n27
global free trade in renewable power, 214–215

global warming. *See* global climate change/global warming
GNP (gross national product) on Spaceship Earth, 206–207. *See also* GDP
Go, game of, 193–194 (194f)
Gobi Desert wind farms, 92, 95
Goldman Sachs (*Dreaming with BRICs*), 35–37
Goldwind (China), 81, 166
Gore, Al, and *An Inconvenient Truth*, 60, 245n18
government, role of, 172–176, and government procurement, 173
GPI (Genuine Progress Indicator), 218
Graetz, Michael J., 249n48
Gramsci, Antonio, 204
Gray, John, 243n7, 288n37
Great Britain. *See* Britain
Great Convergence, 37–38, 239n3
Great Divergence, 37–38, 245n26
Great Transformation, 3–4; drivers of first, 25–34; and global expansion, 34–48; looking toward next, 34, 225, 230, 231
The Great Transformation (Polanyi), 21, 23–24, 243n4
green and black model, 9–14 (12f–14f)
"green and black" paradox, 120
green banks, 137–138, 142–145
green/climate bonds: advantages of, 134, 140–142, 149; and carbon offsets, 147; Climate Bonds Initiative, 131, 140, 142, 268–269n10; Kexim 2013 issuance of, 132, 285n15; not a cost but investment, 43; risk of, 271n29; scale of, 214
Green Credit Guidelines, China (CBRC), 145
green development, Beijing model of, 42–48

green economy, 212; as capitalist, 212, 220–223; and creative destruction, 216; eco-finance driven, 213–214; emergence of, 180–181; finance as a utility, 218–219; global free trade in renewables and clean tech, 214–215; governance of, 223–225; green GDP, 186–187, 218; not as cost but investment, 43; public investment in green shoots, 217–218; reconciliation with ecological principles, 223; renewables and clean tech preferred, 212–213; resource circulation preferred, 213; smart grid/smart economy, 215–216; tax on pollution and virgin resources, 216–217

green energy, abundance of, 43

green growth, 4, 6–7, 15–16, 38, 43, 64, 74, 86, 93, 96, 130, 172, 191, 198–199, 211–212, 220–221, 230–231, 236, 241n23, 242n24, 280n19, 282n31; as development model, 16–17, 38, 225–232, 287n28; and green growth industries, 86

green growth economy, axioms, 211–219, 221

greenhouse effect, 60; Arrhenius' formulation of, 253–254n36; China's projected emissions, 45; as input limit, 115. See also global climate change/global warming

greening of agriculture, 230. See also perennials

greening of cities, 230

green leapfrogging, 43, 141

green paradox, 72, 191, 256n52

The Green Paradox (Sinn), 72

Greenpeace, 48, 116

green shoots, of new economy, 142, 192, 212, 217–218

"greenwashing," 70, 71

Griffith, Saul, 109–110

growth, economic: conventional definition of, 191; and degrowth, 195–198; green, 191–192; intensive versus extensive, 195–196; as perpetual goal, 210

"growth-maniacs," 190

Growth Recurring (Jones), 182

Guaranteed Carbon Collateral Units, 147. See also IETA (International Emissions Trading Association)

Guitang Group (China), 125–126 (126f)

Gulf War, 40

Hanergy (China), 81, 177–178

Hansen, James, 240n12

Harappan collapse, 54

Hardin, Garrett, 53, 73–74, 231, 206–209, 224, 231. See also lifeboat ethic; "tragedy of the commons"

Hargadon, Andrew B., 274n20

Harrison, John, 255n47

Hart, Stuart L., 175, 276n36

Hawken, Paul, 185

hedge borrowing (in Minskyan sense), 270n24

Heinberg, Richard, 251n17

Helm, Dieter, 228

HFC-23 carbon market manipulation, and Clean Development Mechanism, 70

Hicks, John Richard, 185

hidden hand parable (Adam Smith), 73, 75, 231

high-voltage direct current (HVDC) cables, 82–83, 93, 95, 101

Ho, Peter, 248n45

Hoffman, Andrew J., 254n38, 264n3

holistic biomimesis, 278n2
Holling, C. S., 189, 203, 283n36
Hua Guofeng, 246n27
Hu Angang, 2, 4, 42
Hubbert, M. King, 56
Huberty, Mark, 287n28
Hughes, J. David, 253n30
Hulme, Mike, 227, 289n42
Human Development Index, 218
Hu Mei-Chih, 274n23
Hunt, T. L., 251n15
HVDC (high-voltage direct current)
    cables, 82–83, 93, 95, 101
hydraulic fracturing ("fracking"), 58–
    59, 88, 273n10
hypercycles, industrial, 123, 199. See
    also closed loops

ICO2 (Carbon Efficient Index), 72
ICTSD (International Centre for Trade
    and Sustainable Development), 215
ideal types (Weber), 222–223
IETA (International Emissions Trading
    Association), 147, 271n27
Illinois Central Railroad, 153, 271n1
income: distribution of in green econ-
    omy, 221; industrialization and, 3,
    5; and standards of living, 23
inconvenient truth, 60
increasing returns, and manufactur-
    ing, 192, 196–197, 241n21, 284n7
India: as "back office of the world,"
    35; and CSP, 99, 166; eco-industrial
    parks in, 46; income trends in, 3;
    long-term economic fluctuations in,
    36–37 (36f); and National Solar
    Mission, 86; oil dependency and
    energy insecurity in, 38–42 (39f);
    solar-power goals of, 261n33. See
    also BICs (Brazil, India, China)
industrial banks, 135–136

industrial capitalism: filling the planet,
    51–52; and Great Transformation,
    23; initial global expansion of, 34–
    42; need to change rules of, 75; pos-
    itive and negative effects of, 5; third
    phase of, 2; as unnatural abstrac-
    tion, 23–24; up- and downswings
    in, 154–155, 156t, 161, 272n4,
    273n8; "wild" version of, 50. See
    also capitalism
industrial ecology (IE)/symbiosis, 116,
    121–127, 184
industrial hypercycles, 123, 188–189,
    199, 279n12
industrialization: achievements of,
    4–5; diffusion of over time, 36–42
    (36f, 39f, 41f); Industrial Revolu-
    tion, 3, 22f, 243n10; preceded by
    energy revolution, 25–26, 244n14;
    scale of compared with human la-
    bor, 53; separating benefits from
    drawbacks of, 4–5; third phase of,
    2–3
industrial substitution, 167, 168f
industrial symbioses/ecology, 116,
    121–127, 184
industry promotion policies, 88, 90
information technology (IT), and
    technoeconomic paradigm shifts,
    155; as applied to energy systems,
    158
Information Technology Trade Agree-
    ment (ITA), as WTO agreement,
    215
institutional investors, and green/cli-
    mate bonds, 33, 131–132, 139–
    140, 160, 214, 271n29, 285n15
integrated circuits, market creation
    for, 174
intelligent/smart economy, 129,
    267n29

interest charges, 133, 138, 141–142, 148. *See also* green/climate bonds

Intergovernmental Panel on Climate Change (IPCC), 37, 60, 64, 106–108, 253n33

intermediate suppliers, 275n27. *See also* value chains

International Emissions Trading Association (IETA), 147, 271n27

international tourism, growth in, 31f

"Internet of things," 128–129, 215, 267n28. *See also* eco-tagging

intervention, 8, 107, 112, 202, 220. *See also* new default option

IPCC (Intergovernmental Panel on Climate Change), 37, 60, 64, 106–108, 253n33

Iraq War, 40, 111–112

Italy, and feed-in tariffs, 171

IT application to energy systems, 128–129, 215–216. *See also* smart grids

ITIF (Information Technology and Innovation Foundation), 165, 177, 180, 215, 289n44

ITRI (Industrial Technology Research Institute), Taiwan, 165–166

IT Trade Agreement (ITA), 215

Jackson, Tim, 190, 195

Jacobsson, Staffan, 276n34

Japan: and Asian Super Grid, 94–95; and circular economy, 47, 119; Fukushima disaster, 47, 81, 87, 92, 111, 234; industrial banks in, 136; long-term economic fluctuations in, 36–37 (36f)

Japan Renewable Energy Foundation (JREF), 92

Jawaharlal Nehru National Solar Mission (India), 86

Jevons, William Stanley, 21, 25, 116, 264n6; Jevons paradox, 115, 264n6

Jones, Eric, 182, 195

JREF (Japan Renewable Energy Foundation), 92

Kåberger, Tomas, 92

Kaldor, Nicholas, 192, 193, 196–197, 269n16, 281n20, 282n28. *See also* "chain reactions," in green economy; circular and cumulative causation (C&CC)

Kaletsky, Anatole, 225, 288n36

Kalundborg, Denmark, 122, 126, 127f

Kaminker, Christopher, 131, 245n22

Kant, Immanuel, and perpetual peace, 48, 112

Kattel, Rainer, 158

Kawasaki (Japan), 126

Kenney, Martin, 274n20

Kexim. *See* Korean Export-Import Bank (Kexim)

Kim, Sung-Yung, 275n29

Kingston, Bill, 272n4

Klare, Michael, 49, 58

Kondratiev waves (K-waves), 155, 158, 161f, 272n6

Korean Export-Import Bank (Kexim), 132–134, 268n2, 285n15

Korotayev, Andrey, 158, 160–161, 272n6

Krugman, Paul, 250n5

Kurz, Heinz D., 201

Kuznets, Simon, 272n4

Kuznets curve, environmental (EKC), 67–69, 75, 254n39

Kwinana, Australia, 122

Kyoto Protocol, 69, 134, 147, 223, 228. *See also* National Appropriate Mitigation Action (NAMA)

labor: as a commodity, 34; in a green economy, 221; invention of concept, 24; land, labor, money categories, 23, 211
LaConte, Ellen, 182
land, as a commodity, 23, 211
land requirements for renewables, 30, 97–98, 101–103, 109, 260n29
Law for the Promotion of the Circular Economy (2009, China), 119–120
lean production system, 120
leapfrogging possibilities, in renewable energies, 43, 141
learning curves, 99, 105–108 (106f), 285n17. See also cost reduction; experience curves
LeCarre, John, 290n52
Lee, Keun, 275n23
The Lever of Riches (Mokyr), 153
Lewis, Joanne, 277n42
lifeboat ethic (Garrett Hardin), 206–208, 231, 284n5
Life Rules (LaConte), 182
Li Ganjie, 10–11
light-emitting diodes (LEDs), 15
limited liability doctrine, 224–225
limiting factors, for agrarian and industrial economies, 209–211
Limits to Growth (Club of Rome), 53
linear economy (cf. circular economy), 114–115, 117, 129, 153
Lipo, C. P., 251n15
lithium-ion batteries, 108
logic, organizational, 219–220
logistic (S-shaped) curve trajectory of renewables, 13–14 (14f), 46, 84–86 (84f)
logistic industrial dynamics, 80, 167, 168f
Lomborg, Bjørn, 257n58, 278n47, 289n44

long waves theory, 156–160 (156t), 272–273nn4–8
Lovins, Amory B., 185
Lovins, L. Hunter, 185
low-carbon economy, 90
Lund, Henrik, 262n48

Macarthur, Ellen, 265n12
machismo and resistance to renewables, 101, 105
Maddison, Angus, 245n25
Making Peace with the Planet (Commoner), 49
Malthus, Thomas, 22, 209–210
Malthusian trap, 3, 5, 22–23, 51, 210, 236. See also neo-Malthusian
mandates, markets and necessity for, 130, 222
Mandeville, Bernard, 73
Mann, Michael, 61, 109–110, 226–227, 288n39; and sources of social power, 109, 226
manufacturing vs. extractive industries, 43. See also diminishing returns; increasing returns
market-based disincentives, 169, 216–217, 222. See also carbon taxes
market-based incentives (MBIs), 168–172, 217, 222, 275n28. See also SLCP (Sloping Lands Conversion Program)
market expansion: accelerating penetration, 168–170; to compete with China, 179; by EU, 178; vs. innovation, 87–88; through consumer support, 170–172
market failure, anthropogenic climate change as, 60
market fundamentalism, 7
market mandates, 130, 169–170, 222

market society (Polanyi), 23
Marshall, Alfred, 202
Marx, Karl, 1, 35
mass production system, 120
material and energy flow accounting, 116, 123
Mathews, Freya, 279n4
Maugeri, Leonardo, 249n48, 251n20
Mayan collapse, 54
MBIs (market-based incentives), 168–172, 217, 222, 275n28
McCloskey, Deidre, 9, 74, 240n11, 247n37
McDonald's restaurants, 31f
McDonough, William, 114, 115–117, 264n7, 265n9, 290n51
McNeill, John, 51, 249n3
merit-order effect, 108
Merkel, Angela, 87–88
Merrill Lynch, 162
Mesopotamian collapse, 54
methane, 50, 60, 61f, 66
METI (Ministry for Economy, Trade, and Industry), Japan, 94, 119
Mill, John Stuart, 190
Ming Yang, 81
Minsky, Hyman, 131, 146, 203, 218, 270nn23–24, 283nn35–36
modular/cellular organizational principle, 183
Mokyr, Joel, 153, 154
molten salt, as storage technology, 97, 99–100, 104
money, land, labor categories, 23, 211
Mongolian wind farms, 96
Montalto di Castro power station, 102–103
mortality rates, 5
Mozambique (hypothetical case of green bond), 141
Musk, Elon, 273n11

Myrdal, Gunnar, 192, 196, 281n20, 282n27

Naess, Petter, 284n5
Nair, Chandran, 247n38
Namibia, 99
National Appropriate Mitigation Action (NAMA), 271n26. *See also* Kyoto Protocol
National Development and Reform Commission (China), 12, 117, 121
national system for technology diffusion, 165
natural capital, 184–187, 279n9
"naturalized capitalism," 225, 230
Nature, conceived as boundless, 52, 74, 115, 129
negotiable securities (finance), 135
Nemet, Gregory F., 277n43, 278n47
neoclassical economics, 173; aversion to industry policy, 180; and "natural capital," 185–186; and production function, 279n10; view of economy vis-à-vis nature, 187, 188f; weaknesses of, 202
neo-Gerschenkronian, 6, 232–233
neoliberalism, 243n7
neo-Malthusian, 42, 53, 280n15
neo-Olsonian, 6, 233
neo-Schumpeterian, 6, 156, 158, 162–163, 232
Netherlands, 25, 29, 32, 95
Neumayer, Eric, 279n10
Newcomen, Thomas, 26
Newfoundland cod fisheries, 52–53
Nexen, 59
"Next Great Transformation," 4
next/new convergence, 229, 231
nickel-metal-hydride batteries, 108
Nokia, 110
Nolan, Peter, 42

non-conventional fossil fuels, 57–59.
    See also CSG (coal seam gas);
    shale oil
no-regrets approach, 234
North Africa, 98
Norway, 95, 287n29
nuclear energy: Fukushima disaster,
    47, 81, 87, 92, 111, 234; Germa-
    ny's about-turn on, 47, 87–88, 179;
    proponents of, 263n50

ocean acidification, 66
OECD: advocating green investment,
    139; shifting wealth model, 38; total
    material requirement aggregate, 116
offsetting carbon credits, 71–72
off-the-grid renewable technology,
    104–105
oil: and energy insecurity, 38–42
    (39f); "ethical oil," 58; gap in, 39f;
    oil powers, 247–248n42; peak oil,
    36, 56–59, 111–112, 115; Pegasus
    oil spill, 252n25; random distribu-
    tion of, 233; shale oil, 57–59,
    248n47, 252n24; tar sands oil, 57,
    252nn25, 27; "tight oil," 57,
    253n30; US State Department as
    "Ministry of Oil," 226
Oil and the End of Globalization
    (Rubin), 284n8
Olson, Mancur, 6, 176
Olsonianism, 6, 8, 176–177
open-source technology, 291n58
O'Reilly, Tim, 247n41, 290n54
organizational logic, 219–220
Ostrom, Elinor, 256nn54, 55
O'Sullivan, Patrick, 251n16
"overshoot and collapse" resource us-
    age, 52–57

paper consumption, 31f
Pareto eco-efficiency, 198–200

"Pascal wager," circular economy as,
    44, 247n41
path-constrained amelioration, 200
path dependence, 200–201, 216, 220,
    283n33
peak oil, 36, 56–59, 111–112, 115
Pearce, David W., 185, 241n20,
    265n10, 279n9
peat, as semi-fossil fuel, 25
Pegasus oil pipeline spill, 252n25
pension funds, 269n13. *See also* insti-
    tutional investors
perennials, shift to in agriculture,
    289–290n49
Perez, Carlota, 156–158, 160,
    272nn4, 8
Perez and Freeman, 156–157
permanent magnet direct drive
    (PMDD) technology, 166, 262n43
Pernick, Ron, 162
perpetual peace (Kant), 112
Persian Gulf, 111–112
Persson, Åsa, 54
Petrobas, 170
photosynthesis, artificial, 112, 263n51
photovoltaics (PVs). *See* solar power/
    photovoltaics
"picking winners" criticism, 8–9
Piore, Michael, 157
planetary boundaries, 280n13
planetary impact, direct measurement
    of, 223
Plimsoll line of economy, 189–190
PMDD (permanent magnet direct
    drive) technology, 166, 262n43
Polanyi, Karl, 4, 21, 211, 242–
    243nn4–6. *See also* Great
    Transformation
polar ice cap, 63–64 (63f)
"Pollution Rights," 254–255n42
"Ponzi scheme" financing, 146,
    270n24

population: contraception and economic development, 284n6; global, 208–209; and income, 3; urban, 31f

Porritt, Jonathan, 227

Porter, Michael, 285n14

precautionary principle vs. anything goes, 290–291n57

preindustrial collapses, 54–55

Preonas, Louis, 276n32

prestiti, 135

price shocks, 26, 210; and oil supplies, 234

Prins, Gwyn, 228

Proalcool Program, 169

procurement, government, 173–176; and tool of market expansion, 173

producer subsidies, 173

production systems, 120

production tax credit (PTC), 248n46

product responsibility, 118

property rights claims and common law, 8

public investment and transfers, 217, 227

Pueblo culture collapse, 54–55

PV. *See* solar power/photovoltaics

Qatar, 99

Q-Cells, 177

Qing Dynasty, 22–23, 37

QWERTY keyboard, 282–283n33

The Race for What's Left (Klare), 49

Radkau, Joachim, 251n16

railroadization, 153, 163

Randers, Jørgen, 250n11

Rayner, Steve, 228

RE² (renewable energy and resource efficiency) principles, 8, 203; in China, India, Brazil, 10, 46; genera-

tion systems and, 159; and projected financial bubble, 160; and Schumpeterian creative destruction, 192

Reagan, Ronald, 173, 175

"real options" theory, 291n59

Reap, John, 278n2

rebound effect (Jevons paradox), 116, 264n6

"recharge" industrial system, 211

reciprocal control mechanisms (Amsden), 240n10

recycling, moving beyond, 118–119

regenerative economy, 117–118

regulation, of eco-finance, 145–146, 219; of the green economy, 222

Reinert, Erik, 158, 282n30

Reinhardt, Forest L., 285n14

relative interest charges, 142

"Renewable and nuclear heresies" (Ausubel), 102

Renewable Energy Law (China), 176

Renewable Energy Sources Law (*Erneuerbare Energien Gesetz*, Germany, 2000), 47, 176

renewables: benefits of, 104–105; in BICs, 86–87; capital costs, 105, 133, 210; costs of, 105–108 (106f), 159; diffuseness of, 104–105; investment in, 273n13; price of, 285–286n17; rebutting objections to, 100–104. *See also* RE² (renewable energy and resource efficiency) principles; solar power/photovoltaics; wind energy

Renner, Michael, 249n48

Renova Energia, 87

rent seeking, 240n10

resilience of ecosystems, 189

resource efficiency, 5, 7–8, 10–11, 91, 117, 119, 122, 130, 138, 154, 177, 202, 213, 278n45 resources: abundance of green energy, 43; colonialism and acquisition of, 29–32; continuing extraction of, 5, 31; CSP requirements, 97–98; as economic inputs, 212; eco-tagging of, 129; and green paradox, 72; hoarding of, 112; natural capital and, 185–186, 210; need for "steady state," 195–196; ownership of, 221–222; and "Pascal's wager," 44; peaking/overshoot of, 55–59; peak oil, 36, 56–59, 111–112, 115; pollution from throughput of, 5; regenerating/circulation of, 117–121, 187–189 (188f), 193, 211; on Spaceship Earth, 204, 205–209, 283n3; from "subterranean forest" of fossil fuel, 26; thought of as boundless, 52, 74, 115, 129; throughput of, 48, 191; virgin, tax levy on, 216–217

RFID (radio-frequency identification) tagging, 128–129

Rifkin, Jeremy, 158, 162

"ring-fencing" (of green/climate bonds), 141

The River Runs Black (Economy), 52

Robinson, James, 154, 243n9, 245n26, 271n2

Rockström, Johan, 189, 280n13

Rosen, William, 244n13

Rosenqvist, Åke, 288n34

Rosenstein-Rodan, Paul, 197, 282n29. See also "big push"

Rubin, Jeff, 284n8

Ruhr Valley coal deposits, 34

ruptures, 113. See also techno-economic paradigms (TEP)

Russia, 37

Sabel, Charles, 157

salmon farms in Chile, 53

Sandia National Laboratories, 91

satellite monitoring, 224, 288n34

satiety (as economic assumption), 284n9

Saudi Arabia, 99

Sayle, Murray, 254n36

SBIR (Small Business Innovation Research), US, 164

scaling up, 10, 133, 165, 179, 214

Schauvliege, Joke, 118

Scheer, Hermann, 46, 79, 90, 153, 175, 277–278n44

"Schinskyan" approach, 202–203

Schmalensee, Richard, 284n11

Schumacher, E. F., 79

Schumpeter, Joseph: Business Cycles, 21, 153, 158, 203, 272n4; on creative destruction, 216; on engine room of capitalism, 131, 133; and long waves theory, 156–160 (156t), 272–273nn4–8

Schuster, Peter, 123, 266n24

sea-ice, 63–64 (63f)

seawater desalination, 230

SEB (Skandinavska Enskilda Banken), 268n2

securitization, 135

Selections from Prison Notebooks (Gramsci), 204

Sen, Amartya, 218, 286–287n24

Serra, Antonio, 284n7

SGCC (State Grid Corporation of China), 82–83 (83f), 96, 258n7

shale oil, 57–59, 248n47, 252n24

Shams 1 CSP plant, 260n29

Shi, Zhengrong, 96

shifting of wealth, 2

Shiller, Robert, 287n27

Sieferle, Rolf Peter, 26

silicon, 107

silicon wafer supply, 275n27

Simmons, Matt, 56, 251–252n21

Simon, Herbert, 183; and fable of watchmakers Tempus and Horus, 278n1

Simon, Julian, 40–41, 246n34, 247n37

Sinn, Hans-Werner, 72

Sinovel, 81

sixth techno-economic paradigm: clean tech and, 162; and creative destruction, 216; emergence of, 155–160 (156f), 214; Rifkin and, 162. *See also* green economy; TEP (techno-economic paradigm)

SLCP (Sloping Lands Conversion Program), 74–75

Small Is Beautiful (Schumacher), 79

smart grids: China's "smart and strong" grid, 82, 83f, 101, 234; Germany, 88; as green infrastructure, 215–216

smart/intelligent economy, 129

Smith, Adam, 73, 184, 231, 281n20

Smith, J. C., 31

socialism, 221–222

socio-technical standards, and green loans, 144

SoftBank Renewables, 92

Solana generating station, 260n29

The Solar Economy (Scheer), 79, 153

solar power/photovoltaics: current technology, 102–103; declining costs of, 262n44; estimated costs for, 277nn38, 39; experience curve for, 106f; generator sets, 174–175; in Germany, 88; land requirements for, 102–103; in United States, 173–176

Solibro, 177–178

solid-state ammonia synthesis, 112, 263n51

Solow, Robert M., 279n7, 280n15, 281–282n26

Solyndra, 177

Son, Masayoshi, 92–96

sound material-cycle society (SMCS, Japan), 119

Sources of Social Power (Mann), 109–110, 226

South Africa, 99

Southern Power Grid Co., 83

South Korea, 6, 126, 132–133, 165

Soviet Union, 27–28

Spaceship Earth metaphor, 204, 205–209, 283n3

Spain, 261n34

spectral analysis, 273–274n14

speculation in carbon market, 70, 160

"speculative borrowing," 270n24

Speenhamland system of labor, 24

Spence, Michael, 3, 229, 239n3, 289n47

Spender, J. C., 234

Speth, Gus, 226

SPIDERS (US Armed Forces), 91, 259n21

Spitznagel, Mark, 289n40

state action, need for, 9, 74, 163–165, 180, 222

State Grid Corporation of China (SGCC), 82–83 (83f), 96, 258n7

"stateless innovation," 180

Statoil, 71

steady-state economy, 2, 16, 189–191, 195, 203, 206, 280n16

steam power, 25, 26, 244n13, 249n1

Steffen, Will, 51, 54

Stern, David I., 254n39

Stern, Nicolas, 60

Stewart, Fiona, 131, 245n22

Stiglitz, Joseph, 286–287n24

Stoll, Steven, 281–282n26

stranded assets, 72, 137. *See also* unburnable carbon

Stroup, Richard L., 287n32

"subterranean forest," fossil fuels as, 26
sugarcane-based ethanol, 170
sun, as resource base, 212–213
Sundrop Farms, 263n52, 286n23
Sun Yat-sen, 37
super grids, 92–96 (93f), 214
supply-side acceleration, 167, 168f
"survival of the greenest," 274n18
sustainability, science and management of, 184
Sustainable Energy Trade Agreement (SETA), 215
sustainable supply-chain networks, 193
Suzhou eco-industrial park, 194–195, 281nn23, 24
Sweden, 92
"sweet water," 115

Tactical Garbage to Energy Refinery, 92
Tainter, Joseph A., 54, 251n14
Taiping Rebellion, 22–23
Taiwan, 165–167
"take, make and dispose" thinking, 115
Taleb, Nassim Nicholas, 289n40
Tan, Hao, 65, 85, 126, 240n12, 240–241n15, 248n43, 258n6, 266n18, 266n22, 279n11, 281n25, 282n32
targets, setting of, 169. See also market mandates
tariffs, 170; against Brazilian ethanol, 248n46; degression of, 171; reductions on clean-tech goods, 215. See also feed-in tariffs
Tarling, R. J., 282n28
tar sands oil, 57, 252nn25, 27. See also non-conventional fossil fuels
tax policy, 216–217, 220. See also environmental taxation

techno-economic paradigms (TEP). See TEP (techno-economic paradigms)
technological substitution, trajectory of, 13–14 (14f)
temperature increase, historically, 62
ten principles of green growth economy, 211–219
TEP (techno-economic paradigms), 157–158, 272n4; and analysis of long waves, 160–162; criteria for new, 158–159; and debates, 14, 18; fifth techno-economic paradigm, 155, 157–158, 213, 215; resistance to new, 160. See also sixth techno-economic paradigm
Tesla, Nikola, 79, 80, 257n1, 262n40
Tesla Motors, 273n11
TGCs (tradable green certificates), 171–172, 276n34
The Theory of Economic Development (Schumpeter), 131
thin film solar photovoltaics (TF-PVs), 103, 107, 166, 178f, 275n26
Thirlwall, Anthony, 197, 282n28
"3-D" property rights, 287n32
3Rs (reduce, reuse, recycle), 120–121
Three Gorges Dam, 104
Thurbon, Elizabeth, 175, 276n37
Tianjin Economic Development Area, 195
"tight oil," 57, 253n30. See also non-conventional fossil fuels
total material requirement, 116
toxicity of solar cell components, 103–104
Toynbee, Arnold, 243–244n10
Toyota's lean production system, 120
tradable green certificates (TGCs), 171–172, 276n34
tradable pollution permits (TPPs). See cap-and-trade; carbon markets

tradable renewable electric power, 92–96

"tragedy of the commons," 73–75, 206, 224, 231. *See also* Hardin, Garrett

transition: to green economy, 153–155; to green energy, 108–111; and industrial revolution, 25–26. *See also* sixth techno-economic paradigm

transnational investment regulations, 147–148

Tsirel, Sergey, 158, 160–161, 272n6

tundra, Arctic, 66

Turner, R. Kerry, 185, 265n10, 279n9

Twelfth Five-Year Plan (China): accelerating green investments, 10; as blueprint for green economy, 6, 229; circular economy strategy in, 119–120; clean technology goals in, 81; CSP capacity, 81; "green and black" paradox of, 120–121; "Internet of things" in, 267n28; renewable power-generating capacity in, 12, 45–46

Ulsan, Korea, 126

The Ultimate Resource (Simon), 40–41, 246n34

ultra high-voltage direct current (UHVDC) systems. *See* smart grids: China's "smart and strong" grid

unburnable carbon, 72, 76, 137, 233, 268n9, 290n53. *See also* stranded assets

UNDP (UN Development Program), 195

UNEP (UN Environment Program), 195

UNFCCC (UN Framework Convention on Climate Change), 69, 74

UN-GEA (UN Green Economy Agency), as proposed in this book, 195

United Arab Emirates, 99

United Nations, 195

United States: coal and industrialization, 27, 28f; congressional inconsistency, 47–48, 173; consequence of turn from PVs, 175; floundering energy policy in, 47–48; long-term economic fluctuations, 36–37 (36f); military interest in renewables, 48, 90–92, 101, 226, 249n50, 259–260n23; preference for government procurement, 175–176; protection of fossil fuel interests, 6; State Department as "Ministry of Oil," 226; trade sanctions against China, 178, 180; WWII industry scale-up, 165

Unruh, Gregory, 271n3, 278n45

"unsubsidized solar revolution," 107

upswings and downswings, 154–155, 156t, 161, 272n4, 273n8

US Battery Consortium, 103

US Congress: inconsistency of, 47–48, 173; military bypassing of, 91–92, 249n50

USS *Makin Island*, 91

utility, finance as a, 219, 287n27

Value and Capital (Hicks), 185

value chains, 189, 281n23

Valuing the Earth (Daly and Townsend), 182

van der Ploeg, Frederick, 256n52, 284–285n11

Vanke Center (Shenzhen, China), 290n51

vegetation cover, monitoring, 288n34

venture capital, 274n20

Victor, David G., 263n49

Victor, Peter A., 186
virtual eco-industrial parks, 193

Wade, Robert, 256n55
Wall Street, 136–137, 146, 227
war, causes of, 112
Ward, Barbara, 1
waste as food, 117
watchmakers parable (Simon), 183
water: and artificial photosynthesis,
    265n51; and collective action prob-
    lem, 256n55; depletion of, 7, 51;
    desalination, 112, 230; fracking
    and, 59; and green industrialization,
    217; industrial symbioses in Den-
    mark, 127f; Newcomen's beam en-
    gine, 26; North-South Water Trans-
    fer, 121; pollution of in Chile,
    250n12; pollution of in China, 52,
    121; to strip tar sands, 252n24;
    "sweet water," 115; use of, 31f; use
    of seawater, 230; use of since Indus-
    trial Revolution, 31f
Wealth of Nations (Smith), 184
Weber, Max, 1, 222, 225
Weiss, Linda, 276n37, 277n38
Weitzel, Matthias, 289n45
Western Europe economic fluctua-
    tions, 36–37 (36f)
Why Nations Fail (Acemoglu and
    Robinson), 271n2
"wild capitalism," 42, 50, 67, 219, 220
Wilder, Clint, 162
wind power: (ASG) Asian Super Grid
    proposal, 92–96 (93f), 99, 214; in
    Brazil, 86–87; in California,
    277nn40, 43; declining costs of,
    107, 159, 262n44; generating ca-

pacity of, 107; German Ener-
    giewende, 88
Winston, Andrew, 255n48
Withagen, Cees A., 256n52,
    284–285n11
Wolf, Martin, 38
Wong, Shiu-Fai, 275n29
wood, price shock in seventeenth cen-
    tury, 26, 27f
"workshop of the world," China as,
    35
World Bank, 290n55
World Business Council for Sustain-
    able Development, 116
WTE (waste-to-energy) initiative, 92
WTO (World Trade Organization):
    and China joining, 80–81; and ITA
    (Information Technology Trade
    Agreement), 215, 286n18; and pro-
    posed clean-tech trade agreement,
    214–215; rules and procedures of,
    147–148, 179
Wu, Ching-Yan, 274n23

Yanosek, Kassia, 263n49
Yergin, Daniel, 249n48, 251n19
Young, Allyn, 196, 203, 281n20
Young, Soogil, 265n23

Zero Emission Campus (Birkenfeld,
    Germany), 118
zero emissions vehicle (ZEV). See elec-
    tric vehicles (EVs)
Zero Emission Village (Weilerbach,
    Germany), 265n15
zero growth, 15–16, 195, 198
Zhengrong Shi, 260n27
Zysman, John, 287n28